WORDS OF LOVE

ALSO BY PAMELA NORRIS

The Story of Eve

WORDS OF LOVE

Passionate Women
from
Heloise to Sylvia Plath

PAMELA NORRIS

HarperPress
An Imprint of HarperCollins*Publishers*

HarperCollins*Publishers*
77–85 Fulham Palace Road,
Hammersmith, London w6 8jb

www.harpercollins.co.uk

Published by HarperCollins*Publishers* 2006

1

Pamela Norris asserts the moral right to
be identified as the author of this work

A catalogue record for this book
is available from the British Library

ISBN-13: 978-0-00-257178-4
ISBN-10: 0-00-257178-1

Typeset in Granjon with Historical-Fell Type Display by
Rowland Phototypesetting Ltd, Bury St Edmunds, Suffolk

Printed and bound in Great Britain by
Clays Ltd, St Ives plc

For my mother, Peggy Norris,
whose love of reading and romance
has enriched both our lives

Contents

'There is such a magic in affection that I have been more gratified by your clasping your hands round my arm, in company, than I could have been by all the admiration in the world . . .'

Mary Wollstonecraft to William Godwin,
10 November 1796

Introduction

For centuries, the history of love in the Western world has been dominated by male writers and their ideas. In Jane Austen's *Persuasion*, when Captain Harville debates love with the heroine Anne Elliot, he insists on women's fickleness. 'I do not think I ever opened a book in my life which had not something to say on woman's inconstancy,' he tells her. Songs, proverbs, every form of literature tells the same story. Stop there, cries Anne, do not quote examples from books. Men have always had the advantage over women when it came to telling the story of love. 'The pen has been in their hands.'

Anne's playful rejection of Captain Harville's 'evidence' is spoken from a heart burdened with faithful love for a man she fears no longer cares for her. At this period, the early nineteenth century, the novel was only just beginning to become established as the medium in which women writers were to flourish, and through which the tale of women's love in all its variety, depth and passion might finally be made public. Up until this time ideas of love had been dominated by the tradition of male longing promoted by the troubadour poets of southern France. According to the troubadour ideal of *fin'amor* (fine loving), the male lover worshipped a woman who was both desirable and untouchable. The tradition evolved through the Italian poets Dante and Petrarch, and was taken up with enthusiasm by Elizabethan poets and their heirs. Keats's Belle Dame whose kiss condemned her lover to the ghastly Life-in-Death of unrequited love, the dangerous enchantresses of Pre-Raphaelite paintings and Dickens's icy Estelle in *Great Expectations* were all manifestations of the troubadours' *domna*, the controlling mistress for whom the lover would risk his life.

In this outpouring of words and images, women's experience was barely noticed. Educated women may have taken up their pens, but their writings lay neglected in private journals, or were briefly published and then vanished for lack of a reading public committed to understanding and valuing women's words. 'I look everywhere for Grandmothers & see none,' exclaimed the poet Elizabeth Barrett, when she was beginning her career as interpreter of women's experience of love and marriage. Even in the 1920s, when Virginia Woolf was researching *A Room of One's Own* she was disheartened by the lack of information about women in history. Such works as were available seemed all to have been written by men. The pen had indeed been in their hands. Since Woolf delved disconsolately in the archives of the British Library, there has been a revolution in public awareness of women's history and writing. Women's words have been excavated from the musty vaults and chambers of obscurity, and it is finally possible to address the question that so baffled Freud: '*Was will das Weib?*' ('What does Woman want?')

Words of Love begins and ends with the stories of two exceptional women. The writer Sylvia Plath committed suicide in 1963, at the age of thirty and at a point when her reputation as a writer had barely been established. She died alone, in a sparsely furnished flat in north London, during one of the coldest winters on record, her two children sleeping in an upstairs room. Almost exactly eight hundred years previously the abbess Heloise died peacefully at the convent of the Paraclete near Nogent-sur-Seine, after a long and fruitful career as director of the foundation and its daughter houses, and as mentor to the nuns under her care. What has ensured the survival of these two women in the popular imagination is not Plath's poetry and fiction, nor Heloise's outstanding career at the

Paraclete. Like Shakespeare's pathetic heroines Juliet and Ophelia, both are remembered for doomed love.

The connections between the women extend far beyond their romantic reputations. Both were highly intelligent and exceptionally well educated. Both were personally ambitious and pushed against the boundaries of what was considered appropriate or possible for women during the times in which they lived. Both fell in love with exciting, clever men and dreamt of an intellectual partnership, a marriage of minds that would parallel and complement the physical passion each expressed for her lover. In both cases their marriages failed in tragic circumstances. While Heloise survived the wreckage of her hopes, Plath was ambushed by depression. The struggle to come to terms with love and its demands was only a part of each woman's story, but it was of overwhelming significance. Looking at how these two writers, separated by a gulf of time and differing social customs, approached the challenge of passion reveals surprising similarities and even more unpredictable contrasts. Both left records of their love affairs: Heloise in the letters she wrote to Abelard years after their separation; Sylvia Plath in the journals that tell the story of a young woman's experiments in sex and love, and her yearning for the 'strong potential powerful mate who can counter my vibrant dynamic self'. Their histories provide fruitful contexts, one from the recent and well-documented past, the other from the partially irrecoverable Middle Ages, within which to explore two women's experience of love, and to see how their lovers responded to their dreams and desires. Part 1: 'Farewell, my only love' tells Heloise's story.

Heloise was the product of medieval Europe, a culture increasingly dominated by the Christian Church and the dynastic ambitions of the nobility, and in which Latin was still the language of literature and communication. Even if a woman dared to write about her desire for a man, unless she was highly educated, her words had little chance of survival. The situation for women at the Heian court in Japan was rather different. Although their lives were similarly bound by convention and prohibition, they were able to write in vernacular Japanese and within a culture that valued women's words as evidence of their elegance, style and sensibility. Behind the shutters and blinds that concealed noblewomen from prying eyes, Lady Sarashina, Lady Gossamer and the court poet Izumi Shikibu explored their experience of love in memoirs and poems, which were circulated and eagerly read among their peers. One woman even tried her hand at fiction, producing a novel that is still considered a masterpiece. An astute observer of court life, Murasaki Shikibu imaginatively recreated a picture of Heian society in the lives and loves of the first romantic hero, Prince Genji. Like the court memoirs and Izumi's poems, *The Tale of Genji* is predominantly an account of women and their experience of love and marriage in the claustrophobic atmosphere of Heian Japan. Explored in Part 2: Shimmerings of a Summer Sky, the writings of these Japanese women are as fresh and frank as if they had been penned in the time of Jane Austen, and offer a glimpse of how women thought and felt in a time and place that are barely remembered.

Medieval women also wrote intimately about love, but their writings were more dispersed and often quickly vanished, leaving barely a trace in the cultural heritage passed on from generation to generation. Heloise lived in Paris at a time when troubadour views of love were beginning to filter through from the south. Their influence seems scarcely to have touched her. Her letters look back to a more ancient tradition, to classical ideals of friendship, love and companionship. She probably knew nothing of the women troubadours, the trobairitz, whose songs were heard in the castles of Occitania, a vast region of what is now southern France. While the male troubadours were celebrating *fin'amor* and showing off their linguistic dexterity, the lady was stepping off her pedestal to tell her side of the story. Castelloza, the Countess of Dia and their sister trobairitz wrote boldly of women's desire and disappointment, of the *domna*'s trust and bitter betrayal. Their tales of love and loss were taken up by a very different kind of storyteller, the poet Marie de France, whose 'Breton lays' reveal a magical world of fairy lovers as well as human knights and ladies, a realm where animals can speak and humans metamorphose into birds, and the only rule is fidelity to the heart's promptings. Part 3: The Heart's Desire tells the story of these medieval women writers, of the trobairitz and Marie de France, and the feminist and bluestocking Christine de Pizan, who lived by her pen in a society dominated by authoritative men. Even so, she dared to praise women for their skill and contribution to society, and criticised the code of *fin'amor* for the damage it inflicted on women who embraced the *domna*'s role.

The fate of Anne Boleyn is a tragic example of what can happen to a woman who plays the game of love without due care. Muse, mistress and finally wife to Henry VIII, she was elevated, then ruined by love, charged with sexual crimes and conspiracy, and beheaded within days of her arrest. If Anne wrote poetry it has not survived, but another aristocratic woman, Lady Mary Wroth, tried her hand at the sonnet cycles popular with male poets in the Elizabethan golden age of poetry. Developed by Dante and Petrarch, the love sonnet was the natural heir to the troubadour lyric, with a poetic vocabulary and repertoire of attitudes that continued to express male fantasies of the ideal mistress. While her uncle Sir Philip Sidney had celebrated a lady known only as 'Stella' in sonnets that showed off his wit, brio and poetic virtuosity, Lady Mary wrote a series of poems describing her fluctuating hopes and fears during the course of a troubled love affair. Hers was an isolated voice. The next English female poet to tell the woman's side of the story in a sonnet sequence was Elizabeth Barrett, whose *Sonnets from the Portuguese* were written during her courtship by Robert Browning. They offer a bewitching account of a woman's recall to love, in which the sick, reclusive poet is pulled back from the brink of the grave to warm, pulsating life as wife and mother, and a rewarding poetic

partnership. The American poet Edna St Vincent Millay also chose
the sonnet to explore her love affair with a man many years younger
than herself. Millay's experience as a gifted, beautiful woman
attempting to find a voice in a world just emerging from the straitjacket of Victorian morality was very different from that of Lady
Mary Wroth or Elizabeth Barrett. Part 4: The Heat and Violence
of the Poet's Heart explores the histories and love poems of these
three writers, and the downfall of the tragic muse Anne Boleyn.

With the development of the novel, women found a medium
ideally suited to their skills as storytellers, psychologists, gossips
and social observers. Relatively unexplored, the novel had also
the advantage of not having been earmarked for centuries as the
preserve of the male writer. Women could at last begin to explore
the issues so important to a heroine attempting to make her way
in the world. Part 5: Dreams and Reality discusses some of the ways
in which women novelists have written about love. Jane Austen was
only too aware of the pressure on women to marry, but was it love
or money that a heroine should try to achieve? Charlotte Brontë
imagined a new kind of heroine in poor plain Jane Eyre and beady
Lucy Snowe. George Eliot and Edith Wharton sympathetically
explored the fate of the penniless young woman for whom her
beauty and accomplishments were her only path to financial security.
Again and again, talented women writers wrestled with the tension
between relationships and work. If a woman attempted to balance
love with a career as artist or writer, what was the outcome? And
what was the connection between a writer's personal experience and
the stories she told? Louisa May Alcott and L. M. Montgomery
wrote books for girls that ended with happy wife- and motherhood.
Despite these satisfying romances, their authors led passionate,
troubled lives. Looking at their own experience, often marked by
disappointment and failed love, what kinds of hero did women
authors dream up to match their feisty heroines? What kind of
lover did women want? Jane Austen created Mr Knightley as the

only man capable of winning fastidious Emma; Charlotte Brontë matched Jane Eyre's originality and spirit with the flawed Mr Rochester, a Dark Hero who re-emerges in women's writing about love to the present day.

The book ends with a real-life heroine, the writer Sylvia Plath, in whose brief history so many of the themes explored in *Words of Love* coalesce. Ambitious and highly talented, she willed herself into excellence, whipping herself to meet her own exacting standards as a poet, a writer and a twentieth-century woman, committed to marriage and childbearing as much as she wanted fame. Like Edna St Vincent Millay, she was eager to learn about love and the ways of men, although she never developed Millay's sang-froid and self-protection in dealing with her lovers. Passionate and curious, she was puzzled by and angry about the double standard that permitted men sexual licence and kept its girls frustrated virgins. When she eventually met her own 'Dark Hero', the poet Ted Hughes, she recognised her male counterpart, the gifted lover with whom she could share her energy, ambition and longing for love. Like Jane Eyre with Mr Rochester, she claimed him as her equal, the glittering prize after a girlhood of confusion over quite how a clever, passionate woman was to make her way in the world of literature and love. Despite its unhappy ending, their partnership was an attempt, like Heloise's with Abelard or Mary Wollstonecraft's with William Godwin, to find a way for men and women to live together as lovers, as creative co-workers, and as friends and equals in their journey through life.

PART 1

'Farewell, my only love':
The Passion of Heloise

The sword has fallen truly
between us, . . .
and there is no returning.

Sally Purcell, 'Abelard Solus'
(*Collected Poems*, p. 66)

The Story of Heloise and Abelard

'God is my witness', wrote the nun Heloise to the husband from whom she had been separated for more than a decade, 'that if Augustus, Emperor of the whole world, thought fit to honour me with marriage . . . it would be dearer and more honourable to me to be called not his Empress but your whore.'[1] It was a demand for freedom in love revolutionary for a woman in the Middle Ages, and indeed at any period of Western history until the very recent past. The story of Heloise and Abelard has attracted attention for over eight hundred years. It was gossiped about by contemporaries and became the subject of prurient speculation by generations of male commentators aroused by Heloise's outspoken passion. The love affair that captured the imagination of romantic readers can be briefly summarised.

In the early 1100s a clever young woman, Heloise, living in Paris under her uncle's guardianship, was seduced by her tutor, the famous scholar and philosopher Peter Abelard, and gave birth to a child. When her uncle found out about the affair he had Abelard castrated and the lovers were separated. Heloise spent the rest of her life in a convent, mourning the loss of her lover. The myth of Heloise's youth and beauty, her self-sacrificing love and tragic incarceration, and most of all her undimmed desire for Abelard, inspired such emotional treatments of the story as Alexander Pope's poem 'Eloisa to Abelard' (1717). Typically, Pope glossed over the details of the story to focus on Eloisa's sexual yearning. The real story of Heloise and Abelard is more complex and interesting than

Pope's sensationalist treatment, although it does include sex and frustrated passion. Heloise is one of the most eloquent writers ever to describe a woman's desire, either in the Middle Ages or subsequently. We know a good deal about her thoughts on both love and marriage because she is one of the few medieval women to leave an intimate record of her feelings in the letters she wrote to Abelard.

Heloise's letters were written many years after her sexual relationship with Abelard had finished, and were a pained response to Abelard's own account of their affair in his memoir, *Historia calamitatum* (*The Story of His Misfortunes*), written in his early fifties.[2] At the time she wrote her letters, probably in the early 1130s, Heloise was very likely already abbess of the religious community at the Paraclete, a foundation established by Abelard and handed over to Heloise and her sister nuns when they were forced to leave their refuge at the convent of Argenteuil. The private self that Heloise exposes in her letters is in marked contrast to her public position and responsibilities. Carefully composed in polished and eloquent Latin, and drawing on Heloise's remarkable scholarship, the letters nevertheless present the image of a body and soul in torment, a woman in thrall to sexual yearning and emotional deprivation. Just as the desperate Jane Eyre, in Charlotte Brontë's bold novel about a woman's capacity for love, challenged Mr Rochester to meet her as an equal, spirit to spirit, across the social gulf that divided them, so Heloise in writing to Abelard made a last desperate bid for recognition from the lover whom she feared that she had lost for ever.

Peter Abelard's Version of Events:
The Story of His Misfortunes

Peter Abelard, the lover and then the husband of Heloise, was one of the outstanding scholars of his generation, a brilliant and innovative thinker, who had built up an international reputation as a philosopher and charismatic teacher. When he met Heloise in around 1116, he was already master of the prestigious cathedral school at Notre Dame in Paris and, at the age of thirty-seven, believed that he was 'the only philosopher in the world'.[3] The portrait he paints of himself in his autobiography, *Historia calamitatum*, is of an ardent, handsome man, still a novice in love, who was eager to satisfy the desires he had held so long in check. At this time Heloise was living in the cathedral close with her uncle Fulbert, her mother's brother, a canon of Notre Dame. It is often claimed that Heloise was very young, perhaps just seventeen or eighteen, when she met Abelard. The idea of her youth feeds the romantic legend of an impressionable girl in thrall to her distinguished mentor. Given Heloise's own reputation for learning, however, which had spread beyond the confines of Paris (Abelard boasted that in scholarship 'she stood supreme'), Heloise may well have been in her twenties.[4] One scholar places her birth as around 1090 or earlier, which would have made her twenty-six or -seven when she met Abelard.[5] What is certain is that Abelard set out quite deliberately to seduce this brilliant woman. For all his intelligence, Abelard was burdened, as he himself acknowledged, with a volatile temperament, which tended to sabotage his prospects at his greatest moments. His pursuit of Heloise was typically audacious, ill-judged and eventually cruelly damaging to both partners.

Writing to Abelard after the catastrophic outcome of the affair, a fellow cleric, Fulco, Prior of Deuil, taunted him with promiscuity and hinted that Abelard had squandered his earnings on harlots and prostitutes.[6] In his autobiography, perhaps in response to such gibes, Abelard protested that until this time he had been sexually chaste. He had never consorted with whores and his dedication to learning had prevented him from enjoying the company of socially respectable women.[7] What, then, attracted Abelard to Heloise? Why, if we are to believe his assertions of chastity (and they must, given his subsequent behaviour with Heloise, be viewed with some degree of scepticism), did he decide at the comparatively mature age of thirty-seven to embark on a sexual relationship with a younger woman and one, moreover, entrusted to his care? Perhaps, as was claimed by the philosopher William Godwin, who was a similar age when he fell in love with Mary Wollstonecraft, he had simply never before 'met with an object so consummately worthy'.[8] The *Historia calamitatum* is a polished document, written many years after the events it describes, and it was intended to explain Abelard's misfortunes as part of God's plan of salvation for his lowly servant. Despite his anxiety to give an account of his life that would satisfy his critics, Abelard's impetuous and essentially truthful nature undermined his careful phrases with explanations that have the ring of truth. In writing about Heloise it is clear that he was drawn to her at least partly by personal vanity, attracted not so much by her looks, about which he was rather dismissive, as by her gift of letters, so rare in a woman. He was the toast of Paris, she too had a reputation for outstanding knowledge. For this arrogant man, in the full flush of professional success after years of struggle, bedding the clever Heloise would be one more proof of his supremacy over his fellow men. She was also unmarried, known as a virgin scholar, and one can imagine the ribald jokes that would have gone the rounds among the male students at Notre Dame. For Godwin, an ever-closer proximity to Mary Wollstonecraft was productive of the tenderest 'friendship melting into love'.[9] By contrast, Abelard's seduction of Heloise was, by his own account, a cynical, worldly conquest. It was also, given her uncle's standing in the community and his unusually strong affection for his niece, foolhardy in the extreme.

As Abelard tells the story, having decided to seduce the book-ish Heloise, he insinuated himself into Fulbert's house as a lodger and was given sole charge of Heloise's education, an extraordinary concession at a period when young unmarried women were carefully guarded. Even Abelard was astounded at Fulbert's simplicity: 'if he had entrusted a tender lamb to a ravening wolf it would not have surprised me more.'[10] There was little need for further explanation. 'We were united, first under one roof, then in heart; and so with our lessons as a pretext we abandoned ourselves entirely to love.'[11] Like Dante's errant lovers, Paolo and Francesca, ceaselessly tossed on the tempests of carnal yearning, Abelard seduced Heloise through their shared enthusiasm for the written word.[12] Dante's *Inferno* was written many years after both Abelard and Heloise were dead, but the poet's understanding of the power of passion to undermine rational behaviour and even self-interest reflects Abelard's account of the devastating effects of his desire for Heloise.

Writing about these events many years later, Abelard was at pains to distance himself from sexual games which, as a Christian monk and ascetic, he could only recall with horror and regret. But his moral purpose was subverted by the force of his memories. His confession of lust segues seamlessly into a frank celebration of the lovers' physical delight in one another. Licensed by Fulbert to shut themselves away in private tutorials, they quickly abandoned reading for the language of love, and scholarship for kisses, caresses and even blows. In his anxiety that his niece should benefit fully from her tuition, Fulbert had given Abelard permission to strike her (at that period, Latin was often quite literally beaten into a student's head). Tender correction supplied a titillating element of sado-masochism to a relationship Abelard confessed (or boasted) 'left no stage of love-making untried'.[13] The effects on the great philosopher were dramatic. Just as Erec, in Chrétien de Troyes's verse-romance *Erec and Enide* (written a few decades later), becomes unmanned by paying too much attention to his beautiful new wife, so Abelard collapsed under the strain of sex. Exhausted by nights of pleasure, he neglected his studies and dismayed his students by repetitive lectures. Any surplus energy was devoted to composing love songs, which once again made Heloise the talk of France, but this time as the famous Abelard's notorious mistress. Almost everyone in the small community was aware of what was going on, except Fulbert. As St Jerome, never one to overlook an opportunity for moralising, had once remarked, 'We are always the last to learn of evil in our own home[.]'[14] Eventually the lovers were caught, as Mars and Venus were discovered by Vulcan in Ovid's *Metamorphoses*, in the very act of lovemaking. Soon afterwards Heloise wrote joyfully to Abelard to say that she was pregnant, and he secretly abducted her from her uncle's house and left her with his sister in Brittany, where she gave birth to a son, the curiously named Astralabe.

From this point the situation escalated to a terrible denouement. As Abelard was only too aware, he had placed Heloise's uncle in an untenable position. If Fulbert took action against her seducer then Heloise, still living with Abelard's family, might suffer harm. Finally taking pity on Fulbert's rage and anguish, Abelard offered to marry Heloise, with the proviso that the marriage be kept secret in order to protect his reputation. A public front of celibacy was essential for a man in Abelard's position. There was a movement at that time towards celibacy for all members of the priesthood and clergy, and marriage would have restricted his chances of promotion in the Church, an important career option for a scholar of Abelard's standing. Privately, it seems that sexual jealousy was a significant component in Abelard's wish to marry Heloise. He may have feared that her uncle would try to marry her off to another man in an attempt to rescue his niece's reputation, and in a later letter he admitted to her, 'At the time I desired to keep you whom I loved beyond measure for myself alone[.]'[15] Heloise, up till now a rather shadowy figure in Abelard's narrative, strongly opposed marriage, arguing that it would not appease her uncle for the insult to his honour. As a wife, she would be a disgrace and burden to her ambitious lover. Finally recognising that Abelard was adamant, she capitulated, but she was under no illusions about the outcome: 'We shall both be destroyed. All that is left us is suffering as great as our love has been.'[16]

Leaving the baby Astralabe with Abelard's sister, the lovers were secretly married in Paris. Despite this concession to decorum, Fulbert, still wincing under his niece's disgrace, began to spread news of the marriage, which Heloise, anxious about Abelard's reputation, as strenuously denied. To protect his wife from Fulbert's reproaches and (probably) physical assaults, Abelard removed her to the convent at Argenteuil in the countryside near Paris, where Heloise had been brought up and educated as a small girl. He also persuaded her to adopt the habit of a novice. Whatever his motives for this, and again sexual possessiveness may have played a part, it was the final straw as far as Heloise's family was concerned. Believing that Abelard had rid himself of an unwanted wife by persuading her to become a nun, Fulbert and his friends plotted a savage revenge. Bribing a servant to gain access to Abelard's lodgings, Fulbert's hirelings caught the philosopher unawares as he was sleeping and, in Abelard's laconic account, 'they cut off the parts of my body whereby I had committed the wrong of which they complained'.[17] Humiliated and bitterly repenting the loss of his reputation, he resolved to take orders, having first instructed a reluctant Heloise to embrace the veil. Abelard then retired to the Abbey of St Denis and Heloise remained at Argenteuil. This may have been the last the couple saw of one another for several years.

Heloise Speaks Out

Like Augustine's *Confessions*, its great predecessor in Christian autobiography, Abelard's *Historia calamitatum* is an account of spiritual regeneration, intended to bear witness to God's merciful intervention in a sinful life. It was composed in the style of *consolatoria*, a formal letter of encouragement generally written to a friend suffering from misfortunes and, as was customary with such letters, Abelard attempted to cheer up his unnamed recipient by pointing out how much worse his own life had been. His love affair with Heloise was just one of the many setbacks that Abelard described to his friend and he was anxious to justify the tragic events as part of God's plan of salvation for the guilty lovers. Castration was the necessary disgrace that shocked Abelard into awareness of his sinful behaviour and his enforced seclusion as a monk brought him face to face with God. Ted Hughes, centuries later, was similarly fatalistic in his *Birthday Letters*, the collection of poems published shortly before Hughes's death, in which he finally broke silence about his relationship with his wife Sylvia Plath. Like Abelard, Hughes saw the tragedy of his marriage as predetermined, in his case by some mysterious force, call it fate or the quasi-demoniac image of Plath's dead father Otto, which swept Plath irresistibly to her premature death. It is a curious parallel between the two men that, in their public statements about their marriages, both sidestepped personal responsibility by calling on external forces – God or fate – to justify the outcome. It is impossible to know how Plath would have responded to this attempt to hive her off into the realm of myth or destiny. Heloise was seriously disturbed by what she saw as Abelard's misrepresentation of their love affair and her anxiety to set the record straight inspired her letters. Refusing to be marginalised by Abelard's redemptive agenda, she told the truth about God and love, and in the process offered a unique perspective on a medieval woman's attitude to sex, marriage and a supportive partnership between intellectuals who were also intimates and lovers. The fact that one of these learned thinkers was a woman made their relationship all the more challenging. So outspoken was she that for years scholars debated whether such 'unmaidenly' letters could have been written by a woman. The history of (generally male) attempts to disprove the authenticity of Heloise's letters makes fascinating reading and offers a disheartening insight into scholarly misogyny towards erudite women writers. It is now generally accepted that the letters are genuine and that the personality which breaks so ardently through the careful Latin phrases is indeed that of Heloise.[18]

It is not clear whether Heloise read the *Historia calamitatum* by chance, or through Abelard's deliberate intention.[19] Whatever the circumstances, although she took up the letter with eagerness, she was appalled by Abelard's account of his woes, and determined to confront him with the truth about her own feelings and behaviour. By this time settled at the Paraclete, the foundation Abelard had established in the Champagne countryside near Troyes, and probably already promoted to the influential role of abbess, Heloise composed an extraordinary letter. Like Abelard in the *Historia calamitatum*, she wrote in Latin, still the customary medium of scholarship and communication. In accordance with her classical training, she constructed an *epistola deprecatoria*, a letter intended to convey a request, in which the writer uses every art at her disposal to persuade her recipient to agree to what she asks.[20] Heloise's apparent purpose was to urge her claim to the same degree of comfort as Abelard had offered his 'friend' in the *Historia calamitatum*. She went far beyond this, however, using the formal framework of the letter to pour out her heart to Abelard, both about their relationship as lovers and her feelings in the fifteen or so years since their marriage had been ruptured. Carefully crafted, drawing on every resource of rhetoric and knowledge at her disposal, Heloise's letter was a reminder of mutual passion and also of the intellectual partnership that she had once shared with her lover. It is a formidable assault that rarely collapses into emotionalism. Heloise, whom Abelard had described as supreme among women, addresses her husband in a virtuoso *contrappunto* of form and content intended to impress and to guarantee a response.

By this time Abelard's fortunes had reached a new low. He was living in virtual exile as abbot of the community at St Gildas de Rhuys on the coast of Brittany, a wild and, in Abelard's view, barbarous environment. With characteristic self-dramatisation, he describes himself, at the end of the *Historia*, as buffeted between murderous monks and the roaring ocean, at the rim of the known world. Heloise seizes on this alarming finale as a starting point for her letter. She claims to be writing on behalf of the Paraclete community to say how distressed the nuns have been by Abelard's account of his misfortunes, how they worry about the dangers he faces and how much they crave reassurance about his welfare. From this graceful and unthreatening introduction, Heloise moves rapidly into a plea for personal support, recalling the close marriage tie that binds her to Abelard and his responsibility for her present situation. Despite her reluctance to become a nun, she had obeyed his command implicitly, resolutely rejecting her own hopes for happiness: 'at your bidding I changed my clothing along with my mind, in order to prove you the sole possessor of my body and my will alike.'[21]

What had particularly upset Heloise was the account Abelard gave in the *Historia* of her reasons for wanting to avoid marriage. There was a long-standing tradition among classical and Christian male authorities that marriage was a distraction from study and spirituality, and Heloise had similarly criticised the constraints of

domestic life. 'What harmony can there be between pupils and
nursemaids, desks and cradles ... ? Who can concentrate on
thoughts of Scripture or philosophy and be able to endure babies
crying ... ?'[22] These are questions that may well have preoccupied
Sylvia Plath, torn between poetry and potty-training in the early
1960s. As Heloise explains, her objections to marriage extended far
beyond such mundane considerations. What she had in mind was
an entirely disinterested relationship, based on her appreciation of
Abelard's merits. 'The name of wife may seem more sacred or more
binding, but sweeter for me will always be the word mistress[.]'[23]
In preferring 'love to wedlock and freedom to chains', Heloise was
laying claim to a view of partnership that valued emotional ties
beyond material considerations or even the woman's reputation.
'God is my witness that if Augustus, Emperor of the whole world,
thought fit to honour me with marriage and conferred all the earth
on me to possess for ever, it would be dearer and more honourable
to me to be called not his Empress but your whore.'[24]

Heloise supports her argument that love is more important than
social position or wealth by reference to another learned woman,
the classical Aspasia, who, as the key to a happy partnership, had
recommended husband and wife to maintain what Heloise describes
as the 'blessed delusion' that each was living with the perfect mate.[25]
Her accusation that the woman who marries for money is offering
herself for sale is, by contrast, strikingly modern, chiming with the
views of twentieth-century feminists, who criticised marriage as a
form of barter discrediting to both partners. But Heloise's love for
Abelard is as far from the self-assertion of modern feminism as it
is from classical ideals of discipline and moderation. She seems quite
simply to have worshipped him. In an extraordinary outburst of
feeling, this dignified nun breaks into frank celebration of her lover,
who she has no doubt was the most seductive partner any woman
could desire. 'What king or philosopher could match your fame?'
she asks him. 'Every wife, every young girl desired you in absence

and was on fire in your presence; queens and great ladies envied me my joys and my bed.'[26] Heloise's zest in her reputation as the mistress of the famous philosopher is unmistakable and she recalls the many love songs Abelard wrote in her honour. Who would not pity her for the loss of such joys, she persuasively enquires. Who, indeed?

As for those who had envied and criticised her as a young woman, Heloise feels that now she deserves their sympathy, for her motives have always been good. She is arguing the point that 'It is not the deed but the intention of the doer which makes the crime' and she reminds Abelard, 'What my intention towards you has always been, you alone who have known it can judge. I submit all to your scrutiny, yield to your testimony in all things.'[27]

Given all this, why does Abelard now neglect her? Is it because, as the world suspects, he pursued her out of lust rather than affection? Heloise closes with a plea for Abelard to write to her, to give her at least 'some sweet semblance' of himself in a personal message.[28] All that she has done has been for him; she can expect no reward from God, 'for it is certain that I have done nothing as yet for love of him'.[29] Without Abelard, her heart, believed in the twelfth century to be the site of the soul, cannot exist and she reminds him of the many letters he once wrote when he sought her out for 'sinful pleasures'.[30] Would it not be better now, she cunningly suggests, to use his famous eloquence to summon her to God? And she concludes simply, *'Vale unice.'*[31] The force and intensity of Heloise's *'unice'* is untranslatable. 'Farewell, my only love / unique one / my one-and-only' are pale approximations of her meaning.[32]

Not surprisingly, Abelard seems to have reacted to Heloise's letter with dismay and he hastened to distance himself from her demands. From his point of view Heloise may well have been something of a loose cannon. Her frank admission of her feelings posed a worrying threat to his rehabilitation as a Christian leader and scholar. Not only was she harking back to the scandal of their affair and his castration, which he had for fifteen years been attempting to lay to rest, but her letter was potentially blasphemous in putting her devotion to the all too human Abelard above her duty to God. His response was chilly in the extreme. Where she begged for intimacy and loving-kindness, he offered Christian precepts and a shared community as God's servants. His aim seems to have been to remind Heloise that the only possible relationship they could have was one that acknowledged their changed status. His greeting stresses that they are now brother and sister in Christ, and Abelard counters her plea for personal comfort with the request that she and her nuns pray for him in his troubles. As for their marital relationship, he notes coldly that the prayers of a devoted wife are considered to be particularly efficacious. Far from reassuring her about his current situation, he closes by asking Heloise, if his enemies do kill him, to bring his body to the burial ground at the Paraclete, where it can be laid to rest among the community of pious women. Prayers for the salvation of his soul will be proof of the love she bears him.

This is all very negative and unconsoling. Not surprisingly, Heloise's response is a cry of anguish and need, which is all the more striking given the time that had elapsed since she last had any sexual contact with Abelard. Anxious even in extremity not to antagonise him nor to lose his respect, she begins with some polite flimflammery about her husband's gloomy plans for his burial, but moves rapidly on to her real concern, which is her own unhappiness. At the heart of her complaint is her unassuaged desire for Abelard. Despite all that has happened and the years of separation, the 'pleasures of lovers' they shared continue to haunt her. Even during Mass, 'lewd visions' distract her thoughts to wantonness. 'Everything we did and also the times and places are stamped on my heart along with your image, so that I live through it all again with you.' Even in sleep, she is not free from desire: her body moves inadvertently, her murmurings betray her. God may indeed have been kind to

Abelard, for 'a single wound of the body' freed him from sexual torment. 'But for me,' she wails, 'youth and passion and experience of pleasures which were so delightful' increase her longing and the anguish of frustrated desire.[33] Her reputation for holiness and chastity is undeserved; her pious behaviour is a sham. God knows the secrets of her heart. And she plays her last, best card: it is Abelard who can effect her spiritual regeneration. Abelard must not be taken in by her hypocrisy; he must understand how much she needs his prayers and support. With his help, she may hope at least to avoid danger; the crown of victory is beyond her strength.

Now, at last, Heloise stings Abelard into a considered and indeed heartfelt response. He dissects her letter and answers her grievances point by point, in the process offering a remarkable insight into their sexual relationship. In particular, he responds to what he calls her 'old perpetual complaint', her blaming God for the circumstances in which she and Abelard were forced to enter religious communities.[34] Abelard had taken the line in the *Historia calamitatum* that his castration and its aftermath were acts of divine mercy that permitted both partners to repent their previous sinful way of life. Heloise will have none of this and still clings to the memory of the pleasures she has lost. Most of all, she cannot understand why God punished Abelard after they had regularised their relationship by marriage. Abelard, in explanation, reminds her of the day he visited her at the convent at Argenteuil, when she was hiding from Fulbert after their marriage. '[Y]ou know what my uncontrollable desire did with you there, actually in a corner of the refectory, since we had nowhere else to go.'[35] He recalls other 'wanton impurities' that had preceded their marriage, his deception of her uncle and her disguising herself as a nun when she fled to Brittany during her pregnancy. These sins against Christian morality and even the sanctity of a holy place deserved the punishment Abelard received, while the couple's commitment to God was a fitting restitution for the sacrileges they had committed: 'See then, my beloved, see how with the dragnets of his mercy the Lord has fished us up from the depth of this dangerous sea[.]'[36]

Abelard then turns to his own 'unbridled lust' for Heloise, which led him to ignore the Church's prohibitions on intercourse during certain holy festivals and fasts. Even when Heloise was unwilling, Abelard had forced her consent 'with threats and blows'. Through lust, he had set 'those wretched, obscene pleasures, which we blush even to name' above his duty to God or himself.[37] What surprise, then, that God should punish him by making it impossible ever to indulge those pleasures again?

Abelard's rejection of their shared sexual history is absolute. There is no hint, from him, of nights tormented by desire and the memory of shared eroticism. He does, however, write eloquently and tenderly to Heloise, 'my partner both in guilt and in grace', of their future companionship in God.[38] Just as St Jerome, one of Abelard's and Heloise's favourite Christian authors, wrote words of consolation and encouragement to his female supporters, so Abelard now rouses himself to answer Heloise's plea for spiritual support. He tells her that in naming her Heloise, as if after his own Hebrew name of Elohim, God has marked her out as 'especially his'. Their marriage, despite Abelard's selfish motive 'to keep you whom I loved beyond measure for myself alone', was part of God's plan for their joint conversion. Had Heloise not married, she might have 'clung to the world' to please her family, or to satisfy her own sensual nature.[39]

There are other benefits. As spiritual mother to so many daughters, Heloise has released herself from the squalor of childbearing and has 'turned the curse of Eve into the blessing of Mary'.[40] Carried away by his own eloquence, Abelard falls back on the conventional clichés of the time, forgetting or ignoring Heloise's reluctance to disrupt their scholarly partnership by bearing children, and seeming too to have disregarded her experience of pregnancy and the birth of their son Astralabe. He is trying, within the constraints of his own sense of vocation, to cheer and enhearten Heloise, reminding her that, as a nun, she is now the spouse of Christ, and Abelard compares the great love of her spiritual bridegroom for his bride with his own human feeling. What he felt for Heloise was lust, he claims: 'I took my fill of my wretched pleasures in you, and this was the sum total of my love.'[41] Brutal indeed, but Abelard is speaking, now, not as the ardent lover of Heloise, but as a monk chastened by suffering and committed to asceticism. Looking back through the distorting prism of Christian teaching on sexuality, he can only acknowledge his desire as something tainted, sinful and valueless to Heloise.

As for Heloise's claim that she cannot aspire to the crown of victory, he tells her gently that it is precisely because she still suffers from her youthful desire that the martyr's crown will be hers. In Abelard's case there is nothing to strive for: 'the thorn of desire is pulled out.'[42] Then he returns to his idea that Heloise must pray for him, but now he makes this a more urgent, personal plea by reminding her of their marriage: 'we are one in Christ, one flesh according to the law of matrimony.'[43] As the bride of Christ, Heloise can intercede for her earthly husband and he tells her the prayer of supplication she must offer to God: 'those whom thou hast parted for a time on earth, unite forever to thyself in heaven[.]' He ends, 'Farewell in Christ, bride of Christ; in Christ fare well [sic] and live in Christ.'[44]

With this partial but open response, Heloise has to be satisfied. Finally, Abelard has given her a clear statement of where he stands and how she can best hope to keep his attention in future. In her reply, she says quietly that she will not trouble him further with her grief. In writing, at least, she can control the words that gush spontaneously from her overflowing heart, but she suggests that the best way to drive out her obsessive thoughts is to find new interests. She asks him to explain the origins of the order of nuns and sends him a list of enquiries relating to the organisation of the women under her care. With this bold stroke, Heloise acknowledges that her former relation to Abelard has gone for ever and that the most persuasive claim she can make on him is in their shared work to develop the community at the Paraclete.[45] It was a wise move on Heloise's part and the beginning of a fruitful partnership in many matters concerning the nuns. Over the next few years, apparently at Heloise's request, Abelard produced a body of writing that included his proposals for the Rule for the community, sermons, hymns and a commentary on the Book of Genesis. Heloise also sent Abelard her *Problemata*, a set of forty-two theological questions, which she invited him to answer. What we don't know is how Heloise responded to Abelard's writings or, indeed, whether she ever addressed him on any personal matter again.

Heloise's Dream: A Loving Partnership

In Christian terminology the word 'passion' refers not to sexual ardour, but to the agonies of Christ, from the commemorative farewell of the Last Supper to the painful and humiliating death on the green hill of Calvary. 'Passion' here is closely related to its Latin meaning of 'suffering', which implies 'allowing to happen' as well as 'feeling pain', and brings together ideas of sacrifice, separation and death. It is one of the many ironies of Heloise's story that, for her, the intense joy of sexual passion led to unwilling renunciation and lifelong cloistration in a Benedictine convent. After a frustratingly brief period as the lover of Peter Abelard, she spent nearly half a century as the spiritual bride of Christ. How far she came to accept her divine spouse is still a matter for conjecture. What is evident is that for years she was tormented by physical longing for Abelard. Writing to her lover, her voice speaks to us from the remote twelfth century with a resonance as powerful as that of Sylvia Plath, so unmistakably a modern woman with her appetite for sex, a family and professional success. In the letters that describe her love, perhaps only six thousand words in all, Heloise lays bare her feelings, her expectations and regrets, with a frankness that goaded squeamish scholars into claiming that her letters were too sensual to have been written by a woman. In these brief and preternaturally vivid texts, her words emerge momentarily and with piercing clarity from an unfathomable silence, like the tantalising call of a mermaid who beckons from the waves before dissolving into foam.

It is Heloise's voice that has ensured her survival as one of the great romantic heroines. Translating the letters in Paris around a hundred and fifty years later, the poet Jean de Meun was captivated by what they revealed of Heloise's personality. To the impressionable Jean, her capacity for love and her intelligence were equally remarkable. At one fraught moment in the relationship, his textual note exclaims, 'Still she loved Abelard like one beside herself!' In another place, 'never did a woman speak more wisely,' he comments approvingly.[46] Petrarch was also an admirer, making a list of dates in his manuscript copy of the correspondence, which he marked with a secret code of dots and dashes recording his own attempts to master sexual desire.[47] Like Jean de Meun, he responded to Heloise with tender chivalry, approving the sweetness and gentleness of her conduct, and praising the feeling and elegance of her style.[48] Alexander Pope was one of many later poets to fall under Heloise's spell and he introduced her to a whole new generation of readers as a heroine tormented by sexual longing in his influential 'Eloisa to Abelard'.[49]

It is understandable that a woman's devotion might appeal to male readers, but was there more to Heloise's love than slavish assent to Abelard's sexual games? Was she one of those abject women described by Simone de Beauvoir in *The Second Sex* as capable of realisation only through her commitment to a superior male? 'Since she is anyway doomed to dependence,' de Beauvoir comments of such a woman, 'she will prefer to serve a god rather than obey tyrants – parents, husband, or protector. She chooses to desire her enslavement so ardently that it will seem to her the expression of her liberty; ... through her flesh, her feelings, her behaviour, she will enthrone him as supreme value and reality: she will humble herself to nothingness before him. Love becomes for her a religion.'[50] De Beauvoir's description resonates uncomfortably with many of the expressions used in Heloise's letters. There is no doubt that she elevated Abelard to the status of a god; she even insisted that all she did was for him. Such a view of Heloise, however, ignores what is perhaps most interesting about her commitment to Abelard: her achievement as the supreme woman of letters in France, her suitability to be the mistress of one of Europe's leading philosophers, and her plans for a scholarly partnership with Abelard based on mutual love and shared interests, a relationship very similar, in fact, to Simone de Beauvoir's theoretical arrangement with her lover Jean-Paul Sartre. Above all, as the scholar Constant Mews has so perceptively observed, she valued sincerity and love beyond social convention: 'In wanting to deepen her relationship with Peter Abelard, Heloise was fascinated by the possibility that a woman and a man could share in the most intimate form of friendship.'[51] So why did it all go wrong?

In order to answer such questions, one has to strip away the prejudices and beliefs of a more feminist and romantic age, and to recreate the social climate of France in the early twelfth century. The expectations of men and women at this period were very different. Peter Abelard's background may well have had something in common with Heloise's family origins and aspirations, but his experience was quite separate from hers. Abelard was a knight's son, who grew up on the borders of the Duchy of Brittany in the town of Le Pallet. His father, Berengar, belonged to the minor nobility and was probably one of the knights who guarded the castle of Le Pallet in return for land. As Abelard explains in his autobiography, Berengar had a passion for learning and was determined that his sons should be educated before they trained as soldiers. Abelard embraced his father's plans with relish and eventually renounced his privileges as eldest son, withdrawing 'from the court of Mars in order to kneel at the feet of Minerva'.[52] Despite this choice, some of his knightly inheritance remained with him. As a philosopher, he studied the arts of the trivium (Latin grammar, rhetoric and logic), but he was also a talented musician, who became renowned for the melodious love songs he composed for Heloise.

Abelard's musical abilities and the suggestion of something light-hearted and even comical in his nature – he was famous for his jokes – connect him with the troubadour poets just beginning to emerge from Poitou and Aquitaine in the south, and their often self-mocking songs of love, longing and loss.[53] Eventually, he found his way to Paris, attracted by the presence there of William of Champeaux, master of the cathedral school at Notre Dame and renowned for his knowledge of logic.

Abelard's account in the *Historia calamitatum* of his fortunes until his meeting with Heloise focuses on his struggles to win supremacy over William, for whom he quickly came to feel contempt. It is a record of a brilliant young pupil's attempt to challenge what he regarded as the plodding methods and outmoded ideologies of a once revered teacher. Abelard tells the story with energy and self-righteous indignation, but without attempting to gloss over his own pride and ambition. By 1114, after several attempts to set up rival schools and a period of breakdown back home in Brittany, an episode that hints at his emotional fragility, Abelard was finally master at Notre Dame. By now he had become a considerable personality, his learning, personal charisma and innovative style of teaching attracting students from all over Europe and even as far afield as Ireland. During his years of struggle he had enjoyed moving freely in scholastic circles, engaging as an equal in the intellectual debates of the time. As a young man he had studied with Roscelin, a famous and controversial master of logic. He had dared to challenge William of Champeaux on his theory of universals and criticised another distinguished teacher, Anselm, for his methods of teaching the Bible. These disputes attracted the adverse notice of more conservative opponents and sowed the seeds of Abelard's later clashes with ecclesiastical authorities, but, as he commented ruefully, 'success always puffs up fools with pride'. Convinced that his reputation as a philosopher would protect him from criticism, he succumbed to 'the lusts of the flesh'.[54]

Abelard's impulsiveness, so important in his relationship with Heloise, was in some senses his downfall, although his daring and recklessness enabled him to make intellectual journeys denied to more cautious thinkers. He was well known for his disputatious approach and arrogance, and a lack of tact when dealing with influential opponents. His admission of pride and wilfulness in the *Historia calamitatum* may have been a conventional trope of spiritual confession, but he was clearly a tricky, contentious character, whose innovation and enjoyment of verbal cut and thrust made him sparkle in the classroom, but caused problems with more circumspect colleagues. His polemical pyrotechnics and doctrinal originality antagonised such influential churchmen as Bernard of Clairvaux and culminated in 1140 in his being sentenced by Pope Innocent II to perpetual silence as a heretic. Although he may have manipulated his life story into an account of spiritual regeneration, Abelard was truthful in the emphasis he gives in the *Historia calamitatum* on his career, first as the famous philosopher, then as the innovative (and much-maligned) churchman. His seduction of Heloise and his later behaviour towards her have to be seen in the context of his public career, because that was his own order of priorities.

Heloise, by contrast, like the majority of women of the period, had little prospect of public life, except perhaps in the role of prioress or abbess of one of the many religious foundations for women then proliferating in France. Little is known of her parentage and family. In the Paraclete's necrology, a calendar used to record the deaths of members of religious houses, her mother's name is given as Hersindis, but who her father was and the circumstances of her parents' relationship remain obscure. It seems likely, however, that Heloise was born into local minor aristocracy in the region of Paris. This would explain her placement, probably as a child, at the convent of Ste Marie at Argenteuil in the countryside near Paris, on the north bank of the Seine. At a time of rapid growth in the number of female religious houses, it was customary for young daughters of the minor nobility to be sent to a convent to be cared for until old enough to take vows, or, if circumstances were propitious, to marry.[55] In a society that practised primogeniture, the available girls far outnumbered the young men who could afford to marry. Becoming a nun was often the only career choice open to a young woman without the attraction of a substantial dowry. By the time Heloise met Abelard, both her parents had vanished from the scene, perhaps already dead, or themselves retired to some monastic foundation.

The idea of female religious houses as bleak environments populated by saintly women has perhaps never had much currency, at least among those familiar with such establishments. Human nature will prevail, whatever the circumstances, and women herded into religious life without vocation will inevitably seek outlets for worldly tastes and pleasures. Chaucer's prioress in the *Canterbury Tales* is a vain and self-indulgent woman, who feeds expensive treats to her little dogs (nuns were not supposed to keep pets) and whose rosary is decorated with a medallion that reads *Amor vincit omnia* (Love conquers all). God's love was not what the prioress had in mind, although it is unlikely that she would have followed up her blatant invitation. A study of nuns in sixteenth-century Venice reveals a community of women committed to gossip, frivolous shoes and embroidered underwear, and given to forming unsuitable allegiances with serving women. They even accepted roses through the convent grilles from admiring youths.[56] In Heloise's time there was considerable concern about the worldly behaviour of clerics. Legislation was passed to prohibit deacons and priests from aping contemporary fashion by 'wearing long hair, beak-shaped pointed shoes, sewn clothes' and 'having laces on tunics or shirts'.[57] If religious men were so attentive to the niceties of dress, it is unlikely that young girls cloistered together would have escaped the seductions of pretty clothes and flirtation with any male allowed within the precincts. There would have been other tensions, to do with the relationships between girls and nuns, and among the girls themselves. Antonia White's novel, *Frost in May*, about girls growing up in a Catholic boarding school shortly before the First World War, is a painful account of the spiritual and emotional pressures of such an environment. In the convents of twelfth-century France, where young girls read Ovid along with the Bible, an awareness of the body and its temptations would have been inevitable.

In the light of Heloise's subsequent career, her early years at Argenteuil are of tremendous interest in tracing her development as scholar, lover and, eventually, respected abbess. As a grown woman, prioress and then abbess of an important religious foundation, she was alert to the difficulties of protecting and controlling a community of disparate girls and women. Some years after her separation from Abelard, she and her fellow nuns were thrown out of the convent of Argenteuil on charges of immorality, trumped up on flimsy evidence by the Abbot of St Denis who was anxious to get his hands on a wealthy convent. The fact that Abbot Suger could pursue such charges with little investigation by the authorities indicates a moral climate in which the venery of nuns was regarded as commonplace, one of those stereotypes that might have held some grains of truth. It was, in any case, a convenient way of getting hold of women's buildings and benefits on behalf of rival communities of monks. Later still, as abbess of the Paraclete, Heloise wrote anxiously to Abelard to enquire whether Benedictine habits of hospitality were appropriate for female communities. 'It is all too easy for the souls of men and women to be destroyed if they live together in one place, and especially at table, where gluttony and drunkenness are rife, and wine which leads to lechery is drunk with enjoyment,' she commented rather primly.[58] Considering that Heloise had herself once succumbed to Abelard's lust in the refectory at Argenteuil, her anxieties were well founded. In writing to Abelard about the Rule for her community, Heloise revealed a concern for the particular needs and requirements of women that is strikingly modern and recalls the plea of Virginia Woolf eight hundred years later, in her essay *A Room of One's Own*, for women writers and students to be permitted the conditions best suited to their mental and physical make-up, and to enabling them to cope with the many competing responsibilities peculiar to women.[59]

Growing up amid a gossipy community of girls, some intended to be nuns, others for marriage, Heloise may have shaped her unique vision of her female destiny in reaction to what she learned from her fellow students about women's limited choices. Although the Church paid lip-service to the idea of consent in marriage, personal preference was a low priority. A girl with a substantial dowry would be used as a pawn in the game of strategic alliances between great families anxious to consolidate their wealth and power. Even the daughters of minor nobility rarely married for love. Handed over by father or brother to her husband's control, a woman was expected to produce children: sons to secure the family inheritance and daughters to extend its possessions. Implicit in the role of wife was a woman's subordination to her husband. Although there were exceptional women such as the noblewoman Adela of Blois, who managed her husband's estates and financial affairs for many years while he was absent on crusade, this level of female status and power was unusual. As for a woman's rights as mother, these were again a low priority. Even when a woman survived childbearing, she might be separated from her children when they were very young. A daughter betrothed to another juvenile might be sent to live with her future husband's family; a son was often lodged with relatives for military and courtly training.[60]

At Argenteuil, Heloise would also have observed the alternative career option for women, the life of a nun, and she seems again to have been unimpressed by what she saw. Writing to Abelard years later, she made it clear that she had no vocation for monastic life, even though there were substantial benefits for senior women in the community. A Benedictine order, the convent of Ste Marie had been richly endowed by Queen Adelaide in the late tenth century. Its abbess would have been expected to keep in touch with local land-owners as well as churchmen, and had an important role as administrator of a substantial foundation. In that busy and prosperous environment a clever girl could have picked up a useful working knowledge of the profitable management of rents, agricultural land, vineyards and fish ponds, of the combination of tact and flattery required to court influential patrons and sponsors, and the flexibility to meet the diverse needs of a community of nuns. These skills, learnt by proxy at Argenteuil, came to the fore during Heloise's highly successful years as abbess of the Paraclete and its daughter houses. At this early stage of her life, however, her interest seems to have been above all in scholarship, through which she perhaps saw an opportunity to transcend the limitations on women's possibilities. Like Mary Ann Evans (later the writer George Eliot) and the young Virginia Woolf scrambling to acquire the classical education that was automatically available to male members of the family, Heloise may have been energised by the enthusiasm of the autodidact, or she may have been one of a group of bluestocking convent girls, eager to participate in the intellectual vitality that filtered through to Argenteuil from neighbouring Paris. The kind of community in operation at Regensburg in south Germany in the late eleventh century or at Le Ronceray in Angers may well have reflected the environment at Argenteuil. At Regensburg, well-born young women lived in the convent with the sisters, and were allowed association with the outside world through visits from family and clergy. They were taught the liberal arts by a scholar from Liège and Heloise may have received her education in a similar fashion.[61] However she acquired her learning, from the evidence of references in her letters it seems that Heloise was formidably well read, and had a thorough knowledge of the learned and literary texts then available in Latin, including large sections of the Bible, the letters of St Jerome, the essays of Cicero, the poems of Ovid, and epics by

Virgil and Heloise's favourite, the 'silver poet' Lucan, who, like John Keats, was gifted, prolific and dead by the age of twenty-six. Abelard even credits her with a knowledge of Greek and Hebrew.[62] This education was the basis of Heloise's intellectual partnership with Abelard; her ardent, erotic nature the lure that enticed the self-proclaimed sexual novice.

At some period, perhaps in her late teens, possibly some years later, Heloise came to live with her uncle Fulbert in the cathedral close of Notre Dame. The Paris of the early twelfth century was considerably smaller than the modern city, more or less confined to the Île de la Cité, the larger of the two islands on the River Seine. At the eastern end was the cathedral of Notre Dame, an earlier building than the current Gothic edifice. Around two sides of the cathedral was the cloister, a walled close containing a number of houses, each with its own garden. It was probably here that Heloise lived with Fulbert, in close proximity to the school of Notre Dame, where Peter Abelard became master in around 1114. Her love of learning may have brought her to the city. Even though it is unlikely that she was allowed to mix in scholastic circles (Abelard had to lodge with Fulbert in order to meet Heloise), in leaving Argenteuil for the metropolis, she may have been responding, like Abelard himself, to the attraction of living in an important intellectual and cultural centre. She had the benefit of family support. Despite his conventional notions about female chastity, her uncle seems to have played a significant role in encouraging Heloise's scholarly aspirations.

Fulbert is frequently portrayed as a bully, whose incestuous feelings for his niece explain the viciousness of the blood feud he waged against Abelard once the love affair was discovered. It is possible, however, to see Fulbert in a more sympathetic light. In a series of poems meditating on Heloise's story, the modern poet Hilary Davies offers a sensitive interpretation of Fulbert as a devoted brother, who regretted his sister's wasted opportunities. When they were children,

Hersindis was 'spirit, counsellor, adversary and friend' to her brother, but her dragonfly glamour was frittered away on the 'banal things men expect of women'.[63] Her daughter must have a better chance in life. It seems unlikely that Fulbert was an early feminist in quite the way Davies imagines, but he was evidently proud of Heloise and actively supported her education in Paris. His enlightened attitude towards his niece may have made her fall from grace all the more difficult for Fulbert to accept and there is again the question of personal vanity. Just as Abelard wanted the kudos of bedding the learned virgin, so Fulbert seems to have relished the notoriety of his clever niece and may have enjoyed boasting about employing the famous Abelard as her teacher.

Why did Heloise fall in love with Abelard and what kind of relationship did she dream of having with him? Sex was evidently deeply important, but she seems also to have craved intellectual and emotional companionship. Her letters attest to their shared reading and her desire to impress him with her erudition and literary skill. She freely confesses that she adored his fame and status, and relished being known as his mistress. But Heloise also cries out for intimacy, for the personal word and gesture, which would distinguish her as Abelard's chosen soulmate from among the nuns at the Paraclete. She addresses him in one letter as *'unice'*, her only one, and in another as *'Suo specialiter, sua singulariter'*, which the medieval scholar Peter Dronke, one of Heloise's most fluent interpreters, suggests can be translated as 'To him who in a special way is hers, she who is uniquely his'.[64] Heloise's desire for validation recalls Simone de Beauvoir's rather contemptuous description of the dependent 'woman in love', but at a profounder, more recognisably human level it asserts her claim on Abelard to acknowledge the special place she has in his life. It attests, as well, to a passionate desire, which recurs in women's writings about love: the need to strip away all veils and pretences, and to be known and loved for oneself alone. In his poem 'For Anne Gregory', Yeats mocks the aspiration of women to be loved for their essential selves; only God is capable of such love. In Heloise's case, however much Abelard directed her to turn her thoughts to God, what she wanted was Abelard's devotion.

Heloise's plea to Abelard also reflects her isolation. Her relationships with other women remain a mystery. As a young woman and then as a nun, she does not appear to have had a coterie of female companions with whom to share her feelings and interests, although it is difficult to know where evidence of such friendships might survive. One can only turn to Heloise's letters to Abelard and her record as an abbess responsible for women of all ages, a role that might not have lent itself to intimacy with her charges. When she mentions female role models, it is not her contemporaries, or even women from the recent past whom she cites. Her notions of female heroinism and possibilities for good and evil are drawn from the classical past, the Bible and the Church Fathers: texts that were written by men and often tainted by misogyny. Her letters to Abelard, casting herself as a woman in need of succour and consolation, connect her with Ovid's *Heroides*, a series of poetic letters ostensibly written by women to their absent lovers.[65]

Ovid was widely read in the twelfth century and, in the repinings of such abandoned heroines as Dido, Ariadne and Medea, Heloise may have found comfort and imaginative stimulus for her own sad reveries of a vanished past. However sympathetic Ovid's treatment, these are generally unhappy tales, where the outcome is at best equivocal and where the women are constrained to follow the destinies and wishes of their men. Penelope, waiting for Ulysses during his extended absence after the fall of Troy, is better off than Queen Dido casting herself into the flames when Aeneas abandons her, but these are hardly positive images of female authority and independence. Similarly, when Heloise blames herself for the seduction of Abelard, she follows his lead in the *Historia calamitatum* in citing the traditional Christian view of women as responsible for men's downfall. Eve condemned Adam to hard labour and death,

Delilah unmanned Samson, even the wise Solomon was plunged into idolatry on the advice of a persuasive wife. Given such evidence, well might the sage in Ecclesiastes warn: 'And I find more bitter than death the woman, whose heart is snares and nets, and her hands as bands[.]'[66]

Even in formulating her personal vision of a loving relationship, Heloise draws on models from the past. In her rejection of marriage and disdain of 'squalid' domestic life for scholars, she looks back to the ascetic ideals of the classical philosophers, the teachings of St Paul and the lives and writings of the early Church Fathers. Her fantasy of the perfect partnership draws on Cicero and Ambrose, although both authorities, of course, only envisage such an arrangement between men. In his essay *De amicitia*, Cicero proposes a wholly disinterested friendship, in which each partner is loved without any thought of personal gain or benefit. The feelings that play between the two friends veer across the spectrum from friendship (*amicitia*) to love (*amor*) and Cicero paints a charming picture of the harmonious life of two such good companions, recalling his own relationship with Scipio: 'We shared the same house, we ate the same meals, and we ate them side by side.' Every spare moment was 'devoted to study and research, withdrawn from the eyes of the world but enjoying the company of one another'.[67] Ambrose draws freely on this ideal of friendship for his definition of Christian *amicitia* in *De Officiis*:

What is a friend if not a consort of love, to whom you can join and attach your spirit, mingling it so that out of two you would become one? One to whom you are united as to another self, from whom you fear nothing, from whom you yourself seek nothing dishonourable for the sake of advantage – for friendship is not calculating, but full of beauty, full of grace. It is virtue not gain ... What is more precious than friendship, which is common to angels and men?[68]

This attractive image of loving companionship would have been almost impossible to fulfil between a man and a woman within the restrictive sexual and intellectual climate of twelfth-century France. In practical terms, what Heloise may have had in mind was some kind of formal concubinage, models of which were possibly available among clerics at Notre Dame.[69] But the Church increasingly frowned on such arrangements and her uncle in any case would probably not have permitted it.

Writing in an age that long pre-dated romanticism, Heloise's dream of companionate love resonates with the aspirations of such talented, innovative women as Mary Wollstonecraft and Simone de Beauvoir. In her adulation of Abelard, she recalls Charlotte Brontë and the artist Gwen John, both clever (and motherless) women who fell in love with men whom they worshipped as their 'master', and to whom, like Heloise, they were prepared to offer their devotion with almost masochistic zeal. (Sylvia Plath, heroically typing up Ted Hughes's poems to mail to magazines and journals, belongs to the same tradition.) Isolated and ambitious in a society that did not value female intellect and talent, Charlotte Brontë fell in love with her teacher Constantin Heger because he talked to her, encouraged her to read and judged her writings with an impartial eye.[70] Living within the cloisters at Notre Dame, the 'supreme' scholar Heloise was similarly solitary. When she met Abelard she relished the opportunity to taste the fruits of knowledge with a famous, gifted man. It was a relationship George Eliot was to evoke as an ideal in her novel *Daniel Deronda*, although she underestimated Heloise's contribution to the learned dialogue:

> . . . more potent still is frequent companionship, with full sympathy in taste, and admirable qualities on both sides; especially where the one is in the position of teacher, and the other is delightedly conscious of receptive ability which also gives the teacher delight. The situation is famous in history, and has no less charm now than it had in the days of Abelard.[71]

Letter-writing Women

Heloise's isolation may have been self-imposed, a result perhaps of her unique gifts and unusual sense of personal destiny. Despite her apparent lack of female confidantes, her bluestocking enthusiasms and wish for a close relationship with a male mentor were shared by other women at that period. Surviving manuscript collections offer intriguing examples of letters and poems in Latin sent to and fro between men and women.[72] Many of these exchanges were preserved in manuscript collections as models of good writing, at a time when the elegant and appropriate use of Latin was the mark of an educated person. These examples of women's skill in Latin composition suggest an environment in which women were able actively to participate in contemporary literary enthusiasms, and were closely involved in debates about the appropriate relationship between men and women in religious and secular life. They are also personally revealing. The language used by the correspondents is often astonishingly sensual. Some decades before Heloise was writing to Abelard, the monk Baudri of Bourgueil was enjoying a suggestive exchange with a young nun at the wealthy abbey of Notre-Dame du Ronceray in Angers. Writing to his goddaughter Constance to declare his spiritual friendship, Baudri pens a letter-poem in eighty-nine couplets in which he employs the worldly language of erotic love and recalls the *grandes passions* celebrated by Ovid, the favourite love poet of the Middle Ages, in his *Metamorphoses* and *Heroides*:

> You are more to me, better and greater,
>> than goddess, than maiden, than any love there is;
> You are more to me than Paris was to Helen,
>> Venus to Mars, Juno to Jupiter.

He teases Constance with a daring reference to physical contact, which he then dismisses:

> Your naked hand will touch my naked page . . .
> You can safely lay it in your lap.[73]

Constance's response, a letter-poem that exactly matches Baudri's in length and form, wittily acknowledges her godfather's ribaldry: 'With my hand I have touched your naked songs.' She too can be suggestive:

> I put the letter under my left breast –
>> they say that's nearest to the heart . . .
> At last, weary, I tried to get to sleep,
>> but love that has been wakened knows no night . . .
> I lay asleep – no, sleepless – because the page you wrote,
>> though lying on my breast, had set my womb on fire.[74]

For all her flirtatiousness, Constance is conscious of her spiritual destiny. 'Oh if only I could live as bride of God!' she exclaims, a reminder of the reality of her situation.[75] The idea of the nun as Christ's cherished spouse, which Abelard also urges on Heloise, derives from a long tradition of Christian teaching on the Song of Songs, which Bernard of Clairvaux, a contemporary of Heloise and Abelard, was to reintroduce to the medieval Church as a sublime allegory of the reciprocal love of Christ and his servants. The sensuality of the image was both emphasised and nullified by its Christian setting of continence and self-denial. Heloise's marriage of minds might have been permissible in such a context as Baudri's carefully modulated correspondence with Constance. In a religious atmosphere in which the Church reluctantly conceded that it was better to marry than to burn, and in which sex was regarded as a necessary evil for the sake of procreation, Heloise's attempt at a bodily relationship with her teacher was scandalous and, in the eyes of their critics, only redeemable by the religious life she and Abelard subsequently embraced.

Other women faced similar conflicts. The young women at the convent in Regensburg sent tender, admonitory letters to their tutor, proposing an approach to love that valued the classical qualities of *virtus* and *probitas*, and respected honour rather than Ovidian dalliance.[76] A twelfth-century manuscript from Tegernsee (also in Bavaria) contains a diverse collection of women's letters, which were preserved in a monastic library because of their literary style, but they include material of great human interest.[77] Underlying the smooth Latin phrases are the tensions and conflicts of men and women struggling to express their need for sex, friendship and love in a social climate in which churchmen prated about female chastity and women were seen as true daughters of Eve, gossipy, lecherous and prone to mischief. One woman reproaches a lover for abandoning her; another declares her devotion to a female friend despite the great distance that separates the two. The writer of a third letter is torn between her male correspondent's demand that she offer him absolute trust, her fear that this may compromise her reputation and a rueful awareness that love demands both effort and suffering. 'Take care that no one sees this letter,' she warns, but somehow her words have survived, offering a tantalising glimpse of a woman in the grip of contradictory emotions.[78] Such exchanges provide an illuminating context for the love affair between Abelard and Heloise, in which letters were a crucial aspect of courtship and intimacy.

Particularly intriguing among these collections are the *Epistolae*

duorum amantium, the 'Letters of Two Lovers', which were tran-
scribed from an earlier manuscript at Clairvaux in 1471 by a young
monk researching suitable material to include in an anthology.
Although the exchange is incomplete and open to a variety of
interpretations, the *Epistolae* chart the trajectory of a love affair with
its quarrels and reconciliations, protestations and sulks. One possible
reading suggests a train of events that sounds unexpectedly familiar.
An older man falls in love with a younger woman, towards whom
he has some formal relationship as teacher or mentor. He declares
his passionate attachment; she wants a probing conversation about
love to support their sexual relationship. The man evades her
attempts to establish intimacy; she is disappointed, but eventually
accepting. He worries about his career and what people will say
about their relationship; she is less concerned with public opinion.
A period of stand-off is abruptly terminated by her joyful announce-
ment that she is pregnant. The man is horrified at the news.[79]

Such a reading would support the argument that these were
letters written by Heloise and Abelard during the early stages of
their courtship, although scholars are still divided over this question.[80] Abelard suggested in the *Historia calamitatum* that an
exchange of letters with Heloise was part of his plan in seducing
her and, writing from the Paraclete, Heloise nostalgically recalled
the stream of notes Abelard had once sent her. Whether or not the
Epistolae are part of this lost early correspondence, they offer a
fascinating account of a man's resistance to his lover's demand for
close engagement. Instead of the thoughtful analysis of the nature
of their love the woman requires, the male writer offers compliments. It is an evasion of intimacy that Mary Wollstonecraft was
later to mock in her correspondence with William Godwin. The
cautious philosopher seems, touchingly, to have written a poem
dedicated to Mary, but she was dissatisfied with the result and
admonished him not 'to choose the easiest task, my perfections, but
to dwell on your own feelings – that is to say, give me a bird's-eye

view of your heart'.[81] Her tone is gay, but the theme is serious. 'Talk to me,' she is saying to Godwin, as Heloise, Charlotte Brontë and the unknown woman in the 'Letters of Two Lovers' similarly begged their lovers to be open with them.

Abelard's Rejection of Love

Abelard's responses to Heloise throughout their affair and its aftermath were conditioned by differences in expectation and opportunity which were largely functions of gender. When they met, he had already achieved public status; her fantasy was of supporting his career, gladly relinquishing conventional female domesticity and even respectability in order to promote his interests. As Heloise pointed out to Abelard, she wanted to prove the integrity and disinterestedness of her love; she wanted him to be free from legal and familial ties. All this appears to have passed over Abelard's head. When it came to the crunch, he wanted marriage so that he could keep her for himself.

Was Abelard driven solely by lust? At this distance of time and given the rather different notions of sexual and marital love that prevailed in the early twelfth century, it is impossible to be certain about his motivation. In his later rejection of his sexual self, Abelard was acting within a well-established framework of spiritual penitence and the Christian ascetic ideal. When he wrote about the affair in the *Historia calamitatum* and in his letters to Heloise, he had been castrated for many years, a factor for which Heloise appears to have made little allowance, but which must have had profound psychological as well as physical effects. Abelard's biographer, Mike Clanchy, suggests that the castration would have been carried out with 'surgical care'.[82] Judicial castration appears to have been performed by drawing the scrotum tight with a cord in order to limit bleeding, while the testicles were cut out with a knife. This method

48

was probably employed in Abelard's case. He records that he felt little pain and he may well have been secretly drugged by his servant. He writes that he was peacefully asleep when his attackers burst in. Whether Abelard would have continued to feel sexual desire after castration is arguable. Eunuchs subject to similar mutilation apparently retained sexual feelings and were even able to have erections. As Clanchy comments, whatever the medical evidence, Abelard and his contemporaries believed that castration caused impotence.[83]

This belief was reflected in folk legends of the period, many of which were connected with Abelard's birthplace of Brittany. In *Chaitivel*, one of the Breton lays recorded by Marie de France, a knight is pierced in the thigh by a lance during a tournament. Such a wound was a circumlocution for castration and the knight later complains to his lady that he is the most wretched of men. He constantly keeps company with the woman he loves, 'yet I cannot experience the joy of a kiss or an embrace or of any pleasure other than conversation'.[84] It is clearly not simply the conventions of *fin'amor*, the courtly code of love, that are holding him back. Chrétien de Troyes's *The Story of the Grail*, with its mysterious account of the Fisher King, also derives from Celtic myth. In Chrétien's tale the king's wound, again clearly resulting in impotence, has laid bare his territories. Bleak and infertile, they have become a wasteland, the inspiration for T. S. Eliot's poem of that name, and a symbol for the vacuousness of the inter-war years in twentieth-century Europe.

Abelard's condition had further links with medieval mythology. In a biography of St Goswin (an intellectual who, in his youth, had the temerity to challenge Abelard during one of his explosive lectures), Abelard is described as *rhinoceros indomitus*, a reference to Pope Gregory the Great's commentary on the Book of Job, in which he described the rhinoceros as 'altogether indomitable in its nature'. The rhinoceros was seen as an allegory of pride, linked with heresy and voluptuousness. Like the mythical unicorn, a graceful creature with a coiled horn in the middle of its forehead, it can be tamed by the sight of a virgin's breast.[85] In the mysterious tapestries of the Lady and the Unicorn, now in the Musée du Moyen Age at Cluny, the hanging representing 'Sight' shows the unicorn reposing in the lap of a beautiful young woman, who holds up a mirror so that it can view its own reflection. Like the rhinoceros and the unicorn, the dangerous Abelard was also tamed by a virgin, but the process cost him his 'horn'.

Whatever Abelard's physical experience of castration, it was evidently psychologically traumatic. He wrote that he suffered extreme humiliation, which may well have caused repugnance at the thought of sex. In such a context, Heloise's still vivid memories of the pleasures of love may have repelled Abelard. Indeed, it was the sense of shame that drove him to take orders and, as the *Historia calamitatum* records, he swiftly sought refuge in the idea of spiritual regeneration. His new zeal for asceticism was essential to his reputation and success as a monk. It was also necessary to rebuilding his self-respect. In accordance with Jesus's prescription, he had claimed his right to enter the kingdom of heaven by quite literally becoming a eunuch.[86]

There is another difference between the lovers, which is one of emotional honesty or perhaps simply focus of feeling. In the *Historia calamitatum* and the letters, Abelard maintains a distance from Heloise. As a priest with a public position to uphold, he rejects their love affair, condemns and belittles his sexual feelings, and confines his generosity to encouraging her spiritual well-being. By this time Heloise herself has a position to maintain, but she ignores her worldly and spiritual standing to throw herself at Abelard's feet. She is not a pious woman, she claims; she suffers the torments of desire; she longs for her lover to acknowledge what they have lost. His answer is to guide her to God.

The love affair of Abelard and Heloise has sometimes been compared to the tragedy of Tristram and Yseult, which was current in

Europe from the twelfth century and again possibly originated in Abelard's native Brittany. There is another less well-known story, which more closely mirrors their experience, a romance written three hundred years later by René, King of Sicily and Duke of Anjou. René's *Le Livre du Cueur d'Amours Espris*, often called his 'Book of Love', tells the painful story of the Heart as Love's knight. Instructed by Love, Cueur (the Heart) and his page Desire set out to liberate the lady Sweet Grace, who is being held captive by three enemies of Love: Denial, Shame and Fear. Despite the intercession of Amour, the young God of Love, and the successful release of Sweet Grace, the party is ambushed on its joyful journey to the Chateau of Pleasure. Desire is killed, Cueur is sorely hurt and Sweet Grace is taken back into captivity. Cueur's later days are spent in prayer and silent remembrance. René's exquisite tale reflects the influence and development of the courtly code of *fin'amor*, which swept through Europe from the early twelfth century in the wake of the troubadour poets. Its allegory of love's burning imperatives is carefully placed in a framework of Christian renunciation and self-discipline. This formal fable of the perils of love offers insight into the forces arrayed against Abelard and Heloise. Love's sweetness is challenged by opponents whom the life-loving René represents as mean-spirited and uncourtly. For all the Heart's debonair courage, it is the enemies of Love who prevail in the end.

~

Despite the years of self-discipline and leadership that followed the end of her marriage, as Heloise became Abbess of the Paraclete and established the daughter houses spawned by the foundation, it seems that she never repented of her love affair. In the final years of his life Peter Abelard wrote a poem of advice for their son, Astralabe, in which he spoke about the value of repentance and referred to those who are unable to repent because their past sins are still so attractive:

This is the burden of complaint of our Heloise,
whereby she often says to me, as to herself,
'If I can not be saved without repenting
of what I used to commit, there is no hope for me.
The joys of what we did are still so sweet
that, after delight beyond measure, even remembering brings
    relief.'[87]

Fascinating as evidence of Heloise's continued refusal to repent what was clearly the most significant event of her life, the poem also suggests that Abelard at least carried on some kind of correspondence with his son. He talks about Heloise's complaint as if it were a matter well known to Astralabe and still frequently discussed between his parents. Did Heloise write to Astralabe about his parents' love affair? Did she ever see her son? All that is known about him is that he was left as a young baby with Abelard's family and later, after Abelard's death, Heloise wrote to Peter the Venerable asking if he could find Astralabe a prebend in Paris or some other diocese. Recording Heloise's death in either 1163 or 1164, the nuns described her affectionately as 'mother of our order', but how she felt about Astralabe, her real child, can only be conjectured. Abelard described her as delighted to be pregnant, despite her horror of nappies and nursemaids in the scholar's household, but she was very quickly separated from her baby and may have had little opportunity to see him as he grew up. We know from the handbook written in the ninth century for her young son by a Carolingian woman, Dhuoda, how passionate a mother's love could be even when forced to live separately from her child.[88] Might Heloise not have loved Astralabe, if only as a reminder of the passion she once shared with his father? Abelard's poem tantalisingly suggests a family trio of which the evidence has almost entirely disappeared.

Like the story of Tristram and Yseult, the love affair between

Abelard and Heloise entered the realm of romantic legend in which so many details become obscured. There was a surprising coda to their relationship, a human response, which was both touching and spiritually significant. After Abelard's condemnation for heresy following the Council of Sens in 1140, he was offered shelter by Peter the Venerable, the Abbot of Cluny, who made it possible for Abelard to spend his final years in peaceful pursuit of the ascetic, scholarly life he had long craved. When Abelard died around two years later, Peter wrote to Heloise, paying tribute to her lifelong reputation for learning and her dedication to the spiritual life. In Peter's theology, at least, Heloise's sinful commitment to Abelard had long since been redeemed by her dedication to God, and he concluded with a remarkable image that gracefully acknowledged the relationship between the former lovers and hallowed it with the shining light of God's benignity. Writing tenderly of her dual union of flesh and spirit with Abelard, he promised Heloise that 'him, I say, in your place, or as another you, God cherishes in his bosom, and keeps him there to be restored to you through his grace at the coming of the Lord, at the voice of the archangel, and the trumpet-note of God descending from heaven.'[89] In this daring vision of God cherishing Abelard on Heloise's behalf until the lovers were united at the Last Trump, Peter paid tribute to a love affair that seems, despite all the scandal at the time, to have left an indelible imprint on the imaginations of those who heard about it. Whether Heloise smiled wryly at Peter's praise of her piety it is impossible to know. She would have seen nothing incongrous in the idea of her own restoration to God once her life was finished. Writing to Abelard to confess her spiritual weakness, she nevertheless had the confidence to assure him, 'In whatever corner of heaven God shall place me, I shall be satisfied.'[90] Heloise was convinced that she would find a niche in heaven. In Peter's beatific vision, her place was to be with Abelard in the bosom of the Lord.

PART 2

Shimmerings of a Summer Sky: The Transient Loves of the Japanese Court

'I want to reveal all to you, the good and the bad, worldly matters and private sorrows ...'

Murasaki Shikibu, *The Diary of Lady Murasaki*[1]

The Romantic Hero and His Loves: Murasaki Shikibu and 'the Shining Prince'

A beautiful woman is hounded to death by jealous rivals. A little girl is kidnapped by a wealthy aristocrat, who schemes to make her his mistress. A mother is persuaded to hand over her only child to another woman's care. In a moment of bitterness Lady Murasaki, the heroine of the novel in which these stories are told, reflects on the self-restraint which society requires of women.[2] Whatever her feelings about the pleasures and sorrows of this fleeting world, a woman was expected to be 'sensitive but silent'.[3] Written around one thousand years ago by a woman known as Murasaki Shikibu, *The Tale of Genji* (*Genji Monogatari*) challenges the convention of woman's silence by revealing the realities of life for aristocratic women at the high point of Japanese Heian culture. The novel tells the story of 'the shining prince', Genji, and the wives and courtesans whom he loves, beds and finally houses at his splendid mansion in Heian Kyō, the City of Peace and Tranquillity, for centuries the capital of Japan and home of the emperor and his court.

Murasaki Shikibu's novel is a remarkable achievement. Its fifty-four chapters span seventy-five years and involve four generations. There are over four hundred characters, many of whom are related. The plot, while more or less chronological, weaves in and out of different characters and locations, sometimes anticipating future events or recalling a situation that has happened many pages previously. Her expert handling of complexity implies either prodigious feats of memory on the part of the author, or else that she kept systematic charts of who did what and when. In translation, the novel runs to around 625,000 words. All this was achieved by a woman writing with brush and inkstone on whatever scraps of paper she had to hand and, as she mentions in her diary, with no safe place to store her manuscript.[4] Quite how she managed to create what is generally recognised as a masterpiece of world literature and the first psychological novel in its history is almost as remarkable as the work she produced.

Little is known about Murasaki Shikibu's life, although tantalising details can be gleaned from her diary, in which she recorded her life at court from 1008 to 1010. Even her real name has not been discovered. The name by which she is commonly known may combine the name of the heroine of her novel, also Murasaki, with a reference to her father's position in the Ministry of Ceremonial (Shikibu Shō). The Japanese word *murasaki* means 'lavender', the colour of *fuji* or wisteria, perhaps an allusion to Murasaki's illustrious family, the Fujiwara clan, who dominated Heian politics from 967 to 1068.[5] Murasaki was born in about 973 to a junior branch of the Fujiwaras, and included a distinguished poet and a literary statesman among her forebears. She appears to have inherited her bookishness from her father and early showed signs of a taste for learning. Although official links with China had ceased almost a century previously, Chinese culture had retained its prestige, and the young Murasaki seems to have delighted in delving into Chinese history and literature. In her diary she records how she would listen to her brother's lessons, quickly becoming proficient at translating and memorising passages that he found too difficult. But a classical education was regarded as a handicap for a girl and 'Just my luck!' her father would complain. 'What a pity she was not born a man!'[6] Perhaps because prospective suitors were wary of her bluestocking reputation, Murasaki was married at a comparatively late age for a Heian noblewoman (about twenty). She was certainly aware of the problems of too much education. There is an amusing scene in the early chapters of *The Tale of Genji* in which a group of young men discuss what attracts them in women. Too much knowledge is frowned on as unfeminine, and the Chinese language in particular is criticised as 'muscular and unyielding' when used by women.[7] Worst of all, perhaps, is the woman who tries to show off her scanty knowledge of the Chinese classics, while knowing nothing about everyday matters that interest her lover. As Jane Austen observed in *Lady Susan*, a woman is rarely courted for her learning. '[T]o be Mistress of French, Italian, German . . . will gain a Woman some applause,' declares her worldly heroine, but such acquirements 'will not add one Lover to her list'. For Georgian misses and Heian ladies alike, 'Grace & Manner after all are of the greatest importance'.[8]

Murasaki's husband, Fujiwara no Nobutaka, probably a kinsman, was considerably older than her and had at least three other wives, so the marriage may have been a matter of family interest rather than of love. He seems to have been a confident, rather arrogant character, whose high-handed approach caused dissent when he was a provincial governor.[9] The court lady Sei Shōnagon commented on his unusual habit of dressing up for pilgrimages to Mount Mitake at a time when most travellers wore their shabbiest clothes for the gruelling journey. His flamboyance paid off. When he was appointed governor of the large province of Chikuzen, people whispered that the God of Mitake must have approved of his stylish dress.[10] Murasaki left no record of her feelings towards her husband, who died in an epidemic in 1001, leaving her with at least one daughter. Although her diary records regrets for the past, she refers only obliquely to her husband and never mentions her child.[11] It may have been during a period of seclusion after his death that Murasaki began work on the novel that was to make her reputation in her lifetime. After several years in retirement, she became lady-in-waiting to the Empress Akiko, consort to the reigning Emperor Ichijō, a position that placed Murasaki at the centre of court life and politics. After a tentative start, in which she seems to have intimidated her young employer, Murasaki won the Empress's heart by secretly reading Chinese poetry with her. If even the Empress found it advisable to pursue her intellectual interests in private, the pressure on women to avoid 'unfeminine' behaviour must have been considerable. In spite of this, the Emperor seems to have been charmed by his wife's clandestine studies. When he discovered their secret, he and his powerful courtier Fujiwara no Michinaga, Akiko's father, arranged for copies of favourite Chinese works to be presented to the women. Although Murasaki makes much of her efforts to be self-effacing, her talents evidently caused something of a stir in court circles. Chapters of *The Tale of Genji* were already in circulation, arousing envy as well as admiration, and Murasaki records her indignation at being nicknamed 'Lady Chronicle' by a spiteful lady-in-waiting.[12] In spite of her disclaimers, she seems to have enjoyed her reputation for learning, but like many clever women she found it difficult to abandon scholarly reserve for the trivial gossip so popular among the women of the imperial court.

In a revealing passage in the diary she describes the rather stuffy impression she made on her fellow ladies-in-waiting. By reputation she was regarded as 'pretentious, awkward, difficult to approach, prickly, too fond of her tales, haughty, prone to versifying, disdainful, cantankerous and scornful; but when you meet her, she is strangely meek, a completely different person altogether!' In short, she claims, she was regarded as 'a dullard' face to face, but she adds defiantly, 'I am what I am.'[13] Murasaki's assertion of identity reverberates down the centuries, repeated again and again by women writers who felt themselves at odds with prevailing ideas about female behaviour. The riches of Murasaki's inner world, the source of her rebellious 'I am', are revealed in her perceptiveness and the compassion and sensitivity with which she describes her characters in *The Tale of Genji*, as well as in her unusual gifts as narrator and poet. Given her unfashionable interests and tendency to introspection, it is not surprising that she failed to win popularity in the hurly-burly of the Empress's court. The extrovert Sei Shōnagon, who served for some years in the entourage of Akiko's rival, the Empress Sadako, was far more adept at the social skills required of a court lady and her commonplace book, known as *The Pillow Book* (*Makura no Sōshi*), is crammed with amusing anecdotes about her zestful negotiation of the pleasures and perils of waiting on an empress.[14]

Murasaki's later life is unknown. She may have accompanied the Empress Akiko into her long retirement when Emperor Ichijō died in 1011. She is mentioned in the historical *A Tale of Flowering Fortunes* (*Eiga Monogatari*) for 1025, but has vanished from the record six years later, which suggests that she may have died or sought seclusion in a convent by then.[15] All that can safely be said about the writing of her novel is that chapters were in circulation at court by 1008 and most, if not all, of the work had been completed by 1022.[16] As for her personal experience of love, apart from the fact that she was married, we know almost nothing about Murasaki's most intimate relationships. In contrast to the worldly tone adopted by Sei Shōnagon, Murasaki's diary suggests that she kept aloof from the sexual intrigues that thrived in the imperial court, even daring to slap the wrists of the lecherous Michinaga when he made advances. When he wrote her a suggestive poem, Murasaki was prompt with a cutting response:

His Excellency [Michinaga] saw *The Tale of Genji* lying about in the Empress' apartments. He made his usual stupid jibes, and then handed me a poem written on a piece of paper to which he had attached a branch of plum-blossom: 'What with these ardent tales of love, little can I think that men have passed you by, as they might this plum-tree's sour fruit.' And so I replied,

'If no man has tasted, who can say if the fruit is sour, or if the writer of these tales herself has known such love?'[17]

Soon afterwards she was disturbed by a tapping on the window shutter of her room and lay awake all night in terrified silence. In the morning another brisk exchange of poems left Michinaga in no doubt that his attentions were unwelcome. This is all that Murasaki was prepared to reveal of her adventures with court gallants, and how she acquired the knowledge of love and passion that is so evident in *The Tale of Genji* remains a matter for conjecture.

Trying to piece together a sexual biography of Murasaki Shikibu is even more difficult than in the case of Jane Austen, another writer whose prodigious powers were hidden behind a waspish persona. Despite the centuries that separate the two women (Jane Austen was born in 1775, almost exactly eight hundred years after Murasaki Shikibu), they had much in common as writers. They shared a keen and ironic observation of the society in which they found themselves, and an acute sensitivity to the narrowness and constraints of women's lives. Both were literary pioneers, developing fledgling forms of the novel into a flexible instrument for exploring human behaviour, particularly in regard to love, courtship and marriage. Both pioneered new ways of revealing character through subtly layered perspectives and a nuanced use of language. By the late eighteenth century the English language had been evolving for centuries as a literary medium, but most published works had been written by men. One of Jane Austen's great achievements was to refine English prose into a suitable vehicle for her unique and female talents. In the case of Murasaki the use of vernacular Japanese for literary works was comparatively recent, but, for once, sexual differentiation operated in favour of the woman writer. While male writers were still obliged to employ the prestigious Chinese language and characters for any serious composition, women were free to use the *kana* phonetic script, developed from a native syllabary known as the 'woman's hand'. This enabled them to reproduce the Japanese language as it was spoken, a tool that Murasaki and other women writers used with great freedom and fluency. The Heian period saw an astonishing flowering of vernacular literature and its reliance on the 'woman's hand' rather than 'men's letters' (Chinese characters) gave women an opportunity to develop their skills in a variety of literary fields, including diaries, travelogues and the *monogatari* (prose fictions), of which *The Tale of Genji* is such an outstanding example.[18]

Like Jane Austen, Murasaki wrote about what she had observed at first hand. Love, marriage and sexual intrigue are her themes, but an interaction between politics and sex was fundamental to Heian society. From the very first page of *The Tale of Genji* the reader is plunged into the competitive world of the Heian court, and the snobbery, jealousy and power struggles that made life fraught for so many courtiers, especially the women. In the novel the emperor's reckless passion for a young lady 'not of the first rank' causes ripples of anger among the other imperial consorts. When the lady gives birth to a son, the senior wife is in a fret of anxiety in case her own child should lose his position as successor to the imperial throne. Furious at the hours the emperor spends in his private rooms with this minor concubine, the court women treat her with hostility and contempt. Worn out by their antagonism, the lady falls ill and eventually dies. Gentle and unassuming, she was too fragile to cope with the emperor's passion or its consequences. Like many young girls, her father's hopes had brought her to court, but his premature death left her without support. Even the emperor's love could not protect her. While his women fumed at the flouting of proprieties, what was most at stake was control of the emperor and the all-important question of the succession. But Murasaki is less concerned with dynastic issues than the vulnerability of young women and the cost to girls of parental ambition, themes she will return to again and again in the novel.[19] The child of this unfortunate lady is the beautiful Genji, nicknamed 'the shining prince' for his remarkable talents, a hero who will become a source of suffering as well as pleasure to the many women he seduces.

Although she changes names and deals with fictitious situations, the opening chapters of Murasaki's novel reflect the dynamics of the imperial court and provide the context for much of the subsequent action. By the late tenth century the emperor had become no more than a puppet authority dominated by the Fujiwara family, who maintained control of the throne by judicious marriage. Fujiwara daughters were bred to the role of imperial consort and Fujiwara no Michinaga, the senior statesman at the centre of court life in Murasaki's diary, married four daughters to successive emperors. They in turn gave birth to a further three emperors. During the thirty years in which he controlled Heian political life, Michinaga avoided high office, never becoming chancellor and only serving as regent for a brief period.[20] Like the Medici in fifteenth-century Florence, he made canny use of family connections, patronage and an enthusiasm for the arts to establish his predominance, which is chronicled in another work by a female writer, *A Tale of Flowering Fortunes* (*Eiga Monogatari*). Believed to have been written by the celebrated poet Akazome Emon, this is a record of court life from 887 to 1028, but is largely devoted to celebrating Michinaga's achievements.[21]

While Michinaga enjoyed decades at the centre of government, the authority of the reigning emperor was short-lived and paradoxically compromised by his powerful family connections, who treated him as a convenient figurehead. Typically, the emperor succeeded to the throne when very young and was obliged in his early thirties to abdicate in favour of his son, the crown prince, whose mother would almost inevitably have been a Fujiwara daughter.[22] This process and the pressures on imperial spouses can be observed in the history of Ichijō, the reigning emperor at the time of both Sei Shōnagon's *The Pillow Book* and Murasaki's diary. The son of an emperor and a Fujiwara consort, Ichijō succeeded to the throne at the age of six and was married at ten to a first cousin, Fujiwara no Sadako, who was five years his senior. Sadako's joy at the birth of a son nine years later was overshadowed by the introduction of Michinaga's daughter, Akiko, as a secondary royal consort. Eight years younger than her husband, Akiko quickly became his preferred wife. When Sadako died in childbirth in 1001, Akiko's prospects (and those of her father) must have looked good, but her first son was not born until 1008.

Murasaki's diary begins with an account of the ritual attending the birth of this important imperial baby and describes Michinaga's extravagant joy in his grandson, born after years of anxious waiting. Akiko's second son arrived in 1009, but two years later Emperor Ichijō suffered a serious illness and abdicated at the age of thirty-one. Within days he was dead and Akiko began her long retirement as Dowager Empress, possibly with Murasaki Shikibu as a member of her establishment.[23] Each of her two sons eventually became emperor, helping to perpetuate Fujiwara authority. This is the context in which Genji and his companions act out their love affairs, against a background of powerful family interests, shifting allegiances and the pomp and ceremony of the imperial court. There were advantages to the Fujiwara stranglehold on Japanese political life. Although the ruling class's myopia about life outside the capital eventually proved disastrous, the Fujiwara regime provided an extended period of peace and prosperity in which the arts of civilised living could evolve and flourish. These arts, the pursuit of style, taste and sensibility, were what gave meaning and occupation to the vacant hours of the well-born woman.

Murasaki's novel deals with a tiny stratum of Heian society, an aristocratic clique distinguished by wealth, leisure and an obsession with good taste. The vast majority of women and men in Japan at this period were peasants living in abject poverty, but their lives and struggles barely impinged on the 'good people' whose prosperity depended on their labour. These included the nobility of the Heian court and the lesser officials who administered the provinces. Although many of the men in Murasaki's novel hold high-ranking office in the government, there is almost no mention of their formal duties. Of supreme importance to both men and women was the cultivation of aesthetic skills: the exchange of impromptu poems, designed to display the writer's sensitivity and written in exquisite calligraphy on carefully chosen paper, and the related arts of dress, carefully dyed fabrics and sophisticated perfumes. Most of all, the 'good people' enlivened their idle moments by the pursuit of love. A wealthy man with a talent for amorous games might marry a 'senior (or principal) wife' and collect a harem of secondary wives and concubines, although these women typically maintained separate establishments. Preoccupied with the consequences of such arrangements, Murasaki's novel has justly been described as 'a study of the varied manifestations of sexual and romantic love'.[24]

The shining prince's relationship with women is the central theme of *The Tale of Genji*, which charts its hero's progress as a Heian nobleman, his fall from favour and temporary exile, and the prosperous middle years before ageing and death. The final chapters of the book record the history of a very different hero, Prince Kaoru. The contrasts between these two men and the multiple sub-plots involving their comrades and competitors allowed Murasaki to explore the sentimental life of the Heian noble in great depth. Equally important are the women who are pursued, seduced, neglected or even abandoned. Although her heroines rarely protest, Murasaki Shikibu speaks out on their behalf, recording women's sexual lives in a society where polygamy was the norm for the high-ranking male. So great, indeed, is her sensitivity to women's woes that it is tempting to claim Murasaki as an early feminist. In her frank portrayal of female experience, she may have been influenced by an earlier manuscript, a Heian noblewoman's account of her life as minor wife of a powerful statesman. The author, a distant relative of Murasaki and connected to other talented literary ladies, wrote in angry rebellion against the comforting lies peddled to women in the *monogatari*, the traditional prose fictions that were the staple reading matter of Heian noblewomen.[25] Her memoir, known as *The Gossamer Diary* (*Kagerō Nikki*), is a painful account of jealousy and isolation, and may have encouraged Murasaki to write candidly about women's feelings.

Murasaki's own commentary on popular fiction is pointed but oblique. One rainy day, Genji finds his young ward Tamakazura whiling away the time with illustrated romances. He makes fun of her for believing what she reads, but acknowledges there may be some truth in the tales. The writer, he speculates, is 'so moved' by what he observes happening to men and women that he 'wants to commit it to writing and make it known to other people'. As for the fiction writer's relationship with reality: 'Sometimes the author will want to write favourably about people, and then he will select all the good qualities he can think of; at other times, when he wants to give a fuller description of human nature, he introduces all sorts of strange and wicked things into his book. But in every case the things he writes about will belong to this actual world of ours.'[26] Genji's unexpected support for romantic tales is not to be trusted. *In loco parentis* to Tamakazura, he is sexually attracted to his ward and takes advantage of his rights of access to pursue his infatuation. His sympathy with her reading is a ploy to disarm her. If the tales with their illicit love affairs present a true picture of the world, then there is nothing unusual about his own behaviour. 'Suppose the two of us set down our story,' he suggests, pressing closer to the embarrassed girl, 'and give the world a really interesting one.'[27] In the case of his own daughter, Genji prefers to dwell on the dangers of fiction. When he hears that Lady Murasaki has been reading romances with the little girl, he insists that the child's reading must be censored. It wouldn't do to give her wrong ideas.[28]

Although the old romances were unreliable guides to reality,

Genji's description of telling the truth about 'the things of this world' suggests Murasaki's own methods as a storyteller. In *The Tale of Genji* she tried to give a portrait of the world she knew, in which her readers would recognise and empathise with the trials that her characters faced. She was well aware of the ambivalence in human nature, the potential for a person to be both good and evil, and she made this an essential strand of the truth she wanted to reveal. Genji's capacity for thoughtlessness and even bad behaviour is an important part of his character. Quite early in the novel, after telling the story of an elopement that ends in tragedy for a young girl, Murasaki writes that she would have preferred to conceal 'these difficult matters'. She had told the truth about Genji because she had been 'accused of romancing, of pretending that because he was the son of an emperor he had no faults'. Now, perhaps, she continues mischievously, 'I shall be accused of having revealed too much.'[29] Murasaki's 'warts and all' approach to her hero allowed her to explore and weigh the effects of his behaviour on the women for whom he had assumed responsibility. Confused by her protector's behaviour, Tamakazura takes refuge in marriage to another powerful man, the unattractive Higekuro. Maybe she feels that she will be safe with him, but the marriage upsets his principal wife, a woman to whom he has been married for many years. The wife turns violent and is packed off to her father's house on the grounds that she has gone mad. This in turn traumatises Higekuro's teenage daughter, who is upset at leaving her childhood home. Murasaki's account of the far-reaching consequences of Genji's behaviour to Tamakazura is typical of her approach. While she never underestimates the emotions and motivations of her heroes, she explores with sympathy and insight the inner lives of their wives and concubines, the women's limited powers to control their destinies and the misery of their suppressed feelings. 'Such a difficult, constricted life … a woman was required to live!' laments her heroine, Lady Murasaki. Women were regarded as 'useless, unfeeling creatures' who should be 'sensitive but silent', but the 'balance was certainly very difficult to maintain'.[30]

Angela Carter described Genji as 'the first great romantic fictional hero in the world', a description that anticipates Lovelace and Julien Sorel, as well as Mr Rochester and Maxim de Winter.[31] Murasaki Shikibu makes it clear that he is a flawed hero and she never loses sight of the effect of his actions on the women he pursues. Her ability to look at a situation from several points of view is evident in her exploration of the relationships that establish Genji's amorous career and determine the course of his emotional life. In describing Genji's feelings for his father's favourite, Fujitsubo, she anticipates Freud's analysis of archetypal family rivalry: a son's subconscious wish to oust his father and marry his mother. In Genji's case this incestuous yearning is projected on to the young woman who takes his mother's place in the emperor's affections. Genji's mother dies soon after he is born and the emperor later becomes deeply attached to another beautiful girl, Fujitsubo, who closely resembles her. From an early age, Genji fixes his heart on Fujitsubo, regarding all other women as substitutes for this one great passion. The attentions of a young man blessed with legendary good looks and an equally impressive array of talents finally prove irresistible to Fujitsubo. In a moment of frailty she succumbs to Genji, falls pregnant and is terrified that the emperor and court will discover that she is carrying Genji's child. The strain of this secret makes her ill, but when her son is born, although he bears a close resemblance to his real father, the emperor remains blind to the connection.

After this one lapse, Fujitsubo insists on an arm's-length relationship with Genji, but their thwarted love affair taints her happiness and after her early death her spirit returns to haunt her lover, blaming him for the wrong to the imperial inheritance. Their son, too, suffers from his parents' 'frail, fleeting union'. The sense of some secret attaching to his birth taints his pride in his rank and gnaws at his self-esteem and, when he becomes emperor, he takes the opportunity to abdicate early. Later, in a parallel twist of the tale, Genji has the unpleasant experience of himself being cuckolded when a young rival seduces his wife, the Princess Nyosan, and he is forced publicly to acknowledge a son he knows is not his. This young man, Kaoru, is similarly haunted by a sense of something amiss in his origins, and the final chapters of the novel deal with his increasingly desperate attempts to find himself through love and spirituality.

In Heian society women were the prize in the game of love, recipients of attentions they did not always want and could only passively solicit. Their ploys for attracting attention ran the gamut of the Heian aesthetic, from a reputation for beauty and skill in calligraphy and composing poems, to the exquisite tints of their sleeves, casually dangled from the ox-drawn carriages in which they sometimes ventured into public. Like the troubadours of twelfth-century Provence who evolved their own elaborate code of forbidden love, the Heian male enjoyed a challenge and Genji's love for Fujit-subo was enhanced by her unapproachability. High-class women in Heian Japan led rigorously secluded lives. Screened from the intrus-ive male gaze by an array of blinds and curtains and a charmingly decorated fan, women could only reveal their faces to members of their own sex and to their husbands. Even close male relatives were frequently kept at a distance. Although it is evident from first-hand accounts of court life such as Murasaki's diary and *The Pillow Book of Sei Shōnagon* that these restrictions might be relaxed in day-to-day exchanges at imperial residences, Genji's wooing is usually conduc-ted from behind a screen, or peeping through a shutter at a carefully averted profile. This can lead to embarrassing consequences as in the case of the 'safflower' princess, whose bulbous red nose he discovers at a late stage in the proceedings. Murasaki's account of Genji's courtship of this lady, a prince's daughter who languishes in poverty and isolation until Genji seeks her out, can be read as a satire on popular romances of the period, the Heian version of

Tennyson's wistful Mariana, in which beautiful maidens wait in remote and hidden villas until rescued by handsome young men.

As the emperor's favourite, Fujitsubo is kept apart from the common gaze, and the mystery and inaccessibility of her pavilion enhance her allure for Genji. His success in seducing her is testimony to the somewhat haphazard arrangements for protecting Heian women. Japanese houses lacked solid doors and walls, and a lady had to rely on the presence and goodwill of her female attendants to keep unwanted admirers at bay. Again and again in *The Tale of Genji*, women are kidnapped, seduced or even raped at moments when, by chance or trickery, they have been left alone. Even the loyalty of their waiting women is susceptible to the persuasions of a plausible suitor. These female servants, busily intriguing to secure prestigious lovers for their mistresses, form an amusing and sometimes pathetic chorus to the love affairs of the 'good people'. Like the *lauzengiers*, the court gossips and slanderers who plague the troubadour poets, they can make or break reputations, and it is generally court ladies who suffer most from their innuendo and malicious interventions.

Genji's love for Fujitsubo recalls the minstrel Tristram's forbidden love for Yseult, the wife of the King of Cornwall, a romance that captured the imagination of medieval Europe. Free from the constraints of Christianity and the code of chivalry, Genji is able to pursue his rake's progress without sexual guilt or reverence for female chastity. Married at twelve to the haughty Princess Aoi, he finds little satisfaction in his wife, who is several years older and one of the tiny minority of women indifferent to his charms. Instead, he enjoys entanglements with a potpourri of partners, from the ageing court coquette Naishi to the mysterious Yūgao, a lover whose talent for passion and sudden, shocking death haunt Genji's imagination. The most significant of his mistresses is Lady Murasaki, the gentle, exemplary heroine who seems in her understated commentary on woman's lot to act as the author's spokeswoman.

Just as Genji, for all his faults, represents the epitome of the romantic hero, so Lady Murasaki embodies all that was considered most pleasing in a woman, an ideal of feminine charm that was to remain constant for a thousand years and was symbolised by the association of her name with *fuji* or wisteria. In an account of the flowers and gardens of Japan written in the early years of the twentieth century, the horticulturalist Florence du Cane commented:

> To the Japanese mind the *fuji* is essentially feminine, and they find in the wistaria [*sic*] their ideal of woman, – the Japanese woman – whose charm of temperament and whose beauty has been so praised. It is a pretty idea, and it is not difficult to understand their ideal of woman when one observes how the wistaria clings to the undaunted pine, and how gently she falls down, easily moved by a breath of wind and yet firmly holding her own place. The wistaria is regarded as the emblem of gentleness and obedience, and these are the keynotes of a Japanese woman's character.[32]

Du Cane was writing during the last gasp of Victorianism, when woman was treasured as a clinging vine. Her account of the wisteria's constancy and pliancy corresponds to Lady Murasaki's steely self-possession. For all her hard-won docility, she is a woman of great character and sensitivity. Her handling of her wayward lover draws on formidable resources of tact and self-control, but the reader is fully aware of the cost of her forbearance.

Lady Murasaki's history reveals the brutality and suffering for women that underlay the Heian sexual code. Genji first comes across her when she is a charming child and is struck by her resemblance to Fujitsubo, who turns out to be her aunt. Once again, Genji falls in love with a girl who reminds him of his dead mother. Like Genji's mother, Lady Murasaki's mother had been hounded to death by female jealousy. When the child's grandmother, her chief protectress, dies, Genji kidnaps the little girl and carries her off to his palace. Here he brings her up in secret, hidden from the father and family servants who might have protected her. Genji treats the child as a plaything, visiting her whenever he can escape from his official duties and love affairs, and training her in the arts of calligraphy and good taste. The young girl is shocked out of this idyll of romps and dolls' houses soon after Genji's wife suddenly dies in childbirth. Overnight, her guardian changes from playmate to lover, an experience that leaves her too shocked and mortified to speak. Lady Murasaki has become, at the age of around fourteen, an official secondary consort and her fate from now on will be indissolubly linked to Genji's. She is the woman to whom he will always return after his love affairs. Murasaki Shikibu leaves the reader in no doubt of Lady Murasaki's pain, jealousy and curiosity about her rivals, and the skill and self-restraint with which she deals with Genji's evasions and subterfuges. Even after years of marriage, she continues to feel insecure. Her anxieties reveal the strain of being a secondary wife to a wealthy aristocrat, as well as the problems for the polygamous male who has to juggle the needs of wives and mistresses.

For Genji, the demands on his energy, time and purse are prodigious. One of his virtues is his genial habit, unusual among Heian noblemen, of taking care of previous lovers, even after the sexual relationship has ceased. In doing this, he is pleasing himself – Genji loves to feel that he is a benefactor – but he also offers a material service to these women, most of whom lack male support, and it is his loyalty in this matter which particularly marks him out as an ideal hero. As well as visits, ceremonial gifts and other personal attentions, Genji takes responsibility for his women's housing needs. At the peak of his wealth and influence, he builds a four-winged mansion with an annexe nearby to house his principal wives, wards and other women who require his protection. His attempts to pay each woman her due, including spending nights with official wives, cause tension with Lady Murasaki. New loves arouse particular anguish. Hot in pursuit of the sophisticated Princess Asagao, Genji excuses his absences by saying he didn't want to be taken for granted 'like a familiar and rumpled old robe'. Lady Murasaki's response is bleak: 'So this . . . was marriage. She had been too confident.' Her women shake their heads: 'It continues to be his great defect that his attention wanders.'[33]

Not surprisingly, given Heian tolerance of polygamy, *The Tale of Genji* is crammed with incidents involving jealousy among men as well as women, but the woman's position was particularly vulnerable. Seclusion and passivity took a terrible toll. Gwendolen Harleth was to complain centuries later to her suitor Grandcourt in *Daniel Deronda*, 'We women . . . are brought up like the flowers, to look as pretty as we can, and be dull without complaining.'[34] Boredom was not the only trial the secluded Heian lady had to endure. In a culture in which 'a woman was rooted like a flower in her house' while 'a man had the mobility of a bee', it was inevitable that she should yearn to have her husband or lover to herself, and would fear and even loathe the women who competed for his attention.[35] Such feelings had to be kept secret. Jealousy was regarded as an unacceptable emotion, particularly repugnant in women, to be rigorously repressed or at worst suffered in silence. Lady Murasaki wisely refrains from nagging Genji about his affairs, but another lover, known as the Rokujō lady (after the street where she lives), is a proud and passionate woman who feels herself cruelly wronged. Robbed of expression, her jealousy takes the form of a vengeful spirit with horrific consequences.[36]

Murasaki's portrait of the Rokujō lady weaves in and out of the story of Genji and his loves, a troubling undercurrent of pain and dissent. Vengeful and disruptive, she embodies the emotions that bubble below the surface of compliant femininity. Like so many young girls in the novel, ambitious parents sent her to the emperor's court. Her father, one of the imperial ministers, had prepared her with the greatest care for high position. Married at sixteen to the crown prince, heir to the imperial throne, she was devastated by his premature death four years later. With husband and father both dead, the Rokujō lady becomes isolated and vulnerable, and her affair with Prince Genji leaves her further exposed. Attracted by her elegance and hauteur, Genji had won her by passion, but his ardour rapidly cooled, leaving the lady prey to sleepless nights and anxiety. His callous treatment causes a minor scandal at court and may seem out of character, but Genji is always resistant to strong-minded women who make claims on him. Already married to Aoi who disdains his frivolity, he cannot bring himself to marry a second censorious woman. The situation reaches a crisis when Aoi, finally pregnant after ten years of marriage, insults the Rokujō lady at a public festival.

Soon after this, both women fall ill and it seems that Aoi is gripped by a malignant spirit. As the exorcists grapple with the succubus, the Rokujō lady dreams that she is savagely beating an unknown lady. Aoi goes into labour and her baby is safely delivered, but Aoi suddenly dies. The Rokujō lady recovers from her illness, but is puzzled to find the scent of poppy seeds, customarily burnt at exorcisms, permeating her clothes and hair.[37] As in the case of Lady Macbeth, obsessive washing fails to erase the incriminating evidence and the Rokujō lady realises that she has possessed Aoi and probably caused her death. Subsequently, after the Rokujō lady herself is dead, Genji becomes guardian to her daughter, but this fails to mollify the mother's restless spirit. One evening, many years later, he tells Lady Murasaki about the Rokujō lady's demands and jealousy. Depressed by hearing about Genji's love affairs, Lady Murasaki has her women read her some of the old romances, tales that ended comfortingly with the hero settling down with just one woman. Why, she wonders, should she have to live in such uncertainty with Genji: 'were the ache and the scarcely endurable sense of deprivation to be with her to the end?'[38] There is worse to follow.

When Lady Murasaki falls ill, it becomes evident that the Rokujō lady has returned to inhabit her greatest rival. Speaking through a medium, she tells Genji that her spirit was recalled by his unkind and wounding criticism of her. She can find no peace in holy rites, which further inflame her tormented feelings. She begs him to pray for her sins and to warn her daughter of the dangers of jealousy.

Murasaki's representation of jealousy as a psychological force so powerful that it can possess and even kill rivals is handled with great subtlety and restraint, and has tremendous dramatic force. The Rokujō lady targets women who have offended her pride and her revenge is exacted without her conscious will, almost against her wishes. Aoi's death is not the first of her murderous assaults; she is implicated in the unexplained death of Yūgao, another rival. Her attack on Lady Murasaki is particularly shocking, since she too can be seen as a victim of Genji's promiscuity and her situation might be expected to arouse some sisterly feeling in her aggressor. Even after their many years together, Genji's wife is still hurt by his stories about other loves; she yearns for the security of a faithful husband, but the Rokujō lady seems impervious to her pain. At first, Lady Murasaki recovers from her illness, but some months later, fatally weakened by the malignant spirit, she dies.

Love and Longing:
Lady Gossamer and Her Diary

In writing about the evil effects of jealousy, Murasaki Shikibu may have had in mind the real-life history of a lady known only as 'the mother of Michitsuna', the author of one of the most gripping accounts of female jealousy and frustration ever recorded.[39] This lady was the secondary wife of Fujiwara no Kaneie, a powerful statesman who eventually assumed the position of regent and who is known to have had a large number of secondary wives, perhaps as many as eight. Little is known about 'Michitsuna's mother' beyond what she herself discloses in the memoir known as *The Gossamer Diary* (*Kagerō Nikki*), which describes her courtship by Kaneie in 954 and their subsequent tempestuous relationship, which had dwindled to coldness and reproach some twenty years later. Like many of the major Heian women writers, Lady Gossamer, as it is convenient to call her, was born into the provincial-governor class, which was of lower social status than her husband and the other great Fujiwara statesmen. Her father held minor appointments in Heian Kyō during her childhood and moved to a provincial post soon after her marriage to Prince Kaneie in a promotion probably due to his son-in-law's influence. Respect for parents was a basic requirement for a well-brought-up Heian girl, but Lady Gossamer seems to have worshipped her father and suggests in her diary that her husband, with his unreliability and penchant for amorous adventures, was a poor replacement.

Because she only bore him one child, Lady Gossamer would always be a secondary wife to the well-born Kaneie, with fewer claims on his time than the woman she calls 'the lady in the main house', his first wife, Tokihime.[40] Although the two women were roughly equal in rank, Tokihime was to produce three sons and two daughters, giving her unquestionable superiority over her rivals.[41] Whatever Lady Gossamer's eventual status in the marital pecking order, marriage to such an up-and-coming young man would have been regarded as highly advantageous and her mother seems to have chivvied her to encourage the prestigious suitor. The couple were emotionally ill matched. Lady Gossamer's passionate and demanding nature required a commitment from the Prince that he was unable to provide because of his position and responsibilities. As she writes in her diary, she wanted a husband 'thirty days and thirty nights a month'.[42] Few Heian gentlemen could offer such attention to a wife, but Kaneie, with his love of fun, pleasure and the pursuit of new lovers as well as the many political and domestic demands on his time, was particularly unsuited to the role. He may have pursued Lady Gossamer because of her good looks (she was one of the three remarkable beauties of her day), but in temperament they were almost entirely at odds.[43] She was earnest, obsessive and romantic, prone to sulks and melancholy sighs. He was ardent, brisk and noisy, and bewildered by his wife's failure to be happy and appreciative of his efforts to look after her. What makes *The Gossamer Diary* so gripping is the author's skill in communicating the Prince's character as well as her own. While she never seems to understand how her reproaches drive him away, she captures the essence of her wayward lover with a few deft strokes of her writing brush. He stands before us, busy, prosperous and self-important, eager for smiles and entertainment, disposing largesse before hurrying on to his next important engagement.

What with visiting his wives and promoting his career, Kaneie's days (and nights) must have been crowded with activity, but his political machinations are scarcely mentioned in the diary. There is barely a whisper that he may have had worries about his own status or future, although Lady Gossamer reveals that he was assiduous in promoting the interests of 'the boy', Michitsuna, the child they shared. Kaneie's battle for the regency and the temporary dip in his career during the 970s appear to have passed his wife by, perhaps because she intended to write only a personal record. After her one brief account of a political event (the banishment of the Minister of the Left, Minamoto no Takaaki, which paved the way for Fujiwara supremacy for the next hundred years), she says that the true aim of her diary is to 'set down only things that immediately concern me'.[44] The seclusion of her life may also have kept Lady Gossamer ignorant of the power struggles and day-to-day gossip of the court. Like many Heian noblewomen, she continued to maintain her own establishment throughout her marriage to the Prince, who customarily visited her at her own home, the cause of much anxious waiting and disappointment when he failed to show up. There is only one account of her going to see him, when he was seriously ill, a visit conducted with great secrecy and embarrassment on the lady's part.

Lady Gossamer's restriction of movement was not unusual. Unless she was in active court service, like Sei Shōnagon and Murasaki Shikibu who acted as waiting-women to imperial consorts, the upper-class Heian woman spent most of her life hidden behind closed blinds, eagerly waiting for a letter, a visit, or even the pleasurable anxiety of a neighbour's house burning down to vary the monotony of her daily routine. Since the Heian mansion was typically constructed of wood, with rooms separated by screens, blinds or curtains, warmed by braziers and lit by lamps or tapers, fires were a frequent occurrence and are one of the few excitements recorded in the diary.[45] Although entitled to inherit property in her own right, and therefore often economically independent, the Heian noblewoman was constrained by ideas about female duty and value that made her reliant on male protection and kept her secluded indoors. According to Chinese teaching, an unmarried woman owed obedience to her father, a wife to her husband and a widow to her eldest son. Customary interpretation of Buddhist doctrine further emphasised her inferiority. However well a woman behaved in her present life, she would first need to be reincarnated as a man before she could be reborn into one of the higher categories of being.[46] The system of polygamy current among the aristocracy further weakened her position, ensuring that women were frequently in competition for the attention of the same male partner. The only serious alternative to marriage (or concubinage) and childbirth was living in retirement as a nun, either running one's own establishment (a possibility for wealthy women), or as part of a religious community. But for a young noblewoman, commitment to the harsh and comfortless life of a nunnery was a last resort, and onlookers at the ceremony would weep as the young girl took her vows and the priest cut off her long black hair, the distinctive mark of a woman's beauty and desirability.[47]

As the years and disappointments accrued, Lady Gossamer often thought wistfully of retiring from the world. Pilgrimages to temples provided her with the change of scene, the bustle of activity and chance to relish the beautiful countryside that her parched spirit craved, but she never finally made the break. Instead, in around 971, at a time when she was starting to withdraw from Kaneie and his erotic intrigues, she may have begun to compile her diary.[48] As she explains in a brief introduction, she had spent years poring over old romances, but found them to be 'masses of the rankest fabrication'.[49] *The Tale of Genji*, in which Murasaki Shikibu attempted to paint a picture of the world as she saw it, had yet to be written. From the few examples that survive, its predecessors would have had little to offer a reader as discriminating as Lady Gossamer.[50] *The Tale of the Bamboo Cutter* (*Taketori Monogatari*), for example, the oldest surviving *monogatari*, is the story of Kaguya-hime, a tiny girl who is discovered in a bamboo stalk. Within three months the exquisite child has become a fully grown woman, whose beauty attracts a flock of suitors. She keeps them at bay by imposing impossible tasks as the price of marriage and finally admits that her true home is with a race of celestial beings in the moon, to which she eventually returns. In contrast to this tale of supernatural beings is *The Tale of the Lady Ochikubo* (*Ochikubo Monogatari*), which is set firmly in the world of the tenth-century Heian court.[51] The interest of this tale for the modern reader is in its links with the Cinderella story, which can be traced to an even earlier Chinese tradition.[52] Ochikubo is the neglected daughter of a Heian gentleman, whose second wife maltreats her stepchild in favour of her own less attractive daughters. Luckily, a handsome young nobleman courts the beautiful waif, carries her off to a position of wealth and consequence, and devises a series of nasty surprises to punish her persecutors.

It is not surprising that Lady Gossamer found little to sustain her appetite for authenticity in tales of this kind, amusing as they might have been for a contemporary audience. As an antidote to such fantasies she proposed to set down the true story of 'her own dreary life', recounting events exactly as they happened, from past to present.[53] Looking back from the perspective of her middle years (she was possibly in her mid to late thirties), alone and disenchanted, she pieced together a unique record of a woman's life and of the love affair that dominated her thoughts and actions for twenty years. Like St Augustine in his *Confessions*, or Abelard constructing the *Historia calamitatum*, what she sought was a rationale for apparently random happenings. Had her life been 'one befitting a well-born lady'? she mused.[54] It was an extraordinary enterprise. Much of the diary must have drawn on letters, poems and other documents preserved by Lady Gossamer or garnered from the writing boxes of friends and relatives. Even Kaneie may have been a party to this critique of his failings as a husband, since it was also a record of his poems and of the many attentions he paid her, along with the neglect, slights and hurts that she felt he so liberally bestowed. The first book of the diary, the shortest, covers the fifteen years from Kaneie's courtship in 954; the second and third books each cover three years, with events probably increasingly being recorded as they occurred, taking the narrative to the end of 974 when the diary abruptly stops with a pounding at the door on New Year's Eve.[55]

The story begins with Kaneie's energetic pursuit of this reluctant and romantic beauty. Whether he actually saw her in person before their marriage is unlikely. She would have been kept closely secluded, with tantalising reports allowed to circulate about her charming appearance and deportment. He presses his suit through letters, mainly poems protesting desolation and longing, but from the start Lady Gossamer is critical of her suitor's behaviour. He approaches her father openly rather than seeking access through a female go-between, thus losing an opportunity for romantic intrigue. He sends a messenger to beat on her gate, putting her women in an uproar; his poems are brief and the handwriting appalling. They finally spend the customary three nights together, which mark the beginning of their marriage, but almost immediately she is upset by his absences and cavalier ways. Soon she falls pregnant and gives birth to 'the boy', but the following month she finds a note intended for another woman. She has the Prince followed to a certain alley where he has become a regular visitor and even writes to his principal wife to condole with her on her husband's inconstancy. So begins the long war of attrition between these ill-suited lovers. Each winds the other up to rage and frustration. Her house is on his direct route to the palace, which he often visits at night. Passing to and fro, he coughs to catch her attention, but fails to stop. Lying sleepless, she writhes with irritation. 'He used to be so fond of her,' her women whisper.[56] Meanwhile, the lady from the alley has fallen from favour and Lady Gossamer revels in her discomfort. 'I had prayed, at the height of my unhappiness, that she would live to know what I was then suffering, and it seemed that my prayers were being answered.

She was alone, and now her child was dead ... The pain must be even sharper than mine had been. I was satisfied.'[57]

Humourless, self-obsessed and vindictive towards her low-born rival, Lady Gossamer nevertheless compels our sympathy. She is so unhappy, so exacting, and so eloquent and open about her miseries. Even the child mocks her, with his stumbling chant, 'I'll come again soon, I'll come again,' parroting his father's hurried promise as he dashes from the house.[58] True to character, Kaneie robustly refuses to accept that there is a problem: ' "Have I done something wrong?" he would ask innocently, and his injured and guileless manner made it impossible for me to speak.'[59] Eventually, she writes a long poem to explain her terror of abandonment and neglect, and leaves it on a shelf for him to find. His response is pained, but practical: 'True, the newly gathered leaves will fade. Love is but love.' He points out that she has played her part in alienating him. Frequently angry, she smoulders like Mount Fuji and her women turn her against him, driving him away to 'kinder places'. If she wants to find someone to cherish her better, they must separate. But what, he wonders, will become of the boy, the fatherless colt, 'sadly neighing'?[60]

Michitsuna, the boy, becomes the cement that keeps this warring couple together, since the Prince takes pride in his son, and makes an effort to introduce him into the court ceremonies and festivities that will promote his career. But as Michitsuna grows up, Lady Gossamer uses him as a pawn in her battle with his father, cruelly manipulating the boy's attachment to both parents and exploiting his torn loyalties. As the years pass, she becomes increasingly estranged from Kaneie, who loses patience with her waywardness and refusal to be happy. There are no more children, but she adopts a young girl, a by-blow of Kaneie's relationship with a rejected mistress, introducing a brief phase of harmony with the Prince, who is delighted with his pretty daughter. When the girl is courted by a presentable man (probably Kaneie's younger brother, Tōnori), Lady Gossamer is thrilled by her role as duenna and flirts like mad with the persistent suitor.[61] Her account of their negotiations is both comic and touching. He appears at her garden fence, 'as dashing as a hero in a picture', but her serving women spoil things by rushing out 'wrinkled and undressed' to gawp at the handsome man. The wind blows, their protective screen flutters up and the suitor catches a glimpse of the dishevelled crones, desperately trying to hold down the flapping shade.[62] Repeated meetings between Lady Gossamer and the young man satisfyingly arouse the Prince's jealousy, but the marriage plans collapse when the suitor unexpectedly runs off with another man's wife. As the year dwindles, Lady Gossamer lapses into sadness and apathy, and finally even the diary grinds to a halt. The last note that she records from her husband suggests the tenor of their future relationship. Ominously, it was 'written by someone else' and 'attached to a branch to which but one leaf was clinging'. The message is succinct and pointed: 'The Prince is very busy today.'[63]

The Gossamer Diary was written to challenge the pleasing myths of the old romances with the reality of a woman's life. The author evidently intended it to be read by others and one of its pleasures is her great skill as a narrator. She is unsparing of herself and Kaneie in her relentless dissection of their differences, but there are brief, lyrical phases when the Prince finds time to give her the affectionate companionship she craves. Modern interpretations of the diary have even suggested that Lady Gossamer took pride in her marriage, particularly in the early years, when Kaneie's visits were so frequent that she was able to make an issue of his absences.[64] (Other less fortunate, less visited women would have understood the point.) Kaneie took the time to write her many poems in response to her carefully worded missives and this aspect of their relationship seems to have been significant to both partners. *The Great Mirror (Ōkagami)*, a gossipy collection of stories and anecdotes about Fujiwara no Michinaga and his times, describes Lady Gossamer as an accomplished poet; she is known to have entered poetry competitions and some of her poems were included in imperial poetry anthologies for the next two centuries.[65] The exchange of poems with such a reputable writer and her willingness to preserve his work for posterity may have been enormously attractive to Kaneie. Despite their differences and only having one child, he seems to have been genuinely fond of his demanding wife and took an active interest in her well-being for many years.

If, for the modern reader, the overall effect of *The Gossamer Diary* is of a sense of waste, Lady Gossamer did manage to reclaim a great deal from the wreckage of her dreams and hopes. Writing the diary perhaps as a kind of letter intended for her adopted daughter, she developed the newly fledged 'woman's hand' into a medium sufficiently flexible to accommodate the record of external events and the difficult journey into the emotions. She dared to write about the domestic and the mundane, as far as these pertained to her privileged life. For posterity, she has left a vivid self-portrait of a stubborn, gifted woman and an unequalled account of the day-to-day existence of an upper-class lady in Heian Kyō. Her own summing-up of her life, however, was bleak. At the end of the first section of the diary she looks back at the events she has recorded and wonders whether she has been describing anything of substance. 'Call it, this journal of mine, a shimmering of the summer sky,' she wistfully concludes, an image that suggests the insubstantiality that lies at the heart of the Heian aesthetic.[66] This sense of the fleetingness of life informs *The Gossamer Diary* and much of the love poetry of the period, where longing and regret are the predominant emotions. *The Tale of Genji* is similarly steeped in a sensibility that mourns the passing of happiness even as its pleasures are savoured on the tongue. It is the Keatsian dilemma of 'beauty that must die', evolved in Heian culture through the conjointure of the Buddhist premise that life is suffering and the Japanese literary tradition of *mono no aware*, sometimes described quite simply as the 'ah-ness of things', the heartfelt sigh that simultaneously responds to joy and recognises its transience. Lady Gossamer's diary has to be read within this tradition. Whatever the realities of her life, literary decorum required that it should be viewed through the azure lenses of sadness and loss.[67] *Kagerō*, often translated as 'gossamer', the term she uses to describe her diary and from which she derives the name by which she is commonly known, has the double meaning of 'mayfly', an insect famous for its exquisite, ephemeral existence, and 'the shimmering of heat waves', again a symbol of evanescence and even incorporeality.[68] Do such images have any real existence, or are they just a mirage, a trick of the eye? In asking herself and her readers such questions, Lady Gossamer reveals her artistic ancestry, which was entirely in tune with her despondent, regretful temperament. Her ability to capture the essence of *mono no aware*, to render the ineffable in a sleek turn of phrase, may well have been, paradoxically, the key to Kaneie's passion, and the source of his admiration and persistence in wooing such an elusive mistress and capricious wife.

It is one of the great ironies and joys of literary history that the diary of the mistress of transience has in fact survived, to tell the story of a love affair whose characteristic mood, whatever its literary wrappings, seems to have been one of anger and reproach. Turning the pages, one sees a woman sequestered in a darkened room, waiting anxiously for the lover whom she will greet with frowns and complaints when he eventually finds the time, or the courage, to pay her a visit. Despite her resentment at Kaneie, she never manages to wean herself from her craving for his attention. It seems that on the emotional level, to borrow the words of an unhappy wife in one of Doris Lessing's stories, Lady Gossamer 'knew finally – and this was stronger than anything else – that without him there would be no meaning in her life at all'.[69] As an artist, and here she was a worthy precursor to Murasaki Shikibu, she managed to break free from the constraints of language, convention and isolation to create a form of expression ideally suited to her task. 'Perhaps, she

ule fauurs bien atriufe
omment helours lawelle
urodit pierres alulart

ienes alulait le confesse
Qui fuet helouys lawesse

belard and Heloise in
arnest debate, perhaps
bout her innovative
iews on marriage,
4th century.

ngelica Kauffman's
omantic painting (1778) of
belard and Heloise parting
t the nunnery door.

On this 14th-century ivory casket (*top*), the lovers Tristram and Yseult sit on the left, while Yseult's husband King Mark secretly watches from the tree above, his face reflected in the water. On the right, a unicorn is stabbed as it lies in a lady's lap, a warning of the dangers of adultery.

In this late 15th-century tapestry (*above*), the unicorn seems entranced by his own image. The ermine at the lady's feet symbolizes chastity, but rabbits suggest fertility.

Jupiter castrating Saturn in a graphic illustration to a 15th-century edition of *Le Roman de la Rose* (*left*).

Comment esperance tire le cuer hors de leaue et dit lacteur

E quant le cueur se vit de hors sil fust joyeux ce ne
fait pas ademander et regarda qui estoit celle dame
qui lauoit aide ayssir hors deleaue Si congneut q̃
cestoit dame esperance sa bonne maistresse qui ja autres
fois luy auoit tant fait et enseigne de biens Et adonc le
cueur osta son heaulme de la teste et abaissa la ventaille
et puis ilz sentrebaiserent et sentrefirent tel feste et tel

Iope comes to the rescue of the knight Cueur in *Le Livre du Cueur d'Amours Espris*, 1457.

Amalthea, a female scribe, with the tools of her trade: books, scrolls, knife, compasses, pen and inkpot (*above*).

Oenone writing to her faithless husband Paris in this illustration to Ovid's *Heroides*, 1496 (*left*).

An 18th-century engraving of the bustling convent parlour at San Lorenzo, with nun receiving visitors from behind their grilles.

On the left, Genji talks to Lady Murasaki about his romances with other women, while her little maids make snowballs in the moonlit garden, in this 17th-century Illustration to *The Tale of Genji*.

On this 17th-century screen, Genji spies on Utsusemi, a married woman whom he is pursuing, while she plays a game of go with her stepdaughter.

A maid brushes a court lady's long black hair, while another woman reads aloud, probably from a popular romance, on this 12th-century scroll of scenes from *The Tale of Genji*.

Michinaga inspects the boats specially made for the Emperor's visit to his newborn son in this 13th-century illustration to *The Diary of Lady Murasaki*. '[Y]ou could almost imagine that the dragon and mythical bird on the prows were alive.'

Living for a time in a mountain village, Lady Sarashina is awoken at dawn by the cry of a deer in this 1704 illustration to *The Sarashina Diary*.

On a snowy night, Prince Niou carries Ukifune off to the Islet of Oranges in Tosa Mitsusada's 18th-century illustration to *The Tale of Genji*. He admires the rich, enduring green of the pines, but she murmurs, 'The colours remain, here on the Islet of Oranges. / But where go I, a boat upon the waters?'

said to herself, even the story of her own dreary life, set down in a journal, might be of interest . . . they must all be recounted, events of long ago, events of but yesterday. She was by no means certain that she could bring them to order.'[70] She could, and did, and the result is a masterpiece. With great skill and economy, Lady Gossamer shaped the events of her marriage into a compelling drama, in which Kaneie acts the role of the neglectful lover while she broods behind her curtains, scheming for his homage. At the beginning of her diary she wrote of her contempt for the old romances, but she is herself the embodiment of the romantic heroine, a woman who, like Emma Bovary, craves the devotion of a lover whose passion will survive marriage, a child and what Genji called the 'rumpled old robe' of familiarity, and who will daily woo her anew with his poetry of love, loss and longing, his tributes to her beauty and his witty dependence on her goodwill.

～

Not all Heian love affairs were anguished. Indeed, the popular fantasy of love was of a meeting between two exquisite beings, in which the participants' elegance, style and sensitivity were matched by the beauty of their natural surroundings. In *The Pillow Book* Sei Shōnagon describes the pleasures of love in the summer season, when the garden becomes an extension of the room where the lovers meet:

> To meet one's lover summer is indeed the right season. True, the nights are very short, and dawn creeps up before one has had a wink of sleep. Since all the lattices have been left open, one can lie and look out at the garden in the cool morning air. There are still a few endearments to exchange before the man takes his leave, and the lovers are murmuring to each other when suddenly there is a loud noise. For a moment they are certain that they have been discovered; but it is only the caw of a crow flying past in the garden.[71]

This delicious encounter, so nostalgically evoked by Sei Shōnagon, epitomises the romantic bonding between man and woman Lady Gossamer craved, but which seems so often to have eluded her. In the extremity of her longing she has connections with many ardent, anxiously waiting women, both in fiction and real life. Constrained by gender and culture, she resembles Jane Austen's mutely suffering heroines: Jane Bennet in *Pride and Prejudice*, wondering if Mr Bingley will seek her out in London, and Anne Elliot in *Persuasion*, pining for a tender gesture from Captain Wentworth. In her dependence on her lover's favour she recalls Charlotte Brontë at Haworth yearning for a letter from Constantin Heger, Gwen John in her Paris studio wearing her prettiest clothes in case Rodin comes to call, or Sylvia Plath at Cambridge listening for Ted Hughes's all-conquering step on the stair. Fretting alone at home, she was cut off from the imperial court with its coteries of literary ladies, its gossip and love affairs, its glamour and ceremony, which might have satisfied her appetite for drama and flirtation. Unlike most of the surviving Heian women writers, Lady Gossamer never entered into service for the emperor or one of his wives. Craving love and attention, she lacked the opportunity and possibly the talent to enjoy the freer relations between men and women so cunningly described by that supremely gifted observer, the professional court lady Sei Shōnagon.

A Woman's Eye View of Courtly Love: Sei Shōnagon

Sei Shōnagon was born some thirty years later than Lady Gossamer, in around 966. Little is known about her life. Her father and grandfather were distinguished poets; she herself possibly married once or even twice and may have had a son, although she never mentions this child and seems to have found babies rather a nuisance. She appears to have entered court service in the early 990s as attendant to the Empress Sadako, consort to Emperor Ichijō. For a while, court culture revolved around Sadako's entourage, but her primacy was challenged when Fujiwara no Michinaga introduced his daughter Akiko as imperial consort. Younger and possibly less threatening than Sadako, Akiko was quickly promoted to Second Empress and set up her own court, with Murasaki Shikibu among her literary ladies. After Sadako's death in childbirth, Sei Shōnagon vanishes from the records, although Japanese legend, always fond of a gloomy fate for uppity women, claims that she died alone and in poverty. Her legacy is a remarkable collection of notes and observations on court life, generally known as *The Pillow Book of Sei Shōnagon*. The title refers to an account at the end of the book of how it came to be written:

> One day Lord Korechika, the Minister of the Centre, brought the Empress a bundle of notebooks. 'What shall we do with them?' Her Majesty asked me . . .

'Let me make them into a pillow,' I said.

'Very well,' said Her Majesty. 'You may have them.'

I now had a vast quantity of paper at my disposal, and I set about filling the notebooks with odd facts, stories from the past, and all sorts of other things, often including the most trivial material. On the whole I concentrated on things and people that I found charming and splendid ... it is written entirely for my own amusement and I put things down exactly as they came to me.[72]

There has been much debate about what is meant by making 'a pillow'. Paper was a costly and much-prized commodity, so Sei Shōnagon's booty would not have been used literally to sleep on. Court ladies slept on wooden pillows to protect their carefully styled hair, so it may have been tucked into a pillow drawer for easy reference when Sei Shōnagon was in the mood for jotting down her thoughts. In any case the title suggest the personal, informal nature of the collection, which includes descriptions of the people, places and events that caught the writer's attention, as well as impressions, opinions, lists and poems.[73] The work was probably begun while Sei Shōnagon was still at court and completed after Sadako's death, and can be described as a kind of commentary on court life, seen through the eyes of a witty, knowing and partisan observer. In its mingling of anecdote with details of ceremonial, character sketches with appreciations of nature, and its amusing lists of things the author either likes or loathes, it provides a view of the everyday life of the Heian aristocracy that can be read in parallel with Murasaki Shikibu's attempt in *The Tale of Genji* to share her experiences of the society in which she lived. In the purity of its language, the quality of its prose and the unique character of its author it has claimed a place as one of the great works of Japanese literature, the oldest surviving example of the *zuihitsu* genre, literally 'following the [impulses of] the brush', which is still in vogue in modern Japan.[74] It also provides an invaluable insider's view of the practice of love at the Heian court.

Flirtation and intrigue seem to have been the favourite occupations of privileged courtiers, burdened by leisure. At a time of peace and prosperity for the 'good people' of the Heian aristocracy, deaf to mutterings of discontent from the provinces, the days would have seemed unendurable without the distractions of ceremonies and festivals to enliven the monotony. In their constant comings and goings through the imperial chambers, court women had a freedom denied to secluded wives and consorts such as Lady Gossamer. Congratulating herself on her favoured status, Sei Shōnagon pours scorn on the narrow lives of 'women who live at home, faithfully serving their husbands'. Such women have 'not a single exciting prospect in life', yet they 'believe that they are perfectly happy'. As for the accusation that court ladies are frivolous and wicked, Sei Shōnagon robustly defends the equality at court, which permits women as well as men to 'see everyone face to face'. Women at court 'do not spend their time hiding modestly behind fans and screens, but walk about, looking openly at people they chance to meet', permitted even to gaze on the august countenances of the emperor and the high court officials (Sei Shōnagon was an ardent imperialist).[75] It is clear, however, that women did at times resort to fans and screens to seclude themselves from the rude male gaze, leading to pleasing games of Peek-a-Boo and Peeping Tom, which enhanced the sexual excitement.

The flimsy construction of the women's apartments in the Imperial Palace meant that women had constantly to be on their guard against intrusive males, especially at night. There were no solid doors to lock or windows to bar, and even Murasaki Shikibu was forced to endure Michinaga's drunken assault on her sleeping space. It is all pleasure, however, to the doughty Sei Shōnagon:

But I rather enjoy all this. Throughout the night one hears the sound of footsteps in the corridor outside. Every now and then the sound will stop, and someone will tap on a door with just a single finger ... Sometimes the tapping will continue for quite a while without the woman's responding in any way. The man finally gives up, thinking that she must be asleep; but this does not please the woman, who makes a few cautious movements, with a rustle of silk clothes ... Then she hears him fanning himself as he remains standing outside the door.[76]

A lover's behaviour is of particular concern and Sei Shōnagon has tremendous fun with her critique of the boorish male. Secrecy was an essential component of love affairs, particularly at court, and she is merciless about the man who reveals his presence in a lady's room by snoring, or dropping the blinds with a great rattle. Even worse is the vain or fussy courtier, the man who spends time adjusting his headdress or cloak before he leaves, or noisily hunting for his fan, which he then opens with a great snap. Protocol demanded that a lover should leave silently at dawn and a good lover is concerned only with the lady he is leaving. He drags himself out of bed with a look of dismay and resists attempts to urge him to make haste. His whole demeanour suggests that it is agony to leave and, before he goes, he confesses how much he dreads being separated during the coming day. In contrast is the brute who rushes off without a backward glance:

When he jumps out of bed, scurries about the room, tightly fastens his trouser-sash, rolls up the sleeves of his Court cloak, over-robe, or hunting costume, stuffs his belongings into the breast of his robe and then briskly secures the outer sash – one really begins to hate him.[77]

Equally obnoxious is the man who is emotionally dishonest, pretending a woman can rely on him, when in fact he finds her tiresome
and repugnant. The lover who speaks ill of a lady behind her back
and the churl who abandons a court lady when she becomes pregnant feature prominently in Sei Shōnagon's list of 'Shameful
Things'.

In exposing the realities of sexual manners at the imperial court,
Sei Shōnagon throws into relief the caring behaviour of the peerless
Prince Genji, who acts the perfect gentleman to the women he
seduces. Murasaki Shikibu's heroines resemble the cloistered, stay-
at-home wives despised by Sei Shōnagon and it was Murasaki's great
art to reveal the possibilities of pain for such women, constrained by
a sexual code that favoured the wandering, predatory male. What
Sei Shōnagon celebrates is the pleasure to be enjoyed by the sophisticated court woman, who knows how to play the game, to reel in
the assiduous lover and revel in his attentions. Such men seem to
have been in short supply and Sei Shōnagon's descriptions of romantic perfection may belong to the realm of fantasy rather than real
life. The handsome young bachelor who returns at dawn from an
amorous adventure and immediately sits down to write a 'next-
morning' letter to his lover is a charming sight (the 'next-morning'
letter typically protested love, desolation at the need for separation,
longing for the next meeting and so on). But Sei Shōnagon tells an
alternative story of the 'morning after', which reveals the transient,
extemporaneous nature of Heian love affairs. In this incident a
woman lies in bed at dawn, her long hair tumbled and her robes in
disarray. It is clear that she is sleeping after a night of love. A man
rushing home after a similar encounter passes the open lattice of
her room. Seeing an opportunity, he leans through to talk to her,
but his overtures are interrupted when a messenger arrives from
the woman's lover, bringing his 'next-morning' letter. Finally the
interloper leaves, smiling at the thought that a similar scene may be
taking place at the home of the woman he had left earlier that

morning. He, however, has yet to write his own 'next-morning' declaration.[78]

Worldly and sophisticated, Sei Shōnagon was the antithesis of the woman, like Lady Gossamer, who waited in solitude and longing for the infrequent visits of a man she shared with other wives and mistresses. Her savoir faire ensured that she held her own at court among backbiters and predatory males. Famous for her wit, acerbity and encyclopaedic knowledge of poetry, she thrived in the atmosphere of gossip, competition and snobbery that prevailed among the imperial entourage. She probably had love affairs, but they seem to have left her untroubled. Love was not the centre of her life, as it was for Lady Gossamer or even Lady Murasaki, Genji's favourite wife. There was, however, another woman at the Heian court who combined Sei Shōnagon's worldliness with an outstanding talent for passion. A brilliant poet, Izumi Shikibu pursued the game of love with curiosity and emotional intensity, and her poems offer unusual insight into the private feelings of an amorous Heian lady.

The Life of an Amorous Woman:
Izumi Shikibu

The gossip and scandal that signposted the career of the poet Izumi Shikibu resemble the attention paid to modern media stars. Part of her notoriety derived from her distinguished lovers: she had affairs with two princes, brothers to the heir to the throne, in rapid succession. A tantalising glimpse of her in *The Great Mirror* reveals the panache with which she played the crowd. When she appeared in public with her lover Prince Atsumichi at the celebrations for the annual Kamo Festival, the front blind of their carriage was split down the middle so that it could be raised on the Prince's side to display his magnificence to the admiring public. The lady was supposed to remain screened from prying eyes, but Izumi, always happy to play the crowd, allowed her tinted sleeves to trail through the apertures of the panel, while her striking scarlet trousers hung to the ground. As an exercise in attention seeking it worked admirably: 'Everyone seemed to be looking at the two of them instead of watching the procession.'[79] Nothing could be further from Lady Gossamer's reclusive life, but Izumi shared her predecessor's sensitivity to the sufferings of the woman in love. Passion was Izumi Shikibu's favourite theme and what Murasaki Shikibu described as the 'rather unsavoury side to her character', her enjoyment of a succession of lovers, gave her ample opportunity to explore its possibilities.[80] Her reputation as a poet was inextricably linked to her fame as a femme fatale.

The public were only allowed a glimpse of Izumi's trailing robes, but what would such a woman have looked like to the lovers permitted to share her private rooms? Heian standards of beauty were very different from those of the Western world. Had a visitor from medieval Venice or London been allowed a glimpse behind the screens of the seductive Izumi Shikibu, he might have been startled by her bizarre appearance. To create an impression of beauty and fragility, a Heian woman's eyes were supposed to be narrow slits, her nose small and refined with an upward tilt, and her chin and neck well-rounded. A striking fall of hair was a great asset. It should be dark, glossy, very thick and straight, should part in the middle and flow over the shoulders in an abundant stream, and be long enough to trail on the ground.[81] In her descriptions of the ladies-in-waiting at Empress Akiko's court, Murasaki Shikibu is particularly interested in their hair. Lady Dainagon's hair falls to three inches beyond her heels; another lady has to thicken her glossy locks with a hairpiece; a novice nun boldly cuts off her flowing mane before a farewell visit to the palace.[82] In the list of 'Things That Make One's Heart Beat Faster', Sei Shōnagon includes the pleasure of taking care of her hair and dress. 'To wash one's hair, make one's toilet, and put on scented robes; even if not a soul sees one, these preparations still produce an inner pleasure.'[83] (She had no illusions about her own appearance: in a moment of frank self-appraisal, she describes herself as an old woman, whose frizzled, dishevelled hair would disqualify her as the heroine of a courtly romance.)[84] In contrast to their black hair, women were expected to have chalk-white skin, a mark of aristocracy often enhanced by powder. Married women might rouge a little and lips were painted into a rosebud pout. It was also the fashion for women to pluck their eyebrows and paint in a substitute pair, shaped like a blob rather than a crescent, and to blacken their teeth with a dye made by soaking pieces of iron in vinegar or tea mixed with powdered gallnut.[85] Sei Shōnagon listed 'Well-blackened teeth' among her 'Things That Give a Pleasant Feeling'.[86]

Court women seem to have been conventional about matters of dress and appearance, those essential components of the desirable woman, but a curious story has survived from the period, which describes a girl who refuses to conform to these practices. The heroine of *The Lady who Loved Insects* is a clever and thoughtful young woman, a philosopher interested in Buddhist ideals.[87] Her favourite occupation is watching caterpillars transform themselves into moths and butterflies, and she persuades small boys to hunt reptiles and insects so that she can observe their habits. As if this eccentricity were not enough to dampen her marriage prospects, she also insists on keeping her appearance in a state of nature, refusing to pluck her bushy eyebrows or to blacken her white teeth. Intrigued by reports of this feisty bluestocking, a captain of the horse sneaks up to her garden gate to see if he can catch a glimpse of the freak. The girl is leaning through a window to inspect her latest specimens, too interested in her studies to care about being seen, and he shakes his head over her beetling brows and unpleasantly gleaming teeth. Something about her determination and liveliness attract him, even so, as does her beautiful (if dishevelled) hair. The tale breaks off at the beginning of this unlikely courtship, but it strikes an unusual note, as if Jo March from *Little Women* or tomboy Maggie from *The Mill on the Floss* had suddenly been transported to Heian Japan.

Izumi Shikibu seems to have had something in common with the insect-loving lady, in particular her intelligence and curiosity, and a willingness to flout convention. There are no reports, however, that she broke the rules as far as her appearance was concerned, and she can be imagined as a classic Heian beauty with blackened teeth and an almost featureless face. Her audacious self-display at the Kamo Festival with Prince Atsumichi suggests that she took a keen interest in the details of dress and presentation so vital to success in Heian society. A woman's clothes were designed to obscure rather than display her body.[88] They were statements of

her imagination and aesthetic taste, and their style and arrangement were matters of huge concern. Formal court wear consisted
of layers of long loose clothes, which included an unlined dress, a
set of lined robes, a gown and mantle, and a train and jacket. The
lined robes were usually made of a light gauzy material, allowing
the colour of the lining to shine through. This would produce a
third colour, often referred to by the name of a flower. In order to
demonstrate a woman's subtlety in the choice and preparation of
dyes, the sleeves of her robes were often of different lengths so that
the full effect of the layered colours could be appreciated.[89] In her
court diary, Murasaki Shikibu includes minute accounts of the many
ravishing outfits worn by the ladies-in-waiting. On the day of a visit
from the emperor everyone is dressed to the nines. A lady carrying
the ceremonial sword wore a 'plain yellow-green jacket, a train
shading at the hem, and a sash and waistband with raised embroi-
dery in orange and white checked silk. Her mantle had five cuffs
of white lined with dark red, and her crimson gown was of
beaten silk.' Peering behind the blinds at the women watching the
emperor's arrival, Murasaki describes their gowns as 'a miscellany
of autumn leaves of varying tints', while their lined robes were of
'saffron of differing shades, purple lined with dark red, and yellow
lined in green'. Even the fans had been specially decorated for the
occasion.[90] Gorgeous as these costumes were, the weight and volume
of cloth must have been a serious impediment to any kind of
mobility for the wearer.

However she might have appeared in private moments with her
lovers (and the evidence suggests that a woman's dishabille was
equally carefully arranged), on formal occasions Izumi would have
been a static beauty, hampered by layers of cloth and the weight of
her long black hair. Her reputation for stylish dressing was matched
by her prowess as a poet, a powerful attribute for a woman. One of
the stories told by Sei Shōnagon is about the daughter of a senior
official. The girl's father advises her that the essential skills for

any young woman are mastering the arts of calligraphy and the seven-string zither, and memorising all the poems in the twenty volumes of the imperial poetry collection, the *Kokinshu*. Needless to say, the girl obeys her father's instructions and stupefies the court by her ability to recite any verse of any poem the emperor cares to name from the anthology.[91] A knowledge of writing, music and poetry was essential to the education of an aristocrat, and women were expected to be as adept in these arts as men. Most important of all was the art of poetry, a response to the events of life as natural to the Heian nobility as breathing or eating, and a fundamental requirement for success in the game of love. In his preface to the *Kokinshu* the court noble Ki no Tsurayuki wrote that poetry was the irresistible outcome of human emotion:

> The poetry of Japan has its seeds in the human heart and mind and grows into the myriad leaves of words. Because people experience many different phenomena in this world, they express that which they think and feel in their hearts in terms of all that they see and hear. A nightingale singing among the blossoms, the voice of a pond-dwelling frog – listening to these, what living being would not respond with his own poem? It is poetry which effortlessly moves the heavens and the earth, awakens the world of invisible spirits to deep feeling, softens the relationship between men and women, and consoles the hearts of fierce warriors.[92]

It is a description that recalls Dante's ecstatic vision at the end of the *Paradiso* of '*l'amor che move il sole e l'altre stelle*' ('the love that moves the sun and the other stars'). As a medieval poet, Dante interpreted humanity's relationship to the universe in terms of the divine. His responses to nature and the numinous, and to his beloved Beatrice, were filtered through the lens of an ardent Christian spirituality, but, like Heian aristocrats, poetry was the medium through which he expressed his sense of wonder and reverence. For the Japanese writers of the Heian court, all powerful emotions could best be expressed through poetry, whose effect was in turn healing and transformative. As Tsurayuki pointed out, its influence was paramount in mellowing relations between men and women. Lady Gossamer used poetry as the most effective means of communication with her husband, the path to his heart when all else failed. For Izumi Shikibu poetry offered an essential outlet for her passionate nature. Notorious alike for love and poetry, she recorded her affairs in poems that enable the reader to enter the emotional atmosphere of an amorous woman in eleventh-century Japan, and to experience her world through an imagination simultaneously alert, original and playfully ironic. At the same time she frankly explored her own sensuality, introducing a sense of the female body and its desires largely absent from the yearnings of Lady Gossamer and Murasaki Shikibu's refined heroines.

Izumi Shikibu was probably born some time in the late 970s.[93] Like most Heian women writers she came from the provincial-governor class. Possibly in her late teens, she married another provincial official, the governor of Izumi Province, from whose posting she takes her name. She was already beginning to gain a reputation as a poet. Some years after her marriage and the birth of a daughter, she met Prince Tametaka, brother to the heir to the imperial throne and grandson to Fujiwara no Kaneie, the husband of Lady Gossamer. Like the fictitious Prince Genji, Tametaka was acclaimed as a radiantly beautiful child, whose subsequent career followed a similar pattern of numerous love affairs, although Tametaka was to die in his twenty-sixth year. His grandfather Kaneie, another cheerful libertine, was closely involved in the upbringing of Tametaka and his two brothers, since their father, ex-Emperor Reizei, was insane, a kind of 'holy fool'.[94] With this combined inheritance of the powerful, pleasure-loving Kaneie and the deranged ex-Emperor, it is not surprising that Prince Tametaka had a reputation for being flighty.

His wife, a daughter of the Fujiwara clan, was a deeply religious woman, determined not to allow marriage to interfere with her devotions.[95] Her beliefs did not impose on Tametaka, who was described in *A Tale of Flowering Fortunes* as a 'tireless gallant, indiscriminate in his pursuit of women'.[96]

Little is known about Tametaka's relationship with Izumi Shikibu, but its consequences were unfortunate for both partners. There was plague in the capital and the streets were clogged with heaps of decaying corpses. The Prince continued his habit of roaming about at night to visit his lovers, despite warnings from his followers and disapproving gossip among the courtiers. Eventually, he fell ill and died. Izumi Shikibu went into mourning and, soon after this, she separated permanently from her husband. She may even temporarily have been disowned by her parents and her family's strong reaction reveals the social stigma attached to a married woman who strayed. While a single woman might have as many lovers as she wished provided she was discreet, a wife was expected to remain faithful to her husband for as long as they were officially married, even if the man, like Kaneie, chose to share his favours between several wives and concubines.[97] There is evidence that Izumi kept in touch with her husband and continued to feel fond of him, and she did not remain alone for long. Before her year's official mourning for Prince Tametaka had ended, she had fallen in love with his younger brother Atsumichi.

When the affair began, Izumi Shikibu was probably in her mid twenties, a woman whose sexual life was already the subject of scandal and speculation in court circles. Atsumichi's interest in her may have resulted from fraternal competition, a subconscious wish to take over his brother's mistress. He may also have been tempted by her growing reputation as a poet. Perhaps it was simply her sophistication and allure that won him over, her ready wit, her passion and her long black hair. Izumi's savoir faire in matters of appearance and public display may also have been a profound relief to the Prince, whose first marriage to a mentally unstable girl had been a source of humiliation.

Atsumichi seems to have been a somewhat raffish character whose affairs, like those of his older brother, attracted gossip and censure. As younger brother to the heir to the throne, he was under constant scrutiny by the imperial household and its hangers-on, but he seems, too, to have been a magnet for unwelcome notoriety. His first wife, a daughter of Fujiwara no Michitaka and thus also a grandchild of Kaneie and cousin to her husband, was described as immature in manner and appearance.[98] In a marriage brokered by family interests Atsumichi ignored his wife, who took revenge by attention-seeking behaviour. According to the chronicler of *The Great Mirror*, she took to raising her blinds and baring her breasts in front of male guests, a shocking breach of decorum. 'I used to sit there with my eyes averted, too embarrassed to move or think,' the Prince reportedly complained. She belittled his cultural aspirations by loudly criticising the Chinese poems recited by guests and pelted students with gold dust during a poetry-writing session, resulting in an unseemly scramble.[99] This troublesome woman was eventually packed off to her family and ended up 'eking out a precarious existence', secluded from public view in one of the less reputable alleys between the great avenues where the nobility lived.[100] Whether she was truly deranged can only be conjectured, although inbreeding may have affected a number of Fujiwara offspring. It is tempting to interpret her behaviour as a feminist protest against her position as a neglected wife, or a Heian version of Princess Diana in revolt against a stuffy spouse, but it is more likely that, like her husband's father, she was mentally unstable without the status that would grant her licence as a 'holy fool'.

Atsumichi's second marriage was blighted by his affair with Izumi Shikibu. When he fell in love with the poet, his wife's distress was understandable. After months of clandestine meetings, Atsumichi moved his mistress into the family home with the excuse that he needed a woman to dress his hair. His wife could not bear the humiliation and returned to live with her grandmother.[101] These marital scandals, as well as his open association with a woman regarded as partly responsible for his brother's death, raised courtly eyebrows. Izumi's lesser rank as daughter of a provincial governor only added to the scandal.

Izumi tells the story of her courtship by Prince Atsumichi in *The Izumi Shikibu Diary* (*Izumi Shikibu Nikki*), a curiously arm's-length account of a romance in which the lovers seem almost as eager to escape entanglement as they are to pursue their mutual attraction.[102] The work covers the nine months between the Prince's first approach and the day when his official wife leaves his palace. The story is told in the third person and at times reads more like fiction than a record of actual events. The Prince seems torn between passion, jealousy and a fear of scandal; the lady, too, blows hot and cold, partly because the Prince's ardour is so volatile. While he can choose if and when he will approach her, even finally carrying her off to his palace without consultation, Izumi is condemned to anxious waiting and feels all the awkwardness of her position when she is finally installed in the Prince's home. The brief text is crammed with the poems exchanged by the lovers, of which the dominant note is that of melancholy, loss and *mono no aware*, the Heian anguish at the beauty and fleetingness of life.

The sudden death of Prince Atsumichi some few years later can only have confirmed Izumi's view of love as sudden, stormy and evanescent. After a period of mourning, she entered the service of Empress Akiko and later married again, but found time as well for many lovers. Indeed, Michinaga, the Fujiwara magnate who had attempted to flirt with Murasaki Shikibu, boldly inscribed Izumi's fan with the words: 'Fan of a Floating Woman'. A 'floating name' meant that a woman was subject to gossip and the inscription could only be seen as insulting. With her customary tartness, Izumi Shikibu did not hesitate to put Michinaga in his place:

> Some cross the Pass of Love,
> some don't.
> Unless you are the watchman there
> it is not your right
> to cast blame.[103]

Izumi's diary may have been written in an attempt to justify her behaviour to censorious courtiers. It comes across as a stilted work, in which she plays only too well the traditional role of the lonely, yearning lady. Prose narrative may not have suited Izumi's gifts; her poetry gives a very different impression of her intelligence and emotional depth. In structure, it is conventional and highly polished. The classical *waka* (now known as *tanka*) poem is very short and consists of five metrical units (each the equivalent of a line in Western poetry, although there are no line breaks). These are arranged in a pattern of 5, 7, 5, 7 and 7 syllables. There is no rhyme scheme, but the sound of words is very important, and there is also great play with the *makurakotoba* or pillow word, a traditional phrase with its own repertoire of meanings, and the *kakekotoba* or pivot word, which had two separate meanings, each significant to the poem's interpretation.[104] The result is a deceptively brief poem capable of communicating complex ideas and intense emotion.

The *waka* was ideally suited to the poetry of love, whether rebuking a neglectful suitor, bemoaning loneliness or jealousy, sharing a joke or celebrating sexual pleasure. Izumi Shikibu developed the form to suit her diverse experience of love, which she seems to have regarded as a supreme opportunity for exploration and self-knowledge. Many of her poems attempt to bridge the gulf between the physical and emotional experience of passion. Love itself may be colourless, but her body is deeply stained by her lover's, she claims in one poem.[105] In another:

This body,
remembering yours,
is the keepsake you left.[106]

'Lying alone,' she muses elsewhere, 'my black hair tangled, uncombed, I long for the one who touched it first.'[107] The poet's own body is rarely mentioned in Japanese poetry, but Izumi willingly engages with the physical consequences of a lover's neglect.[108] She is only too aware of love's destructive potential, which she records in poem after poem. Love consumes and transforms her like a summer moth burning in flame, a metamorphosis which, as she does not need to remind the reader, inevitably ends in death. Sometimes the all too fleeting scents of spring awaken nostalgia. The fragrance of the flowering plum recalls an absent lover; blossoms scattered by a storm cut her to the quick. Time drags for the woman who waits alone, but no one plunges through the grasses, which have overgrown the pathway to her door. Listening eagerly, she mistakes the knocking note of a bird for her lover's impatient summons at the gate. At night she tosses restlessly on her pillow, longing for sleep so that she can at least meet him in her dreams. When she sees a lover again after a long absence, he finds himself lost for words. Wiser than he, she tells him there is no need for speech: 'Only concentrate on this, / on this . . .'.[109] The ellipsis in the English translation stresses the sense of a moment endlessly prolonged in silent contemplation. (Or, perhaps, sensation. Does her poem record the eloquence of touch?) Her eagerness to wring the last drop of feeling from every encounter is matched by her capacity for grief when a lover departs for ever. Mourning Prince Atsumichi, she wrote 249 poems lamenting his loss.[110] In one, she longs for him to return, if only for the second it takes for lightning to flash in the twilight sky. In another, with dignity and resignation, she reflects on the drabness of life after her beloved has died:

> Left behind
> to grow old in this world
> without you,
> the flowers I pick lose their beauty,
> dyed with dark ink.[111]

Perhaps the secret of Izumi's courage and unquenchable zest for life lay in her Buddhist faith. In one of her most famous poems, popularly believed to have been written on her deathbed (but possibly composed many years earlier when she was still a young woman), she wrote:

> The way I must enter
> leads through darkness to darkness –
> O moon above the mountains' rim,
> please shine a little further
> on my path.[112]

This moving poem recalls the bleakness of Samuel Beckett's vision in *Waiting for Godot* of birth taking place astride a grave, or Bede's description of life as a sparrow's brief passage through a lighted hall before it re-enters the enclosing dark. Izumi, however, calls on the Buddhist moon of enlightenment to accompany her for at least part of her journey into the unknown.[113] In another poem the solitary moon at dawn becomes a symbol of her own nature, into which she delves until she knows herself through and through. But, as she ruefully admits while on retreat one autumn at a mountain temple, although she tries in her heart to focus on the Buddha's teaching, the cricket voices of the world clamour in her ear.[114]

Izumi Shikibu's poems are a unique reminder of a woman's experience of love in Heian society. Sensitive and exploratory, she tested the possibilities of love for a woman of feeling. For another woman writer, known only as Lady Sarashina, romance took place mainly in her imagination, a fantasy life that was more rewarding than the conventional milestones of marriage and childbearing. All that she wanted to know about life she found in the pages of fiction, and she left a record of her relationship with reading as vivid and surprising as Lady Gossamer's account of her troubled marriage, or Izumi's lyrical meditations on the effects of love.

Lady Sarashina:
A Heroine in the Making

For many Heian women popular fiction was a pleasant way of passing time, when there was nothing particular to do between breakfast and retiring for the night. Genji's ward Tamakazura loved to lose herself in the old stories, a passion for fantasy that Genji attempted to manipulate to his own ends. When Prince Niou made unwelcome overtures to the young girl Ukifune, in the final section of *The Tale of Genji*, her half-sister consoled her with illustrations to the romances, while a lady-in-waiting read aloud from the accompanying texts. One of life's great romantics, Lady Gossamer had believed the idea of love portrayed in these seductive stories and it had ruined her life. *The Gossamer Diary* begins with its author's rejection of popular fiction. Sickened by her gullibility, she will attempt to write the truth about a woman's life. Throughout history, writers have been alert to the dangers of reading. For some women, like Ruth Weiss in Anita Brookner's cautionary novel *A Start in Life*, belief in fairy tales can take over from reality, with perilous consequences. 'Dr Weiss, at forty, knew that her life had been ruined by literature. . . . [I]t had started . . . when, at an unremembered moment in her extreme infancy, she had fallen asleep, enraptured, as her nurse breathed the words, "Cinderella *shall* go to the ball."'[115] Madame Bovary is perhaps the extreme example of a woman destroyed by fiction, but many a young woman has been deluded into imagining that her prince really will arrive some happy day, holding out the cutest glass slipper, or even, like the prince in 'Sleeping Beauty' or the lover in Izumi Shikibu's poem, plunging boldly through an overgrown garden to the maiden's door.

Perhaps, if she had read *The Tale of Genji*, Lady Gossamer might not have been quite so scornful of fiction. Murasaki Shikibu's empathy with her female characters might have struck a chord, even if Genji's easy charm and perfect good looks were less persuasive. For a young Heian woman generally known as Lady Sarashina, reading tales became the greatest pleasure of her life, an escape from reality and responsibility, and a precious resource in times of trouble. *The Sarashina Diary (Sarashina Nikki)* is no more a daily record of events than Izumi Shikibu's story of her love affair or Lady Gossamer's anatomy of a failing marriage.[116] It is a carefully structured narrative of a woman's life, in which certain key themes are highlighted: the author's love of tales and her early neglect of religion, dreams and their warnings, and the consolations of pilgrimage and prayer. Lady Sarashina was born in 1008, the daughter of a provincial official, and the diary covers the years from her childhood in the remote province of Kazusa until her early fifties when, her husband dead and her family moved away, she lived alone, like a lady in a fairy tale, in a house rapidly becoming overgrown by plants.[117]

Lady Sarashina's description of her isolated widowhood reflects Heian conventions about a woman who lived alone. As a helpless creature without male protection, a solitary woman should live in picturesque neglect. 'When a woman lives alone,' wrote Sei Shōnagon, 'her house should be extremely dilapidated, the mud wall should be falling to pieces, and if there is a pond, it should be overgrown with water-plants. It is not essential that the garden be covered with sage-brush; but weeds should be growing through the sand in patches, for this gives the place a poignantly desolate look.'[118] Lady Sarashina had a profusion of sagebrush, or at least pretended she did when writing to a friend, and this final incident in her life story confirms what the reader intuitively perceives all through this astonishing 'diary'. From start to finish, Lady Sarashina is a heroine in the making. The principal way in which her real life differs from the tales she so enjoys is in its lack of incident. She is always waiting for her story to begin. She makes a virtue of this, writing the history of a woman's inner life, in which the customary milestones of courtship, marriage and children are barely registered. What is important to Lady Sarashina is her fascination with the world of her imagination and its possibilities for ardour, love and spiritual redemption.

She begins with a bold statement of her life's great enterprise. Brought up in a remote province, she discovered the *monogatari*, the romantic tales that delighted the court ladies, only by hearsay. To while away the time, her sister and stepmother would tell her all that they could remember of the stories, including episodes from *The Tale of Genji*, which was already beginning to circulate. It was not enough to satisfy the little girl's curiosity. What she wanted was to read the tales for herself. Eventually, she had a statue of the Healing Buddha built in her own size.

> When no one was watching, I would perform my ablutions and, stealing into the altar room, would prostrate myself and pray fervently, 'Oh, please arrange things so that we may soon go to the Capital, where there are so many Tales, and please let me read them all.'[119]

Finally, when she was twelve years old her prayers were answered and her diary records her family's long journey from the east coast of Japan to Heian Kyō. Even before their bags were unpacked she persuaded her stepmother to write to a cousin who was a lady-in-waiting at the palace. Back came a collection of notebooks containing the stories the young girl had prayed for. 'I plunged into the Tales and read them day and night.' It was not enough. 'I was eager for more. But who in the Capital was going to help this newcomer in such a quest?'[120]

Her stepmother leaves, her beloved nurse dies, finally even her sister, her close companion in girlhood, dies in childbirth. Always morbidly sensitive to illness and death, Lady Sarashina feels these tragedies deeply. Her father's fortunes appear to be on the wane and they move to a less attractive house, although finally he secures another provincial post, leaving his daughter in the capital. Throughout these griefs and worries Lady Sarashina is sustained by reading. However insecure the real world, she can always lose herself in the trials of fictitious heroines and fantasise that she herself may similarly be redeemed by love. One day an aunt gives her a set, fifty-odd volumes, of *The Tale of Genji*, along with a number of other tales, now lost without trace. 'Oh, how happy I was when I came home with all these books in a bag!'[121] At last she could read the whole story of the Shining Prince, comfortably tucked away behind her curtain, and she quickly became familiar with all the many characters in the book. Steeped in Genji's romantic entanglements, she seems barely to have registered the real world.

One night, she had a dream in which a handsome priest ordered her to learn a section of the Lotus Sutra. Was this her conscience, warning her that there were more important things in life than Prince Genji? In any case, she disregards the dream.

> . . . I was much too busy with my Tales to spend any time learning sutras. I was not a very attractive girl at the time, but I fancied that, when I grew up, I would surely become a great beauty with long flowing hair like Yūgao, who was loved by the Shining Prince, or like Ukifune, who was wooed by the Captain of Uji.[122]

Despite her indifference, there are further dreams directing her towards a more spiritual way of life. At one point her mother, concerned about this unworldly girl who showed no signs of attracting a lover, commissioned a priest to dream about her daughter's future. The mother had presented a mirror to a temple and the priest reports dreaming that a beautiful woman showed him reflections in the two-sided surface. On one side he saw a figure rolling on the floor weeping and lamenting; on the other a well-dressed woman sat behind her curtain, overlooking a beautiful garden full of birds and flowering trees. The message seems unequivocal: Lady Sarashina must take steps to secure her future happiness. Her thoughts, however, are far from religion, or even the realities of finding a husband.

> I lived forever in a dream world. Though I made occasional pilgrimages to temples, I could never bring myself to pray sincerely for what most people want. . . . The height of my aspirations was that a man of noble birth, perfect in both looks and manners, someone like Shining Genji in the Tale, would visit me just once a year in the mountain village where he would have hidden me like Lady Ukifune. There I should live my lonely existence, gazing at the blossoms and the Autumn leaves and the moon and the snow, and wait for an occasional splendid letter from him. This was all I wanted; and in time I came to believe that it would actually happen.[123]

She was forced to emerge from her fantasy life. An opportunity arrived for her to attend the imperial court as a lady-in-waiting at the comparatively late age of thirty-one. It was not the exciting experience she had dreamt about. Having been totally absorbed in tales, she had made no attempt to cultivate other court ladies and the only people she knew were the women she had visited to borrow books. On her first tour of duty she survived just one night before rushing home to her quiet routines and old-fashioned parents. She was not the only person to feel daunted by her encounter with the

court. Even the robust Sei Shōnagon confessed that she had felt
overwhelmed by shyness on her first venture into that treacherous
atmosphere. While Sei Shōnagon quickly took the measure of how
to survive court politics, Lady Sarashina was temperamentally
unsuited to intrigue and flirtation. Her father's loneliness when she
was away from home meant that her attendance at court was in any
case too random for success as an imperial handmaid. Even so, the
one romantic encounter of her life, or at least the only one she cares
to share with the reader, took place at court.

One evening, she and another lady-in-waiting were quietly listening to some priests chanting in a nearby chapel when they were
approached by a gentleman. Usually shy in the presence of men,
Lady Sarashina was attracted by his beautiful manners and exquisite
taste. He engaged the women in the kind of conversation so dear
to the hearts of Heian aristocrats: the sadness of the world, the
charm of the moonless night with the rain pattering on the leaves,
the contrasting beauties of autumn and spring (an apparently in-
exhaustible debate as far as the 'good people' were concerned).
The courtier recalled a wintry night which had made an indelible
impression on his heart, and gracefully assured the ladies that, in
future, dark rainy evenings would seem equally moving. This was
to be Lady Sarashina's longest encounter with this civilised man,
the poet and statesman Minamoto no Sukemichi.[124] Some months
later they had a second, eerie exchange, when he happened to chant
a sutra on the veranda outside her room. She spoke to him and
the sound of her voice recalled their rainy night meeting, but his
companions joined him and the moment was lost. He sent a message:
'I should like to play the flute for you.' She longed to hear him and
waited for a suitable moment. 'It never came.' There was another
missed opportunity one spring evening and then nothing more. 'He
was an unusual man,' Lady Sarashina explains, '. . . not the type to
bustle about.'[125] This fragile love affair was perhaps the supreme
emotional experience of Lady Sarashina's life. The briefness of the

encounter, the man's respectful attention, their soulful conversation, and the missed opportunities that assured her of his continued interest: these are the stuff of dreams, which she had no chance, and perhaps no wish, to test against the realities of courtship, a physical love affair, maybe even marriage to this congenial man.

Real life did eventually catch up with Lady Sarashina. At about this time her diary reports a period of activity when her tales had to be laid aside, partly because of her court duties and also because of a new religious awareness. She even began to question her own romantic credulity. 'How could anyone as wonderful as Shining Genji or as beautiful as [Ukifune] really exist in this world of ours?'[126] What a fool she had been to let the years slip by, neglecting prayer and pilgrimage for the delusions of the storytellers. She does not explain this change of heart, although her personal circumstances must have forced her into a new awareness of reality and responsibility. Astonishingly, she married at what was, for a woman in Heian society, the very ripe age of thirty-six and she even had three children, but these crucial relationships are barely mentioned in the diary. Instead she writes, beautifully, about her retreats and pilgrimages to various temples. Like so many Heian noblewomen, she found the bustle and change of travel refreshing, and was trained in an appreciation of nature that made journeys into the countryside and mountains deeply fulfilling. As the tales loosened their hold on her imagination, her engagement with the natural world and its exquisite scenes deepened, offering consolation and refuge from the ups and downs of married life. Although she says almost nothing about her feelings for her husband in her diary, she was traumatised by his unexpected death and recalled the priest's dream about the writhing figure. Pondering this sad event, she again regretted the time she had wasted on tales: '. . . I had wandered through life without realizing any of my hopes or accumulating any merit.'[127] A dream of the Amida Buddha shimmering with a golden light seemed to promise hope of salvation, but her diary ends with Lady

Sarashina living alone, like the heroine of an old romance, in her neglected house with the sagebrush choking the garden.

Like *The Gossamer Diary* and Genji's musings about fiction in *The Tale of Genji*, Lady Sarashina's diary poses a question that seems to have been deeply important to Heian women writers. Is fiction harmful to women? Is it a pack of lies, or is it capable, as Genji asserts, of telling important truths? Lady Gossamer preferred the realities of her own life to the fabrications of the tales, but her expectations of her husband were conditioned by romantic ideals, which he consistently failed to match. Lady Sarashina's imagination dwelt in the magical realm of high romance, and she did not even attempt to address the discrepancy between her dreams and the realities of marriage and bringing up three children. Finally, she relinquished love for the surer consolations of pilgrimage and religion, although she was still presenting herself as a romantic heroine at the end of her diary. Other writers took a more realistic attitude to love. For Sei Shōnagon, courtship was primarily a question of good manners, while Izumi Shikibu plunged into sexual experience to test the possibilities of feeling between men and women. Honest and courageous, she bypassed the lies and emotional manipulations that seem to have been an inevitable consequence of Heian sexual arrangements. Like Mary Wollstonecraft and George Sand, her natural successors, she had the strength to challenge social convention and dared to use her public platform as a writer to explain her philosophy of love. Despite the attractions of spirituality, it seems never entirely to have replaced the struggle for passion and emotional commitment.

Unusually among these writers, Murasaki Shikibu in *The Tale of Genji* turned to fiction to expose male subterfuge and female suffering. She wrote about the perfect hero, but dared a 'warts and all' portrait. Even she seems to have come to the conclusion that the cost of love was sometimes too great. One of Lady Sarashina's heroines was Ukifune, the young woman whose story concludes

The Tale of Genji. No doubt it was Ukifune's seclusion and her pursuit by two remarkable princes that captured Lady Sarashina's imagination. Even so, Ukifune was a strange role model for an ardent young woman. Her story is dark and terrible. Like Lady Sarashina's diary, it concludes with a farewell to love.

Ukifune Takes Up Her Writing Brush

The Tale of Genji ends on a note of such ambiguity that some commentators have wondered whether the novel is, in fact, incomplete. The final stages of the book tell the story of a young girl, Ukifune, whose efforts to make her way in the world have been sabotaged by her dubious parentage and the rival attempts of two suitors, Prince Niou and Prince Kaoru, to control her sexual favours. Traumatised by her lovers' demands and with no independent financial support, she decides to throw herself into the river at Uji, the mountain hideaway where she has been living under Kaoru's protection. Her attempt to commit suicide fails when she is possessed by a mysterious spirit. When she finally awakens from her trance, she cuts off her beautiful long hair and embraces the ascetic life of a nun. Pretending that she can no longer remember her former life, she evades attempts by Kaoru to re-establish contact. As a nun, her future will be uncomfortable. She faces a life of hard work and physical deprivation, and everyone who sees the charming novice deplores her decision. Ukifune, however, is content. She has found an existence free from sexual jealousy and the threat of abandonment. While Kaoru broods possessively over what has become of her, she takes refuge in her brushes, inkstone and some sheets of paper. 'She had never been an articulate girl, and she had no confidante with whom to discuss the rights and wrongs of what had happened. She seated herself at her inkstone and turned to the one pursuit in which she could lose herself[.]'[128]

As in the case of Lady Gossamer, Lady Sarashina and the other remarkable women discussed in this chapter, writing offers Ukifune a way of giving meaning and order to the apparently random events of an unhappy life. Liberated from sex and its torments, she forgets herself in the pleasures of the brush and the consolations of imagination.

PART 3

The Heart's Desire: Medieval Women Write About Love

'[A]s for pleasure, rest assured that in love there is a hundred thousand times more grief, searing pain, and perilous risk, especially on the ladies' side, than there is pleasure.'

Christine de Pizan,
The Book of the Duke of True Lovers[1]

Women's Voices from the Distant Past

In 1405, the French writer Christine de Pizan completed *The Book of the Duke of True Lovers*, the story of a clandestine love affair between a young knight and a married woman. De Pizan was a bluestocking and feminist, who nevertheless established herself as a successful writer within the male-dominated culture of the French court. Although her book was written, like many romances of the period, as a narrative poem, it is a fascinating early attempt at the psychological novel, a form in which women were later to excel. It is also a clear-sighted critique of the cost to women of the cult of *fin'amor* ('fine loving'), which was developed by the troubadour poets in Occitania (now southern France) and swept through Europe during the twelfth and thirteenth centuries, influencing chivalric romance from Chrétien de Troyes to Chaucer.

Over two and a half thousand troubadour poems survive, written by more than four hundred poets, a literary treasure trove to delight the general reader, who can enjoy it in translation, and to tantalise generations of scholars, anxious to tease out the realities of life in medieval Europe from what the poems reveal. The songs deal with many topics besides love (politics and war, jokes and arguments, satire and self-mockery), but the troubadours are most famous for their love poems and the ideal of love that they promote. The concept of *fin'amor* endured long after the last minstrel had laid down his harp: European lyric poetry absorbed many of its themes. It has influenced attitudes to passion and sex from Dante and Petrarch in Italy and their English literary successors, Wyatt, Surrey and the Elizabethan poets, to the twentieth-century schoolboy William, who, in Richmal Crompton's 'The Sweet Little Girl in White', falls in love with a blonde goddess, whom he yearns to serve with chivalric fervour. Troubadour lyric poetry, charged with love-longing as it so often is, was written almost entirely from the male perspective, and offers a view of female desire and behaviour that conformed to knightly ideals of sexual conduct. In this outpouring of erotic enthusiasm, the reality of love from a woman's point of view was generally disregarded, but the evidence for how women felt about sex, love, passion and marriage survives from the Middle Ages, if one cares to look for it, and suggests that there was a discrepancy between male fantasy and female experience.

By the beginning of the eleventh century in Heian Japan, aristocratic women using the 'woman's hand' had fashioned vernacular Japanese into a literary language capable of producing poetry, memoirs and *The Tale of Genji*, a novel that is regarded as one of the great works of world literature. Women in Europe had to wait many centuries before they too began to find a public voice, which spoke to an audience with the leisure, income and private space to develop a taste for reading. Women *did* write, however, long before Jane Austen took up her pen in the late eighteenth century and some of their words have survived, as was the case with Heloise's passionate letters to Abelard. Women's words of love lie scattered among the relics of the Middle Ages that litter libraries, museums and private collections. Sometimes they are found in unexpected places, in the ecstatic outpourings of mystics, or the confession of a Cathar girl to her Catholic accusers. Women's voices are also to be found in the poetry that has become synonymous with the medieval code of love. The poems of the trobairitz, the female troubadours in Occitania, provide a muted *contrappunto* to the songs of the male poets, and question the prevailing view of desire and suffering as male prerogatives.

The Troubadour and His Lady

'Worthy, joyful lady, / your lover is dying,' sang the troubadour Bernart de Ventadorn, renowned alike for his poetry and a probably fictitious passion for Eleanor of Aquitaine.[2] It was a plea for compassion that typified the lovelorn male poets of southern Europe. Troubadour poetry and culture flourished for almost two hundred years from around the time of the First Crusade in 1095. Its homeland was Occitania, an area stretching from the Pyrenees and Alps in the south and east of modern France, and incorporating Aquitaine, Limousin and the Auvergne. United by a common language, the region was dominated by noble families who represented powerful, independent and often conflicting political interests, and its closest links were with Spain and the Mediterranean rather than northern France. If one sets aside the anonymous composers of popular songs, the troubadours were the first European lyric poets to write in the vernacular, using the *langue d'oc* of Occitania rather than Latin.[3] As time went on, they developed their own poetic language, a form of literary Occitan, which was intelligible across local variations in speech and dialect. Despite its high polish and sometimes elevated themes, their work would have been accessible to all ranks of society and the male poets themselves came from a variety of backgrounds, probably including clerks and professional musicians as well as great lords and nobles. Their poetry was written to be sung in public performance, often accompanied by harp or vielle, or some other stringed instrument, and they wrote about anything that might appeal to their patrons, and to the lords' retinues and guests. Most

famously of all, they wrote about love, inspired, perhaps, by Arab
erotic poetry, which filtered through from beyond the Pyrenees, by
Ibn Hazm's treatise *The Dove's Neck-Ring*, which describes the
power of love to strike violently and unawares, by native traditions
of popular songs and the Latin poems of clerks and scholars, and by
Ovid's tales of desire and its discontents, which found an enthusiastic
audience in medieval Europe.

The term 'courtly love', often used to describe the medieval code
of love, was invented as late as 1883 by the critic Gaston Paris.
The troubadour phrase *fin'amor*, with its suggestion of emotional
refinement and good manners, is a more appropriate description.
Broadly summarised, *fin'amor* represented an idealised relationship
in which the male lover worshipped a noble lady with almost
religious fervour and performed chivalrous deeds to win her favour,
while barely daring even to address her. The lover's relationship to
the lady was that of the knight to his feudal overlord: he offered
unquestioning loyalty, fidelity and respect. The lady's role was to
be worthy of devotion through her graciousness, beauty and virtue.
Secrecy was an important component of the transaction and the
lady's name was often disguised under a *senhal* or secret name. In
modern interpretations the beloved *domna* or lady is generally
assumed to be a married woman, so that *fin'amor* has become identified with adultery, an idea which the critic C. S. Lewis did much
to promote.[4] However, in its heyday it was seen as a civilising
influence, which ennobled the knight, encouraging him to acts of
gallantry and courage, and honoured the lady who inspired his
deeds of valour.

The troubadour view of love is frequently described as if it were
set in stone from the time of its first known exponent, William IX,
Duke of Aquitaine. As a glance at some of its practitioners will
reveal, *fin'amor* was a fluid concept (almost as varied as the men
who wrote about love), metamorphosing by subtle gradations from
William IX's frankly venal view of women to the sublimated ador-

ation of the later troubadours. The ideal of love as a route to virtue was to culminate in Dante's veneration of his muse Beatrice, by which time lust had been refined into spiritual yearning. As the emotional content evolved, so did the poetry, since the troubadours increasingly used their celebration of *fin'amor* as a means to demonstrate verbal dexterity. What was important was the ability to create an impressive tapestry of words and ideas, a striking design cunningly constructed within the formal constraints of rhyme and metre and drawing on the stock themes associated with love-longing. Behind these protestations of love for an unattainable beloved, one senses the alert ego of the poet on the make, eager to exhibit his skill and virtuosity to an admiring public. A detailed account of troubadour diversity would take many pages, but a brief tour of three very different poets may sketch an impression of their interests and themes.

While the lives of many troubadours remain unknown or depend on their *vidas*, the fanciful biographies often written decades after their deaths, Duke William ix emerges from the records with surprising freshness and vigour. He is known as the first of the troubadours because his poems are the earliest to be recorded in the manuscript collections, but his fame depended as much on his colourful personal life as on his literary inventiveness. William became Count of Poitou and Duke of Aquitaine on his father's death in 1086, an inheritance that made him one of the most powerful landowners in France. Nominally owing allegiance to the king in northern France, William and the other magnates who controlled the southern territories were able to exert independent authority over the lands they owned. The greatest check on William's activities was the Church, which he defied by seizing Toulouse while its lord was absent on crusade and by his open pursuit of women, including a married lady perhaps aptly named Dangerosa. William's *vida* illustrates his legacy in the popular imagination and for once the details may bear a close resemblance to the truth:

> The Count of Poitiers was one of the most courtly men in the
> world and also one of the greatest deceivers of women; and he
> was a good knight-at-arms and generous in his gallantry; and
> he could write good poetry and sing well. And for a long time
> he wandered about the world seducing women.[5]

Something of William's energy and subversiveness lingers on in
the ten or so songs of his that have survived, and which seem to
confirm his scandalous reputation. 'Companho, faray un vers tot
covinen' ('My friends, I'll write a song that's made for the occasion')
begins as an apparently innocent account of trying to choose between
two horses.[6] It quickly becomes apparent that the 'mares' are women,
whom the poet aims to 'break in' to suit his taste. The mutual
antagonism between the women and William's casual comment that
he had given one when still a 'foal' to her current 'master' suggest
the lord's absolute power over the men and women in his entourage
and the lowly status of women, who were pawns in the male game
of property and inheritance. In another poem the tables are turned,
although still to William's advantage, when he comes across two
noble ladies, who take him home thinking he is a dumb pilgrim.
They test his inability to tell tales by dragging a vicious cat up and
down his naked back. When he manages, heroically, to stay silent,
the women settle down to a week of sexual fun, which allows
William to boast about his virility:

> You know how many times I screwed them?
> One hundred and eighty-eight to be precise;
> so much so that I almost broke my girth
>   and harness . . .[7]

Elsewhere he claims that 'there is no woman who, after a night /
with me, will not want me back the next day'.[8] William's bawdy
enjoyment of his sexuality contradicts the later stereotype of the

bashful troubadour and may reflect a transitional stage in court manners and morality, before the Church asserted its authority over sexual behaviour. It may also hint at the degrees of latitude permitted to men and women at the Duke's court, although there is a suspicion that William's love affairs exist only in his own fantasy. The poem about the two rival 'horses' implies that he can take his pick of the wives of local knights, but is there anything more to this than braggadocio? In the cat anecdote, the women are apparently in control of their sexual adventures, although they take care to choose a lover who is unable to gossip. Once again, however, this sounds suspiciously like the titillating accounts of randy women in modern sex magazines for men. Genuine emotion or even the respectful *fin'amor* of the later troubadours is entirely lacking. The two 'mares' suffer from jealousy, but in neither song does William appear to have any serious feeling for the women he beds.

Bawdiness is not William's only note. His lyric 'Ab la dolchor del temps novel' ('With the sweetness of the new season') exchanges raunchiness for sincerity and suggests that he was capable of real sensitivity in love.[9] The poem begins in spring, when leaves are freshly budding, the birds are trying out new melodies and men yearn to fulfil their dreams. His lady's silence keeps the poet sullen and sleepless; he can do nothing until he knows the outcome of his suit. These were to become stock themes in the troubadour repertoire, but William insists on the flesh-and-blood reality of the lovers. They veer between coldness and passion like a frozen branch of hawthorn revived by sudden sunshine. Theirs is a tempestuous relationship, but he recalls a happy morning of truce, when the lady gave him the gift of a ring and, more preciously, her love. 'May God grant that I live long enough / to have my hands beneath her cloak' is his heartfelt response to this happy memory.[10] Like his literary heir, the Tudor poet Sir Thomas Wyatt, William falls back on plain language to communicate the urgency of sexual desire.

Nothing could be more remote from William's hands-on

approach to women than the ethereal passion of Jaufre Rudel. Again, a *vida* records the legend of this troubadour, whose songs were composed some time in the mid-twelfth century, but whose fame as an exemplary lover lingers to the present day and was celebrated by the Finnish composer Kaija Saariaho in her opera *L'Amour de loin*, which was premièred at the Salzburg Festival in 2000. According to legend, Rudel was a Prince of Blaye, a town between Bordeaux and the western coast, which became famous as the site of the tomb of Roland, a popular stopping-off place for pilgrims en route to the shrine of St James at Compostela in northern Spain. Rudel's legend emphasises the prodigious travels people happily undertook at this period, and the close contacts between the European continent and its neighbours to the east and south. Captivated by reports of the goodness and grace of the Countess of Tripoli, which pilgrims brought back from Antioch, Rudel fell in love with the distant lady and wrote many songs in her honour. Finally he decided to pay her a visit, taking the Cross as a crusader and setting out on the perilous voyage across the Mediterranean. Sadly, he fell ill on the journey and arrived at Tripoli on the point of death. Hearing of his plight, the Countess hastened to Rudel's bedside and embraced him, momentarily reviving her exhausted lover. This orgasmic encounter is captured in a delightful manuscript illustration in which an ecstatic Rudel swoons in his lady's arms. After his death, she buried him in the house of the Knights Templar and took the veil for grief that very day.[11]

The truth of this romantic story cannot be proved, although there was a Countess of Tripoli at the time, Hodierna of Jerusalem, who was famously headstrong and pleasure-loving, and was kept in seclusion by her jealous husband.[12] Even so, Rudel's *vida* should probably be scanned for its inner meaning rather than its authenticity. It is a tale about love, pursued faithfully and almost without hope, in which love itself is the goal. The lady's significance lies in her absence and the emotion this arouses, and death, not sexual fulfilment, was the only appropriate resolution to Jaufre's yearning. The theme of '*amors de terra loindana*' ('love from a distant land') dominates the few songs of Rudel's that survive, testimony to the power of the imagination to inspire overwhelming longing.[13] The simplicity of his style and language enhance the impression of the poet's single-mindedness. Love for Rudel has the force of a spiritual quest.

One of his most beautiful poems, 'Qan lo rius de la fontana', begins with the poet's ardent response to the natural world.[14] The clear water from the fountain, the wild rose in bloom, the nightingale polishing its song, inspire him to record his heartache. Only the sound of his lady's voice, tempting him to love in an orchard or a secluded bed chamber, could cure his lovesickness. In another poem he fantasises about the pilgrim's journey, which would allow him at least to see her and to enjoy her conversation.[15] If he does manage to visit his love, '*Iratz e gauzens m'en partrai*,' he says, 'Sad and happy I shall leave'.[16] Elsewhere he says that, even though he knows his obsession is futile ('never . . . will she promise herself to me'), she makes him uniquely happy, '*ni per nuill joi aitan no ri*.'[17] What is most striking about Rudel's passion for the unknown Countess is her absence from the story. She exists almost entirely in his fantasy and his poems delicately explore his own psychological processes.

Rudel's romance lingered on in the European lyric tradition and found particular resonance with nineteenth-century writers. In Heinrich Heine's 'Geoffroy Rudel und Melisende von Tripoli' the Countess weaves a tapestry from which the ghosts of the lovers emerge, finally allowed to enjoy their love in death. In *La Princesse lointaine* the French playwright Edmond Rostand introduced a rival attraction between the Princess and a second troubadour, employed by Rudel as go-between. According to Lord Wavell, with whom the story was a favourite, the part of the Countess was played by Sarah Bernhardt, which perhaps explains why her essentially passive role was so dramatically expanded.[18] Robert Browning, a poet fascinated by questions of identity, imagination and worldly reputation, summed up the futility of the troubadour's fixation in 'Rudel to the Lady of Tripoli' (1855). In this version of the story Rudel weaves a personal emblem to send to the Countess. The device he chooses is the humble sunflower, which worships the sun 'like a sacrifice / Before its idol', and becomes 'but a foolish mimic sun'. Just as the sunflower ignores the bees that gather its pollen, so Rudel is indifferent to men's applause for his poetry. He looks only to his lady for recognition:

> Oh, Angel of the East, one, one gold look
> Across the waters to this twilight nook,
> – The far sad waters, Angel, to this nook![19]

Browning's complex poem anatomises the relationship between the writer and the world, the poet and his subject, the person and his individuality. In every sphere of possible engagement Rudel refuses to play an active role. Even as a lover he fails, preferring the safety of a fantasy that can never be realised. Like the sunflower, he foolishly follows the distant and indifferent sun, and neglects his responsibilities as poet and human being.

Rudel's wistful passion for the Countess of Tripoli contrasts with the more robust approach of Bernart de Ventadorn, writing during the golden age of troubadour poetry in the second half of the twelfth century. A greater body of his work survives (forty or so poems to Rudel's six), of which the majority deal with the theme of love. Here is a master troubadour at work, as Bernart marries technical virtuosity to a dramatic realisation of the emotional ups and downs of *fin'amor*. Bernart's origins were possibly humble. His *vida* suggests that he was a baker's son, who had the good luck to find a wealthy patron, the Viscount of Ventadorn, in the Limousin.[20] Gossip connected him with the Viscount's wife, but the Viscount discovered the relationship, or so the story went, banished Bernart from his territories and had his wife locked up and guarded. The imprisonment of a charming wife by her jealous husband seems to have been popular with medieval storytellers (it features in several of the lays of Marie de France), and the incident (and the poet's nostalgia for his lost lady) was atmospherically recalled by Ezra Pound:

> 'My Lady of Ventadour
> Is shut by Eblis in
> And will not hawk nor hunt
>   nor get her free in the air
> Nor watch fish rise to bait
> Nor the glare-wing'd flies alight in the creek's edge
> Save in my absence . . .'[21]

Later, Bernart's name was linked to the heiress Eleanor of Aquitaine, William's granddaughter, who married Henry of Anjou and became Queen of England and co-founder of the Plantagenet dynasty. Whatever the truth of these rumours, Bernart's songs project an emotional intensity and sensitivity that suggest lived experience of love. At the same time he is the quintessential troubadour: he loves and suffers in secret, he barely dares to speak to his beloved, who is, of course, the most beautiful and gracious of ladies, and he fears malicious gossip from the *lauzengiers*, the spies who hang around virtuous women. 'Joy' is a favourite word with troubadours, expressing an abundance of happiness often associated with springtime and the ecstasy of being in love. Bernart's joy when trees burst into leaf and blossom and the nightingale is heard once more is irrepressible:

> Joy I have for it, and joy for the flower,
> And joy for myself and for my lady even more;[22]

Bernart's sophistication as a poet can be relished in what is possibly the best known of all troubadour songs, the haunting 'Can vei la lauzeta mover' ('When I see the lark'), whose fame spread to faraway places, carried perhaps by its melody, which echoes mournfully in the memory, like the love that is its theme.[23] Beginning with a lyrical evocation of the lark beating its wings in the sunlight, then dropping from the sky in a swoon of rapture, Bernart reflects bitterly on his own lack of joy, since he has lost his heart to a lady who has left him nothing but 'desire and a yearning soul'.[24] Adrift in the desolation of unrequited love, he turns against all women, but cannot leave off loving. Bereft of meaningful life, the only solution is exile and silence: 'I shall renounce and give up singing, / and hide myself from joy and love.'[25] Even in this moment of renunciation and anguish, the poet's sense of his identity never wavers. Like Narcissus, who fell in love with his own reflection in a fountain, Bernart admits that he has been mesmerised by seeing his image in his lady's eyes. He is the true subject of his poem. His wilful lady has value as a mirror of the poet's character and worth; in herself, she is merely a stereotype. The only detail he reveals about her is that she is 'truly' a woman in desiring most what is prohibited. For a twelfth-century audience this casual reference would have been rich in meanings. The lady is like Eve, history's favourite scapegoat, a foolish woman who condemned men to death by her fondness for gossip, her fickleness and appetite for forbidden fruit. By refusing to pity the poet, the lady condemns him, as Eve did Adam, to displacement and death.

William ix, Jaufre Rudel and Bernart de Ventadorn are just a few of the medieval poets who wrote so eloquently about love. Did women have any value to the troubadours who so assiduously praised their beauty, grace and charm, deplored their indifference and cruelty, and developed the *canso*, the love song, into a form exquisitely suited to express the pain of thwarted desire? Reflecting on the role played by woman in history, Virginia Woolf came to the conclusion that 'Imaginatively she is of the highest importance; practically she is completely insignificant'.[26] Mary Wollstonecraft would probably have agreed. On hearing that her lover, the prosaic philosopher William Godwin, had written her a poem, she responded tartly, 'Do not make me a desk "to write upon," I humbly pray . . .'. She was thinking of Samuel Butler's quipping couplet: 'Shee that with *Poetry* is won / Is but a *Desk* to write upon.'[27] Were the women in troubadour lyrics simply 'a Desk to write upon', at best an imaginative stimulus to poets looking for themes that would appeal to their overlords and the women in their households? In the thirteenth-century Occitan romance *Flamenca*, the king of France pays attention to the new wife of one of his barons, Lord Archambaud, unwittingly arousing the latter's jealousy. The king's act of homage to pretty Flamenca is intended to honour her husband rather than initiate a love affair, and it is only the queen's envy that sows the seeds of doubt in Archambaud's mind. When troubadours sang about the grace and beauty of the unattainable *domna*, were they complimenting their patrons by praising the excellence of their wives? When they called a lady *midons*, 'my lord', the title by which a vassal addressed his feudal lord, were they confirming their service to the master rather than the mistress of the house?

During the period in which the troubadours developed the language of *fin'amor*, sexual relationships and the balance of power between men and women of the Occitan nobility were dominated by considerations of property, social custom and the Church. Marriage was the means through which great nobles such as William IX and Henry of Anjou increased their land, strengthened their political dominance and confirmed alliances with their peers. When the marriage of Eleanor of Aquitaine and Louis VII of France was annulled in 1152, Eleanor, a great heiress in her own right, was pursued by fortune hunters who plotted to kidnap and forcibly marry her, greedy to acquire her territories of Aquitaine, Gascony and Poitou. By rapidly marrying Henry of Anjou, she cemented an alliance that brought a vast tract of land stretching from the English Channel to the Pyrenees under one marital umbrella. She also satisfied her sensual appetites, thwarted by years of marriage to the monkish Louis, and saved herself from less attractive suitors. The sexual chemistry between the newly weds was legendary and led to the birth of a succession of sons. Eleanor's infamous reputation for sex (apart from her attraction to the virile Henry, there were reports of at least one affair during her marriage to Louis) was not customary among women of her class. Daughters of Eve and therefore prone to promiscuity and deceit, they were also daughters of the Church and expected to marry as virgins and cleave only to their husbands thereafter. As far as the Church was concerned, marriage was better than fornication, but the purpose of sexual intercourse was procreation not pleasure. Legitimate heirs were a prime consideration for the nobility and a straying wife was a threat to a man's dynastic ambitions as well as his honour. As for marrying for love, no doubt some arranged marriages did develop into love matches, but the emphasis was on property, power and inheritance. Once married, even a substantial landowner like Eleanor was expected to defer to her husband. Despite the emphasis on masculine superiority and authority, a minority of aristocratic women in Occitania such as Ermengard of Narbonne and the mother of the troubadour Raimbaut d'Orange did wield considerable power over lands and property.[28] In the case of the formidable Ermengard, the honorary title '*midons*' would have been no more than her due. As a gesture in the rhetoric of *fin'amor*, it probably had as much relationship to true reverence as John Dowland's praise of Elizabeth I as 'Queen of Love and Beauty' when she was already well into her final decade.[29]

The troubadour songs were not addressed to an ageing and childless queen, whose courtiers found it useful to promote an image of youth and sexuality. Many of the women they celebrated would have been young and attractive. With such tempting bait, was adultery commonplace among the Occitan nobility? Since the troubadour lady was both high-born and unattainable, it has generally been assumed by scholars that either her admirer was too poor to marry – a landless knight, perhaps, or someone even lower on the social ladder – or else that the woman was already married. Even if the latter were correct, the frank eroticism of some troubadour poems should not be taken too literally. As historians delve into ecclesiastical and civic records, it becomes apparent that, like the social code in Victorian England, rules of behaviour for the nobly born in medieval Europe aimed to protect the chastity of women, and to maintain male power and dynastic interests. Although legislation on sexual conduct varied from region to region, the double standard for men and women was the norm. Even so, men were expected to respect women who were their social superiors and those of their own rank. As the story of Heloise and Abelard indicates, illicit love affairs were not unknown in twelfth-century France. Human nature suggests that some lovers did take the risk of being found out and engaged in more than the formal kiss of greeting on a lady's lips, which so delighted an English ambassador.[30] Most aristocratic women were more likely to have been preoccupied with childbearing and domestic duties. With husbands and retainers absent on crusades, they were also responsible for maintaining property, land and crops. *Fin'amor* was a sophisticated game, an elegant way of defusing sexual tensions, so much so that a cleric known as Andreas Capellanus even went so far as to compile an advice manual, the ironic *De Arte Honeste Amandi* (probably written in the 1180s), which pretended to offer a guide to appropriate behaviour for noble lovers. Despite his apparent liberality, Capellanus ends his work by condemning love outside marriage, reinforcing his argument with citations from the Bible and the more misogynistic comments from such authorities as Juvenal, Jerome and their successors in the 'women are evil' brigade.

A modern critic succinctly summarises the situation on adultery in troubadour circles: 'unless a *fin'aman* sings of his desire for his own wife, or for a woman of an inferior social rank, he is transgressing both the lay and ecclesiastical models of marriage in some way[.]'[31] Reading the troubadours' polished phrases, *fin'amor* seems no more than a literary entertainment, a medium through which talented poets could practise their skills, flatter their employers and, like the modern pop singer, provide a safe outlet for impossible yearnings. When women write their side of the story, however, the game of love is seen from a fresh perspective. The words of the women troubadours, the trobairitz, reveal the pain and tension of the *domna*'s role. Reading their confessions of joy, jealousy and loss raises once more the question of authenticity. How far were troubadour love affairs all in the mind? The songs of the Countess of Dia and her fellow trobairitz seem to permit a more intimate glimpse behind the castle walls of ancient Occitania, into secret chambers where lovers exchanged glances and rings, and lay awake with beating hearts through the long dark nights of the Middle Ages.

The *Domna* Tells Her Story

'I must sing on a theme I would rather avoid . . . I am deceived and betrayed,' begins one poem by the Countess of Dia.[32] Her lament resonates as plaintively today as it did in the latter part of the twelfth century. The music for this song, 'A chantar m'er de so q'ieu no volria', was jotted down in a surviving manuscript fragment and something of its flavour can still be recaptured. Sung on a modern recording by an unaccompanied female voice, the repetitive melody mirrors the lady's obsessive retelling of her lover's treachery and asserts her claims to his attention. Almost certainly written for public performance, perhaps for a castle community or circulation among fellow poets, the song is nevertheless intensely intimate. While the words speak of disappointment and suffering, the music invites emotional release of the purest kind. What is unexpected about the Countess's song is that, like the poems by the trobairitz Castelloza written a decade or so later, it reveals the *domna*'s sense of disillusionment and betrayal. When the lady alights from her pedestal, it is to describe how she feels when abandoned by a knightly lover.

The trobairitz were active in the courts of Occitania for only a limited period, from the mid-twelfth to mid-thirteenth centuries. In contrast to the many male troubadours in southern France, only twenty named trobairitz are known, along with a handful of anonymous female poets. Their collected works today number fewer than forty songs. Because of the scantiness of records, it is not always clear what rank of society they occupied, although it is generally assumed that they were noblewomen rather than professional musicians. Their *vidas* typically identify them as courtly and accomplished, and often link them romantically to men who were not their husbands. So-called 'women's songs', the *chansons de femme* in France, the *cantigas de amigo* in Portugal and the *Frauenlieder* in Germany, love poems in which the woman is the speaker, were widespread in the European vernacular traditions, but it is impossible to know how many of these were actually composed by women. The trobairitz seem to have been an isolated example of a group of medieval women writers working within a literary tradition, and one which was dominated by male poets and a masculine ideology of love.

The trobairitz poems that survive in manuscript collections were probably preserved because of their public nature. Written for performance in front of a mixed audience, several songs communicate a sense of fun and flirtation, as male and female speakers argue the nicer points of courtly behaviour. Courteous and often jocular in tone, these *tensons* or debate songs between a troubadour and trobairitz reveal the issues at stake between women and their admirers. One *tenson* discusses the possibilities for equality in *fin'amor* if the man is vassal to the lady. According to the male speaker, once a lover has proved his loyalty he is entitled to the same authority as his *domna*. The trobairitz argues that even when a lady has granted her love, the man is still her servant. In another *tenson* the trobairitz presents the case of a woman with two lovers. Before she will let either of them come near her, they must swear not to trespass further than a hug or kiss. The first lover, casual about oaths, immediately gives his promise; the other, a more honest fellow, does not trust himself to keep the agreement. Which of these two was the truer lover, is her enquiry. The troubadour upholds the honest lover, fearful of harming his lady. The trobairitz argues that passion justifies bad behaviour. So much for the idea that medieval women were shrinking violets! In a third poem, a dialogue rather than a *tenson*, a woman asks her lover why he has grown cold; he craftily blames the *lauzengiers*, the court gossips, and claims he has been trying to protect her reputation.[33]

The *tenson* is a game that permits the contestants to demonstrate their wit and expertise. If the songs referred to real-life lovers known to the audience, the verbal sparring would have been all the more enjoyable. The balance between male and female speaker maintains a sense of sprightliness and good manners, and even when the tone veers towards bitterness or a more heartfelt complaint, the *tenson* is self-consciously courtly. The songs of individual trobairitz are more intimate and personal. While the troubadour convention expected men to pine for an unattainable mistress, the trobairitz had to find a way to put the woman's point of view. Given that she was supposed to be simultaneously haughty, virtuous and kind, it was difficult for a woman to say anything without making a fool of herself. *Fin'amor* was male territory. Giving the *domna*'s point of view demanded courage and honesty, and exposed women to the possibility of derision or even accusations of immodesty. Their songs had to negotiate a fine line between the female conduct prescribed by the rules of *fin'amor* and shaming revelations of vulnerability, need and sexual desire.

For most of the trobairitz their work has to be assessed on the basis of a single poem. Even so, the songs that survive communicate a strong sense of the poet's female identity. In what is probably the earliest known trobairitz song, a mere fragment of eight lines, a woman known as Tibors confirms her feelings through a series of negatives: she has never lacked desire for her handsome lover, she has never failed to long to see him, she has never regretted their affair, she has never felt a moment's joy after they have parted in anger. It is a teasing poem, which may reflect the self-confidence of happy love, or a woman's spirited defence against accusations of indifference.[34] Clara d'Anduza is equally devoted to her lover, but her freedom to enjoy his company and even to write poetry has been damaged by tittle-tattle. The *lauzengiers*, court gossips and spies, have been all too succcessful in separating the lovers, and now she seethes with anger and resentment. Despite disquieting undertones, these songs assert the *domna*'s loving-kindness and good faith, although her status in relation to the lover remains indecisive. Was Tibors a married woman writing to a clandestine lover? Clara d'Anduza writes that her body may belong to another man, presumably her husband, but her loyalty is entirely to her '*belhs amicx*', her fair friend.[35]

In the case of the poet Castelloza a rather different picture emerges. Castelloza has left three or possibly four songs, which all explore unhappy love. Her poem 'Amics, s'ie.us trobes avinen' ('Friend, if I had found you kind') paces restlessly around her feelings of loss and rejection, her desire to protect her lover even as she damages his good name by her revelations, and her confession of fidelity and ardent love.[36] The poem reads like a letter or an entry in a diary, catching the movement of her thoughts with the spontaneity of eager speech. If her lover had been kind, how she would have loved him! Instead, he's a beast, but she praises him anyway; she wants him to be publicly admired. She has considered being nasty in her turn. Perhaps this would make him like her more, but she doesn't want to give him any excuse for saying she's been deceitful. Maybe it is improper for a lady to make begging speeches to her lover, but it relieves her unhappiness. Anyone who blames her for loving this man is a fool; she remembers his kindness on one occasion and lives for the moment when such joy may come again. No other love has any value for her; she revels in her lover even as she suffers. She's under no illusions about his character and yet, still, he fascinates her. She's bypassing the go-between (the customary bearer of love's messages) to tell him this to his face. If he doesn't relent, she will die and the sin will weigh against him. Castelloza's pain and agitation cast new light on troubadour courtship. If the lady responds to pleas to be gracious and kind, she exposes herself to terrible suffering when her suitor turns cold. It is fascinating to see how often the possibility of estrangement and loss lurks in the interstices of women's writing on love, from Lady Gossamer's memoir and Heloise's yearning letters to Rosamond Lehmann's *The Weather in the Streets* (1936), a novel haunted by its heroine's terror of losing her married lover.

Did women support one another through the heartache and perplexities of *fin'amor*? The trobairitz poems record a variety of relationships between women. In one poem Lady Iseut begs Lady Almuc to be kinder to an erring sweetheart, but 'He hasn't repented!' is the tart response.[37] In another Bietris de Roman pens a love song to her friend, Lady Maria.[38] Was Bietris a lesbian and were such friendships common among aristocratic women? Was it the custom for women to address one another in exaggeratedly affectionate terms, as sometimes happened in Victorian England? Or was Bietris simply adopting a male persona to demonstrate her skill as a lyric poet? It is impossible to be sure. Another poem follows a conversation between three women.[39] Two sisters, young, beautiful and well-born, ask a third woman, Lady Carenza, for advice on love and marriage. The girls are ambivalent about marrying: although it might be amusing to have a husband, childbirth leads to sagging breasts and a wrinkled belly. Carenza, perhaps an older woman acting as duenna to the girls, returns an unexpectedly serious answer to their jokes. Her advice to these giddy girls is to betroth themselves to Christ and bear the fruit of lifelong virginity. The author of this pithy poem is unknown, but her song, today barely read except by academics, offers a privileged opening into the private conversation of courtly women in the Middle Ages. In their preoccupation with their looks, relationships and the dilemma between marriage and independence, these could be three young women gossiping in a wine bar in London, New York or Sydney.

The abyss between the lives of women then and now is clearly marked by Carenza's sombre, but also joyful, recommendation of becoming a nun.

The trobairitz corpus is so limited that it is difficult to reach firm conclusions about the identity and status of the women poets and how far they wrote within a female poetic convention, drawing, like the male troubadours, on a repertoire of stock themes. The four surviving poems of the Countess of Dia offer a rare opportunity to assess the versatility of an accomplished trobairitz. Once again, we do not know how far the Countess was speaking personally or through a series of poetic masks, but her poems suggest the range of possibilities when a *domna* speaks. She is not afraid to assert her value, nor to talk openly about desire. Her complaint in 'A chantar m'er de so q'ieu no volria' ('I must sing on a theme I would rather avoid') springs from her own worthiness to be loved.[40] She points out that she is in every way an exemplary mistress, fulfilling all the requirements the troubadours praise in women. She is beautiful, intelligent and high-ranking; she demonstrates the courtly virtues of graciousness and mercy. Above all, she is faithful and passionate in love. Despite all these claims to his esteem, her noble lover has turned against her, offers haughty looks and cruelty where once he was kind, and now prefers another lady. With her accusation of bad faith, the Countess challenges the troubadour account of love and gives the lie to male protestations. Beauty, worth, courtliness and truth do not win a man's heart, at least not for ever. '[R]emember how it was at the beginning of our love,' she begs him.[41] Those happy days are gone; all she can do now is to send her song and remind him that pride has been the downfall of many men.

The identity of the Countess of Dia remains a mystery. Her *vida*, written many years after her death, is tantalisingly brief and probably reflects its audience's relish for romantic anecdote rather than providing any facts about the Countess's life. While the details are suspect, they offer an intriguing confirmation of troubadour mores.

The *vida* claims that the Countess was married to one man, Guillem de Poitiers, but in love with another, Raimbaut d'Orange, possibly the famous troubadour, to whom she addressed her *chansons*, or love songs.[42] At the same time the Countess is described as 'beautiful and good', conventional female attributes at that period, but arresting when used of a woman who apparently indulged in adulterous longings.

When the *domna* writes about her sexual feelings, the social rules are dramatically flouted. The Countess of Dia's 'Estat ai en greu cossirier' ('I have been in grave distress') reveals just how open a trobairitz was prepared to be.[43] Her poem is a frank debate about sexual intimacy. It seems that her knight has abandoned her because she refused to sleep with him. Now she regrets her mistake and longs to have him back. In a daringly sensual image, she confesses that she yearns to hold him in her naked arms and pillow his head against her breast. She even thinks about taking him as her husband, which would give him authority over her and the right to share her bed. She adds an anxious proviso: only if he promises to do everything she asks.

This apparently playful song raises a serious issue: 'My handsome friend, . . . when will I hold you in my power?'[44] It is a struggle the Countess seems long ago to have lost. Although she compares their situation to that of Floris and Blancheflour, legendary lovers who were famous for their fidelity and courtesy, she and her lover do not have a magic ring, as Floris did, to protect their love. Even if she gave him a husband's rights, there is no guarantee that her knight would remain faithful. The Countess's challenge is for her lover to prove his reliability. Like her poem, 'A chantar m'er de so q'ieu no volria', it is an adroit rewriting of the customary rhetoric of *fin'amor*.

The Countess's conflicts as a female artist echo through women's words from Heloise to Lily Briscoe in *To the Lighthouse* and are an important theme in women's creativity today. On the one hand she has to cope with the limitations and constraints of male fantasy. The *domna* in troubadour poems is a muse rather than a flesh-and-blood woman. When she becomes human and makes demands on her lover, he fails to live up to his pretensions to *fin'amor*. The Countess is also an artist in her own right. Like Ellen Ash, the wife of the great Victorian poet in A. S. Byatt's novel *Possession*, she wants to be a maker as well as a muse. Pondering the tensions in her marriage, Ellen reflects sadly, 'My recent reading has caused me . . . to remember myself as I was when a young girl, reading high Romances and seeing myself simultaneously as the object of all knights' devotion – an unspotted Guenevere – and as the author of the Tale. I wanted to be a Poet and a Poem . . . No one wishes a man to be a Poem.'[45]

Although it is impossible to know how many medieval women aspired to be 'a Poet and a Poem', the tiny number of trobairitz poems that survive suggest how difficult it was for women to penetrate the male stronghold of the love lyric. When they do so, their wish to be taken seriously as women, as lovers and as poets resonates through their words. Centuries later, Virginia Woolf was to write about women's indignation, the plea by Jane Eyre for the right to be ambitious and the freedom to learn and explore which men took for granted. Woolf saw this anger, the note of querulousness and rebellion in Charlotte Brontë's writing, as a weakness.[46] It undermined the woman writer's achievement and conflicted with the psychological androgyny that Woolf felt was the mark of the great writer. And yet, how could the Countess of Dia or any of the women struggling to find a voice in medieval Europe hope to achieve such purity of tone? Their position as women was dinned into them from early childhood by religious custom and preaching, and by the example of their mothers, sisters and female servants. As women, they knew what was expected of them. They might dream, like Heloise or the young Eleanor of Aquitaine, of expanding the horizons of their female destiny, but they could never forget their sex, its constraints, or their true position in relation to men. When the Countess of Dia questioned her lover's good faith, she had centuries of custom and experience behind her. What is remarkable is that she dared to speak out so frankly, or at all.

Complaint was not the Countess's only mode, and the versatility of her themes as well as her technical skill may have ensured the popularity and hence survival of at least some of the poems of this protean composer. Her work would certainly have appealed to her female listeners, responsive to songs that reflected their own fears and secret longings, and perhaps their experience of the realities of the *domna*'s role. Two of her surviving songs deal with the pleasures of love. In 'Fin ioi me dona alegranssa' ('Perfect joy brings me happiness') she gaily challenges the malicious gossips to do their worst.[47] Their spiteful words cannot impose on her delight. 'Ab ioi et ab ioven m'apais' ('With joy and youth I prosper') celebrates her knightly lover, and claims that a woman should be bold in revealing her feelings.[48] The Countess's lightness of touch, her delight in loving and zest for joy, mirror the ecstasy of reciprocated love.

It is in the bed chamber, the site of passion's consummation, that love becomes difficult for the Countess, or at least for her poetic persona. The lady's anxiety about sleeping with her lover in 'Estat ai en greu cossirier' is in marked contrast to the insouciance of Arnaut Daniel, the troubadour whom Dante praised as *'miglior fabbro'*.[49] In 'Doutz brais e critz' ('I hear sweet calls and cries') he writes happily about secretly kissing his lady.[50] She shields him with her blue robe from the 'adder tongues' of the *lauzengiers*, and he looks forward to coaxing her, 'amid kisses and laughter', to uncover her body so that he can gaze at its loveliness in the lamplight. Arnaut's clever poem begins with the chirruping of birds calling their mates to love; his words will similarly persuade his lady, just as his poem will captivate his hearers. It is a masterly performance by a supreme practitioner, who is relishing showing off his skills. Caught in the web of Arnaut's verbal flourishes, the lady has no chance of resisting his advances. That saving laughter hints at intimacy, but Arnaut's emotional commitment is to his genius. The lady vanishes into a whirlpool of virtuosity. What is also absent is any hint of the Countess's worry about sharing her body with her lover. Arnaut's only fear is that love will distract him from his duties as a knight.

The word 'trobairitz' appears in only one medieval text, the thirteenth-century Occitan romance *Flamenca*, a poem running to well over 8,000 lines which, with more than a hint of satire, demonstrates *fin'amor* in action, with all its possibilities for misunderstanding, misery and overwhelming joy. Little is known about the author, who appears to have been well versed in both knightly and clerical culture, but the story he tells brings together ideas about love popularised by the troubadour songs and takes them to a logical conclusion. A jealous lord locks his beautiful wife Flamenca in a tower, only allowing her to venture out, heavily veiled and under his close guardianship, when she attends church on major feast days in the Catholic calendar. A young nobleman hears of her plight and falls in love with her, solely on the report of her virtue and good looks. True to his role as a knightly lover, William suffers longing and despair on account of his unseen lady, before he finally contrives to approach her in church. Disguised as a cleric, he is able to whisper a few words under pretext of offering her the Holy Book to kiss. Over a period of weeks (and pages of text), the couple use church ritual as an opportunity to conduct a courtship, skilfully manipulated by Flamenca and her two resourceful maids. When William manages on one occasion to gasp 'Alas!' as he hands her the book, Flamenca responds the next time they meet with, 'Why grieve?' 'I'm dying' is William's reply, some days later. 'Of what?' 'Of love.' 'For whom?' 'For you.' 'What can I do?' 'Cure me!' 'How?' and so on. Rearranging the words of a well-known troubadour song to conduct this attenuated courtship, the women gradually encourage the bashful William to plan a rendezvous. Delighted with the success of their stratagem, Flamenca congratulates her maid, Margarida, on being an excellent 'trobairitz'. The word *trobar* means 'to make or compose', but, like the real-life trobairitz who were writing in Occitania at this period, Flamenca and her girls compose with a difference, restructuring the conventional troubadour lyric to assert their own emotional needs. Through their linguistic dexterity, William's narcissistic adoration is transformed into a passionate sexual affair and the maids also find attractive lovers.

Despite its many details of court life and behaviour, *Flamenca* should not be read as an accurate portrayal of adulterous love in the Occitan court. It is a romance, designed perhaps to feed the escapist fantasies of women married to ageing and brutal husbands, as well as the love-longing of sex-starved cadet-knights. Flamenca, with her golden hair and willingness to grant love as a mark of her good breeding, and the handsome, virile, almost superhuman William (he is more than seven foot tall) are idealised rather than human lovers, although Flamenca's husband is a compelling portrait of jealousy and madness. Unkempt and smelly through depression and self-neglect, Archambaud alienates his wife by his unjust suspicions and drives her into the arms of the chivalrous William. The close relationship between the two maids and their mistress, and the women's clever tricks for evading Archambaud's vigilance, are an appealing portrait of female feistiness, but may equally have exploited male anxieties about women's guile and readiness to deceive. The wily Eve chatting to the serpent or tempting Adam to try the forbidden fruit would have been all too familiar images for *Flamenca*'s courtly audience. *Flamenca* also takes the idea of love as a religion to its extreme, with the courtship conducted in church, cloaked by sacred ritual. At one stage the women even re-enact the whispered exchange between William and Flamenca, substituting a copy of a popular romance for the Holy Book.[51] The poem's exaggerated discourse of love admits a note of irony and even condemnation, as the pursuit of love's rules leads William and Flamenca into blasphemy. Had he paid the same attention to God as he gave to love, the poet remarks tartly at one point, William 'might have ruled all heaven'.[52]

Love was a consumer activity for the wealthy leisured nobility of medieval Europe, just as it is for modern Western society, with its Valentine's Day cards and presents, and insatiable appetite for romantic novels and films. As the art historian Michael Camille points out, looking, talking, touching and kissing were signposts in the lover's journey, in which eyes and heart played significant roles. Craftsmen incorporated such insignia into the design of domestic articles, clothing and the tiny personal items that could be exchanged between men and women.[53] In his *De Arte Honeste Amandi* Andreas Capellanus lists the gifts a lady might freely receive from her lover, as long, he adds, as her motives are pure. These included a handkerchief, a hair band, a gold circlet, a brooch, a mirror, a belt, a purse, a comb, gloves, a ring, or indeed any small gift that might be useful in making her toilette, or would remind her of her lover.[54] Such gifts provided an opportunity to press the lover's suit through images of successful love and purveyed an atmosphere of erotic possibility. A mirror case made in northern Italy shows a lover giving his lady a long-tined comb; a similar two-sided ivory comb, now housed in the Victoria and Albert Museum in London, depicts a lady crowning her lover with a garland of leaves, a symbolically circular token of success or conquest. A man's belt buckle pictures a woman's acceptance of her dashing knight; an enamelled pendant case, perhaps intended to be hung from a belt, reveals a more ambiguous scene. A lady leans over a castle parapet to address a mounted and visored knight. Is she handing him the lance, which both grasp in their right hands, or is the knight's impressive weapon a blatant symbol of his virility, as he lays siege to the lady in her tower of chastity?[55]

Medieval love is fraught with such ambiguities, which the troubadour poems and the romances of the twelfth and thirteenth centuries do little to dispel. Sexual behaviour among the European aristocracy at that period continues to be debated among scholars. Anthropologists, evolutionary psychologists and social historians are still at odds over the origins of romantic passion, although it is gradually becoming acknowledged as a human universal rather than the specific creation of Western culture.[56] Equally contested is the question of why medieval male poets perversely chose to celebrate women as the unattainable other, although anyone who has spent time with teenage boys will be aware of the emotional and physical turmoil that might make such a pose seem highly desirable. The sons of the nobility were often sent away at an early age, perhaps as young as seven, to live in the households of family members or friends, where they were trained up to knightly accomplishments. Separated from their mothers and female siblings, plunged early into the arts of war and obedience to male mentors, boys faced their testosterone-rich teens with little insight into women and their needs. Biologically programmed for sex, but forbidden to touch girls of their own rank and confused by church teaching about the dangers and damnation inherent in female sexuality, it is hardly surprising that young men identified women as both desirable and threatening. John Keats's 'Belle Dame', who tempts and then abandons a knight to a ghostly life-in-death, owes a subterranean ancestry to medieval debates about the fatal allure of women, a theme that continues to fascinate storytellers.[57] (Brigid O'Shaughnessy in *The Maltese Falcon* and Julia Roberts's murderous mole in the film version of *Confessions of a Dangerous Mind* are just two of the Belle Dame's more recent manifestations.) For many noblemen marriage was not an option. The demand for heiresses outnumbered the supply, and there were quantities of portionless younger sons and other indigent knights roaming the European courts in search of patronage and income. In such conditions it is hardly surprising that love-longing, its pleasures and discontents, flourished among the Occitan nobility.

Unfulfilled desire, however imaginary or puffed up by the fashion for *fin'amor*, could bring real illness. Lovesickness was an identifiable disease in medieval Europe, believed to affect young noblemen rather than women, and with a long history of research and learned commentary in Greek and Latin medicine and in medieval Islam.[58] In *Flamenca* the young lover William demonstrates classic symptoms of love's malady: he grows pale and hollow-eyed, he loses weight and suffers from a fever. His mental pain is acute and relentless; he can concentrate on nothing except his longing for a woman whom he has barely seen. As the scholar Mary Frances Wack explains, lovesickness is intimately connected with the sufferer's aspirations and self-worth:

> In describing the dysfunction of the mental faculties caused by love, the physicians note the lovers' tendency to idealize the beloved. . . . the patient considers her better, more noble, and more desirable than other women, even though this may not really be so. The misjudgment of her desirability fixes the lover in meditation on her mental image. In medieval lyric the image of the woman, thus internalized, stood as an ideal for the self. The physician William of Brescia . . . said that the patient fears to lose his love object because he believes he will be perfected by her or it. Her overestimated nobility mirrors at a psychological level the lover's own social elevation . . .[59]

If this psychological profile is correct, what happens when the man enters into relationship with the idealised woman, or even goes so far as to have sex with her? Troubadour poets promise fealty to the beloved, but trobairitz poems question their sincerity and point out some of the conflicts for women in realising desire. The women record the anxieties as well as the joy of love, their wish to develop intimacy and perfect trust, the constraints on speaking freely and the bitterness of abandonment. 'I have pledged my heart and myself to a thankless service,' Castelloza tells her lover. Typically, she doesn't recant; good faith, good will and constancy keep her love alive.[60] Her declaration of fidelity against all odds is reminiscent of Anne Elliot's modest plea to Captain Harville in *Persuasion*: 'All the privilege I claim for my own sex (it is not a very enviable one, you need not covet it) is that of loving longest, when existence or when hope is gone.'

Trusting the Heart:
The Lays of Marie de France

A knight suffers a wound, which can only be healed by a woman's love; a young girl prepares the marriage bed for her rival; an unhappy wife undertakes a perilous journey to search for her dying lover. The writer Marie de France offers a wider perspective on love and its possibilities than her sister poets in Occitania. Her *Lais* invite the reader into the realm of magical romance, inhabited by fairy girls and jealous husbands, where a hawk metamorphoses into a handsome lord and a weasel cures a deathly hurt with a crimson flower. While she enchants the imagination, Marie is equally attentive to emotional authenticity. However fairy-tale her settings, and even in the twelfth century many of them would have seemed far from ordinary, Marie's interest is in telling the truth about love. Uniquely in her period, she cut across conventional ideas about sexual behaviour to explore what happens when lovers listen to their hearts.

It is one of fate's ironies that almost all that is definitely known about this great medieval storyteller is her insistence on being identified as the author of her works. At the end of her *Fables*, the earliest extant collection from Western Europe of such tales in the vernacular, she gives her name as 'Marie' and says, 'I am from France.' '[M]any a clerk' (the typically male writers and copiers of texts) may claim her work as his own, but she would be a fool to allow herself to be forgotten.[61] In the two other works identifiably hers she again takes care to record her authorship. 'I, Marie, have recorded the book of Purgatory in order to be remembered,' she writes in her translation of the supernatural tale *St Patrick's Purgatory*.[62] She begins *Guigemar*, the first of her *Lais*, with a confident assertion of her identity and skill: 'Hear, my lords, the words of Marie, who, when she has the opportunity, does not squander her talents.'[63] Her longing for recognition influences Marie's choice of subject matter. In her Prologue to the *Lais* she mentions that she had originally thought of translating stories from Latin, but it had been done too often and wouldn't bring her fame. Marie's honesty is both endearing and illuminating; one wonders how many women writers found their work appropriated by ambitious clerics or swamped by the competition. In any case her tactics appear to have been successful. She remained clearly identified with the *Lais* and *Fables*. An illuminated manuscript of the *Fables* shows two charming likenesses of the author (based on the illustrator's imagination: the real Marie had long been dead). The text begins with a column-width miniature of Marie in a blue dress, with inkhorn in one hand and pen in the other. She is seated at a slanted desk, busily writing in a codex. At the end of the *Fables* she appears again as an illustration in the letter A, still seated, but now holding up her book to display the text she has just completed.[64]

Despite her longing to be remembered, Marie's identity remains elusive. When she wrote that she came from France, she may have meant that she was born on the Île-de-France, or somewhere on the French continent as opposed to in England. She seems at some point to have joined the Anglo-Norman court, writing the *Lais* for a 'noble king', probably Henry ii, Eleanor's husband. Some scholars hypothesise that she was the illegitimate daughter of Geoffrey of Anjou and hence Henry's half-sister, who became abbess of Shaftesbury in around 1181, but there are equally indeterminate claims linking Marie to other known women. Her work confirms that she was educated, fluent in French with a knowledge of Latin and

English, and familiar with the ideas about love and chivalry current among the nobility. She also mentions that she sat up late at night to finish her lays, which suggests that she might have been busy during the day with more conventional 'woman's work'. (Her determination to carve out time for writing recalls the frustration of those clever Victorian girls, Florence Nightingale and Virginia Woolf, at wasting valuable hours on tea parties.)[65] Given the subject matter of the lays, it is unlikely that Marie was already in religious orders, but she may have had duties at Eleanor's court, or even been married, with a family and household of her own. The most interesting 'facts' about Marie are the clues that can be gleaned from the *Lais*. These reveal her interest in human behaviour, her sensitivity to the nuances of words and actions, her wit and iconoclasm, and her relish for the trappings of romance: beauty and grace, fine clothes and rich draperies, love's mystery and the joy and anguish of love-longing. In particular, like the trobairitz in the south, she wrote with great sympathy and understanding about women's experience of love. A contemporary, Denis Piramus, mentioned how popular Marie's stories were with the nobility, particularly the ladies, who 'listen to them joyfully and willingly, for they are just what they desire'.[66] It is no surprise that she appealed to the female members of the court, hungry for heroines with whom they could identify.

Quite when Marie was busily staking her claim to immortality is not known. The *Lais* are believed to have been composed before the *Fables* and *St Patrick's Purgatory*, but even on Piramus's evidence can only loosely be dated to the latter half of the twelfth century. They were written in French in octosyllabic couplets and are typically quite condensed. Marie's treatment of the Tristram and Yseult story, *Chevrefoil*, captures a fleeting moment between the lovers and is only 118 lines long. Even *Eliduc*, the longest of her lays, is considerably shorter than most of the romances that were beginning to flood through Europe. Marie's economy in making her point is unusual in her period and it is one of her great strengths as a storyteller. Not only was her choice of form original: her account of her sources is also intriguing, since she claims that these are Breton lays, short tales of Celtic origin, and based on true stories she is now retelling. The writer John Fowles was captivated as a student by Marie's lays and points out that the term 'Breton' could include the Welsh and Cornish as well as Bretons proper.[67] Marie might have drawn on a broad spectrum of Celtic tales, which included legends about King Arthur and his knights, and the tragedy of Yseult and Tristram, a cycle of stories that travelling minstrels made popular throughout the European courts.

Each of the twelve lays explores an aspect of love between a nobleman and a woman, sometimes posing moral questions about the validity or conduct of their love, as in *Equitan*, a story of betrayal and attempted murder, at others focusing simply on the emotion between the lovers, as in the secret tryst in *Chevrefoil*. Several have fairy settings, or retain mysterious magical elements, which suggest the ancient lineage of Marie's stories, whose roots seem to lie in a distant, barely recoverable past of myth and oral storytelling. One of the most beautiful and evocative is *Guigemar*, the tale of a young knight who is perfect in almost every way, except in his indifference to love. One day Guigemar goes hunting and fatally wounds a curious beast, a white hind with a stag's antlers, who is feeding in the forest with her fawn. Guigemar himself is wounded, since his arrow rebounds and strikes him in the thigh. The hind has the gift of human speech and, to his dismay, she dies with a bitter curse, telling him that no doctor, potion or ointment known to humankind can cure his wound. The only remedy is to find a woman willing to love Guigemar almost beyond endurance, whose love he must reciprocate. Anxious and in pain, Guigemar rides off alone into the woods and eventually reaches a cliff. Looking down at the sea below, he sees a ship, its sails set in readiness although it lacks any sign of a crew. The vessel is richly appointed and, when he staggers on board, he finds a magnificent bed, carved from cypress and ivory, inlaid with gold and covered with rich silks and furs. It proves too tempting for the wounded knight and he lies down for a moment, only to find himself swiftly carried on the high seas to a hidden inlet below an ancient city.

Needless to say, Guigemar does find love, in the person of a beautiful young wife, locked away in seclusion by her ageing, jealous husband. For a time they love in secret until betrayed by a spying servant. Guigemar is allowed to depart on the magic ship, but not before the lovers have safeguarded their love by secret tokens. She ties his shirt into a knot only she can disentangle; he circles her thighs with a belt only he can unfasten. These gages protect them both during the adventures that follow, and finally lead to their reunion and a happy outcome to their romance.

At its simplest level Marie's story declares that true love will find a way to overcome obstacles, a theme emphasised by the paintings that decorate the lady's prison. On the walls are scenes in which Venus teaches the obligations of love, its demand for fidelity and loyal service. In one she even burns the book in which the poet Ovid gave advice on making the most of love affairs. (This was presumably the *Remedia amoris* (*Remedies for Love*), a cynical approach much enjoyed by medieval readers.) By surrounding her with these images the tyrannical husband wants to school his wife in proper feeling, but she can only follow her heart. *Guigemar* tells the tale of a young man's education in love, and there are many possible interpretations of its incidents and symbols. The white hart with its masculine horns and feeding fawn may represent ambivalence in Guigemar about his sexuality, or his fear of the family unit of father, mother and child. It may also symbolise a lover whom the boy has callously rejected and who has taken her revenge by condemning him to death, or to suffering love's anguish. The knotted shirt and locked belt represent the fidelity and commitment of true love. Guigemar is protected from the women who besiege him when he is a knight at arms again, apparently

unattached and free to wander the world. Similarly, the wife is kept
safe from the powerful lord who shelters her when she escapes from
her husband and who falls in love with his attractive guest.

One of the great pleasures of Marie's stories is that they invite
reflection and debate, since they are rarely unambiguous and never
conventional. Her lays support the holiness of the heart's affections,
the true love and fidelity that bind a man and woman irrespective
of social pressures and marriage dues. Another story, which has
affinities with *Guigemar* both because of the situation of the wife
and also its mysterious fairy-tale elements, is *Yonec*. In this story,
too, contemporary rules about female chastity and the sanctity
of marriage are simply not in question; nor, indeed, are the
arm's-length pinings of *fin'amor*. In *Yonec* an unhappy wife literally
wills a lover into being, summoning him to her chamber by the
strength of her need. Once again, a beautiful young woman has
been married off to a wealthy old man, who locks her in a tower
and sets his widowed sister to watch over her. Lonely, childless and
unhappy, the wife fantasises about being rescued by a handsome
knight and is visited by a hawk, which is magically transformed
into the lover of her dreams. The knight declares his love and takes
the sacrament to prove his good faith, visiting the lady again and
again in his guise as a bird. Eventually the wife's new radiance
alerts her husband and he discovers her secret. He privately arranges
for sharp spikes to be attached to the bars of her prison and the
hawk is wounded as he flies into the room. There follows a curious
sequence, like a dream, in which the wife leaps down from her
twenty-foot tower to follow the trail of blood left by the fleeing
knight. The path leads to a dark passage through a hill, then out
into a meadow on the edge of a walled city built, it seems, entirely
of silver. The lady finds a way into the city and follows the blood-
stains to the castle. There, she walks through a series of rooms in
each of which a knight lies sleeping. In the third room she finds
her beloved, close to death and lying on a bed of great splendour.

He gives her a magic ring to protect her from her husband and entrusts her with his sword, which she is to keep for their son Yonec, the child she is now carrying in her womb. This child will grow up to avenge his father's death.

In this strange and lovely story Marie blends human passion and yearning with other-worldly elements of fairy tale and the solemn ritual of Christian sacrament and myth. As in *Guigemar*, the norms of moral behaviour are overturned in the interests of emotional truth. The lady accuses her hard-hearted husband of having been baptised in the river of hell; by contrast, the holiness of the knight's love is proved when he is able to receive the sacrament without harm. Although this is essentially a story about human love, the knight's fate suggests the idea of Christian suffering and sacrifice. The spike piercing the hawk's body recalls the spear that was thrust into Christ's side at the crucifixion and may glance, too, at Arthurian legends of the Holy Grail. The lady's discovery of her dying lover resonates hauntingly with the English 'Corpus Christi' carol in which a wounded knight, identified as Christ, bleeds night and day on a golden bed while a maiden weeps at his side.[68] 'Lully, lulley,' runs the refrain of this exquisite lament, 'The fawcon [falcon] hath born my mak [mate] away.' The falcon and the hawk, the weeping girl and the bleeding man on his gorgeous bed may stem from some common stock of ideas that was diffused through oral traditions to re-emerge in Marie's Breton lays and English folk song. The effect of this cluster of images is both eerie and profoundly moving. The religious echoes enhance the human suffering of the lovers; the woman's journey and the sombre scene that concludes her quest for her beloved resonate on both the human and spiritual planes.

The supernatural similarly plays an important role in the lay *Lanval*, but here the situation of *Yonec* is partly reversed, since it is a fairy lady who visits her knight in secret and the story ends with the young hero Lanval abandoning the tarnished splendour of Arthur's court to follow his beloved to the magic realm of Avalon.

Forgotten by the king in the dispersal of favours, then falsely accused of sexual overtures by the queen, Lanval lingers only long enough to clear his name with the help of his fairy mistress. Once again true love has triumphed, in this case over Lanval's aspirations for fame and honour as a knight. Marie has tremendous fun with the settings and costumes in this story, which emphasise the eroticism of the love scenes and play to her audience's relish for consumerism. Her lavish descriptions of Lanval's meeting with the fairy girl and her maidens, and their later pageant-like arrival at Arthur's court, splendidly dressed and impressively mounted, dramatically contrast the fabulous wealth, beauty and courtesy of the fairies with the malevolence and moral ugliness of the human court and, in particular, its vengeful queen.

Even true love has its ridiculous aspects, however, as Marie shows in *Les Deus Amanz* (*The Two Lovers*), the tale of a young man who has to win his bride by carrying her up a steep mountain. The girl, one of Marie's typically resourceful heroines, does all she can to help her lover by going on a crash diet and arranging for her aunt, a wise woman skilled in potions, to prepare a strengthening tonic for the youth. She even arrives for the test clad only in her shift. Despite her precautions it all ends badly. The lover rushes up the mountain without pausing to take his medicine and dies of exhaustion when he reaches its summit. The girl's heart breaks with grief, while her aunt's potion, which the girl tosses aside in despair, fertilises the soil for miles around. The tongue-in-cheek moral seems to be that happiness in love requires a little common sense and moderation, but Marie is also making the point that *desmezura*, a lack of balance in love, can be fatal, a theme she illustrates in several of her lays.

The final lay in Marie's collection is a story that characteristically resists simple explanations and apportioning of blame. On the surface, *Eliduc* appears to be about a knight and the conflicts he experiences between his obligations to two overlords and his loyalties to two women, his wife and the girl he falls in love with when far away from home. Marie herself says that the lay is really about the two women. She doesn't explain her comment and the reader is left to ponder its implications as the story unfolds. Eliduc is a knight who worthily serves the king of Brittany, but is forced into exile when rivals blacken his name. He leaves his wife at home, assuring her of his fidelity, and travels to Logres, Arthur's kingdom in the West Country of England. Here he enters the service of a local lord, swearing an oath of fealty for a fixed period. Soon afterwards he falls in love with the lord's daughter Guilliadun. There is a brief struggle of conscience when he remembers his wife and his promise, but Guilliadun is young, beautiful and madly in love with Eliduc. He enjoys the company of this lovely girl, pursuing a romantic courtship, but never mentions the wife waiting for him at home.

Their idyll is interrupted when the king of Brittany sends for Eliduc, reminding him of his feudal duty. Eliduc reluctantly returns home, promising the lord that he will come back if needed and secretly arranging a tryst with his daughter. Once home in Brittany, Eliduc quickly sorts out the king's problems, but he grieves his wife by his sullen behaviour. A good, wise and attractive woman, Guildeluec tries to discover what has caused the rift, but Eliduc sets off again to Logres. His service to the lord has been completed and he arranges for Guilliadun to elope with him. They set sail for Brittany, but a terrible storm threatens shipwreck. One of the sailors blames Eliduc for bringing back the girl when he has a faithful wife at home. Shocked by the sailor's words, Guilliadun falls into a profound faint. Believing that she is dead, Eliduc throws the sailor overboard and brings the boat safely to shore. Guilliadun does not recover and he secretly places her body in a chapel near his home, sneaking out to pray by her bier whenever he can find the opportunity.

Guildeluec now shows her mettle. She had joyfully greeted her husband on his safe return from Logres and was met again with a churlish response. By stealth, she discovers his visits to the chapel and resolves to explore the building herself. When she sees Guilliadun lying on the bier, her reaction is unexpected. She examines her closely, admiring her still rosy freshness, and immediately understands that this young woman must be her husband's lover. Hatred and envy seem far from her thoughts; instead, she generously mourns the tragedy, torn between pity for the beautiful girl and love for her husband. As she sits weeping by the bier, a weasel runs over Guilliadun's body and Guildeluec's valet kills the creature with a stick. Soon afterwards the weasel's mate arrives and tries to revive the corpse. When he fails, he runs into the woods and returns with a red flower, which he places in the dead animal's mouth. She revives and starts to run off, but quick-witted Guildeluec tells the valet to strike the weasel again, the flower falls to the ground and she places it in the girl's mouth.

Guilliadun awakens from her coma, only to blame Eliduc for deceiving and now abandoning her, as she believes. Guildeluec reassures her and tells her that she plans to reunite the lovers. So that her husband may be free of his obligations, she herself will take the veil. All turns out as she planned and, with Eliduc's support, Guildeluec establishes a religious foundation for women. After many years of happy marriage to Guilliadun, Eliduc too becomes a monk and his second wife joins Guildeluec in her convent. All three devote the rest of their lives to serving God.

Marie's claim that this lay is really about Guilliadun and Guildeluec reveals her deep interest in women and sympathy for their emotional struggles. Through the character of Guilliadun she traces the excitement and fear of falling in love, as the girl courageously makes her interest known to Eliduc by gifts of a ring and belt. Innocent and loving, she follows him unquestioningly to Brittany and nearly dies of shock when she discovers that he has deceived her. Guildeluec is similarly wholehearted in her love, but she is a mature woman who has had many years of marriage. She is quick to recognise her husband's loss of commitment and at first tries to find out any causes for misunderstanding between them. When she discovers Guilliadun in the chapel, her response is generous and practical. Her prompt action revives the girl from her swoon and she does this with a red flower, a symbol of love and its power to quicken and energise, and also of the heart's blood, the pain that she herself must suffer in parting from her husband. Although she recognises what she must give up, she is quick to reassure Guilliadun about the future. Realising that Eliduc is hopelessly in love, she gracefully withdraws from the triangle and makes a life of her own as abbess to a community of nuns. Guildeluec's generosity to her rival is not unique in Marie's account of women's mutual kindness. In *Le Fresne*, a young girl prepares the marriage bed for her lover and the new wife who will supplant her, an act of selflessness that paves the way for her own restoration to love and fortune.

As for Eliduc, he could be criticised as a false husband to his wife and lover to his mistress; and as a knight who tried to serve two masters and disloyally stole the daughter of the lord who had shown him favour. Alternatively, he might be seen as a man who did his best to accommodate changing circumstances, seeking his fortune in a foreign country and accepting the advances of a lovely woman when the prospects for a safe return to his wife seemed uncertain. Should Eliduc be blamed for seizing life's adventures? Marie doesn't say so. Instead, she demonstrates the difference of opportunity between men and women. The wife has to remain at home waiting for her husband; the girl is dependent on Eliduc to keep his promise to return, then to look after her when she accompanies him to Brittany. Both women reveal their characters by their willingness to commit themselves to faithful love. Eliduc's dilemma is that the choices for him are not quite so clear-cut and, if he acts dishonestly towards the two women, Marie does not judge him, but simply shows the consequences, for Eliduc, for Guilliadun and Guildeluec, and for the unfortunate sailor who dared to speak frankly about Eliduc's elopement with his lover.

Marie's *Lais* drew on Celtic myth and storytelling, but her emphasis on the emotional adventures of her heroines introduced a new element in European storytelling. Ideas about love had, in any case, moved on from the early days of the troubadours in the south. In several of his Arthurian romances, Marie's contemporary, Chrétien de Troyes, explored the tensions for the knight between the demands of chivalry and the claims of love, a view of sexual relationships that upheld conjugal love rather than the adultery implicit in troubadour *fin'amor*, or the tragic *desmezura* of Tristram and Yseult, which challenged civilised values and proved fatal to the lovers. In Chrétien's *Erec and Enide* the hero is mocked for his infatuation with his new bride, which keeps him cloistered in her bedroom when he should be out in the world, pursuing deeds of valour. His romance *Yvain* similarly tests a knight's ability to remain faithful both to his wife and to his worldly reputation. While Chrétien's poems debate important social issues, Marie's approach avoids discussion of right and wrong, and simply demonstrates the primacy of true love over social and moral considerations. Eliduc's fall from favour forces him to leave his wife while he goes in search of adventures, but the tension between chivalry and uxoriousness is not Marie's point. Eliduc's prowess as a knight is never in question; what is at stake is his behaviour towards the two women and, more important, how they respond to the demands he makes on their affection and loyalty. Women were said to have loved Marie's stories, and she created heroines who spoke to women's most intimate feelings and experience. Like the trobairitz, her desirous girls and unhappy wives reveal the suffering of love, but Marie's heroines are not constrained by the male code of love and its service. They ignore or consciously flout convention in order to follow their hearts.

In composing her lays, Marie showed her artistry by inventing a form that exactly suited her skills as a storyteller. Economic, drawing freely on legend and the supernatural, her stories speak to the imagination and are psychologically persuasive. Chaucer wrote his own version of the Breton lay in 'The Franklin's Tale', a virtuoso exposé of *fin'amor*, which draws on classical reference, magic and the full repertoire of love's games and torments, but for all her fine speeches and torn loyalties, the distress of his heroine Dorigen lacks the emotional authenticity of the lady's frenzied leap from her high window in pursuit of the wounded knight in *Yonec*, or Guildeluec's pity for her husband's mistress.

In her perceptiveness about human emotions and foibles, and her sense of irony and fun, Marie has been described by John Fowles as a precursor to Jane Austen.[69] She also has much in common with Murasaki Shikibu. Despite the differences in culture and in form, both women insisted on telling the truth about feeling, and on the centrality of love to happiness and to living a morally viable life. Neither was in any obvious sense hostile to men; they created attractive and plausible heroes, and were sympathetic to their emotional struggles and public aspirations. They took great pains, however, to show the cost to women of limited opportunities and the male values that constrained their lives, and they were not afraid to reveal women's capacity for jealousy, greed and bad faith, as well as their generosity, devotion and passion. There were connections, too, in their approach to writing. In her prologue to the lays, Marie talks about writing as a way of focusing the energies, protecting the writer from vice and warding off sorrow. Her words may hint at some tragedy in Marie's own life, and connect her with Jane Austen, Charlotte Brontë and many other women writers who found consolation in fiction. They also recall Murasaki Shikibu's tormented heroine Ukifune, in *The Tale of Genji*, crouching over her brush and inkstone when love became impossible for her. Both writers shared a need to record experience. Just as Murasaki Shikibu was driven to pin down on paper what she observed of life, so too was the idea of memory important to Marie. Sitting up late at night, eager to finish her task, again and again she stresses the truth of her lays, and her belief that by writing them down, the stories will be remembered for ever.

The Dangers of Love

One of Marie's flawed heroines is exposed in her lay *Chaitivel*, an ironic look at the dangers of *fin'amor*. It is unclear whether the heroine is married, but her beauty, education and nobility attract a swarm of lovers and, in particular, four knights who vie for her attention. Unknown to her suitors, the lady cannot choose between them and is equally encouraging to all, sending love tokens and receiving their advances in a most friendly manner. Finally, the knights fight in a tournament and, carried away by success, they behave incautiously. Three are killed and the fourth is grievously wounded in the thigh. It quickly becomes apparent that he has been castrated. The lady is horrified and does all she can to cheer the wretched hero. One day she tells him that she is going to compose a lay about her lovers, which she plans to call 'The Four Sorrows'. The knight responds that a better title would be 'The Unhappy One'. His rivals suffered terribly through love, but now are dead and beyond human feeling. He endures the torment of being able to see and speak to her, without being able to consummate his love. Of all the lovers, his lot is the worst.

This melancholy story casts the lady in the role of a flirt. Like Anne Brontë's Rosalie in *Agnes Grey*, she encourages adoring swains and keeps them dangling at her disposal. Brontë's Rosalie insists on keeping her engagement secret, so that she can enjoy her last weeks of freedom by breaking as many hearts as possible. Marie's lady is similarly secretive and her song is as much about her powers as femme fatale as her sorrow over the lost heroes. Her taste for admiration reveals the lady's heartlessness. As for the knights, their behaviour was foolish. Obsessed with fame and rivalry in love, they neglected the basic rules of self-protection and exposed themselves to danger and death.

Marie's lay wittily inverts the knight's usual complaint that his lady will kill him by indifference. Troubadour lovers and the heroes of popular romances typically besiege a lady with sighs and tears and vows of instant death if she refuses to be kind. This lady's prodigal kindness really does kill off or else unman her lovers. All that is left is her self-esteem. It is a warning to be careful how and whom one loves, and may represent Marie's contempt for the shallowness of *fin'amor*. Her verse-writing lady is the troubadour's exemplary mistress carried to her cold extreme and she cleverly turns the tables on men who moan about their misfortunes in love. This is the outcome, Marie seems to be saying, if the game of love is played out according to its ridiculous conventions.

Christine de Pizan was writing many years after Marie and in a period when troubadour ideals of love had hardened into the mannerisms of romantic chivalry. She too questioned the posturings of *fin'amor*. In her verse-novel *The Book of the Duke of True Lovers*, she makes plain the risk to any woman who is silly enough to accept a knight as her secret 'friend'. Christine's credentials as supporter and adviser to women were exemplary. Born in Venice in around 1364, she came to France as a child when her father, the renowned physician and astrologer Tommaso da Pizzano, was offered a position at the court of Charles v. Although she later complained about her lack of learning, Christine was educated by her father in the liberal Italian style for young noblewomen, combining study of reading and writing with the social skills of chess, backgammon, music and dancing, as well as proficiency in the courtly arts of riding and hawking. At the age of fifteen she married the notary Etienne de Castel, who appears to have resembled her father in his fondness for learning, and Etienne's encouragement of his wife's taste for scholarship seems to have made for a happy partnership. Her husband's untimely death turned Christine's thoughts and talents in a new direction. Finding herself with sole responsibility for supporting a family of small children, a niece and her widowed mother, she set herself up as a professional writer, possibly France's first woman to live by her pen. Writing to commission or inventing works she thought might attract wealthy sponsors, Christine embarked on a career that lasted until her death forty years later. Her output was remarkable, and revealed the fluency and flexibility of her talent, including a manual on military tactics, the official biography of King Charles v and a poem honouring the victories of Joan of Arc, whom Christine greatly admired. Most interesting, perhaps, for the modern reader are her books celebrating women's lives and possibilities, and her guides to female behaviour. Christine took immense care with the presentation and illustration of her manuscripts, and a favourite self-image reveals her hard at work in her study, dressed in a rich blue gown and peaked white headdress, writing at a table, with her little dog waiting patiently beside her chair.[70]

During her early attempts to establish a reputation, Christine wrote widely about love, producing collections of lyric poetry and a number of longer poems that playfully discussed aspects of the lover's behaviour. Although her early poems were adapted to the conventional tastes of her noble patrons, she soon began to reveal a sharper, more sceptical attitude to the platitudes of courtly romance. In *The Debate of Two Lovers* a group of men and women enjoying themselves at a ball idly discuss the idea, so central in love poems of the period, that a suitor will die if a lady denies him favours. If these stories are true, one woman acidly enquires, where are the graves of men who have died of love? Shakespeare's Rosalind in *As You Like It* was to be similarly robust on the survival prospects of the amorous male.

Christine's increasing self-confidence as a writer took her a step further than gentle irony. Greatly daring, she publicly challenged the misogynous view of women presented by the poet Jean de Meun in the *Roman de la Rose*, a well-known poem about a lover's adventures. The first part of the *Rose*, written by Guillaume de Lorris, presents an idealised account of love, as a young man dreams about an earthly Eden where he falls in love with a single rose, symbol of the pure and unattainable beloved. Jean de Meun's sinewy completion of the romance lifts the story out of the ethereal world of *fin'amor* and debates the practical implications of love, embracing such contentious questions as female lechery, chattiness and fondness for fine clothes. The poem ends with the symbolic rape of the rose, hardly the conclusion de Lorris intended. Christine summarised her objections to the poem in an exchange of letters with the Provost of Lille, one of de Meun's supporters. Other eminent men were drawn into what became known as the *querelle des femmes* and Christine formally presented a copy of the correspondence to Isabeau de Bavière, the Queen of France. Perhaps inspired by her tussle with these worthies, Christine went on to write a passionate account of women's virtues and achievements in *The Book of the City of Ladies*. The book begins with a homely description of Christine sitting alone in her study, wondering why so many men throughout history had found such damning things to say about women. Christine's musings were interrupted by her mother calling her to supper, but the subject gripped her imagination. Mustering her by now considerable resources of scholarship, she penned one of the first serious defences of her sex written by a woman writer, a work that links Christine with those later advocates of women's abilities and potential, Mary Astell, Mary Wollstonecraft and Virginia Woolf.

By the time she wrote *The Book of the Duke of True Lovers*, Christine had had many years to consider the literature of love and to observe sexual intrigue in practice at the French court, the scene of a number of scandals. Her book purports to be a nobleman's account of his love affair with a married woman. As the story unfolds, it becomes clear that Christine's real motive was to expose the selfishness of the hero's passion. The young man, known only as the Duke of True Lovers, sees love as a matter of prestige and his description of the affair is steeped in courtly rhetoric. When he finds a suitable lady, a gracious blonde married to a wealthy lord, the Duke is pierced by Sweet Look's arrow shot from the bow of Love, and his heart happily consents to the wound. This doesn't prevent him from falling prey to lovesickness with its repertoire of faints and tremors, its fevers and flushings and sleepless nights tossing on a tumbled bed. While Desire racks the lover, the husband's jealousy and the malice of gossips hinder his attempts to pursue his suit. Finally, by a series of pantomimic contrivances, the couple spend the night together and the lady promises him every mark of favour except the 'base act' of sex.

The affair allows the young man to conform to the fashionable role of lover, to wear his lady's favours and share delicious secrets, meeting and corresponding by stealth, to show off his daring in tournaments and his skill on the dance floor, and to seek fame in battle to win her regard. The risk is all on the lady's side, whether of discovery by her husband, or of loss of reputation through the gossip of servants and other tattlemongers. The lady's vulnerability is highlighted when a friend, an older woman who functions as a surrogate mother, writes to warn her of the dangers to her reputation and happiness if she continues to encourage her lover.

Christine signals the importance of this friend's advice by naming her Sebile de Monthault, Dame de la Tour, which would have suggested to her well-educated audience the idea of the wise sibyl of the classical past, speaking authoritatively from her high mountain or tower. The Dame de la Tour's letter recalls the standard of behaviour expected from a high-born lady. She warns her young friend of the dangers of exposing herself to gossip and innuendo, the tendency of mud to stick however innocent the recipient and the dishonour to her children if even a whisper of scandal becomes attached to their mother's name. As for the argument that the lady's 'friendship' inspires her lover to valour, the Dame points out that the honour and profit belong to the man, while the woman cannot ask her 'servant' for any practical help because it would damage her reputation. The Dame concludes with a reminder of male deceit and trickery in love, the fleetingness of passion and the tendency of the lover to kiss and tell.

Christine wrote *The Book of the Duke of True Lovers* when she was in or approaching her forties, an age when a woman can consider sexual relationships on the basis of observation and experience. The Dame's letter offers a clear-sighted critique of *fin'amor*, and points out that it only benefits the man and will almost inevitably leave the woman bereft, unhappy and ashamed. Her sensible analysis recalls the bitter songs of Castelloza, the trobairitz who was lured by her lover's enticements, and found herself rejected and alone. Work on your marriage is the Dame's advice to the lady; look after your household, take up needlework, and rear your daughters to be modest and virtuous women. As for passion, its ecstasies will not compensate for the sorrows that inevitably follow. Despite her warnings the liaison continues and the Dame's forebodings are realised. The strain of subterfuge undermines the lady's happiness and confidence, and the lovers are repeatedly separated when the Duke is forced to travel in search of valour and renown. The poem ends with the lady's suspicion that the Duke is in love with another woman, while she is left to her regrets.

For all its promises to women, as Christine makes clear in the Duke's memoir, romantic chivalry could never bring them happiness. Christian values prevented women from following their hearts and desires, and Marie de France's lays must have resonated the more poignantly with her female listeners because they knew that, unless they were lucky in their marriage partners, they might never cherish a beloved lover, never know the joy of reciprocated passion. Apart from Heloise, it is difficult to find a medieval woman who wrote honestly and openly about desire and sex, and the life of erotic experiment that illuminates the poems of Izumi Shikibu seems not to have been possible to European women at this period. From William ix's cheeky song about the two 'mounts' to Chaucer's ribald 'Miller's Tale', men were permitted a licence in subject matter and behaviour forbidden to literary women. It was not just a question of what was decorous for a woman to write, but also of the experience available to women. Marie's Eliduc and Christine's Duke travel in search of adventure and reputation; their women stay at home and wait for the men to return. As a young man, Chaucer fought in France and later travelled widely in Europe on the king's service. For many years he held a prestigious position in Customs and was elected knight of the shire for Kent. Apart from her babyhood in Venice, Christine spent her whole life in France, and established a formidable literary reputation against the odds of custom, education and prejudice against women. While Chaucer sat in taverns and rubbed shoulders with the intelligentsia of Europe, Christine read books and ate supper with her mother. If her writing is sometimes costive where it should flow, and admonitory when it might be gay and adventurous, this is scarcely surprising.[71]

It was only when women denied the world that they were permitted any real licence in self-expression. Although religious writing was expected to be contained within accepted Christian conventions, this framework permitted surprising latitude to extravagant expressions of desire. Mystics wrote in ecstatic terms about their union with Christ, using language borrowed from the Song of Songs, sanctioned by the early Church Fathers and revived by Bernard of Clairvaux, to express yearning whose intensity has sometimes been interpreted as displaced sexuality. Such a reading, fed by post-Freudian knowingness, does these women a disservice. It devalues their spirituality, and refuses the act of empathy and knowledge that would permit a more nuanced understanding of what Mechthild of Magdeburg, for example, intended when she wrote about the consummation of the 'naked soul' with God as a 'two-fold intercourse' in which 'He gives Himself to her / And she to Him'.[72] In attempting to express her perception of the ineffable, Mechthild drew on the songs of love in circulation among the minnesingers, heirs to the troubadours, in her native Saxony, but her rhetoric of adoration takes her far beyond the stale platitudes of knightly love. In its depth of emotion and permissive eloquence, love of God offered a freedom of expression to women that was denied when it came to love of man. Drawing on dream, reverie and imagination, Mechthild, Hildegard of Bingen, Julian of Norwich and other gifted religious women produced works of extraordinary originality and power.

In secular life, however, women had to suppress their passion. Christine's lady, in *The Book of the Duke of True Lovers*, fails to reject the Duke and suffers bitterly in consequence. In *The Princess of Clèves* (1678), a novel that has interesting parallels with Christine's anti-romance, Madame de Lafayette returned to the theme of adulterous love with a heroine whose self-restraint would have satisfied even the Dame de la Tour's requirements for female rectitude. The Princess of Clèves's behaviour is all the more admirable, given the eroticised society she inhabits. Set in the lavish court of Henri II, the novel establishes from the outset an atmosphere of lasciviousness and intrigue. The queen indulges Henri's fondness for the company of women and Diane de Poitiers, his mistress for more than twenty years, dominates the hunting parties, tennis games and ballets, which keep the courtiers entertained. Among the glittering beauties who crowd the state chambers and enjoy the royal parks, we catch a glimpse of the young Mary Stuart, Elizabeth's bane, recently married to the dauphin. Equally splendid are the princes and nobles, although the Duc de Nemours carries the honours for valour, nobility, good looks and an irresistible *sprezzatura*, which delights both men and women, and ensures he has his pick of mistresses.

Married to a man whom she esteems but does not love, the

Princess of Clèves falls passionately in love with the duke, who finds himself equally smitten. Unlike Christine's lady, the princess is in no doubt of how she ought to act. Her mother, a woman with affinities to the Dame de la Tour, has brought up her daughter to prize virtue and protect it with the utmost self-discipline. The princess resists the duke's suit and, when she feels her resolution wavering, courageously enlists her husband's help in removing her from temptation. She has dangerously misjudged the strength of her husband's feelings. Her confession of love for another man plunges him into torments of jealousy and suspicion, and eventually he dies. Faithful to her mother's precepts, the princess rejects the opportunity to marry the duke, and devotes the rest of her brief life to religion and good works.

The Princess of Clèves breaks new ground for its period, providing a study of disappointed love that is psychologically subtle and persuasive. The princess and the duke are not the only victims of passion's caprices. The husband's agonies of thwarted love have an authenticity that takes him far beyond the stock jealous husband in medieval romance. Madame de Lafayette's message, however, is very similar to that in *The Book of the Duke of True Lovers*. Neither Christine's lady nor the Princess of Clèves derives happiness from love and their stories insist that passion fatally compromises a woman's honour. In both these cases, as with many of Marie de France's heroines, the women are married to unsympathetic or unattractive husbands, and they have to look outside the marriage to find a suitable object for their feelings. For the daughters of the nobility, arranged marriages were the norm, and women writers at the European courts imagined heroines whose choices in love were restricted and often adulterous. When the rise of an affluent middle class provided an audience with the income and leisure to make reading more freely available, women's tales of love increasingly focused on the trials and mishaps of the unmarried woman in search of a mate.

In eleventh-century Japan, Murasaki Shikibu made outstanding use of the raw materials of life that she observed among the Heian nobility. In medieval Europe and working within the constraints of time and income (Marie's sleepless nights, the hungry mouths down the stairs from Christine's study), Marie de France and Christine de Pizan found ways to bypass the trite conventions of *fin'amor* and tell the truth about women's desire and disappointments in love. Like Murasaki Shikibu, they can be seen as precursors to the women novelists who took up their pens in droves in late-eighteenth-century Europe. But what of the poets, Castelloza, the Countess of Dia and Tibors? What was the legacy of the trobairitz to women writing about love?

PART 4

The Heat and Violence of the Poet's Heart: Women and the Love Sonnet

'[W]ho shall measure the heat and violence of the poet's heart when caught and tangled in a woman's body?'

Virginia Woolf, *A Room of One's Own*[1]

Illustration on reverse:
The poet Edna St Vincent Millay, already famous for her youth,
beauty and talent, under a magnolia tree, in the spring of 1913.
Photograph by Arnold Genthe

The Muse's Dilemma

Could a woman have written the plays of Shakespeare? In attempting to answer this question Virginia Woolf dreamt up a story about Shakespeare's imaginary sister, a gifted girl called Judith, who mooned about at home with books and papers when she should have been mending stockings. Threatened at sixteen with marriage to the son of a wool stapler, she ran away to London and hung about stage doors begging for work as an actress. Finally Nick Greene, the actor-manager, took pity on her, but she became pregnant with his child, killed herself one wintry night, and 'lies buried at some cross-roads where the omnibuses now stop outside the Elephant and Castle'.[2] While male playwrights kept the London theatres buzzing, writing for the public stage in the age of Elizabeth 1 and the early Stuarts appears to have been unthinkable for a woman, although the enterprising Lady Mary Wroth wrote a play called *Love's Victorie*, probably to feed the vogue for private theatricals, and Queen Henrietta Maria composed a pastoral in which she herself appeared at Somerset House. It took the determination of Aphra Behn and the more liberal social climate of the Restoration for a female playwright to succeed on the English stage. When it came to love poetry, women writers again seem to have been strangely silent. In Europe, Louise Labé in France and Gaspara Stampa in Italy were among the women sonneteers who won fame and admiration for their love poetry.[3] In England, although library shelves are crammed with works by male poets who flourished during the late sixteenth century, women's writing on

177

love is surprisingly sparse. In Wroth's prose romance, *The Countess of Montgomery's Urania*, the hero mentions that he has seen 'some excellent things' in women's writings.[4] It seems that closet scribblings shared among friends were as far as women cared to entrust their thoughts about love.[5]

The problem may have been a result of restricted opportunities for women in the public sphere and their limited education, although many aristocratic women in England, including Elizabeth I, were excellent scholars. As in the case of the trobairitz poets, it was also a question of poetic convention. How were women to discuss their personal experience of love within the parameters set by male poets? When they weren't being bawdy, the troubadours and their heirs typically wrote about a woman of inspirational goodness, adored from afar. For women poets, there was the question of female modesty and chastity, of what a woman was permitted to say in public (or even to think), and how to reinvent the language of a poetry that required a desirable woman as its subject. Paradoxically, the difficulties faced by imaginative, erotic women can be illuminated by looking at the experience of a woman who was not a poet, but, like her daughter Elizabeth I, was both muse and female icon. Anne Boleyn was a highly intelligent and well-educated woman who used the arts of love to negotiate the tricky waters of Tudor diplomacy. Her reign as wife to Henry VIII lasted barely three years, the famous 'thousand days' of legend. Her daughter survived as a spinster ruler for forty-five years, repeatedly dangling the possibility of a diplomatic marriage, but never quite taking the final step. Meanwhile, she allowed her supporters to create her dazzling public image as both Virgin Queen (a function previously fulfilled by the Virgin Mary) and alluring Queen of Love and Beauty, contradictory roles that male poets and artists played a major part in supporting, publicising and mythologising. Elizabeth's strategy ensured that she never had to defer to a husband's authority and kept her courtiers under her own control.

Her mother's fate must have been a lesson that she never forgot. Anne Boleyn's history records a woman's experience of being a Poem rather than a Poet, and reveals the risks of chivalrous love, an admonitory tale for all women foolish enough to believe in their privileged status as the male poet's muse. Like the trobairitz Castelloza, Anne pledged her heart to a thankless service, but she was given little time in which to repent her mistake.

The Downfall of the Queen of Hearts

Christine de Pizan's abandoned lady and the misfortunes of the Princess of Clèves warned women against the risks of adulterous passion. In England the real-life dangers of the courtly game of love were horrifyingly played out in the career of Anne Boleyn, Henry VIII's second wife and one-time 'mistress and friend'.[6] By the early sixteenth century the troubadour model of the worshipping 'servant' and his gracious *domna* had been wholeheartedly embraced by the European nobility, and had become an excuse for lavish pageantry and display. The grand ceremonial of a tournament might be dedicated to some aspect of chivalrous love, with appropriate costumes and play-acting. In a famous entertainment at Westminster, Henry VIII appeared as *Cuer Loyall* (Loyal Heart), at the head of a team of tilters representing the virtues typically associated with the courtly suitor: *Bon Espoir* (Good Hope), *Bone Foy* (Good Faith) and *Amoure Loyall* (Loyal Love).[7] In the lists, a lover might be permitted to sport his lady's gage and hope that her approving gaze would reward his prowess. In the courtly accomplishments of song and poetry a gentleman wooed his mistress by his skill in composition and dexterity in wordplay. Love tokens might be exchanged along with other marks of favour, although, as always, a woman had to be careful of her reputation and marriage prospects.

As a young girl, Anne Boleyn was sent to the magnificent Habsburg court in Brabant as maid of honour to the Regent, Margaret of Austria. There she learned her first lessons in flirtation and the art of handling amorous suitors from the Regent herself. A stickler for convention and skilled in courtcraft, Margaret warned her ladies against male flattery and cunning. Men were deceivers all, she told them:

> In their hearts they nurture
> Much cunning in order to deceive,
> And once they have their way thus,
> Everything is forgotten.
> Trust in them?[8]

Any woman who did so was a fool is the message of Margaret's ironic song, which reflects the bitter experience of Castelloza and the Countess of Dia, now become a commonplace of feminine wisdom. A ready tongue was a lady's best response to such beguilers; women must cultivate fine words to attract the questing male, then hold him, panting with desire, at tantalising arm's length.

It was a technique Anne seems to have taken to heart and was to use with great effect during her courtship by the King. A striking rather than beautiful woman, she attracted Henry's notice through the Continental style and sophistication that made her outstanding among the dowdier women of the English court. Responsive to her sexual charisma, Henry was further captivated by Anne's cultivated intelligence and wit, the easy brilliance of her conversation and what appears to have been her mercurial temperament. Compared to the devoted but, from Henry's point of view, stodgy Katherine of Aragon, Anne Boleyn hinted at possibilities for female sexuality that bewitched the King. Rumours of witchcraft seem indeed to have dogged Anne's relationship with Henry, spread by critics and detractors suspicious of her influence on English public affairs.[9] She in turn played her cards with astonishing brio. Confident of Henry's ardour, she refused to enter his bed without the security of marriage.[10] Suddenly, dalliance was transformed into serious passion, with a mistress holding out for a fabulous prize. Anne's strategy was bold and risky, and flawlessly pursued. It was made possible by the conventions and ambiguities of chivalrous love.

The Burgundian court, where Anne first learnt the arts of attraction, had long been skilled in elaborate entertainments, which dramatically represented the game of love. Intended to keep the nobility busy with activities less threatening than intrigue and plots, such pageants migrated to the English court, where they were caught up with enthusiasm by Henry VIII and his followers. Involving an element of play-acting, as well as dance, music and cunningly devised costumes and scenery, these productions often revolved around the differences between the sexes. They might include a debate about the niceties of conduct, rather as Christine's knights and ladies had bantered about the fate of the rejected lover. Another favourite theme was a mock battle between men and women, sometimes illustrated as *The Siege of the Castle of Love*. This is shown in the margins of the English Peterborough Psalter, where the women are assailed from beneath their tower by a throng of boisterous knights, whom they pelt from the battlements with flowers.[11]

Anne's first recorded appearance at the English court in March 1522 was at a very similar divertissement representing an assault on the '*Château Vert*', a three-towered structure decorated with pennants and green foil, and concealing a band of musicians to harmonise the fun. Eight court ladies staunchly defended the ramparts, while a party of gallants, led by the King, showered them with costly fruits. Each of the women typified an aspect of the ideal 'mistress or friend', with Henry's sister Mary as Beauty, the Countess of Devonshire as Honour and Anne Boleyn representing Perseverance. The men played Nobleness, Loyalty, Pleasure and other qualities of the perfect knight, while eight choristers, representing unpopular aspects of the courtly lady (Jealousy, Scorn, Disdain and so on), protected the lower walls of the castle. The attack was fierce and furious, with rosewater and sweetmeats raining down on the aggressors, but it ended, inevitably, with the rout of the hostile choristers, and the ladies in their yellow and white satin costumes were led out to dance.[12]

Other diversions were less innocent. Like the lovers in *Flamenca*, Henry and Anne sometimes verged on blasphemy in their exchanges. At mass in the royal chapel, they scribbled messages in a Book of Hours, and Anne daringly used an illumination of the Annunciation for a coded promise:

> By daily proof you shall me find
> To be to you both loving and kind.[13]

By her obedience to God, the Virgin Mary was graced with a son; Anne would be equally obedient and productive, her love offering Henry both kindness and 'kind' in the sense of humankind or kin, the son and heir whom by now Henry desperately desired.

Games in the sight of God are one thing and the lovers may even have been unconsciously invoking divine approbation by their scribblings in a book that was an essential aid to devotion for the Christian nobility. There were other more worldly risks. Anne's talents as 'mistress and friend', those arts of enchantment that had insinuated her into the King's bed as his wife (an unusual role for a royal mistress, however passionately she might be desired), led her into danger the more threatening because it was least expected. On 2 May 1536, three years after her triumphant marriage, Anne was arrested for adultery, incest and conspiracy to murder the King. Five men, including her brother and a young court musician, all of whom had connections with the Queen and may have flirted, joked, danced, or simply spoken with her in the course of routine encounters, were tried on related charges. On 17 May the poet Sir Thomas Wyatt, also arrested apparently on suspicion of having been Anne's lover and languishing in the Tower of London, watched from his prison cell their execution on Tower Hill. Anne was beheaded two days later. What had been for Anne and her 'co-conspirators', and for noblemen and women all over Europe, a delicious game of courtship, innuendo and sometimes genuine friendship and emotional support, conducted according to clearly understood rules, had been manipulated by clever opponents into something infinitely more sinister, involving accusations of libertinism and sexual misdemeanour, which threatened the person of the King himself.

The relationship between Anne Boleyn and the Tudor poet Sir Thomas Wyatt, like so many other aspects of Anne's sexual life and the real motives behind her arrest and trial, remains a matter for conjecture. Wyatt's grandson George claimed that at their first meeting her effect on the poet was instantaneous, ravishing his intelligence as much as his sight, testimony to Anne's brilliance and vivacity:

> The knight . . . coming to behold the sudden appearance of this new beauty, came to be holden and surprised somewhat with the sight thereof; after much more with her witty and graceful speech, his ear also had him chained unto her, so as finally his heart seemed to say, *I could gladly yield to be tied for ever with the knot of her love*[.][14]

Despite George Wyatt's hindsight enthusiasm, whether Sir Thomas and Anne Boleyn were ever lovers remains in doubt, although several of Wyatt's poems seem to hint at some kind of passionate attraction. The most famous of these poems, the sonnet 'Who so list to hount, I knowe where is an hynde', links Wyatt and Anne into a chain of love poets and their muses that goes back to the troubadours and forward to Sir Philip Sidney and the 'Golden Age' of Elizabethan poetry.

A single poetic form connects Dante's love poems, the Italian poet Petrarch's *Rime sparse* (Scattered Verses) dedicated to his muse Laura, Wyatt's poem about Anne Boleyn and Shakespeare's sequence of one hundred and fifty-four poems, which first appeared in London booksellers in 1609. Invented by a thirteenth-century Sicilian lawyer, Giacomo di Lentino, the sonnet, a fourteen-line poem with a distinctive rhyme scheme, was used by Dante in *La Vita Nuova* to describe his love for Beatrice. Petrarch developed the form in writing about his passion for Laura, a woman whom he had glimpsed in church, probably never even met and whom he celebrated in verse for the rest of his life. Like the troubadour poets of Occitania, Petrarch used love poetry as a method of exploring his own complex states of mind and emotion. His account of the (male) lover's sufferings borrowed from troubadour conventions and set the style for European love poetry for centuries to come. It is a rhetoric that relishes contrariety and oxymoron. The lover vacillates between heat and ice, between weeping and laughter; the intensity of his pain is balanced only by love's ecstasy; he is enslaved by love, pierced by the darts that volley from his lover's eyes; her image bivouacs in his heart and keeps him wakeful. As for her looks, Shakespeare evoked the golden hair, red lips and dazzlingly fair complexion of the idealised mistress only to mock such clichés. In a witty comparison of the real with the imaginary, he flaunts his independence from the by then worn-out stereotypes of Petrarchan gallantry:

> My mistress' eyes are nothing like the sun;
> Coral is far more red than her lips' red;
> If snow be white, why then her breasts are dun;
> If hairs be wires, black wires grow on her head.
> I have seen roses damasked, red and white,
> But no such roses see I in her cheeks,
> And in some perfumes is there more delight
> Than in the breath that from my mistress reeks. . . .[15]

Wyatt probably came across Petrarch's *Rime sparse* at the French court of Francis I; he also visited Rome and was Henry VIII's ambassador to Spain at a time when the European revival of interest in Petrarch was spawning vernacular imitations. Fascinated by the possibilities of its short, densely structured form, he introduced the sonnet into English poetry, translating several of Petrarch's *Rime* into English and writing poems of his own using the sonnet structure, in which he modified the typical Petrarchan rhyme scheme to end with a rhyming couplet. This has the effect of summing up and finalising the poem with particular force.[16]

Wyatt's poem about Anne Boleyn, 'Who so list to hount', was translated from Petrarch's *Rime* 190, 'Una candida cerva sopra l'erba verde' ('A white doe on the green grass'), in which the poet sees a beautiful white doe on a riverside at sunrise and decides to follow her.[17] The doe wears a jewelled collar, which declares that she is not to be touched; Caesar has set her free. Intent on pursuit, the poet follows her until midday, when he falls into the water and the creature vanishes. Petrarch's sonnet is thought to record his first glimpse of Laura in Avignon, a town where two rivers meet. The poem exquisitely communicates the poet's wonder at the sight of the white doe, his sense of her invulnerability to the taint of human desires, and his pursuit of a muse who was both inspiring and elusive. Modern readers may identify this visionary creature as one of the many aspects of Robert Graves's White Goddess, the goddess/seductress/muse who lures the male poet through the thickets of desire, struggle and loss to vatic utterance.[18]

Wyatt's version is quite different in mood and tone. Far from spiritual, it admirably demonstrates his customary mien as a courtly lover: passionate, acerbic and ironically committed to pursuing what he knows only too well will do him harm:

> Who so list to hount, I knowe where is an hynde,
>   But as for me, helas, I may no more:
>   The vayne travaill hath weried me so sore.
>   I ame of theim that farthest commeth behinde;

Yet may I by no meanes my weried mynde
    Drawe from the Diere: but as she fleeth afore,
Faynting I folowe. I leve of therefore,
    Sins in a nett I seke to hold the wynde.
Who list her hount, I put him owte of dowbte,
    As well as I may spend his tyme in vain:
    And, graven with Diamonds, in letters plain
There is written her faier neck rounde abowte:
    Noli me tangere, for Cesars I ame;
    And wylde for to hold, though I seme tame.[19]

In this wry confession of frustrated passion, Wyatt confronts Petrarch's dream with brutal reality. His pursuit takes place not in some illusory realm of the imagination, but in the cut and thrust of the English court where Henry's will was absolute. Gone is the delicate white doe symbolising female chastity, tenderness and spirituality. In her place is the wayward hind, who leads her admirers a desperate chase. While Petrarch recalls a wistful quest for purity and inspiration, Wyatt's narrative is wry and worldly, alert to the competitiveness and bad faith of the court, and in particular the practised coquetry of its first lady. Where Petrarch is solitary and single-minded, Wyatt is one among many, bitingly aware of the fruitlessness and dangers of his pursuit.

The jewelled collar on Petrarch's doe declares her right to wander at will and the poet is her sole pursuer. In the case of the hind, her owner's message blazoned around her neck is a ruler's imprimatur intended to see off the competition: 'Don't dare to touch me: I belong to the king.' The message is 'graven with Diamonds' suggesting that the prey is wearing a jewelled collar like that of Petrarch's doe, but it also stresses the adamantine force of the taboo. The young Elizabeth, Anne Boleyn's daughter and future Queen of England, is supposed to have used a diamond to engrave a defiant message on the glass window of her prison when held captive by

Queen Mary at Woodstock.[20] Henry's declaration of ownership of his mistress is equally indelibly engraved. Even here, however, there is ambiguity and uncertainty as the final rhyming couplet appears to throw the King's possession into doubt. According to the Latin version of John's gospel, *'Noli me tangere'* ('Touch me not') were Christ's words to Mary Magdalene when he met her outside the sepulchre. The first person to see the risen Christ, Mary had taken him for the gardener and made a spontaneous gesture to caress him when she recognised her Lord. Christ's gentle prohibition reminded her of his separation from his followers, transformed from the corporeality of their earthly leader to his status as God's risen son. By an analogy that is almost blasphemous in its implications, Wyatt suggests that, appropriated by the God-like Henry as his own possession, the beautiful hind is similarly no longer available to the lesser mortals of his court.[21] The ironic final line seems to suggest that even King Henry will find it difficult to keep hold of this slippery creature. For all her acquiescence, Anne's 'wildness', the emotionality and unpredictability that entranced the King, keep her untameable, someone who, in modern terminology, retains her individuality and is her own person, an implication that stretches the possibilities of the hind's freedom and independence far beyond the boundaries suggested or even imagined in Petrarch's vision of his muse.

Despite this hint of an integrity that answers only to itself, there is no freedom for this hunted hind, nor for the men who recklessly pursue her, as Wyatt's densely nuanced narrative makes all too clear. However swiftly she may flee, with men and hounds in full cry behind her, the hind bears a despot's halter round her neck, that famously long and slender throat Anne Boleyn was to finger apprehensively in the hours before her death. Informed that an executioner had been summoned from Calais to perform decapitation with a sword, a more efficient tool than the axe, which could horribly prolong the victim's suffering, Anne had joked about her 'little neck', circling it tenderly with her hand and, according to a witness, 'laughing heartily'.[22]

Anne Boleyn's attempt to fulfil the role of the *domna*/muse and her cruel fate reveal the risks for women who dared to play the courtly game of love. Wyatt was lucky enough to escape execution. His personal speaking voice, and his grim awareness of the vulnerability and folly of the lover caught in the web of court politics and bedroom stratagems, ensure that his poetry has remained accessible even to present-day readers unversed in the rhetoric of Tudor verse. Many male poets followed his example in developing the sonnet into a compact yet flexible vehicle for the expression of sexual feeling, although in later hands it became playful and even vapid, a tool for virtuosity and self-display. In their adoption of Petrarchan motifs Sir Philip Sidney, Edmund Spenser, Michael Drayton and their contemporaries can be seen as natural heirs to the troubadours, to Bernart de Ventadorn and Arnaut Daniel, as well as to Dante and his fellow poets of the *dolce stil nuovo*. Male Elizabethan and Jacobean sonneteers are still familiar to the general reader, and their poems regularly appear in anthologies and collections of love poetry. Apart from poems attributed to Mary Queen of Scots or Elizabeth I, the secular works of English women poets during the sixteenth and early seventeenth century are virtually unknown to the general reader.[23]

Granddaughter to the Countess of Dia: Lady Mary Wroth

Doris Lessing's novel, *Love, Again*, begins with the heroine, Sarah Durham, in her London flat in the late 1980s. She is listening, rather dismissively, to a song by the Countess of Dia about her passion for her beloved 'friend'. Sarah, a gifted and attractive woman in her mid sixties, will soon have reason to smile ruefully at her impatience with the Countess's complaints. She herself will fall in love, not just once, but repeatedly, in a novel that explores love's capacity to strike the unwary with all the force and irresistibility of Cupid's arrow. Lessing may have come across the Countess when researching the portrait of the fictitious nineteenth-century woman 'troubadour' who is one of the central characters in her novel. Her interest is unusual. Apart from the critical texts of academics, this is a rare reference to trobairitz poetry by a woman writer in the eight hundred years since the Countess was composing her songs. Although the troubadours were still writing in the fourteenth century, and their tradition of love was kept alive by the trouvères in northern France, the minnesingers in Germany and the Italian poets of the *dolce stil nuovo*, typically male poets, the trobairitz left no continuous legacy to later female poets. A hidden remnant, a piece in the jigsaw that has still to be fully recovered, they appear to have been the only women who attempted as a literary group and over a period of years to challenge the male bastion of love poetry. They represent the beginning, or early stages, of a tradition that never got off the ground. Their work rapidly disappeared and seems to have been unknown to later women, who struggled, often in isolation, to write about love in ways that conformed to male models of the genre without flouting the conventions of womanly modesty.

More recent writers were to deplore the lack of a female tradition. 'England has had many learned women, not merely readers but writers of the learned languages, in Elizabeth's time & afterwards,' wrote Elizabeth Barrett in 1845, 'and yet,' she continued, 'where were the poetesses? . . . I look everywhere for Grandmothers & see none.'[24] Dreaming of being 'The Poetess of America' (a title she evidently regarded as honourable rather than patronising), Sylvia Plath looked back to Sappho, Elizabeth Barrett Browning and Christina Rossetti as her earliest poetic godmothers.[25] She either had not read or did not value the many European women who wrote poetry in the centuries between Sappho and Mrs Browning. It is likely that their names and works had simply not appeared on any English syllabus she encountered during her extensive education both in the United States and at Newnham College in Cambridge. Those studious girls Elizabeth Barrett and Mary Ann Evans would have found Christine de Pizan an inspiring grandmother had they known about her work, just as Christina Rossetti might have been captivated by the lyrics of Castelloza and the Countess of Dia.

Even at the time the trobairitz were composing and in the period that immediately followed, their work seems to have made little impression on other women writers. Marie de France's lays show the influence of *fin'amor* and the chivalric tradition, but she did not write personal poetry and looked to narrative sources for her inspiration. The widowed Christine de Pizan wrote love poetry glowing with the freshness and tenderness of remembered passion, but it draws on male courtly lyric and there is little hint that she looked south to the trobairitz for models. While male poets developed the sonnet into a sophisticated tool for writing about love, composing treatises about poetry and competing for public acclaim for their brilliance and wit, women across Europe struggled to find a way of expressing their feelings in language which, as Bathsheba Everdene was so ruefully to comment in Thomas Hardy's *Far from the Madding Crowd*, 'is chiefly made by men to express theirs'.

One Englishwoman who did attempt to break the male stranglehold on love poetry during the early 1600s was Lady Mary Wroth, a member of a distinguished family with strong links to the court and the intellectual life of the late Tudor period. Although born to a rather different class and lineage from Virginia Woolf's fictitious Judith Shakespeare, Lady Mary's life and writings about women's experience of love epitomise the 'heat and violence' of the turbulent poet's heart rebelling against social fetters. She was inspired by brilliant literary forebears, who served as both models and reproofs to the ardent, scribbling girl. Lady Mary's uncle was the writer, scholar, patron and statesman Sir Philip Sidney, who dazzled his contemporaries with the polish and erudition of his writing. In his brief life he produced an accomplished sonnet sequence, *Astrophil and Stella*, a prose romance, *The Countess of Pembroke's Arcadia*, which remained popular for decades, and *A Defence of Poetry*, a seminal essay that drew on Sidney's classical education and wide reading to argue the importance of literature. Impatient with loitering at the court of Elizabeth I without a proper job, he sought active service abroad and managed to secure an appointment as governor of Flushing in 1585. One year later and just a few weeks before his thirty-second birthday, Sir Philip died from an infected wound in his thigh after a skirmish with the Spanish near Zutphen. Extraordinarily, he was accorded the honour of a state funeral at St Paul's Cathedral. Accounts of his prowess on and off the battlefield confirmed his heroic status. His close friend and biographer, the poet Fulke Greville, boasted that in the fatal battle Sidney had deliberately left off his thigh armour so that he would be no better protected than other officers. As he was being carried from the field, he gave his water bottle to a dying comrade. These claims to admiration notwithstanding, Sidney failed to impress T. S. Eliot, who declared with lofty disdain, 'The works of Sir Philip Sidney, excepting a few sonnets, are not among those to which one can return for perpetual refreshment; the *Arcadia* is a monument of dulness.'[26] Had Eliot ever read the works of Sidney's niece, he would no doubt have been equally dismissive, but to the lover of romance or devotee of love poetry, delighted to find a woman's voice amid the babble of male sonneteers, Lady Mary Wroth's writings provide welcome relief, the equivalent, perhaps, of her uncle's precious drops of water to the parched combatant.

The eldest daughter of Sir Robert Sidney, Philip's younger brother, and the heiress Lady Barbara Gamage, Lady Mary was probably born in the year following the death of her distinguished uncle, and was no doubt taught to share the family reverence for his achievements and reputation.[27] The women in the Sidney family were equally worthy of her notice. Lady Mary's aunt, Mary Countess of Pembroke, was sister to Sir Philip, and continued his legacy by editing his work and completing his translation of the Psalms. One of the most remarkable women of the Elizabethan era, the Countess was a poet and translator in her own right, and possessed the capacious mind of the Renaissance scholar. Married to a powerful nobleman many years her senior, she satisfied his dynastic ambitions by presenting him with two sons and flattered his *amour propre* by her energy, talent and attention to domestic decorum. The Countess actively sponsored the work of scientists and physicians, presiding over her own chemical laboratory and establishing an informal academy of brilliant minds at her country estate at Wilton. As patron to poets, she was lavished with praise as the Urania, Clorinda and Cynthia of her day, the Elizabethan equivalent of the compliments paid by troubadour poets to the wives of powerful lords.[28] This formidable lady was probably godmother to Lady Mary, and the young girl frequently visited her learned aunt, in company with her mother and some or other of her many siblings. The Countess was an exemplary role model for her niece: a woman who not only coped adroitly with the duties of wife and chatelaine, but was also an active writer, thinker and talker, relishing the company of the (predominantly male) writers and savants who flocked to her entourage.

Lady Mary's mother, Barbara Gamage, provided a rather different example of female possibilities, being a woman who combined maternal tenderness with a strong sense of duty. She gave birth to twelve children, although only six survived to adulthood. A portrait by the elder Gheeraerts, painted in 1596, shows Barbara with six of her children: a handsome family, the boys in long skirts like their sisters and Lady Mary resembling a miniature Elizabeth I, with her red hair, square-necked bodice and string of knotted pearls. Like the majority of women at that period, Lady Sidney may have been largely illiterate: there are indications that she was unable to read fluently or perhaps do more than print her name.[29] This did not prevent her from taking a keen interest in the education of her offspring, an enthusiasm she shared with her husband, who kept closely in touch with family affairs during his overseas service. In 1599, when Lady Mary was around twelve years old, Robert's steward, Rowland Whyte, wrote to reassure him that 'My Lady sees [the children] well taught, and brought up in Learning, and Qualities, fitt for theire Birth and Condicion'.[30] In her familial concerns, Lady Sidney exemplified the personal qualities and skills most prized in noblewomen at that time. She was a modest and fertile wife, a devoted mother and an assiduous administrator of her husband's properties, estates and households of servants in Kent, London and Flushing. She was also an able hostess whose guests included her husband's relatives, members of the court and the ageing Queen Elizabeth herself, who called for a stout stick with which to heave herself up the stairs at Penshurst Place, and strolled about the imposing rooms, no doubt admiring Sir Robert's many costly improvements, until she was exhausted.

Lady Mary's father was also an important influence. At first somewhat in the shadow of his virtuoso brother, Robert Sidney was appointed governor of Flushing in 1588 and later became a valued member of James 1's entourage. Often separated from his wife and children while he was abroad on the Queen's business, he took to writing poetry, although this was never published in his lifetime. A manuscript collection of sixty-six sonnets, songs and other works dedicated to his sister has recently been discovered. This includes a sequence of love sonnets, *Rosis and Lysa*, which may have been inspired by his brother's more famous *Astrophil and Stella*. Robert kept a close eye on his eldest daughter's progress, organising books for her studies and receiving glowing reports of 'Mall's' achievements from Rowland Whyte. '[S]he is very forward in her learning, writing, and other exercises she is put to, as dawncing and the virginals,' Whyte wrote on one occasion.[31] An all-round education to prepare the girl for court attendance and adult life as wife, mother and the mistress of extensive properties was clearly in progress. Despite Barbara Sidney's frequent pregnancies, she made several voyages to Flushing, no mean feat with a crèche of toddlers and their nursemaids. This early experience of travel and the exposure to foreign scenes and languages may have fostered Lady Mary's tendencies to open-mindedness and self-reliance. Intelligent and quick to learn, she grew up with a marked independence of spirit, which later revealed itself in a willingness to flout convention and her determination to pay off her husband's debts after she was widowed in her mid twenties.

Barbara Gamage's marriage to Robert Sidney had taken place barely two weeks after she came into her inheritance, a scramble to carry off an eligible heiress that recalls the frenzied competition for Eleanor of Aquitaine when she was newly liberated from King Louis. In addition to her father's fortune and extensive land in Wales, Barbara brought her husband valuable family connections. Her father had been first cousin to Sir Walter Ralegh and to Lord Hunsdon, the Lord Chamberlain; another kinsman was Charles,

Baron Howard (later Lord High Admiral and Earl of Nottingham). The couple may not actually have met before the wedding, although it is more likely that their paths would have crossed during visits by Robert to Ludlow or Cardiff, and they may even have sought the marriage out of a strong mutual preference.[32] In any event, they were well-suited, consulting together on their many responsibilities and on the maintenance of their domestic economy (often at risk as funds failed to meet the demands of their expanding households), and apparently developing the warmest affection for one another. Barbara carefully saved the hundreds of letters she received from her husband, in which he records his devotion. One letter concludes with apologies for not having written as frequently as he wished, but 'you shall ever bee most deer to me, and whyle I live I will have the same care of you as of mine own life. Sweet wenche farewell till I can see you.'[33]

Despite her parents' frequent separations, the evidence of these letters and other family documents suggests that Lady Mary grew up in a loving household. Her marriage to Sir Robert Wroth was a very different matter. The couple appear to have been incompatible from the beginning. They were married on 27 September 1604 at Penshurst Place in Kent, the country seat of the Sidney family, when Lady Mary was about seventeen. Almost immediately, Robert Sidney was writing to his wife to report Wroth's unease with his new bride. Meeting his son-in-law unexpectedly in London, Sir Robert found that 'there was some what that doth discontent him: but the particulars I could not get out of him, onely that hee protests that hee cannot take any exceptions to his wife, nor her cariage towards him'. This is somewhat ambiguous, but Sir Robert does not develop his comment. He merely reflects rather ruefully that 'It were very soon for any unkindness to begin' and counsels his wife to put a good face on matters until they all meet. Gossip was evidently as pernicious under the Stuarts as it was in the time of Henry VIII and Sir Robert feared that his enemies would relish the opportunity to laugh at him if the disagreement became too public.[34]

The causes of the differences between Lady Mary and her husband remain unclear, but in tastes and temperament they may well have been ill-matched. Although Lady Mary possibly shared Wroth's passion for hunting, his extravagant use of his estates to suit the King's pleasure may have irritated his wife, whose family experience would have made her only too aware of the cost of maintaining public appearances.[35] She was eventually to write to Queen Anne about the loss of income Wroth incurred by allowing deer to feed on his best land rather than hinder the King's sport.[36] The couple may also have had sexual difficulties. Their first child, or at least the first to survive, was not conceived for nine years and was born just a month before the death of his father. Their different tastes and the pull between town and country life may also have caused problems. Preferring to socialise with the King in country pursuits, Wroth may have been jealous of his wife's brilliance and success in court entertainments. Lady Mary had already had a taste of the heady pleasures of display when she danced for Elizabeth I on St Stephen's Day in 1602, performing two galliards with a certain Mr Palmer.[37] As a consequence of her marriage she was drawn into the elite circle of James I and his wife, and acted in a number of the sumptuous court masques so enjoyed by Anne of Denmark, including Ben Jonson's *The Masque of Blackness*, commissioned by the Queen and designed by Inigo Jones. This took place just a few months after the Wroths' wedding, on Twelfth Night 1605. Queen Anne was an enthusiastic dancer, who adored pageantry and dressing up, and was proud of her ample white bosom, shown off to good effect in the elaborate costumes required for masques. A contemporary miniature of a lady dressed as the goddess Flora, with roses and pansies in her hair, daringly reveals its subject in a high-waisted dress cut away around the breasts, which are covered only with a kind of transparent gauze. Such designs showed the influence of the risqué Italian creations of Vasari and Buontalenti, which were probably too extreme in practice for high-born women of the Stuart household.[38] Even so, court costumes were intentionally eye-catching and provocative, and considered rather too Continental by some observers. In *The Masque of Blackness* the Queen, Lady Mary and other attendants appeared as Ethiopian nymphs, with their faces and arms blackened, but their garments were 'too light and Curti-zan-like' to please one disapproving eyewitness.[39]

Following the family tradition, Lady Mary evidently relished the company of talented writers and her own role as patron to leading poets. Her friendship with Ben Jonson may in particular have been a source of friction with her husband. Despite his cynicism about the relationship between sponsor and writer, Jonson was an assidu-ous courter of wealthy patrons, and included the Sidney family and their associates among his chief supporters. His epistle dedicated to Lady Mary's husband, 'To Sir Robert Wroth', is an exercise in classical bucolicism, which extols the harmony and plenty of Wroth's rural estate above the vice and display of city and court, and affects to despise the 'wasted' wit and 'short braverie' of the masque. The poem offers a polished (and possibly ironic) compliment to an influential nobleman, but probably reveals little of Wroth's true character or philosophy. Much as Jonson may have wished on Sir Robert and his other sponsors the contentment of the unaspiring mind combined with prodigal open-handedness, the Sidneys, the Wroths, the Herberts and their peers were competitive players on the chessboard of Stuart politics, as was Jonson himself. Playwright and poet and one of the most important writers of his period, Ben Jonson had been at times an *enfant terrible*, whose reputation still hung in the balance when he met Lady Mary. Responding, perhaps, to her brilliance and enthusiasm for writing, he professed himself her great admirer, dedicating his play *The Alchemist* to her, describ-ing her as 'The Grace, and Glory of women' and lavishly compli-menting her poetry.[40] It has even been suggested that Lady Mary was the 'Celia' mentioned in several of Jonson's love poems.[41] (The

well-known song 'Drinke to me, onely, with thine eyes' was dedicated to this seductive muse.) It seems more likely that Jonson's
relationship with Lady Mary typified the exchanges between a
shrewd author on the make and a noblewoman with influential
connections. However innocent, Lady Mary's friendship with Jonson
and other poets, and her enthusiastic engagement in the cultural life
of the court, may have angered her husband, although she turned
her influence with Queen Anne to good use, obtaining funds to
repair the Wroth family manor at Loughton. Whatever its causes,
Robert Wroth's jealousy was evidently a matter of gossip, or at least
inconvenience to her sharp-tongued admirer. The *Conversations* with
William Drummond of Hawthornden, whom Jonson visited during
his journey by foot to Scotland in 1618, record his laconic comment
that 'my Lady wroth is unworthily maried on a Jealous husband'.[42]

A full-length portrait now in the collection at Penshurst Place
shows Lady Mary casually supporting an archlute, one of the largest
variants of the lute family, which typically provided the musical
accompaniment to court masques. The Puritan lawyer Whitelocke
commented in his memoirs that he had 'engaged forty lutes, besides
other instruments and voyces' for a masque to entertain Charles I,
and the lute had long been a favourite instrument to harmonise
the songs and ballads so popular in European courts.[43] One of Sir
Thomas Wyatt's most bitter lyrics calls on his lute to help him bid
farewell to a proud lady who has spurned him:

> My lute awake! perfourme the last
> Labor that thou and I shall wast,
>   And end that I have now begon;
> For when this song is sung and past,
>   My lute be still, for I have done.[44]

A typical memento mori poem, predicting the decline of human
flesh and the acrid fruits of vanity, Wyatt imagines his love as a

withered old woman lying alone at night, moaning in vain to an indifferent moon. 'Care then who lyst, for I have done,' is Wyatt's grim riposte to this macabre phantom of his own imagination.[45] In contrast to this malevolent vision of courtly games gone sour, Lady Mary's portrait reveals the lutenist in full fig, a woman in her prime elaborately gowned in the fashion of the day, with a starched lace ruff, pointed basque and full brocade skirt. Her capacious forehead suggests intelligence, her gaze is frank if somewhat wary, her cupid's bow mouth stretches a little too widely to conform to Petrarchan rules of feminine perfection. In short, she looks like no one's fool, a self-contained and elegant woman modestly displaying her claims as composer and performer. It is the portrait of a lady of character, painted perhaps when Lady Mary was about to affront the two greatest challenges of her destiny: her husband's death and her passion for a married man.

Robert Wroth died in March 1614 reportedly of 'a gangrene *in pudendis*', an unpleasant-sounding condition, which may suggest he was suffering from some kind of venereal disease.[46] It seems that any differences with Lady Mary had been smoothed over. Twelve days before his death he wrote a will in which he spoke warmly of his 'deere and loving wife', of his 'entire love and affection' for her, and his sense that her 'sincere love, loyaltie, virtuous conversation, and behavioure' towards her husband deserved a better recompense than he had been able to offer, distracted as he was by financial worries.[47] He may have felt both remorse and guilt at the position in which he left his wife and newborn son. His will mentions attempts to pay his debts; despite this, Lady Mary was left with a jointure of £1,200 and a massive debt of £23,000 to repay. When the Wroths' baby son James died only two years later, the bulk of the estate passed to Sir Robert Wroth's uncle, leaving Lady Mary even more heavily encumbered. It is a mark of her steely character and determination that she insisted on dealing personally with the problem and had managed to pay off half the debt by the mid 1620s, but lack of money probably caused anxiety for the rest of her life. Another complication around this time was Lady Mary's entanglement in a love affair which was potentially damaging to her reputation and to her emotional well-being. The lover who tempted this gifted, independent woman was her first cousin William Herbert, the son of Mary Sidney and now third Earl of Pembroke.

Painted in middle life by the Netherlandish portraitist Abraham van Blijenberch, Pembroke is represented as a man of status and authority, who bears the insignia of rank and office: the ribbon and pendant badge of the Order of the Garter, and the white staff and key of his position as Lord Chamberlain.[48] His robust frame communicates a sense of gravitas and power, emphasised by the dense ebony of his robes and the sombre gaze of his brilliant dark eyes. A white lace ruff throws into relief the firm, ruddy flesh of his cheeks and the smooth olive brow, whose central bulge hints at a tendency to choler. Described as 'rather majestic than elegant, his presence full of stately gravity', Pembroke was also reported to have been 'immoderately given up to women', enjoying 'pleasures of all kinds almost in all excesses'.[49] He was to die in his fiftieth year after a period of ill health, possibly resulting from a fondness for good living. An ardent statesman, he was also an entrepreneur, participating in the enthusiasm for overseas trade and colonisation at the beginning of the seventeenth century. Like his cousin, he was a poet and patron of writers, and a supporter of Inigo Jones. Of his affair with Lady Mary almost nothing is known, except that they had two children together. The evidence of Lady Mary's writing suggests that the relationship was tempestuous, tracing a familiar trajectory of pursuit and passion on the man's side, followed by a cooling of ardour, infidelity and finally abandonment. As Lady Mary's financial crises deepened and she became increasingly alienated from the court, she seems not to have been able to turn to Pembroke for support. Her love sonnets imply a period of uncertainty and anguish, followed by resignation. However much he may have delighted in his cousin's brilliance and vivacity, the Pembroke of the portrait, a statesman with so much public dignity at stake and no doubt his pick of more docile court beauties, may have found Lady Mary's debts and the scandal attached to her writing too much to stomach.

It is not suprising that the lovers had been drawn to one another. They had strong family ties and many tastes in common. They first met as children on family visits. Lady Mary's father had been involved in Herbert's upbringing for his future role as courtier and Robert Sidney's family frequently cohabited with the Herberts at Baynard's Castle, their London home. After the death of William's father, Henry Herbert, in 1601, Robert Sidney and the new Earl of Pembroke became good friends, with Pembroke paying frequent visits. The Earl even offered to supply one thousand pounds towards Lady Mary's dowry when she married Robert Wroth. Lady Mary and her cousin shared an interest in music, poetry and the theatre, but whether they were childhood or teenage sweethearts is un-known. As a young man, Herbert appears to have been unprincipled and self-willed, upsetting his mother and causing a serious breach with Elizabeth 1. When he clandestinely courted a maid of honour, Mary Fitton, he was breaking one of the Queen's most rigorous taboos. The young woman audaciously took to cross-dressing to sneak out to her meetings with Herbert. She 'would put of her head tire and tucke upp her clothes and take a . . . white cloake and marche as though she had bene a man to meet the said Earle out of the court'.[50] When she became pregnant, Pembroke admitted his involvement, but refused to marry his mistress, probably hoping for a more advantageous match. He was imprisoned for a while, then rusticated to his country estate at Wilton, from where he wrote grumbling letters to Robert Cecil, attempting to fob off the Fitton family and restore his own damaged prospects. Meanwhile, the baby died and Mary Fitton was left to repent her beguilement by this petulant playboy. A witty and self-possessed young woman, she refused to be cowed by Pembroke's abandonment and went on to bear another child out of wedlock to William Polwhele, whom she later married.[51]

Pembroke was eventually restored to favour under James I and was married in 1604, the same year as his cousin, to Mary Talbot, co-heiress of the wealthy seventh Earl of Shrewsbury. This appears to have been a marriage of convenience and Pembroke strayed from his wife, searching among the court ladies, according to the Earl of Clarendon, for 'those advantages of the mind, as manifested an extraordinary wit, and spirit, and knowledge, and administered great pleasure in the conversation'.[52] Lady Mary Wroth was unusually well-equipped with these rare and enticing qualities, and the cousins may also have been drawn together by shared childhood memories and their literary interests. Married to an uncongenial husband, Lady Mary may have responded to her cousin's charm and fallen for his sophistication in love affairs. She may quite simply have seized on the opportunity to experience passionate sexual love with so suitable (if inconstant) a partner. Quite when the affair started is unknown, but according to a genealogical history of the Herbert/Pembroke family, Lady Mary gave birth to two illegitimate children, William and Catherine, fathered by her cousin.[53] There is a possible reference to 'Wil' in a letter from Sir Robert Wroth to his wife in 1615, which raises interesting questions about when this second son was born, and whether the child born so tardily to the Wroths and recognised as the legitimate offspring of Lady Mary's marriage was actually also Pembroke's son. Both Pembroke's legitimate sons died in infancy, but he never formally recognised William. In 1626 his seven-year-old nephew Philip was named as his heir. The Stuart regime was no stranger to sexual scandal (the Overbury murder was to become a cause célèbre), but as a result of her affair with Pembroke, Lady Mary's star at court rapidly waned. The publication of the first part of her prose romance, *The Countess of Montgomery's Urania*, caused further outrage and damage to her reputation because it appeared to refer to actual people and events.

Such was the uproar that Lady Mary eventually wrote to the Duke of Buckingham, James 1's influential favourite, to say that she had never intended publication of the work and soliciting his help in halting the sale of copies.[54]

Quite when Lady Mary Wroth began to write and circulate her work is, like so many other details of her life, unknown, although Ben Jonson and other eulogisers claimed to have read and admired her poetry. Josephine A. Roberts, Lady Mary's recent editor, suggests that she started writing *The Countess of Montgomery's Urania* between 1618 and 1620.[55] The first part of the romance was published in 1621 along with a sonnet collection, *Pamphilia to Amphilanthus*. Both works are a remarkable achievement and recall the heroic productivity of Murasaki Shikibu in writing *The Tale of Genji*, another work that combines poetry and prose, and offers a panoramic view of contemporary courtly culture. The published section of *Urania* runs to almost 350,000 words and the second unpublished section contains about 240,000 words. The published sonnet collection consists of a hundred and three songs and sonnets, with further poems in manuscript, all purportedly written by Pamphilia, the heroine of *Urania*, to her lover Amphilanthus. In both works Lady Mary was looking back to the writings of her famous uncle in what could be interpreted as an act of literary homage and indeed, she asserts her dynastic credentials on the title page of the 1621 *Urania*: 'Written by the right honorable the Lady MARY WROATH. Daughter to the right Noble Robert, Earle of Leicester. And Neece to the ever famous, and renowned Sir Phillips Sidney knight. And to the most exelent Lady Mary Countesse of Pembroke late deceased.'[56] Even more significantly, Wroth's publication offered a revision of Sidney's two favourite modes to suit a female pen.

Lady Mary was the first woman to write either a prose romance or a sonnet sequence in English, thus transforming the possibilities of what women might write about or publish, although the brouhaha over *Urania* can hardly have been encouraging to other aspirant female writers. Prose romance flourished in Europe from around the mid sixteenth century, with writers across Europe creating, adapting, translating or imitating freely from one another's work. The verse romances that had captivated medieval audiences were reworked to suit new audiences, and in England professional writers such as Robert Greene, Thomas Lodge and George Gascoigne produced their own variations on the genre. Sir Philip Sidney's *Arcadia* was an outstanding example of what could be achieved in the prose romance, and remained popular as a source of entertainment, moral advice and ideas for other writers for the next two hundred years. Considering the role played by nineteenth-century women writers in the development of the novel, it may seem surprising that the romance was almost exclusively the domain of male writers. In the moral climate of sixteenth-century England, however, the modest woman, if able to write at all, was expected to restrict herself to devotional texts. The nearest an Englishwoman had previously come to engaging with romance was the translation by Margaret Tyler in around 1578 of *The Mirrour of Princely Deedes and Knighthood* by the Spanish writer Diego Ortuñez de Calahorra. In her preface 'To the Reader', Tyler attacked the cultural code that demanded women either write about religious subjects or else remain silent, a restraint that was still in place when Wroth dared to write so outspokenly about female passion. If men dedicate prose romances to women, Tyler argued, women should be free to write stories of their own: 'it is all one for a woman to pen a story, as for a man to addresse his story to a woman[.]'[57]

Following the trend for female addressees, Lady Mary dedicated *Urania* to a woman and fellow reader who was both relative and friend, Susan Herbert, Countess of Montgomery, the wife of her cousin Philip, and the romance includes many instances of affectionate relationships between women. It is tempting to read both the romance and the sonnet sequence attached to it as a *roman à clef*, reflecting aspects of Lady Mary's affair with Pembroke. The novel tells the story of Queen Pamphilia's unhappy passion for her first cousin, the Emperor Amphilanthus, in a plot which involves a huge cast of additional characters, multiple sub-plots and numerous twists and turns, as the lovers are persistently separated by ill luck, mis-understanding and deception. The action revolves around a coterie of imaginary noble and royal families, whose adventures take them across Europe, to Greece and surrounding countries. Allegory and dramatic scenes of enchantment, conversation and debate, descrip-tion and poetry are just some of the narrative techniques employed by Lady Mary in her kaleidoscopic exploration of the many facets of relationship and love.

The central theme of the novel is the constancy of Pamphilia ('all-loving') to a lover whose name, Amphilanthus, means 'the lover of two', and whose defining characteristic is knightly valour rather than fidelity. The heroine's ironic recognition of her lover's failing is amusingly summarised during a scene in Book II, where Pamphilia wanders off into a woodland to enjoy some quiet reading. Her book is about Love, 'the affection of a Lady to a brave Gentleman, who equally loved, but being a man, it was necessary for him to exceede a woman in all things, so much as inconstancie was found fit for him to excell her in, hee left her for a new'.[58] In another incident a lady who was abandoned by her lover warns against trusting men, 'for believe it, the kindest, lovingst, passionatest, worthiest, loveliest, valiantest, sweetest, and best man, will, and must change, not that he, it may bee, doth it purposely, but tis their naturall infirmitie, and cannot be helped'.[59] Because of her determination to be faithful, Pamphilia suffers the pain of unfulfilled desire, separation from her beloved, doubt and anxiety, and the gnawings of jealousy. It requires strength and dedication to maintain her good faith, but it is not only as a lover that Pamphilia embodies constancy. She is also a queen, who, like Elizabeth I, has espoused her country, and her commitment to the responsibilities of majesty is another strand in

Lady Mary's exploration of what it means to be a dutiful and heroic as well as loving woman.[60]

While the romance presents Pamphilia's story as an ongoing (and ultimately unresolved) narrative replete with action and drama, the poetry sequence focuses on Pamphilia's most intimate feelings and is remarkable for its study of a woman brooding over the condition of being in love. The sheer difficulty of attempting such an analysis was prodigious. The first problem was one of language and expression. Following her uncle's model, Lady Mary chose the sonnet, the most popular short form for writing about love in poetry since Petrarch. Her choice led her to imitate the ornate language perfected by her uncle, which she handles with great dexterity, drawing on the full range of stock Petrarchan themes, with references to Venus, Cupid and their complex mythology of love. All this requires persistence for the modern reader to disentangle, as Pamphilia struggles to express her fluctuating emotions through a literary form which, in the hands of Sir Philip Sidney at least, had seemed to value performance above personal feeling, and in which a man typically writes about a woman whom he is unable, for one reason or another, to possess.

Sidney's *Astrophil and Stella* anatomised the love of the courtier Astrophil ('lover of a star') for a beautiful court lady, Stella ('star'), believed to have been Penelope Devereux, who married Lord Rich around the time when the sonnets were written. The sonnets express the lady's beauty and power over her lover, and his attempts to conquer sexual desire. In his musings Astrophil reveals both the private face of the lover, a man writing in solitude from his study, and the courtly lover pursuing his public life, appearing at a tournament and debating affairs of state, indifferent to jibes about his absent-mindedness. Despite his protests about love's torments the poet, writing in a long tradition of male poets, never doubts his authority to write about love (for an audience that seems always present to his imagination if not in the flesh), and he remains confidently in control of his subject matter, milking its potential for amusement through his verbal dexterity. Like the troubadour poets who developed the love song as an opportunity to show off their poetic virtuosity, Sidney uses the sonnet as a vehicle to exercise his technical and inventive skills, producing poems whose polish can seem to mask an emotional vacuum. Despite his extended scrutiny of desire, there is little sense of a woman's inviting body behind his sonnets' elegant posturing. His light, ironic approach solicits an equally relaxed response. The sonnets may delight by their playfulness, but they don't arouse empathy or strong emotion. As a statement of the power and persistence of lust, they lack conviction. Fifty years before Sidney, Sir Thomas Wyatt was writing about desire with a raw energy that still delivers across the centuries its message of longing, loss and bitterness. For Lady Mary, the model that was closest to hand, when she came to write her anatomy of thwarted passion, was her uncle's refinement of the language of love into a poetry whose dominant mode was irony, control and self-conscious artistry.

Lady Mary would have known another sonnet cycle, which seems to resonate more closely with *Pamphilia to Amphilanthus* both in approach and in biographical connections. Shakespeare's sonnets had been published in 1609. Their intense, intimate voice and frank discussion of feeling may have influenced Lady Mary in choosing the sonnet as a means of exploring violent and painful emotions, and the fluctuations and ambiguities of desire. She may also have had personal reasons for wanting to associate her poems with Shakespeare's sequence. Shakespeare begins his cycle with a series of poems written to a beautiful 'young man' whose identity has long been the subject of debate. The printer's dedication to 'Master W. H.' has only fuelled the controversy. One strong candidate for the role is Lady Mary's lover William Herbert, third Earl of Pembroke, who was co-dedicatee of the Shakespeare First Folio in 1623. The final sonnets in Shakespeare's sequence revolve around a 'dark lady', whose infidelity (possibly with the young beau) arouses the poet's disgust and heartache. Again, the identity of the lady remains a matter for speculation, but one name mentioned is that of Pembroke's mistress Mary Fitton. It has even been suggested that Lady Mary Wroth might have been Shakespeare's enchantress, in a love triangle that links the two poets with the subject of their sonnets (if indeed Pembroke was Shakespeare's 'Master W. H.' as well as Lady Mary's Amphilanthus).[61]

The question of autobiographical references in both *Urania* and *Pamphilia to Amphilanthus* can only be hypothesised, although the timing of the work, Lady Mary's evidently passionate association with her cousin (she would hardly have borne two illegitimate children to a man she didn't love) and Pembroke's reputation as a ladies' man, as well as many details in the fiction, suggest that Lady Mary drew freely on aspects of her own life in imagining Pamphilia's history. Her courage in venturing into print on such sensitive material should not be underestimated. In theme and approach, she was entering new territory for women writing in England, and it is unlikely that she was able to draw encouragement from European examples of female boldness in print. In *Pamphilia to Amphilanthus* the speaker runs the gamut of emotion from jealousy and depression, to desire and its sublimation through love of God. Constancy remains her mantra, recalling Heloise's declarations of faith in her letters to Abelard and Castelloza's boast of fidelity to her contemptuous lover, neither of which writers Lady Mary is likely to have read, although she may have heard of Heloise. Like Heloise, she may well have drawn on Ovid's *Heroides*, with its images of faithful, yearning women, but there is no guarantee that she knew of the work of Marie de France and Christine de Pizan, both of whom wrote eloquently about female fidelity, or that she was aware of the accomplished love sonnets written decades earlier by Louise Labé in France and by the Italian poet Gaspara Stampa.[62] Indeed, almost the only female poet whom Lady Mary seems to acknowledge is

Sappho, fragments of whose work she may have come across in anthologies or translation and whose history she would have read in Ovid's colourful version in the *Heroides*, where Sappho is presented as driven mad by her passion for the handsome young ferryman Phaon. The myth of Sappho's suicidal leap from the precipice at Leucadia metamorphoses in *Urania* to a cure for love.[63] Marguerite de Navarre's *Heptameron*, a collection of prose stories first published in 1558 and partly available in English translation, included some tales dealing with constancy in love, but again there is no evidence currently available that Lady Mary had read these stories.

Among her near contemporaries the greatest female influence was surely that of her aunt, Mary Sidney, Countess of Pembroke, with whom Lady Mary associates herself on the title page of the published *Urania* and who appears in the romance as the queen of Naples, who was as 'perfect in Poetry, and all other Princely vertues as any woman that ever liv'd'.[64] The connection with her renowned aunt was not entirely to Lady Mary's advantage. Mary Sidney may have edited her brother's *Arcadia*, but she also completed his translation of the Psalms, an exercise in piety which Lord Denny threw in Lady Mary's face during the controversy that followed the publication of the first part of *Urania*. Feeling himself and his family slandered in an episode in the romance, Denny wrote angry letters and a bitter poem to Lady Mary, in which he told her to 'leave idle bookes alone', and advised her to 'redeem the time with writing as large a volume of heavenly lays and holy love as you have of lascivious tales and amorous toys; that at the last you may follow the example of your virtuous and learned aunt'.[65] Lady Mary responded with a witty poem, in which she cleverly mirrors his rhymes and turns his words back against her attacker, but the comparison to Mary Sidney may well have hurt her self-esteem. Its timing was particularly unfortunate. What her aunt and the other female members of her family thought of the *Urania* and its accompanying poems, and to what extent the work had been circulated and commented on in manuscript, is unknown, although it could be speculated that Lady Barbara at least might have counselled caution. By the time the work was on public sale, both Mary Sidney and Barbara Sidney had unexpectedly died within a few months of one another, a double loss that may have influenced Lady Mary's withdrawal from the controversy over the publication of her work.

Lady Mary's relationship with William Herbert, however precious in terms of personal feeling, was an affair with a married man, which jeopardised her public reputation. It no doubt caused embarrassment to her family, and conflict with her parents and other relatives. Herbert's failure to recognise his children and Lady Mary's continued financial difficulties suggest that she could not look to her lover for any practical assistance and this, too, may have been deeply wounding. The difficulties for a woman of a relationship not recognised by law, Church or society reflected the double standard for sexual behaviour characteristic of Western mores throughout the Middle Ages and Renaissance. It was a legacy of guilt and retribution based on the teachings of the early Church Fathers and increasingly embedded in social practice. Whether or not *Pamphilia to Amphilanthus* is to be read as an account of her turmoil over Herbert, Lady Mary's personal experience must have come to her aid in describing Pamphilia's conflicted passion. The sonnet sequence is a study of a woman's responses to a love affair that appears to have been both clandestine and increasingly one-sided.[66] It reads like a novel in verse, an intense psychological drama in which the narrator obsessively records her changing feelings and fluctuating hopes. Unlike the worldly Astrophil, distance and objectivity are far beyond the tortured speaker's capacities. Even her lover seems barely present; what matters is the power of her emotions and her struggle for self-control.

As an emblem of her powerlessness under love's sway, the sequence begins with a dream vision of Venus and her son Cupid, who appear in their classical guise in a chariot drawn by doves. Venus presses a flaming heart to the dreamer's breast and instructs her son to shoot his arrow. The deed is done, the heart is martyred. Since then, 'O mee,' cries the dreamer, 'a lover I have binn.'[67] Controlled by the capricious Cupid, the woman is plunged into a maelstrom of feeling, in which she describes the pain and restlessness of her impassioned imagination, drawing freely and with great fluency on the conventional imagery of the Petrarchan lover, which in turn recalls the favourite themes of troubadour lyrics. Fire and flames, arrows and darts signal love's onslaught on the defenceless victim. Spring arrives with its bounty of blossom and birdsong, but nothing revives the sorrowful heart. Trapped in the winter of unhappy love, Pamphilia remains indifferent to sunlight and heat. Night shrouds her grief from prying eyes; its darkness mirrors love's melancholy and mourning. Sleep is her consolation, since dreams unite her with her lover's image. Hope betrays her, grief destroys her; only love, or death, can bring relief. Or maybe poetry. What is extraordinary in this welter of love, fear and anxiety is the poet's disciplined use of the sonnet to reproduce her mental turmoil. Wrestling with demons, the writer yet brings off the heroic feat of revitalising an almost exhausted literary vocabulary to mirror, with painful fidelity, her suffering subject's skewed responses to the most basic cycles of the natural world.

Pierced by love's arrow, the greatest temptation is to abdicate responsibility. A prey to doubt and jealousy, she imagines Cupid as a mischievous boy toying with human feelings. Then, in a *corona* or crown of fourteen sonnets, where the last line of one sonnet becomes the first of the next, she enters the labyrinth of love, following the thread that will lead her to 'soules content'.[68] For a time, she dwells on love's benefits, worshipping Cupid in his adult, regal mode in words that reflect the bliss of female mystics, bowed at the feet of Christ:

Love is the shining starr of blessings light;
 The fervent fire of zeale, the roote of peace,
 The lasting lampe fed with the oyle of right;
 Image of fayth, and wombe for joyes increase.[69]

'Please him,' she urges herself, 'serve him, glory in his might,' and

 . . . firme hee'll bee, as innosencye white,
 Cleere as th'ayre, warme as sunn beames, as day light,
 Just as truthe, constant as fate . . .[70]

Yet, try as she may, this hopeful vision fades and she plunges, at the end of the *corona*, back into the hell of jealousy and suspicion:

 Yett other mischiefs faile nott to attend,
  As enimies to you, my foes must bee;
  Curst jealousie doth all her forces bend
  To my undoing; thus my harmes I see.[71]

In the closing couplet she returns to the quandary in which she began, lost in love's maze:

 Soe though in Love I fervently doe burne,
 In this strange labourinth how shall I turne?[72]

The sequence ends, in the published version, with a run of poems that appear to accept love's sway, with its due measure of pleasure and pain.[73] The final sonnet, signed with Pamphilia's name, declares her intention to leave 'storys of great love' to younger pens:

 And thus leave off, what's past showes you can love,
 Now lett your constancy your honor prove[.][74]

It is an extraordinary performance, charting the progress of a mind almost literally disintegrating under the stress of thwarted desire, and then the long, slow process of rebuilding equanimity and developing defences against a love that is almost too painful to be borne. Nothing quite like this had ever been written by a woman in English; its closest parallels were with the words of female mystics, struggling through the snags and snares of human frailty to come closer to God.

After the flurry, scandal (and perhaps disappointment) of publication, Lady Mary seems to have retired from public life. Scanty records reveal a pattern of continued debt and frequent changes of residence. She probably died in the early 1650s and her work, including a play, *Love's Victorie*, vanished into a long obscurity. This is a pity, because she deserves both notice and praise. Bold and imaginative, she tried, like Castelloza and the Countess of Dia, to describe a love affair from the woman's point of view. Using the tools to hand, the extravagances of popular romance and the almost moribund language of the Petrarchan sonnet, she explored the possibilities and varieties of women's love through a cast of vividly imagined heroines from Pamphilia to the mysterious shepherdess Urania. Her outspokenness and lack of discretion caused outrage to a courtly audience too blinkered by convention and misogyny to applaud her originality and honesty, but her work has survived, even if few now read it and even fewer would claim her as a literary grandmother. She does, however, have many natural heirs among women writers, not least the poet Elizabeth Barrett who, like Lady Mary, turned both to the novel (in Barrett's case the novel-poem *Aurora Leigh*) and the sonnet sequence to explore her experience of love.

Recalled to Life:
Elizabeth Barrett Browning

How does it feel to be rescued from sickness and seclusion by a passionate suitor? Elizabeth Barrett tried to describe the shock of such a reprieve in the first of her *Sonnets from the Portuguese*, a sequence of forty-four poems written during her courtship by Robert Browning. The sonnet begins with the speaker reflecting on her troubled past: 'The sweet, sad years, the melancholy years'. Her musings are abruptly interrupted:

> a mystic Shape did move
> Behind me, and drew me backward by the hair,
> And a voice said in mastery while I strove, . .
> 'Guess now who holds thee?'—'Death,' I said. But, there,
> The silver answer rang, . . 'Not Death, but Love.'

The violence of love's arrival is emphasised by Barrett's sense of being literally seized by the hair and pulled back from the brink of the grave. Almost from their first exchange of letters, written months before they met, a spark was struck between the two poets, ignited by Browning's ardour and decisiveness. Deeply responsive to passion and its claims, Barrett doubted her worthiness to be loved or her ability to meet her lover's vitality. Despite her qualms, hope stepped into her stuffy bedroom in Wimpole Street along with Browning's first flirtatious letter in January 1845. 'I love your verses with all my heart, dear Miss Barrett [...] and I love you too,' he wrote impulsively, and she was unable to resist his confident demand on her senses and her deepest emotions.[75]

When Elizabeth Barrett received Browning's first letter, she was thirty-eight years old and an established poet, but worn almost to a wraith by illness, grief and the laudanum she took to alleviate pain and steady her nerves. As a teenager she had been struck down by some mysterious ailment, an atrophy doctors treated with regimens that seemed to reinforce her paralysis and isolation from normal healthy life. Although rumour hinted at damage following a riding accident (Browning was at first convinced that she was immobilised by spinal injury), the evidence suggests that Barrett was suffering from chronic lung disease, which smog-filled city air and damp English winters did little to alleviate. For years she led a restricted life in the family home in Wimpole Street, more or less immured in her bedroom, in a seclusion that enabled her to pursue her passion for poetry, scholarship and correspondence. Within a year of hearing from Browning, her life and prospects had been transformed by his friendship. As a consequence of his irruption into her life, she would eventually elope with him to Italy, to a new life as wife and mother, settling in Florence where she would work with tremendous vigour and determination on her political poems and an astonishing verse-novel, her picaresque account of the life and struggles of the feminist poet Aurora Leigh. The stages of Barrett's metamorphosis are recorded in the letters to and from Browning during their twenty-month courtship, and in the poems Elizabeth published some years later as *Sonnets from the Portuguese*. A writer in every fibre of her being, she meticulously documented love's pursuit and mastery in her correspondence with her admirer, and in the sonnets she secretly composed to record the hesitant stages of her recall to life.

Elizabeth Barrett was no stranger to love. She was an avid reader of novels, preferring stories with a strong, thoughtful heroine like Laura in Mary Brunton's *Self-Control* and, like the novelist Susan

Ferrier, another favourite, she was a keen critic of women's wrongs in marriage. Sometimes she had nightmares in which she dreamt she was married and woke with relief to consider her single state: 'I never *will* marry.' At other times she relented, but only if she could find 'an angel at the very least'.[76] Barrett was fascinated by the nature and attributes of angels. She wrote a long dramatic poem about the crucifixion, *The Seraphim*, which is largely a dialogue between two higher angels, Ador and Zerah, and *A Drama of Exile*, which explores Eve's feelings after the expulsion from Eden, a verse-play in which angels again play an important role. In the *Sonnets from the Portuguese* Barrett's early thinking and reading about God and angels came together in a narrative in which she reverses the trend of erotic poetry by relinquishing her claims to God and heaven in favour of earthly love with an (angelic) human spouse.

From an early age Barrett's feminism was an important strand in her thinking. As a teenager she read Mary Wollstonecraft with admiring attention and became a fan of the passionate novels of George Sand, to whom she dedicated two rather muddled sonnets. In 'A Desire', she praises Sand as a 'large-brained woman' and 'large-hearted man', but the best she can hope for such an anomalous being is transformation into the androgynous form of an angel (seraphs, again!), which will allow her to enjoy the praise and glory she so fully deserves. Barrett's confusion over how to estimate Sand, whose cross-dressing, cigar-smoking and love affairs with members of both sexes had scandalised Europe, was never fully resolved. All her life Barrett wrestled with what Virginia Woolf later described as the 'Angel in the House', the spectre of passive womanhood the female writer has to subdue before she can speak out honestly about her opinions and experiences. Her fullest statement of woman's nature and genius was expressed in *Aurora Leigh*, written after marriage and motherhood had enriched her understanding of the possibilities and problems of sexual relationships. In her fledgling years as poet, although she wrote the ballads and lyrics considered appropriate to female sensibilities, Barrett reworked cliché to question contemporary pieties about male and female sex roles. In typically 'tear-jerking' poems such as 'Bertha in the Lane' and the 'The Romaunt of the Page', she managed to feed the public taste for sentimentality, while subtly denouncing the emotional passivity that women were supposed to embrace. On the whole, her reviewers caught the pathos and missed the irony, to Elizabeth's sarcastic delight.[77] In the meantime her own capacity for passion remained undeveloped.

In the letters that poured from her pen in Wimpole Street to her fellow writer Mary Russell Mitford, Barrett reveals a fondness for gossip and an avid interest in her fellow creatures, which suggest a natural bent towards intimacy and the pleasures of companionship. Her secluded lifestyle and an almost pathological anxiety about meeting strangers meant that her friendships evolved through letters rather than in person. As for suitors, it would be a brave man who ventured to court any of the three surviving daughters of Edward Barrett Moulton-Barrett, who had long made it clear to all his children, the boys included, that their duty lay within the family circle. Outsiders in the form of potential husbands and wives would not be welcome. Given his happy marriage to Mary Moulton-Barrett, Edward's possessiveness of his children seems at best ungenerous. From Elizabeth's perspective, her mother's lifelong enslavement to her husband and children, and her premature death at the age of forty-seven were warnings of the toll conventional wedlock could exact from women. Barrett's own early venture into attachment (her adulation of the blind scholar Hugh Stuart Boyd) plunged her into jealousy and self-doubt. The death of her adored brother Bro, for which she partly held herself responsible, strengthened her instinctive recoil from any close relationship outside her immediate family as potentially dangerous and damaging. Barrett's physical weakness, and the myth of invalidism with which her family colluded, further enhanced her remoteness from marriage and child-rearing, the normal concerns of women of her class. Instead, she pampered her spaniel Flush, read till her temples ached and her eyes watered in her airless room and, while her body wasted from inactivity and a persistent anorexia, channelled her restless intelligence and capacious imagination into poetry.

Barrett was nothing if not ambitious, and her subject matter and the forms of poetry she tackled reveal her determination not to be marginalised as a 'poetess' or 'feminine' versifier. A voracious reader of the English poets and a student of Greek and Hebrew, by the age of twelve she had embarked on *The Battle of Marathon*, a long epic poem that mimicked the style of Pope. Her first volume of poetry, *An Essay on Mind*, published when she was only twenty, once again nailed her intellectual colours to the mast. This was followed by a translation of Aeschylus's *Prometheus Unbound* and verse collections that increasingly attracted attention. Her two-volume *Poems*, published in 1844, was a critical success, and one poem in particular, 'Lady Geraldine's Courtship', inspired Browning's first, audaciously complimentary letter. This 'romance of the age', as Barrett describes it, tells the story of the love affair between a penniless poet and an aristocratic beauty, in which the woman takes the initiative to claim the proud poet as her worthy partner and mentor. Among the poems the couple read together is 'some "Pomegranate"' from Browning, which 'if cut deep down the middle, / Shows a heart within blood-tinctured, of a veined humanity', a reference to the *Bells and Pomegranates* pamphlets that Browning was in the process of publishing.

Still struggling for public recognition, Browning was gratified by this mention, which placed him in the company of such well-established poets as Wordsworth and Tennyson. Reluctant to be seen as a literary groupie, he hesitated to approach the famous Miss Barrett, but felt he owed her an acknowledgement of her public praise. His letter, charming, ebullient and extravagant, caught her attention because of the promise it seemed to offer of the literary dialogue her intelligence craved. If Browning were willing to engage in a conversation about what mattered most to her, her 'faults' as a writer, he would 'confer a lasting obligation'.[78]

So began a remarkable exchange between two gifted, emotional poets, a courtship conducted at first entirely by letter. Once Browning had accepted that words were all he was going to receive from Miss Barrett (her taboo was absolute against meeting until a vaguely defined and repeatedly postponed 'spring'), he settled to the challenge of winning the confidence and esteem of his playful but wary correspondent. Obsessed by language and the struggle with words and meaning, both participants in this game of love benefited from the necessity of getting to know one another on paper. Again and again, the letters circled around the problem of Robert's 'exaggerated' response to 'dear Miss Barrett', his bouncing enthusiasm and instant ardour, and Elizabeth's fear that his interest, any man's interest, would inevitably cool, particularly if he met the feeble shadow that she felt herself to be. Used to effusive letters from male admirers, she was distrustful of paper gallantry. Another favourite theme was the question of which was the superior poet (each insisted on awarding the palm to the other) and, in particular, Elizabeth's dislike of being praised. Ultra-sensitive to any hint of patronage or flattery, she demanded to be told the truth about her work. What she wanted was to be taken seriously by a poet whose writing and potential she held in the highest regard. Browning was to be her mentor, pointing out weaknesses and infelicities, and forcing her to aspire towards the highest standard. All this meant that Browning had to rein in his natural impatience and moderate the pace of his wooing to her more cautious measure. The reward was mutual understanding, the gradual movement towards the trust and intimacy Elizabeth craved. Very early in their correspondence she tells him with engaging candour, 'I do not, you say, know yourself . . you. I only know abilities & faculties. Well, then! teach me yourself . . you.'[79] A man who placed the highest value on his personal privacy ('no foot over threshold of mine!' he was to admonish celebrity seekers in his poem 'House'), Browning was compelled by his interest in Elizabeth to reveal his nature and aspirations, an unfolding of wrappings of reserve that gradually exposed the secret self behind his ebullient public mask.

Just as Browning had a persona to protect, so too did Elizabeth. In a moment of apparent candour she spells out for him the myth of solitude on which she had founded her security. 'You seem to have drunken of the cup of life full, with the sun shining on it,' she tells him. Her own life has been very different:

I have lived only inwardly,—or with *sorrow*, for a strong emotion. Before this seclusion of my illness, I was secluded still—& there are few of the youngest women in the world who have not seen more, heard more, known more, of society, than I, who am scarcely to be called young now. I grew up in the country .. had no social opportunities, .. had my heart in books & poetry, .. & my experience, in reveries. [...] It was a lonely life—growing green like the grass around it. Books & dreams were what I lived in—& domestic life only seemed to buzz gently around, like the bees about the grass. And so time passed, & passed—and afterwards, when my illness came & I seemed to stand at the edge of the world with all done, & no prospect (as appeared at one time) of ever passing the threshold of one room again,—why then, I turned to thinking with some bitterness (after the greatest sorrow of my life had given me room & time to breathe) that I had stood blind in this temple I was about to leave[.][80]

This is somewhat disingenuous as a summary of Barrett's early life, which was spent in her father's country house and capacious grounds in the company of loving parents, servants and a troop of younger siblings, with all that such a childhood implies of merriment, companionship and physical exercise, as well as the rivalries and bondings that fluctuate among any group of children growing up together. However, as a statement of her own story about herself it has the seductive charm of fairy tale or legend, recalling the Sleeping Beauty dreaming through the decades before her lover's kiss, or the Lady of Shalott languid in front of her mirror. It was an invitation to disruption, which Browning found almost irresistible. For years, he had kept a print of a favourite painting above his desk: the *Andromeda* of Polidoro da Caravaggio, showing Perseus's rescue of the maiden (naked and chained to a rock) from a fiery dragon.[81] The theme of rescue fascinated Browning, but he was also alert to the reciprocity in the relationship between the maiden and her champion. Andromeda may (desperately) be in need of a rescuer, but, as Browning was far too perceptive to ignore, Perseus is equally dependent on her helplessness in order to fulfil his own destiny or self-image as a saviour. Whatever its mythological inspiration, the thought of Miss Barrett trapped on her sofa aroused Browning's chivalry (a quality for which she frequently teased him) and his unusual sympathy for the weak and suffering. Like St George on his charger, rushing to the aid of Princess Sabra, he was determined to rescue her from the twin dragons of isolation and her formidable father, another weapon in the battery with which Elizabeth attempted to keep her ardent suitor at a safe distance.

The satisfying process of mutual discovery was almost sabotaged by Browning's impetuous response to their first meeting. Longed for by him, dreaded by her, this significant event finally took place on 20 May, four months after his first letter. Michele Gordigiani's portraits of the Brownings, now in the collection of the National Portrait Gallery in London, were painted many years later in Italy, but the representation of Elizabeth at least was apparently very like and the paintings may give an accurate impression of how the couple appeared to one another when they met in her shaded room that

Tuesday afternoon. A petite, delicate figure, Elizabeth worried about her thinness and pallor, and her faint, rather squeaky voice. She was dressed, as always, in black, which added to the general severity of her presentation, but the vitality of her sensitive mouth, her dark eyes and luxuriant dark hair made a profound impact on Browning. In later letters he was to write longingly of her lips and eyes and hair, and her physical presence became increasingly necessary to him as a way of quickly breaking down barriers or clearing up misunderstandings, but also, quite simply, because of her sexual allure for him. He clearly ached to run his fingers through those silky ringlets and kiss the too-wide, talkative mouth. When Barrett eventually allowed him to have a lock of her hair, it was a mark of her acceptance of him as a lover. Like the three stages of his kisses, gradually progressing from fingers to forehead to lips, each significant step in their erotic journey was recorded in her sonnets, in which Elizabeth acknowledged the thrill of sensual love, while cherishing what to her was of the utmost importance, a lover who could meet her high standards of purity and integrity. If God must always be looking over her shoulder, then what He saw must be worthy of His gaze. At their first meeting, the pleasures of sexual exploration still lay in the future. Many months later Elizabeth told Robert that her ambition, when they began their correspondence, 'was simply that you should forget I was a woman'. What she wanted was a friend, to teach her what he knew about art and human nature. Even when they met, she claimed, her feeling about Robert was free 'from the remotest presentiment' of what would later occur. Shy and nervous with strangers, her main preoccupation, that May afternoon, was to acquit herself without embarrassment in the presence of a man whom she admired as a poet ('I am a great hero-worshipper'), and only knew through the written word.[82]

Unlike Elizabeth's reedy whisper, there was nothing sibilant about Browning's voice; indeed, he wrote at once to enquire anxiously whether he had tired her by speaking too loudly, as his friends so often complained. Nor was he in the least retiring. Several years younger than Elizabeth (he was just thirty-three), short-legged, but powerful and vigorous, he was bold and direct in gaze and speech, brisk and energetic, and with a ready fund of ideas and opinions. With his glossy brown hair, clear complexion and well-fitting clothes, he could not have failed to make an impression, although Elizabeth's immediate (and predictable) response after their meeting was a letter arguing about who was benefiting whom by their friendship, and how to name what she insisted on calling his 'kindness' to her.[83] Impatient with such punctilios, Robert replied in terms that caused a shocked withdrawal on Elizabeth's part. His letter was returned, and was immediately destroyed by Browning, so that its contents can only be surmised, but he seems to have made a declaration of love, which she rejected as entirely inappropriate to her situation and indeed the result of his own fantasies and exaggerations.[84] In her reply she ordered him to forget his words for ever, so that they would die out between the two of them alone, 'like a misprint between you and the printer'.[85] Later, Elizabeth was to ask (fruitlessly) for the return of this letter, but at this point in their relationship she seems to have felt bitterly hurt by it, a response that can be explained by her profound sense of herself as a shell of a woman, an intellect rather than a creature of flesh and blood. She flinched from Browning's declaration as from a public humiliation. It was not that she feared he was making fun of her, she already thought too well of him to believe that; but she was wary of his romantic imagination, his power to invent and worship a woman who didn't exist, the troubadour element in the male poet's psyche, which Elizabeth's reading and experience had taught her deeply to distrust.

After this setback Browning learnt to curb his enthusiasm and the courtship progressed at the more leisurely pace that suited Elizabeth's caution and need to understand her suitor through and through. It was an arrangement many women even in more sexually liberated times might have found appealing. For months, she was able to savour the attentions of a passionate and devoted lover, for whom a lock of hair or a kiss on the brow were precious concessions. It also allowed her to probe the depth and nature of his love. '[L]ove me for love's sake,' she begged in Sonnet xiv. Love that depended on good looks, fortune, worldly success and even fallible human responses such as generosity or pity was subject to the erosions of time and mutability. Only quintessential love, which she seems to have defined as spontaneous delight in another's being, survived and would endure beyond the grave into eternity.

In the meantime Browning continued to visit, and when they couldn't see one another they exchanged letters and commented on each other's work. As far as Elizabeth was concerned, here at last was a worthy mentor with whom to explore all the knotty questions about poetry, fame and criticism that she yearned to resolve. It was a partnership, a close collaboration that in turn enriched their poetry. He read her translation of *Prometheus Bound*, making almost eight pages of notes.[86] She in turn read and annotated his poems, writing pages of commentary on his work, including the plays *Luria* and *A Soul's Tragedy*.[87] At one point Browning even fretted that she was too busy writing to him and correcting his verses to produce 'more Berthas and Caterinas and Geraldines, more great and beautiful poems of which I shall be—how proud!'[88] He need not have worried. Elizabeth *was* writing, albeit in secret, and the fruits of her work were offered to Browning some years later when the couple were married, already parents of the beloved boy 'Pen', and living in Florence. Her reticence about showing him the sequence of sonnets is perhaps understandable. However polished and versatile, however innovatory in their account of a woman's reluctant, then joyous acknowledgement of love reciprocated and fulfilled, they are also deeply intimate. In her self-portrait as an ageing, depressed woman brought to life by a virile younger man, Barrett may have felt that she had much to lose by revealing the sonnets too early. Writing to her sister Arabella in January 1851, she described her reticence about showing the poems to Robert, because of his dislike of 'personal' poetry. When he did eventually see them he was 'much touched & pleased' and insisted on publication. They agreed to 'slip them in' to her latest volume, choosing the ambiguous title as 'some sort of veil'. With its suggestion of a work in translation, *Sonnets from the Portuguese* allowed the public Mrs Browning to distance herself from the speaker of these confessional verses. Privately, however, the title was a coded reference to Robert's fondness for Elizabeth's poem 'Catarina to Camoens'. 'In a loving fancy,' she told Arabella, 'he had always associated me with Catarina, and the poem had affected him to tears, he said, again & again. So, Catarina being a Portuguese, we put "Sonnets from the Portuguese"[.]'[89]

Some years after Elizabeth's death, Browning recalled his first sight of the poems in a letter to his friend Julia Wedgwood:

> Yes, that was a strange, heavy crown, that wreath of Sonnets, put on me one morning unawares, three years after it had been twined,—all this delay, because I happened early to say something against putting one's loves into verse: then again, I said something else on the other side, one evening at Lucca,— and next morning she said hesitatingly 'Do you know I once wrote some poems about *you?*'—and then—'There they are, if you care to see them,'—and there was the little Book I have here—with the last Sonnet dated two days before our marriage. How I see the gesture, and hear the tones,—and, for the matter of that, see the window at which I was standing, with the tall mimosa in front, and little church-court to the right[.][90]

Browning's record of the incident is richly suggestive. He describes the poems as a 'crown', recalling the laurel wreath traditionally twisted about the brows of a winning poet, but also love's crown awarded to the successful suitor. At the same time the 'crown' is 'strange' and 'heavy', which implies a certain ambivalence about the gift. The poems weighed him down, perhaps because he became so closely identified in the public mind as their recipient, the passionate lover who recalled the writer to life. To a man as private as Browning, however much he wished to encourage publication of poems whose worth he must instantly have recognised, the commentary and speculation with which the sonnets were received must have been repugnant. There was also the unresolved battle with Elizabeth over which of the two was the benefactor in the relationship. The sonnets forced him to appear, in public at least, as the generous partner, the one who had most to offer and to lose. Browning's detailed recall of the event, his nostalgic reference to the window, the mimosa and the church court beyond, and most of all the memory of Elizabeth's voice and gesture as she offered him 'the little Book', imply that the giving of the sonnets was a deeply significant event, a moment of surprise and revelation when he first learnt of his wife's creative response to his passionate, intense courtship.

The question of how far the *Sonnets from the Portuguese* are autobiographical can never be resolved completely, although the evidence (including Barrett's own description) suggests a close correlation between life and art. A careful reading of the sonnets alongside the courtship letters implies that she used the poems to reflect and comment on important issues in her early relationship with Browning. Many of the sonnets are closely tied in incident and theme to the letters, although Barrett sometimes gives a slightly different spin on events when writing them up in poetry. Each poem establishes a marker in the progress of her thoughts, the next milestone in a journey which reads, in a similar way to Lady Mary's *Pamphilia to Amphilanthus*, like a psychological novel in verse. Wordsworth's dictum of 'emotion recollected in tranquillity' is a helpful description of Barrett's procedure, with its hint of order imposed on the rawness and fluctuation of immediate impressions. There is nothing random about the storyline, which follows a logical, if circuitous, progression from rejection to acceptance of love. Technically, Barrett made every attempt to produce sonnets as carefully wrought as any written by Petrarch and his successors. She had translated several of the *Rime sparse*, perhaps in an attempt to understand the form more fully, and was well read in the male English sonneteers. Her reinvention of the Petrarchan sonnet was in tune with her customary poetic practice, the revival of a traditional form to express new, often subtly subversive ideas.

In writing her account of a woman's experience of love, Barrett did not draw in any significant way on the slender female sonnet tradition, of which her knowledge (like that of almost all women writers of the period) was scanty. In one of her letters to Browning she mentions the Italian sonneteer Vittoria Colonna, but she had almost certainly never read Lady Mary Wroth.[91] There are, however, similarities between the two poets. Barrett's take on the traditional theme of a poet's worship for a distant and unattainable beloved is, like Lady Mary's, innovatory in presenting the woman's point of view. She goes further than Lady Mary in remaking the sonnet to suit her own needs as poet and storyteller. Out goes the enervated vocabulary of Cupid and his darts in favour of language that reflects her own reading and experience and is, for its period, surprisingly outspoken. From that first peremptory tug on her hair, the speaker cannot help responding to her lover's erotic appeal and she writes about her feelings in terms that have a powerful undercurrent of sexual awareness. Even when she rejects his pressing invitation to love, she is conscious of his presence and of the vitality that at first makes her shrink even further into her shell of insufficiency.

Recasting the troubadour roles of poet and *domna*, Barrett begins by seeing herself as a 'poor, tired, wandering singer', who stands outside a lighted window watching her suitor, also a singer but chief musician to a queen, perform in a splendid palace, admired by ladies with brilliant eyes. What can such a man want with a weeping woman or her desolate home, with its broken panes, birds' nests in the eaves and cricket voice chirping in solitude? All that she can offer are the ashes of a heart consumed in grief, barely quenched flames which will scorch him if he comes too close. His presence haunts her, the 'face of all the world is changed' by their meeting, and 'What I do / And what I dream include thee, as the wine / Must taste of its own grapes'.[92] In thrall to his image, how can she reward such a 'princely giver', who has opened the gold and purple of his heart to a woman blanched by tears? From this position of desolation, she moves cautiously to an understanding of the trans-figurative power of love, a tentative acceptance that she may have something to offer, although, for her lover's well-being, she must renounce and set him free.[93] Eventually, she finds the confidence to sink her heavy heart into his 'calmly great / Deep being'.[94] He has seen her 'soul's true face' and not been repelled.[95]

Barrett's debate about love and worthiness insists on the necessity of unconditional love. Love me for love's sake, but also know me for who I am: these are the twin tasks the speaker sets her lover, who, like the fairy-tale prince whose colours he wears, rises splendidly to her challenge. Unlike the troubadours, who preferred to worship across a great void, Barrett demands an intimacy based on unflinch-ing knowledge. When it comes to the choice between earthly and spiritual love, she again breaks with tradition and chooses human passion. In Sonnet XXII she introduces the (surely consciously erotic) image of the lovers' souls, like winged angels, standing:

> erect and strong,
> Face to face, silent, drawing nigh and nigher,
> Until the lengthening wings break into fire
> At either curvèd point [...]

This moment of conjunction is perfect happiness: why aspire higher and spoil their 'deep, dear silence' with the angels' song? On earth, their pure spirits will have a 'place to stand and love in for a day, / With darkness and the death-hour rounding it'.[96] From here it is only a short step to Sonnet xxiii: 'I yield the grave for thy sake, and exchange / My near sweet view of Heaven, for earth with thee!' and, even more extravagantly, her exclamation, 'I who looked for only God, found *thee*!' in Sonnet xxvii. Finally, her lover becomes 'New angel mine, unhoped for in the world!'[97] From some perspectives the substitution of human for divine love might seem sacrilegious, although the speaker qualifies it by her constant reference to the transience and insubstantiality of life. Love, she knows, however deep and true, must in the end forsake its human raiment; by accepting earthly passion, she is only postponing her long engagement with the grave.

Eternity fades, however, in the contemplation of present bliss. Once she was fixed by sorrow like 'a bee shut in a crystalline', but with her lover's purple flung around her the speaker is able tentatively to 'count the ways' of love, and consider its implications for her future.[98] She takes out his letters with tremulous fingers, the 'mute [. . .] white' sheets seeming to have a life of their own.[99] She basks in his affection, twines round him like the vine about a stout tree trunk and loves to hear him call her by her pet name.[100] His kisses fall on her like benisons, enabling her finally to claim him as 'My love, my own'.[101] Already regretting the family affection that she will leave behind, the '[h]ome-talk and blessing and the common kiss / That comes to each in turn', she asks him wistfully, 'If I leave all for thee, wilt thou exchange / And be all to me?'[102] Even these losses, however, she is able to sustain, abandoning the past and its 'pages with long musing curled', as she writes 'new' her 'future's epigraph'.[103]

Like Madeline and Porphyro in Keats's 'The Eve of St Agnes', the lovers did eventually flee away, escaping Mr Barrett's anger and the restrictive atmosphere of Wimpole Street for the milder winters of Italy and, eventually, years of productive companionship and writing before Elizabeth's death in 1861. It is a romantic story and most Victorian critics chose to read the sonnets as exemplars of woman's greatest role in life: to love her mate almost to the point of idolatry. This sentimental reading disregards Barrett's scrupulous analysis of the progress and conditions of love, and her reworking of the sonnet cycle to suit her individual voice. Her achievement captured the imagination of Christina Rossetti, who a few years later published her own sonnet sequence, 'Monna Innominata', the songs of an 'unnamed woman', which Rossetti specifically linked to the troubadour tradition, to Dante's Beatrice and Petrarch's Laura, and to the 'Portuguese Sonnets' of Elizabeth Barrett.

In her introduction to 'Monna Innominata' Rossetti cuttingly describes Beatrice and Laura as 'resplendent with charms', but, in her view at least, 'scant of attractiveness'. Looking back to the troubadour period and unaware of the trobairitz poems, which had yet to be rediscovered, she imagines 'many a lady as sharing her lover's poetic aptitude' and reflects on the 'tender' self-portrait such a lady might have left, could she have spoken for herself. '[H]ad the Great Poetess of our own day and nation only been unhappy instead of happy,' she muses, 'her circumstances would have invited her to bequeath to us, in lieu of the "Portuguese Sonnets," an inimitable "donna innominata" drawn not from fancy but from feeling, and worthy to occupy a niche beside Beatrice and Laura.'[104] Attuned to the poetic possibilities of suffering, Rossetti followed Dante and Petrarch in celebrating a love-longing that had no prospect of earthly consummation. Written by the high priestess of unfulfilled love, her fourteen sonnets, barely read today, tell the story of love deeply felt and resolutely relinquished. Like the songs of Castelloza and the Countess of Dia, they give the woman's perspective on a love affair which is private, volatile and ultimately doomed. They are a poet's tribute to the flesh-and-blood women of the troubadour era, to a fellow poet whose work she valued, and to her own self-conscious renunciation of love.[105]

Siren, Sorceress and Sonneteer: Edna St Vincent Millay

In the late fifteenth century an anonymous Rhenish painter created an image of a beautiful girl. Blatantly erotic, his nymphet challenges the self-control of men in thrall to Christian teaching about fornication, sin and death. Barely twenty-four by eighteen centimetres in measurement, the tiny panel, often called *The Love Charm*, is packed with symbolic detail. Painted in oils, its central figure is that of a young woman, her naked body with its high, rounded breasts, swelling stomach and long slender legs gleaming through the gauze of a diaphanous shift. A wooden chest on a tripod at her side contains a bleeding heart, which she simultaneously inflames with the sparks from a tinderbox and douses with water from a tiny sponge. A fluffy dog, perhaps her messenger in love's rituals or an avatar of Cupid in his bestial, libidinous mode, dozes on a velvet cushion at her feet. Flowers scatter the floor and a parrot, emblematic of lust, perches on a dish of sweets in front of a peacock fan, symbolic of pride, display and maybe the watchful eyes of Juno, goddess of marriage and the family. The girl, with her long golden hair and seductive nudity, is an enchantress, working her spells on the heart that she holds captive at her side. Through the half-open door behind her a young man surreptitiously watches the action, clandestine witness to a ritual that threatens male autonomy at its most vulnerable level.[106]

This fascinating witch represents the shadow side of woman, a threatening female sexuality, which boldly contrasts with the chaste and passive recipient of later troubadour songs. She is the temptress Eve, polar opposite to the Virgin Mary, whose idealised image hovers behind Dante's Beatrice and Petrarch's Laura. 'And do you not know that you are [each] an Eve?' the Christian theologian Tertullian reminded women in Carthage in the second century after the birth of Christ. '*You* are the devil's gateway . . . *you* are she who persuaded [Adam] . . . *You* destroyed so easily God's image, man.'[107] Tertullian's accusation was depressingly tenacious. Medieval art, literature and theology is steeped in references to woman's potential for the coercion and ruin of man. The thesis was still current in Victorian England, spawning a profusion of semi-pornographic paintings of seductive sirens, and influencing social ideas about female weakness and depravity, which rumble on well into the twenty-first century. Witchcraft was a particularly terrifying adjunct of female sexual power, a subtext to Anne Boleyn's trial and beheading, and the excuse for the arrest, interrogation and execution of numerous women during the European witch-hunts. Spell-casting survives in folklore and superstition, the result of an understandable human desire to influence the course of love. For a young woman growing up in Camden, Maine, on the north-east coast of America during the early years of the twentieth century, it was an important ritual, gateway not to hell, but to a new life of love, adventure and recognition of her unique gifts.

The poet Edna St Vincent Millay bore a close resemblance to *The Love Charm*'s witchy subject. Slender and fragile, with a mane of dark-red hair, enormous grey-green eyes and a delicate pale complexion, she became famous for her love affairs and her outspokenness about sex, a celebrity whose public image was enhanced by the potent combination of youth, beauty, scandal and a remarkable literary talent. In 1911, however, she was still unknown, a girl in a white nightgown, crouching over a candle late at night and reciting charms to summon the lover who she believed was to transform her life.

Millay's early life was an education in hardship and self-discipline. Her parents separated when she was eight and Cora Millay eventually settled with her three daughters in an isolated house on the fringes of Camden. Money was scarce and Cora supported her girls by nursing, spending many weeks each year away from home, caring for seriously ill patients. In her absence Vincent, as the eldest child preferred to be known, kept house for her sisters, a life of domestic drudgery, which she pursued with characteristic determination and flair, organising a timetable of chores, and inventing games and songs to enliven the tedium of scrubbing floors, cooking and baking, and hand-laundering the family linen. Apart from the household responsibility, there were real dangers for the sisters, three very young girls living for long periods without adult protection. Years later, in an unpublished memoir, Millay described the gallantry and resourcefulness of the sisters:

> To live alone like that, sleep alone at night in that house set back in the field and near no other house and on the very edge of Millville, the 'bad' section of town where the itinerant millworkers lived,—this was the only way they could live at all. For the house was the cheapest to be found [. . .]
>
> But they were afraid of nothing, which was important,—not of the river which flowed behind the house, coloured with the most beautiful and changing colours,—dyes from the woollen-mills above—[. . .] nor afraid of that other river, which flowed past the front of the house, and which, especially on Saturday nights, was often very quarrelsome and noisy, the restless stream of mill workers [. . .] And once it took all three of the children, flinging themselves against the front door, to close it and bolt it, and just in time. And after that, for what seemed like hours,

there was stumbling about outside, and soft cursing. And after everything was quiet again the children lay awake for a long time, listening, and not making a sound, and thinking sometimes of the inconspicuous little path at the back of the house which they could follow in the blackest of nights without making a sound, through the tall grass of the field to the banks of the river, & how there [. . .] they could swim across as quietly as water-rats to the furthest banks, & [. . .] hide themselves in less than a minute in any one of ten places where nobody on earth—no, not even with a dog and a lantern! [. . .] could possibly find them.[108]

This disturbing memoir echoes the sense of threat and the need for a private refuge or hiding place that lurks in Millay's poetry, and which seems to have been at the heart of her sexual relationships. In an unstable world, the memoir seems to suggest, a wise woman barricades her door and makes sure that she has her escape route carefully planned.

Despite her punishing domestic routines, Millay was eager to excel at school, at times exasperating her teachers by her curiosity and zeal for information. Poetry and writing were essential to her from an early age, and some of her juvenile poems were published in *St Nicholas*, a children's monthly magazine, which offered budding writers an opportunity to see their names in print. When she was fourteen, Vincent won the League's gold medal for her poem 'The Land of Romance', the story of a child's journey in search of romance. The child asks a man to give her directions, but, spindly and uncertain, he says first that he does not know, then that he cannot remember. The child next asks a woman, spinning at her wheel. At first the woman refuses to reply, but then she snaps out:

'Oh! Why do you seek for Romance? And why do you trouble
   me?

'Little care I for your fancies. They will bring you no good,' she
   said,

'Take the wheel that stands in the corner, and get you to work,
   instead.'[109]

The woman's robust advice might stand as the leitmotif of Millay's
adult approach to life. Romantic love was a pleasant diversion,
but what she really cared about was Romance in its storytelling,
imaginative mode, which for Millay involved a commitment to
poetry that required study, dedication and hard work. As for the
wavering man, his characterisation implies that, even as a young
girl, Millay had learnt to regard men as inconsistent, unreliable
guides, perhaps a legacy from her father, whose good looks and
charm could not compensate for fecklessness and even abusive
behaviour towards Cora.[110]

Life for the Millay sisters was not all drudgery. A hugely talented,
intelligent and emotionally dominant woman, Cora was ambitious
for her daughters, and encouraged them to sing and to play musical
instruments, to paint and draw, and read poetry and plays. Later
famous for her dramatic presentations of her own poetry, Vincent
grew up with one foot on the stage, gleefully participating in the
concerts, amateur dramatics and readings that formed an important
part of community life in Camden. The girls also became adept
seamstresses, sewing and embroidering their clothes and household
furnishings. Lacking money for consumer goods, they created their
own decorative effects, keeping scrapbooks, making greetings cards
and pressing flowers, and creating attractive outfits from whatever
scraps of fabric lay at hand.[111] Vincent's showmanship and attain-
ments failed to make her popular with the local boys, who mocked
and mimicked her enthusiasms, and conspired to deprive her of
the coveted class poem at graduation when Millay was seventeen.

Intellectually isolated and frustrated by the lack of suitable outlets for her brilliance and imagination, it is not surprising that she turned to fantasy to find a fitting mate.

The relationship with the dream lover, which began two years after she left school, reflects the passion and frustration of an ardent girl, longing for love but sexually inexperienced, and still in the grip of her childhood devotion to her mother. To win Cora's love and approval, Vincent had frequently pushed herself to the point of illness. Now, to entice the lover of her dreams, she promises to make herself a worthy partner to the paragon whom she describes in her diary as 'strong, clean, and kind'.[112] Her fairy companions will be Strong-Heart, Clean-Hand, Clear-Eye, Brave-Soul and Sweet-Tongue. 'I must keep always before my mind the thought of what you want me to be. I will try harder than ever before,' she promises, but it is hard work struggling without encouragement. 'I am so tired! But when you come I shall rest.'[113] The stimulus to good was not Vincent's only motive in pursuing this imaginary liaison. As her diary entries make clear, what she had in mind was an erotic encounter with a lover whom she invokes with increasing desperation.

Millay's 'Consecration' to her dream lover lasted almost two years, a secret resource that warded off despair until real life unexpectedly began to offer the adulation, success and sexual adventures that she craved. On the third night of every month, if she was alone in the house, she would light a candle and enjoy the company of her phantom lover until the flame burned out. The ritual included wearing a cheap tin ring, retrieved from a 'fortune' cookie, and now solemnly kissed seven times, the magic number from the fairy tales Millay had read in her childhood. Her description of this ring reveals the sleight of hand by which she transformed shoddy materials into the precious brocade of high romance, her willingness to commit herself emotionally to the illusion she so effortlessly created and the staunch common sense with which she calmly took note of the tricks that she was playing on herself. Fully aware that it was 'a cheap little thing in imitation of a solitaire', it was nevertheless 'just the sort of ring to link me to a "Love-o'-Dreams"; I love it with a passion that is painful'.[114]

Just as Millay's ring derived from romantic stories where the exchange of rings symbolised commitment and fidelity, so too did her fantasies of her first encounter with her lover draw on popular stereotypes of the seduction of young virgins. She imagines herself 'wearing a fluffy lavender thing' over her nightdress, a peignoir that anticipates the diaphanous, negligee-like gowns she was to wear to striking effect for her public readings. The lavender robe is 'very soft and long and trails on the rug' behind her bare feet. Despite its seductive promise, Millay's self-image is essentially virginal and even sacrificial: 'My hair is in two wavy, red braids over my shoulders. My eyes are very sweet and serious.' Her lover is sitting in a chair, watching her slow approach across the rug towards him. She falls at his feet and lays her head on his knee, her long braids touching the floor. He gazes deep into those serious eyes, then stands up, lifting her from the ground so that her body lies stretched out before him, flat across his arms. The lavender gown 'falls soft about my feet'. Her eyes tight shut, she feels his kiss on her 'wistful' mouth. 'Oh, Love! I feel your arms about me. I feel—!'[115] He is her 'purpose' and her 'destiny'. 'With you I shall be complete and wonderful, but without you I am nothing,' she assures him.[116]

Given her upbringing in small-town Maine in the early years of the twentieth century, and the literary traditions in which she steeped herself, Millay's abjection to her dream lover is hardly surprising. Lonely and yearning, she fed her imagination with an erotic encounter that stopped short of physical fulfilment: her passionate 'I feel—!' is tantalisingly followed by 'Good night, sweet-heart!'. At the same time the numbing repetitiveness of housework almost overwhelmed her. 'I'm getting old and ugly,' she complained to her dream lover (she was all of nineteen). 'My hands are stiff and rough and stained and blistered. I can feel my face dragging down. I can feel the lines coming underneath my skin. [...] I love beauty more than anything else in the world and I can't take time to be pretty.'[117] It wasn't just her looks that were affected. Disconsolate in snow-bound Camden in January 1912, she confided with characteristic humour and insight: 'I suffer from inflammation of the imagination and a bad attack of ingrowing temperament. [...] I need a man who has been somewhere and done things to graft his healthy ideas into my silly brain.'[118] Her despair, however, was genuine. One month later she told him, 'This is another death—this night.' On the brink of her twentieth birthday, and facing an empty future, she confessed, 'I do not know what will become of me. [...] the thoughts that fill my mind are fearful thoughts. [...] I do not think there is a woman in whom the roots of passion shoot deeper than in me.'[119]

One year later, once more alone with her candle and diary, Millay performed the final ritual for her still elusive lover, sealing the precious ring into a small white box along with hot wax from the candle and 'a drop of red, red blood' from her ring finger. Firmly she wrote in her diary, 'We will have no more vigils.'[120] The perfect lover may not have materialised, but life had come to call for Millay, summoned by her own energy and talent, and by her mother's hopes for her daughter. At Cora's instigation Millay had submitted a long ambitious poem, aptly named 'Renascence', for *The Lyric Year*, a collection of one hundred of the year's best American poems, which was to be published in the late autumn of 1912. The poem is astonishing, describing an encounter with infinity and suffering that condemns the speaker quite literally to a living grave. Crushed by the burden of awareness, he or she (the gender is never clear) calls on God for help, and is eventually released by torrential rain into a rapturous reunion with life and the natural world. Elizabeth Barrett was recalled to life by sexual love; Millay's spiritual rebirth was accomplished through a poetic voice that stubbornly resisted the inertia of circumstance. Years later, the artist Georgia O'Keeffe briefly met Millay and wrote that the poet reminded her of a hummingbird who had once flown into her studio, a tiny creature pulsating with life and determined not to be captured.[121] Millay's energy and independence lifted her out of the obscurity of Camden, but her early experience of poverty and hard work, as well as the claustrophobia of family responsibility, shadowed her life and may partly account for the hummingbird elusiveness that captivated so many of her lovers. What also seems to have influenced Millay was a profound distrust of men.

Considering her family history and her early experience in Maine (the drunken millhands who pressed against her door and envious schoolboys who derided her ambitions), it would not be surprising if the teenage Millay found the specimens of manhood so far available to be wanting in either usefulness or appeal. What appears to have transformed her from the girl pining for the dream lover who would rescue her from the drudgery of Camden to the self-possessed vamp of Greenwich Village some five years later was the perfidy of Ferdinand Earle, the editor of *The Lyric Year*, and the revelation of her own sexual allure when she began to be known and fêted as a brilliant young poet and desirable 'girlfriend' at Vassar. Earle, dazzled by a flirtatious correspondence with Millay, had encouraged her to believe that she was likely to win first prize among the hundred competitors for *The Lyric Year* honours. Millay's disappointment at losing so valuable an award – apart from the glory, there was a cash prize of five hundred dollars, a huge amount to the penniless Millay family – was compounded by her chagrin at Earle's two-facedness. It was a valuable lesson in the limitations of sexual games, which she was never to forget. Whatever (the already married) Earle hinted on paper to his fascinating correspondent, the reality was the decision of the three judges, who awarded the glittering prize elsewhere. Her sense of outrage at Earle's behaviour was soothed by the wave of interest and enthusiasm that flowed from the first publication of 'Renascence' in *The Lyric Year* collection, and her *amour propre* was boosted by the attentions of admirers of both sexes. Although the poem was not selected as one of the three prizewinners, the judges' failure to honour Millay made her a celebrity, and brought her a coterie of fans and an influential sponsor. Within months she had begun a new life in New York, enrolling as a mature student at the prestigious women's college, Vassar, and embarking on three years of study, poetry and flirtation with her fellow students. The 'wistful' maiden of the chilly bedroom in Maine had vanished for ever; in her place was the teasing Vincent, fully alert to her claims to the envy and adoration of the cloistered inmates at the college. From that time Millay made sure that, in the game of love, she held the winning cards.

Millay's reputation as 'the unrivaled embodiment of sex appeal, the It-girl of the hour', as a contemporary described her, was established by her second published collection of poems, *A Few Figs from Thistles* (1920), with its impudent 'First Fig':

> My candle burns at both ends;
> It will not last the night;
> But ah, my foes, and oh, my friends—
> It gives a lovely light![122]

This was considered pleasurably risqué for a young woman, and 'Thursday' with its theme of casual sex as casually forgotten caused even more of a stir. 'I loved you Wednesday,—yes—but what / Is that to me?' the poem ends.[123] As so often in Millay, it is not clear whether a man or a woman is the speaker, but her readers liked to believe that the 'Figs' were the personal record of an audacious female sexpot. By now, Millay had graduated from Vassar and had been living for some time in Greenwich Village, pursuing a precarious career as actress and playwright, as well as writing short stories and poems. That dizzy period of post-war liberation known as the

Jazz Age was sweeping through the garrets and studios of the Village, and Millay took full advantage of the new freedoms, enjoying simultaneous love affairs with a string of men, several of whom left records of her powerful impact. One of the most interesting memoirs was published after her death by the critic Edmund Wilson. In his 'Epilogue, 1952: Edna St Vincent Millay' he recalls how both he and his friend John Bishop fell 'irretrievably in love' with Millay, an 'almost inevitable' consequence of knowing the poet, who exercised a potent 'spell' on people 'of the most various professions and temperaments, of all ages and both sexes'. Looking back on his infatuation after more than thirty years, Wilson acknowledged the importance of admiration to Millay, whose 'intoxicating effect . . . so much created the atmosphere in which she lived and composed'.[124] Confident of her power to bewitch, Millay seems to have been remarkably even-handed in dealing with her admirers. Despite the competition for her favours, her lovers did not quarrel with her or one another, disarmed, perhaps, by what Wilson described as 'an impartiality which was amiably humorous or sympathetic'.[125] As Wilson recorded elsewhere, this humorous impartiality expressed itself one evening after a dinner *à trois* with Wilson and Bishop, when 'sitting on her day bed, John and I held Edna in our arms—according to an arrangement insisted upon by herself—I her lower half and John her upper—with a polite exchange of pleasantries as to which had the better share'.[126] Despite this conviviality, Wilson was seriously in love with Millay, who seems to have known exactly how to 'play' this unsophisticated young man. Her effect was electrifying. He recalled that she

> ignited for me both my intellectual passion and my unsatisfied desire, which went up together in a blaze of ecstasy that remains for me one of the high points of my life. I do not believe that such experiences can be common, for such women are not common. My subsequent chagrin and perplexity, when I

discovered that, due to her extreme promiscuity, this could not be expected to continue, were rather amazingly soothed by an equanimity on her part which was also very uncommon.[127]

Millay's 'promiscuity' is, of course, a moot point. A later generation or a less enslaved lover might have regarded her behaviour as legitimate sexual experimentation. Wilson's account of her detachment does, however, have a note of authenticity. As her lovers soon discovered, her poetry was 'her real overmastering passion'.[128]

Millay's own idea of herself as seductress can be hypothesised from two poems, both apparently flippant and light-hearted, but indicative of the sexual roles which the 'It-girl of the hour' was exploring. 'Witch-Wife' describes an enchanting creature who 'learned her hands in a fairy-tale, / And her mouth on a valentine'. With her abundant hair and evocative voice, the Witch-Wife bears more than a passing resemblance to her creator. Where love is concerned, she does her best, but the speaker is forced to accept that

> she was not made for any man,
> And she never will be all mine.[129]

Elusive but irresistible and, at times, like the Belle Dame, likely to cause serious heartbreak seemed to be the public pose that Millay chose to adopt. Writing poetic self-portraits one evening with Bishop and Wilson, she scribbled the wickedly self-mocking 'E. St. V. M.':

> A large mouth,
> Lascivious, [...]
> A long throat,
> Which will someday
> Be strangled. [...]
> A small body,

Unexclamatory,
But which,
Were it the fashion to wear no clothes,
Would be as well-dressed
As any.[130]

Exhausted by her rackety lifestyle and the attentions of her lovers, Millay eventually fled to Paris, where she became European correspondent for *Vanity Fair* magazine, publishing a series of skits and satires of contemporary sexual mores under the pen-name of Nancy Boyd. Despite the pleadings of her editor, who offered to double her fee if she would write as the infamous Edna St Vincent Millay, she stuck to her pseudonym for what she regarded as pot-boiling journalism. Deceptively light in tone, the Nancy Boyd pieces make fun of social attitudes to women and reveal Millay's awareness of the snares that lay in wait for the unsuspecting female artist. The preoccupation of both sexes with female glamour and artifice is one of Millay's favourite Aunt Sallies. 'Powder, Rouge and Lip-Stick' describes what happens when Robert Avery-Thompson ('subject to recurrent attacks of acute idealism') persuades his wife to abandon make-up. Adorned for an evening at the opera, Gwendolyn appears in a magnificent black and silver evening gown, 'above which rises a rather boyish neck, sun-burned into a V, a fairly well-shaped but sallow face with a pale mouth, a pink and gleaming nose, and no eyebrows whatsoever, from which in turn recedes honestly a flat surface of straight and sand-colored hair'. When Robert exclaims in horror, Gwendolyn disingenuously explains, 'I'm my own sweet, simple, natural, girlish self.'[131] In the case of the female sculptor in 'Madame a Tort!' ('Madam is Mistaken!'), a preoccupation with appearance proves fatal to art. A chance visit to the hairdresser reveals the sculptress's potential as a beauty, and she gives up modelling in clay in order to dedicate herself to the care of her face, hands and elegant clothes. At times she regrets the 'old free days', but 'one glance at my nails, so rosy, so roundly pointed, so softly bright, so exquisite from the loving care of years—and I know that I shall never work again'.[132] In 'The Implacable Aphrodite' another 'graceful sculptress', Miss Black, possessor of 'a long and treacherous throat, full of memories', entertains Mr White, 'a man of parts, but badly assembled'. Mr White claims to want a relationship with a woman where 'the barriers of sex' have dispersed like morning mist, but it swiftly becomes clear that he admires Miss Black's attractions as a woman far more than he respects her work.[133] Amusing and often self-consciously banal, such scenarios suggest the detachment and scepticism with which Millay observed the conventional *beau monde* and the so-called 'liberated' artists with whom she mingled. While the Millay of Greenwich Village or Paris in the early Twenties might be seen as an embodiment of Robert Graves's White Goddess, the elusive muse who goads and inspires the male poet, her work counts the cost of being both a Poet *and* a Poem. Fascinated as she is by sexual relationships, she is equally preoccupied by what it takes to be a woman poet, in terms of commitment to art and relationships with others.

The conflict between love and art for the female poet is lightly sketched in 'Daphne', one of Millay's 'Figs', which offers an alternative perspective on 'The Implacable Aphrodite'. Mr White had been captivated by Miss Black's sculpture of a reclining female nude, for which she cheerfully acknowledged that she was her own model. The subject is the nymph Daphne, who according to classical mythology was turned into a laurel tree in order to escape the amorous pursuit of Apollo. In Miss Black's representation, Daphne has fallen in her flight. Millay picks up this theme in 'Daphne', which is written from the nymph's point of view. In this version the self-possessed Daphne pertly asks the god why he insists on following her when she can so easily escape. If he persists, he will have to accept the consequences:

> Yet if over hill and hollow
> Still it is your will to follow,
> I am off;—to heel, Apollo![134]

On one level cheekily subversive in its view of the male lover as an obedient dog, 'Daphne' also poses the idea of the speaker (Millay herself?) as always in flight, not just from men, but also from her calling. Apollo was, after all, the god of poetry and song. The alternative to running away is to become a laurel tree, which a fleet-footed nymph might find constraining, although it also recalls the laurel wreath placed on the brows of the successful poet in classical times. Daphne's dilemma seems to be between accepting sexual love, or hoping to gain the laurel wreath, the poet's highest accolade. The alternative is the freedom – and exhaustion – of being always on the run. Apparently light-hearted and even throwaway, Millay's 'Daphne' encodes many of the tensions and anxieties that troubled her as poet and as lover. If Millay is Daphne to the world's Apollo, the poem suggests a fundamental distrust both of sexual love and of the world's good opinion, and even of her capacity as a poet. If she did stand still, would the laurel wreath be hers? Would she even have time to claim it before Apollo caught up with her? What loss of artistic selfhood is involved when a female poet is ravished by the god of poetry? In the end, flight may be the only option available to the nymph who values her freedom.

For much of her twenties Millay was herself in flight. Anxious to shake off her pursuers, she hurtled around Europe, restless, often ill and increasingly deracinated, until eventually a chance meeting in April 1923 with a Dutch entrepreneur, Eugen Boissevain, led to marriage and comparative stability at their farm, Steepletop, in New York State. In the meantime she continued to write and became the first woman to win a Pulitzer Prize for poetry in 1923. Boissevain's forte seemed to be marrying remarkable women: his first wife had

An imaginary 13th-century 'portrait' of the trobairitz Castelloza, wearing a striking scarlet overdress and full sleeves, with a chaplet of pearls or ivory beads on her neatly arranged hair.

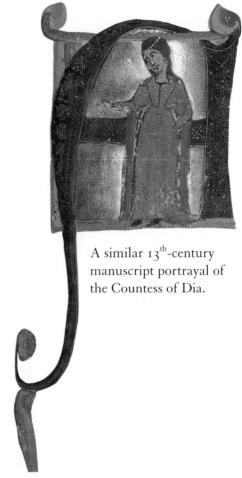

A similar 13th-century manuscript portrayal of the Countess of Dia.

Jaufre Rudel expiring in the arms of the Countess of Tripoli in a 13th-century illustration.

A *joglaresa*, or female entertainer, late 10th century.

ul q̃ ſeuent
de lettreure
deuroient bñ
mettre lor cure
es bōſ luures
⁊ eſ eſcriʒ
⁊ eſ erãmples
⁊ eſ diʒ
Q̃ li phıloſophe trouuerent

Marie de France pictured at work on her *Fables*, *c.* 1300. Seated at a slanted desk, sh
wears a blue gown with a pale sleeveless overdress and a veil. In one hand she holds a
inkhorn, in the other her pen, with which she busily fills the page of her book.

A medieval guide to healthy living, which included the benefits of sex. The male partner's hair is neatly contained in a nightcap.

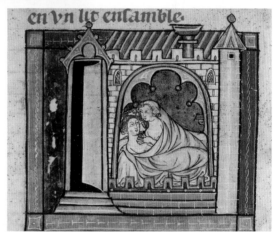

The adulterous Lancelot and Guinevere in bed together, sticking closely to the manual's guidelines.

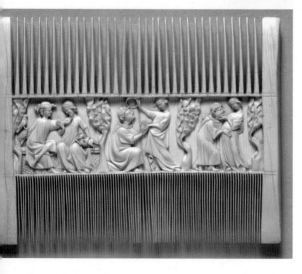

Lovers in a garden: a lady crowns her successful suitor with a garland of leaves on this 14th-century ivory comb.

The Duke courts a lady in a charming wooded glade in *The Book of the Duke of Tru* Lovers.

Christine de Pizan presents a beautifully bound copy of her work to her patron Isabeau de Bavière, Queen of France, c. 1410.

This portrait of Anne Boleyn by an anonymous painter hints at the continental elegance that captivated Henry VIII. Her long oval face and strong features suggest her character. Her hair is confined by a French hood, and she wears a pearl necklace with her initial in gold. In her long slender fingers, she holds a multi-petalled flower, probably a rose, which was an important Tudor emblem, as well as the Virgin's flower and a symbol of love.

In an early 16th-century Book of Hours illuminated by Flemish artists, under an image of Christ as the 'Man of Sorrows', Henry VIII scribbled a note in French to Anne Boleyn: 'If you remember me according to my love in your prayers I shall scarcely be forgotten, since I am your Henry Rex for ever.'

he book was perhaps passed between the lovers during a religious service. Anne
sponded with a verse in English, choosing as her image the Annunciation, with its
omise of new and glorious birth: 'Be daly prove you shall me fynde / To be to you
the lovynge and kynde.' A later hand has cut off Anne's signature, an attempt to
cise a discredited wife from the record.

Lady Mary Wroth, elaborately gowned and holding her archlute, in a portrait th
suggests her intelligence and musical talent, as well as good looks and status.

(*Inset*) Her lover, William Herbert, Third Earl of Pembroke, bearing the staff of t
Lord Chamberlain, in a formal study that asserts his wealth, authority and cultu
c. 1625.

been the suffrage leader Inez Milholland, who had died suddenly from pernicious anaemia. Coddled by her adoring husband, Millay was able to nurture a burgeoning career as one of America's most popular poets, capitalising on her fame by giving readings of her own work, in which she promoted a complex public persona as both femme fatale and enchanting girl-poetess. A journalist's description of an event shared with Robert Frost and other luminaries gives the flavour of her carefully staged performances and their appeal for her audiences. She was wearing

> a robe of gold and bronze and green and her voice was a bronze bell as she read. Back and forth she moved, slender, by turn gay and grave, pompous and flippant. Her robe, because it was traced with gold threads woven into its pattern, whispered and chimed faintly against the floor. If Miss Millay had not been a poet she could easily have been an actress.

At the end of the performance she left the platform 'not as a great poet but as a girl, quite young, of Maine who had done her best'.[135] Syntax notwithstanding, the reporter's response testifies to Millay's subtle allure as an enchantress who somehow also managed to remain the homely girl from Maine. Much as 'Nancy Boyd' might quiz the social attitudes that refused to take women artists seriously, Millay quite deliberately exploited her good looks and seductive speaking voice to enhance her appeal as America's 'unofficial feminine laureate'.[136] It was at one of these readings, when she was thirty-six years old, that she met the poet George Dillon, nearly fifteen years her junior. During the course of their often tempestuous affair, she wrote a sequence of over fifty sonnets, *Fatal Interview*, which charts the progress and eventual decline of a passionate relationship.

George Dillon was a copywriter and poet, at almost twenty-two still living with his parents in their apartment overlooking Lake

Michigan in Chicago. An only child, Dillon adored his mother and seems to have been something of a loner, fond of solitary sports and a compulsive reader. Millay's passion apparently took him by surprise and he was at a loss to know how to deal with her vehemence. His reluctance may have been due in part to a gentlemanly aversion to an affair with a married woman. The obliging Eugen's offers of friendship and hospitality seem only to have made matters worse for this conventional young man. Emotionally fragile, Dillon appears, too, to have suffered terribly when parted from Millay, and to have dreaded the cycle of ecstatic meetings and anguished separations her marriage and public commitments made inevitable. Even when they finally lived together for some months in Paris, the relationship remained volatile, and Millay finally returned to Steepletop and the husband who had made no secret of his yearning for her. 'Couldn't you take a small handkerchief and put it in your Kitty before you take a bath, and mail it to me?' Eugen wrote wistfully, while Millay was in Paris with George. 'I'm longing for your perfume.'[137]

The attraction for Millay of the rather weak and indecisive Dillon may have been quite simply his good looks and vulnerability. Intensely susceptible to beauty and craving the stimulus of novelty after several years of marriage, she may have found the bewilderment and caution of this striking young man an irresistible challenge. They also shared an enthusiasm for poetry and an intellectual rapport, which stimulated her as a writer. Although Millay wrote on many subjects, including a number of political and even propagandist poems, she is remembered chiefly as a love poet, and left a huge body of lyric poetry relating to love in many forms and guises. How far these poems should be read as personal or confessional is open to dispute. As in Sir Philip Sidney's *Astrophil and Stella*, or Elizabeth Barrett's *Sonnets from the Portuguese*, some distancing has to be assumed, even in the *Fatal Interview* sequence, between experience and the poet's use of it. Despite this proviso, Millay's poetic voice has a quality of immediacy and intimacy that seduces the reader into participation with what appears to be deeply felt and personal, an invitation to empathy she shares with other love poets from Shakespeare and John Donne to Christina Rossetti and Thomas Hardy. Like Elizabeth Barrett, she turned to traditional forms, the ballad, sonnet and brief lyric poem, to explore her emotional effects, and the simplicity and accessibility of her poetry, which made her popular with a broad contemporary readership, tend to mask the originality of her response to human relationships.[138] The sonnet was a particular favourite with Millay and she learnt to work within its constrictions to express often quite outrageous ideas.[139]

One of her early love sonnets, 'Love, though for this you riddle me with darts', from *A Few Figs from Thistles*, demonstrates her understanding of the form and her use of it for her own subversive purposes. Instead of bemoaning the pain of love, as convention demanded, the speaker challenges Cupid to arouse passion in a breast so far impervious to the 'puny rain' of Love's darts.[140] She continues her assault on the traditional sonnet in 'I shall forget you presently, my dear', a poem that acknowledges the transiency of passion, for both lovers. 'If you entreat me with your loveliest lie / I will protest you with my favourite vow,' she quips. Despite the brittleness of human promises:

> nature has contrived
> To struggle on without a break thus far,—
> Whether or not we find what we are seeking
> Is idle, biologically speaking.[141]

In 'I, being born a woman' she mocks the 'clouding' effect of passion on the mind. Having succumbed to desire, she warns her partner in sex not to expect love or pity:

> let me make it plain:
> I find this frenzy insufficient reason
> For conversation when we meet again.[142]

For a woman poet, this was audacious stuff.

Perhaps surprisingly, given such boldness, what emerges from many of Millay's love poems is a sense of pain and anxiety, which belies her reputation for easy promiscuity.[143] Ardent and iconoclastic, Millay flouted social expectations of decorous female behaviour in order to be true to her own fluctuating desires. In the case of George Dillon she found herself playing the role of pursuer, an older woman passionately in love with an inexperienced and often reluctant young man. Instead of the fleeing Daphne, Millay had become Racine's Phèdre, burning with forbidden ardour. At the same time she was a writer, attuned to analysing and generalising emotion even as she experienced its turbulence in her fluctuating pulse. The sonnets in *Fatal Interview* tell the story of a love affair, but they are also a poet's mature expression of many years of reflecting on the sexual relationship between men and women.

Millay's title refers to the beginning lines of John Donne's 'Elegie XVI':

> By our first strange and fatall interview,
> By all desires which thereof did ensue,
> [...]
> Temper, o faire Love, loves impetuous rage,

and her sonnets engage in an informed dialogue with classical and Renaissance love poems. In drawing on the tradition of the sonnet sequence, Millay ignores the convention of the distant or alienated lover and instead describes the tortuous progress of a consummated love affair. Although it is not always clear from individual sonnets whether the speaker is male or female, Sonnet II suggests that *Fatal*

Interview is a woman's story, which Millay tells with characteristic frankness. In these sonnets flippancy gives place to irony and lightness of touch to an unremitting engagement with powerful feeling. In Sonnet II she writes of love as a beast that rends her and will leave deep scars, to lie 'like a sword' between the speaker and her 'troubled lord'.[144] In Sonnet VIII she tells her disdainful lover that he cannot escape her. In a mocking reversal of Marvell's 'To His Coy Mistress', she claims that even if he rejects her now, in death her lover will be 'brought to bed' with her:

> And ruder and more violent, be assured,
> Than the desirous body's heat and sweat
> That shameful kiss by more than night obscured
> Wherewith at length the scornfullest mouth is met.

In Sonnet XI she pleads the simplicity of her love; presented not in a jewelled casket, with the 'key withheld', or as an elaborate ring with a secret cargo of poison, but as love 'in the open hand':

> As one should bring you cowslips in a hat
> Swung from the hand, or apples in her skirt[.]

Thinking, in Sonnet XXVI, about the great lovers of the past, of Helen of Troy and Tristram's Yseult, she claims that she alone of modern women shares the ancient 'unregenerate passions'

> of a day
> When treacherous queens, with death upon the tread,
> Heedless and wilful, took their knights to bed.

As their wounded love staggers like a dying bird dragging its feathers in the dust, she begs it to die:

Vanish, be fled, leave me a wingless land . . .
Save where one moment down the quiet tide
Fades a white swan, with a black swan beside. (XLII)[145]

In the final sonnet, 'Oh, sleep forever in the Latmian cave', she compares herself to Selene, the moon, who fell in love with the mortal youth Endymion. While the boy sleeps, the goddess 'wanders mad, being all unfit / For mortal love, that might not die of it'. In this ambiguous ending Millay asserts her ability to survive. She may run mad, but for all her excited coupling with the 'earthen' boy she will not die of love. Millay's sonnet cycle will be similarly resilient. It is a theme that Spenser, Shakespeare and other Renaissance sonneteers used to similar effect. Human passion fails, but the poems that mourn its demise will last for ever.

Millay's *Fatal Interview* is one account of woman's experience of love. In another, much shorter sequence, *Sonnets from an Ungrafted Tree*, she tells the story of a woman who has returned to her estranged husband to nurse him while he is dying.[146] The setting is rural and impoverished, and very little happens. The woman gathers wood and makes a fire; the grocer's man arrives in a wagon and leaves a stack of paper parcels on the dresser. She busies herself with setting the derelict house to order, but is reluctant to welcome the neighbourly women who bring jellies to the door. She had married the dying man because of an incident when they were at school together: he had flashed a mirror in her eyes and somehow she felt chosen. Later, swimming with him in a lake at night, she had mistaken desire for love. These defining moments had committed her to domesticity with a husband who, when he dies, seems a stranger. This simple sequence with its picture of a life spent in drudgery and self-suppression (the woman is alert to the trains that whistle down the track and dreams of the 'magic World' marriage has put beyond her grasp) offers an alternative version of female experience. For the young Vincent, dreaming over her candle in

Camden, such a life would have been a real possibility, had poetry and fame not rescued her in the nick of time. Millay's grim vision of the life unlived may have been the stimulus to her search for experience as a young woman. Love affairs and the world's admiration kept her anxiety at bay, but as she grew older she became increasingly reclusive, and addicted to alcohol and morphine. She died at the age of fifty-eight, following a fall downstairs, probably after she had been drinking. Eugen Boissevain had died from a stroke following surgery for cancer the previous year.

Virginia Woolf wrote about the 'heat and violence' of the thwarted life of the woman poet. Edna St Vincent Millay achieved enviable success as a poet, but her early exposure to hardship and the consequent feelings of vulnerability seem to have damaged her irretrievably. Caught in the family drama of the talented, ambitious mother and her three daughters, struggling to wrestle glamour, hope and the bare necessities out of inadequate materials, Millay was thrown back again and again on her own resources. Being female was deeply significant to all the Millay girls, who had no father or other male relatives to support or protect them. How was a woman to survive in a hostile world? This was the question that dogged them all. In Millay's poem 'Scrub', the speaker defends her bitterness and withdrawal from society on the grounds of youthful suffering: 'It is that a wind too strong / Bent my back when I was young[.]'[147] In an undated poem, a draft found in a workbook, Millay wrote too of the burden of family and her need to shake off the weight of intimate relationships in order to achieve her due stature as a poet:

> Cool on a migrant wing, if I sing at all,
> Down-gliding, up-carried,
> Free must be over mountain and sea my call,
> Unsistered, unmarried.[148]

The cost of not being able to float on that 'migrant wing' is recorded in 'Sorrow', one of Millay's early poems and a moving account of depression. After describing the remorselessness of sorrow beating like 'a ceaseless rain' on her heart, the speaker continues:

> People dress and go to town;
>   I sit in my chair.
> All my thoughts are slow and brown:
> Standing up or sitting down
> Little matters, or what gown
>   Or what shoes I wear.[149]

Her sisters parodied this verse, but it was laughter born of rueful understanding.[150]

Passionate and sensitive, Millay found respite from reality in her response to the beauty of the natural world. Even this, however, was not without pain. In another early poem, 'Assault', a woman takes an unaccustomed walk along a solitary road:

> I am waylaid by Beauty.   Who will walk
> Between me and the crying of the frogs?
> Oh, savage Beauty, suffer me to pass,
> That am a timid woman, on her way
> From one house to another![151]

Fortunately for her readers, Millay's nature did not permit her to 'pass'. There was, in fact, nothing 'timid' about her. Inquisitive, determined and brave, she steeled herself to pause, observe and then record her experiences as a woman, a lover and a poet.

~

Sylvia Plath regarded Millay as one of her poetic godmothers and there are many similarities between the two poets, in the strong, ambitious mothers who drove them to achievement, as well as their careers as sexually active women and female poets. Apart from some early experiments, Plath did not write love poetry, and her style and approach veered dramatically from the lyric verse with which Millay made her name. Perhaps the true modern heiresses of the lost trobairitz tradition are singer-songwriters such as the American Suzanne Vega. Describing herself as a 'solitary troubadour', Vega continues the practice of subversive song initiated by the Countess of Dia and her fellow singers, and made use of by Lady Mary Wroth, Elizabeth Barrett and Edna St Vincent Millay in their feminising of the male stronghold of the sonnet. Vega's enigmatic 'The Queen and the Soldier' is a witty and troubling example of what can happen when a woman rewrites an ancient story. The soldier, a troubadour in modern dress, finds his way into a young queen's private chamber, an inner room lined with scarlet tapestries, which so often symbolises female sexuality. He challenges her to explain why she sends her soldiers out to die on the battlefield, and makes her look out at the sun and sky from her high window. All the queen can say in her defence is that she has swallowed a thread that makes her bleed. The soldier offers marriage and her crown falls to the ground. It seems that she has accepted him, but she sends the suitor outside for a moment and, while he is waiting, orders him to be killed. The queen remains alone, still choking from the mysterious thread, while the fighting continues.

Like the best folk songs, Vega's lyric invites many interpretations. One meaning could be that the queen prefers her own authority to marriage with the soldier, even if it does condemn her to solitude and barrenness. If so, it was a policy pursued to her advantage by an earlier queen, Elizabeth 1, daughter of the woman with whom this enquiry began, the elegant, doomed muse, Anne Boleyn. The canny Queen chose spinsterhood and power; such a choice was generally not available to the woman writer, struggling to make her way in a society that expected women to marry and be dutiful wives and mothers. The tensions between love and money, marriage, art and personal autonomy became the favourite themes of women novelists, happy to find a medium in which the female pen was permitted to succeed.

PART 5

Dreams and Reality: Fictions of Love

'[I]f you please, no reference to examples in books. Men have had every advantage of us in telling their own story. Education has been theirs in so much higher a degree; the pen has been in their hands.'

Anne Elliot to Captain Harville in Jane Austen,
Persuasion (1817)

The Heroine Affronts Her Destiny

In the late 1890s, when Edna St Vincent Millay was still a little girl, a young woman teaching school in a remote corner of Prince Edward Island fell deeply in love. Already secretly engaged to another man, she was horrified by her passion for the son of the family with whom she boarded during the school year. Torn between desire and duty, she turned to her diary as an outlet for her feelings, vividly describing her meetings with her lover and the pain of parting. The young woman was Lucy Maud Montgomery, who was to become the author of one of the best-loved books for girls ever published, *Anne of Green Gables*. Her journals reveal the private life of this accomplished writer and provide a fascinating backdrop to her polished fictions of courtship, marriage and troubled romance among the small-town communities in rural Canada. Like many women writers, Montgomery censored her public writings to suit contemporary ideas about female behaviour, and she used fiction to create relationships in which, whatever the difficulties and misunderstandings, true love eventually triumphed. While she couldn't resist recording her personal experience of love, this history was written for her eyes alone. In public, what she offered her readers was the happiness of love (at last) fulfilled, or at least remembered with bitter-sweet longing if fate or death had separated the lovers.

Women have always sought consolation for the pains of love by writing out their feelings in letters, journals, stories and poems. Tormented by difficult suitors, Ukifune, the young heroine of the final chapters of *The Tale of Genji*, found solace in brush and inkstone. The abbess Heloise vented her longing for Abelard by composing eloquent letters to her lost beloved. Christine de Pizan took refuge from grief at her husband's death in forging a new career as poet and social critic. Busily scribbling at her desk, she earned a living for herself and her dependants by her sophisticated analysis of love and its inequalities, and her spirited defence of the as yet unacknowledged capacities of women in every sphere of human activity. In eighteenth-century England, the woman writing about love became almost a stereotype when Samuel Richardson created a heroine, Clarissa Harlowe, who breathlessly recorded her resistance to a ruthless pursuer, the dashing Lovelace, in a stream of letters that captured the imaginations of readers and writers all over Europe. (To Richardson's horror, Lovelace proved just as appealing as his victim, a prototypical Dark Hero adored by generations of susceptible females.) From Frances Burney's Evelina to Cassandra Mortmain in Dodie Smith's *I Capture the Castle* and Fanny Price in Patricia Rozema's film version of Jane Austen's *Mansfield Park*, the image of the nubile young woman busily scripting her responses to life and love has become a commonplace of romantic fictions. In eighteenth-century Europe, with the growth of a bourgeoisie with leisure and income to indulge their fondness for private entertainment, the novel took over from drama and poetry as the favourite medium for fantasy. It was a form in which women writers were to excel, offering an opportunity for psychological realism and the close study of personal relationships as well as the thrills of sensational plots, melodrama and wish-fulfilment for more escapist tastes. Eager readers, predominantly women, filled vacant hours with the adventures of feisty heroines, whose escapades almost inevitably concluded with love fulfilled and a profitable marriage. Love and the attainment of worldly goods were the happy rewards of a young woman's courage, fidelity and virtue.

The route to happiness was, however, far from untroubled, and it is in the heroine's ability to deal with obstacles and setbacks that the interest of many of these novels lies. Henry James acknowledged the attraction of the struggling heroine in his Preface to *The Portrait of a Lady* (1881). For years an image of 'young feminine nature' had haunted his imagination, and the idea of a 'young woman affronting her destiny' became the 'cornerstone' of his novel. Generally meticulous in his use of words, James's choice of the verb 'affront' implies that a young girl's destiny may frequently be less than desirable. It is a life plot that she may need to tackle or oppose, or at least wrestle into shape, if she is to have any satisfaction. When he considered the middle-class society of America and Europe with which he was most familiar, what impressed James was 'how inordinately' even apparently insignificant women 'insist on mattering'.[1] For George Eliot (as James mentions) their importance lay in their emotional contribution and moral influence. 'In these delicate vessels is borne onward through the ages the treasure of human affections,' she wrote in *Daniel Deronda*. '[G]irls and their blind visions' are 'the Yea or Nay of that good for which men are enduring and fighting'.[2] The Victorians loved to think of women as fragile beings, scarcely able to withstand the pressures of real life, but both Eliot and James created female characters of great strength and integrity. James's heroine, Isabel Archer, represents a clever reworking of the fate of Gwendolen Harleth, the central female character in *Daniel Deronda*. Gwendolen's life is blighted by her lack of private means and insufficient talents; she cannot excel as an actress and has no other way of earning a living except the dull routine of governess or companion. Marriage is her only route to financial security. By contrast, James gives Isabel Archer the benefit of an independent income and greater moral resolution than poor Gwendolen. *The Portrait of a Lady* is a subtle exploration of how a young American woman of taste, spirit and integrity copes with the realities of courtship and marriage in a corrupt world. Isabel does indeed 'affront' her destiny, drawing on resources of strength and moral courage to face, sometimes defiantly, life's surprises and disappointments.

During the period when George Eliot and Henry James were writing, the destiny of almost any well-brought-up young woman was marriage and childbirth, although some women were forced to earn a living. The struggle of women to meet the challenge of these limited options is the theme of most of the novels penned by nineteenth-century female writers. It appears openly in the conventional plot of setbacks and misunderstanding followed by a release into happy love, but also as a muted but insistent subtext in which women authors hint at feelings and responses that convention prohibited their mentioning in public. Even as late as 1931, Virginia Woolf was bemoaning the difficulty for women of speaking the truth about the body.[3] In 1795, when Jane Austen was drafting her epistolary novel 'Elinor and Marianne', frank discussion of a woman's feelings about sex, intimacy and marriage, as well as menstruation, pregnancy, childbearing and lactation, was regarded as inappropriate and immodest.[4] Such common social practices as sex outside marriage, illegitimacy and prostitution were equally unmentionable except in veiled whispers and disapproving hints. What women felt able to say in private was, of course, a different matter. Even in the modern world, many groups of women continue to be controlled by strict rules about their deportment, dress and behaviour. As Marjane Satrapi's comic-strip *Embroideries* (2005) discloses, they still manage to exchange information about their experience of sexual matters. The teatime talk of a group of Iranian women reveals the often comic, sometimes painful secrets of love, sex and marriage in a society where virginity is still a prerequisite for a bride.

It is difficult to imagine Mrs Gaskell or Elizabeth Barrett Browning engaging in such indelicacies, but both writers challenged the hypocrisy and double standard of Victorian sexual practices. Faced with society's limited view of woman's rights and capacities, it is not surprising that the solitary, seeking woman became the mainstay of female fictions. Where writers such as Charles Dickens favoured the infantile heroine, requiring the protection of a stronger, cleverer, more resilient male, or the doomed femme fatale, women writers created heroines who saw themselves as separate and different, brave souls whose independence lifts them out of obscurity, like Jane Eyre, or romantic dreamers like Hetty Sorrel in *Adam Bede*, whose vanity and yearning confirm rather than annihilate her humanity. Such characters speak volumes to the woman reader, attuned to the cost of suppressing female passion. Again and again, women writers have imagined heroines whose every nerve is steeled to affront, to grapple with female destiny. The difference between Jane Eyre, whose adventures first astonished the reading public in 1847, and Martha Quest, the heroine of Doris Lessing's *Children of Violence* sequence (1952–69), is actually very slight, a matter of period and circumstance. In essence, both represent the same striving female consciousness, eager to learn what can be known, and to feel whatever can be endured and beyond. Where female destiny has changed most significantly since the eras of Jane Austen, Charlotte Brontë and George Eliot is that it is no longer linked so absolutely to the idea of one steady faithful (and of course passionate) love, which finds its best resolution in marriage to a suitable partner. The modern heroine – Sara Paretsky's gun-toting private investigator V. I. Warshawski, or A. S. Byatt's disdainful Maud in *Possession* – can fulfil her desire for sex and independence without being exiled like Austen's Maria Bertram to some foreign country in the company of an ill-tempered aunt. Love, however, remains the heroine's goal, and the difficulty of finding a worthy partner is as fraught and challenging today as when Mary Wollstonecraft embarked on her remarkable career as a real-life heroine, writer and lover in the late 1770s. The heroine's struggle for selfhood in life and love is the leitmotif of the female novel from the eighteenth century until today. Tracing the various ways in which heroines have affronted their destinies provides an illuminating journey through changing social customs and ways of thinking about love. It offers, too, a fascinating opportunity to reflect on the differing natures and ambitions of the women novelists who created the Elizabeths and Dorotheas and Cassandras who seem, in Henry James's phrase, to 'matter' so 'inordinately'. Perhaps unsurprisingly, the real-life stories of the writers are often as gripping as those of their heroines, although they rarely end in the 'living happily ever after' of the conventional marriage plot.

'Friendship melting into love': Mary Wollstonecraft's Challenge to Woman's Destiny

If the late eighteenth century can be seen as a period when the heroine came into her own, it experienced an outstanding model of real-life heroism. Mary Wollstonecraft's extraordinary career is rarely equalled in fiction except perhaps by Jane Eyre, or Kate Chopin's Edna Pontellier in *The Awakening* (1899), a novel whose outspokenness about female sexuality permanently damaged its author's reputation and career. Born in modest circumstances, Wollstonecraft's search for authenticity and feeling led her into the volatile life of the freelance writer, and took her to Paris where she witnessed the Terror and fell in love with an American entrepreneur, Gilbert Imlay, by whom she had a daughter. When her relationship with Imlay collapsed, Wollstonecraft tried to drown herself in the Thames. Her slow recovery from Imlay's rejection was aided by friendship, then love, with the philosopher William Godwin, whom she eventually married when she found herself pregnant. She died from puerperal fever after giving birth to a daughter, Mary, who would later elope with Percy Bysshe Shelley and write a novel about the perils of creation, the Gothic masterpiece *Frankenstein*.

Wollstonecraft's most famous legacy as a writer is *A Vindication of the Rights of Woman* (1792), a scathing attack on the social and economic repression of women. Less well known are her letters, but her correspondence with Imlay and Godwin allows private access into this courageous woman's attempts to establish intimacy in love.[5] Sensitive to nuances of feeling and daring in expression, Mary writes from the heart, inviting an equally frank and honest response. With Imlay, she is confident and loving, dwelling on his eyes 'glistening with sympathy', his lips 'softer than soft', and the 'rosy glow' of love, which leaves her cheeks burning.[6] Yet she is aware, too, of the instability of his affection: 'I have found out that I have more mind than you, in one respect; because I can . . . find food for love in the same object, much longer than you can.—The way to my senses is through my heart; but, forgive me! I think there is sometimes a shorter cut to yours.'[7] It is a familiar complaint in human relations: the man is driven by lust, the woman by feeling. The problem was never resolved and Mary had the pain of finding Imlay involved with another woman when she returned to London.

In Godwin, Wollstonecraft discovered a lover more worthy of her affection, although she had to grapple with the caution of this reticent man, already forty when they began their affair and confounded by Mary's boldness and unconventionality. Their letters chart the progress of love, which develops through shared interests in politics and writing, a working partnership in which each member maintained a separate establishment, and met to talk, love and learn. 'It was friendship melting into love,' Godwin wrote later, while Mary described it in a letter to Godwin as 'an increasing affection, founded on a more intimate acquaintance with your heart and understanding'.[8] While William was encouraged to drop his guard and advance into mutual confidence, Mary, like Heloise, accepted the role of pupil, and wrote laughingly that she would not object if her mentor sweetened 'grammatical disquisitions' with affection: 'Fancy, at this moment, has turned a conjunction into a kiss; and the sensation steals o'er my senses[.]'[9] Yet, with Imlay's betrayal still squeezing her heart, Mary suffers anxiety as her feelings deepen. 'I am glad that you force me to love you more and more,' she writes with brave self-mockery, 'in spite of my fear of being pierced to the heart by every one on whom I rest my mighty stock of affection.'[10]

Their relationship might have foundered on the treacherous frontier of sex, had both partners not possessed an unusual degree of self-knowledge and a willingness to break through the barriers that held them tongue-tied and apart. Faced with Mary's ardour, Godwin's first response was conventional and protective. Wary of commitment and possibly physically shy and inept, he tried to dismiss the sexual act as 'trivial', but then confessed his fear that her feelings might not be fully engaged. Their fantasies, too, seemed at odds. While Godwin dreamt of being an all-conquering Jove, when he was faced with a flesh-and-blood mistress his ardour collapsed and he found himself bewildered and chagrined. 'Do not hate me,' he begged her, '[d]o not cast me off.'[11] Chilled by her lover's lack of spontaneity, Mary sent him a poignant fable about a sycamore tree, which foolishly anticipates the spring and has its fresh leaves shrivelled by a hoar frost.[12] Challenged to be human, Godwin responded again with furious blame and withdrawal. 'I have no answer to make to your fable,' he thundered, 'I needed soothing, & you threaten me. Oppressed with a diffidence & uncertainty which I hate, you ... annihilate me.'[13]

Within months, however, these difficulties had been smoothed away, as mutual need, affection and familiarity transformed the awkwardness of their early approaches. Soon Mary was 'acting the part of a wife', sending over Godwin's household linen with a tender note: 'There is such a magic in affection that I have been more gratified by your clasping your hands round my arm, in company, than I could have been by all the admiration in the world, tho' I am a woman[.]'[14] 'It is not rapture' that she feels in his arms, she tells him, but 'a sublime tranquillity', and yet, after a particularly successful night together she writes gaily, 'I have seldom seen so much live fire running about my features as this morning when recollections—very dear, called forth the blush of pleasure, as I adjusted my hair.'[15]

These intimate letters provide a tantalising background to women's fictions of the period. As Wollstonecraft herself recognised, what she made of her circumstances was unique. 'I am . . . going to be the first of a new genus,' she wrote simply, aware that her search for honesty, the holiness of the heart's affections, in every sphere of life required a radical new approach to female destiny. Her tender words of love, her recollection of Imlay's warm cheek resting against hers, and the colour that flooded her face when she remembered Godwin's caresses remind us of the physical reality of sex and love, the excitement and promise of pleasure that drive the plots of innumerable novels even when bodily contact is restricted to the ceremonious gestures of the ballroom, a helping hand over a stile, a supportive arm when tired, or, more daring, Captain Wentworth's flirtatious game of catch with Louisa Musgrove on the stone steps beside the quay at Lyme Regis.

Love or Money:
The Heroine's Dilemma

Jane Austen was a near contemporary of Wollstonecraft, born some sixteen years later, but the contrasts between what the two women chose to write and publish indicate not merely their varied circumstances of family and upbringing, but an immense difference in outlook and interests. Austen was not a reformist in any obvious sense, she led a conventional life, spent mainly in rural Hampshire, and she preferred to make her opinions known through fiction rather than polemic. Her forte was observation and satire, and she delighted in the domestic dramas of her family, friends and neighbours. Love entered her life briefly and inconclusively when she was a young woman. She flirted with a charming Irishman whose family rushed him out of danger from the clever, portionless girl; she later accepted a wealthy suitor several years her junior and renounced the engagement within hours, to the confusion and embarrassment of everyone concerned. There were rumours of the odd admirer, a hint of an attraction here and there, but it all came to nothing and the young woman once sourly described as 'the prettiest, silliest, most affected husband-hunting butterfly' lived quietly with her family, ending her short life in a cottage in Chawton with her mother and spinster sister, sharing a bedroom with Cassandra, and writing in the living room where a creaking swing door between the entrance and the family rooms alerted her to visitors.[16] These are the bare bones of a life, which biographers have fleshed out with fact and speculation relating to her family's history and connections with the theatre, the navy and the French Revolution, with money and inheritance, with trial and imprisonment, and myriad other details that create a vivid panorama in which Jane Austen remains, as in Cassandra's watercolour of her sister, a solitary figure sitting under a tree and gazing out on a blank sky, her back resolutely turned to the viewer. Even in her novels she remains scarcely visible, a self-effacing creator, who permits her characters and stories to take centre stage.

When it came to the question of a heroine's destiny, although her own lack of income never forced her to seek paid employment, Jane Austen was aware of the necessity for some young women to work. Lady Susan's daughter in Austen's early epistolary novel talks wildly of preferring to earn her bread to marrying a hated suitor, and the Bertram girls in *Mansfield Park* have a governess whom they share with their cousin Fanny Price. What happens to Miss Lee when she is no longer needed is not revealed, but her status in the family is unequivocal. As Mary Wollstonecraft and Charlotte Brontë were only too angrily aware, governesses were generally regarded as very small fry. In Miss Lee's case, the fate of a minor employee is unimportant among the grander concerns of the Bertram family and estates, even if she has been with the family for many years. Like Miss Lee, Fanny too is a dependant, a child taken in from an impoverished branch of the family, and she gratefully inherits the schoolroom as her private domain when the girls are too old for lessons. Her prospects as a penniless girl are ameliorated by the benevolence of Sir Thomas, although her aunt, the mean-spirited Mrs Norris, repeatedly reminds Fanny of the precariousness of her stake in the Bertram household. In *Emma*, the plight of the portionless young woman is feelingly demonstrated in the history of Jane Fairfax, brought up as a lady, but without independent means to sustain her social position. For all her accomplishments and polish, Jane is destined to earn her living as a governess as soon as she is old enough to be found suitable employment. Jane's desperate position as the unacknowledged fiancée of the flighty Frank Churchill recognises the humiliation and hard choices awaiting indigent women. Unlike Mary Wollstonecraft, Jane Austen does not protest women's rights in any obvious way, but her writing provides an unobtrusive commentary on the social rules of her period. All her novels deal with the search for love of one or more of the heroines, and in each novel the balance between love, income and property is meticulously calibrated.

The situation facing Jane Austen's heroines is quite simple. As primogeniture, the passing of property to the eldest son, became the norm, the position of unendowed daughters (and younger sons) grew increasingly precarious. The Bennet girls in *Pride and Prejudice*, the Dashwood sisters in *Sense and Sensibility* and the charming hoyden Catherine Morland in *Northanger Abbey* face an uncertain future if they fail to secure suitable husbands. By contrast, a young woman of property or with a substantial dowry would have little trouble marrying, although, like plain Mary King in *Pride and Prejudice* with her unfashionable freckles, or jealous Miss Grey in *Sense and Sensibility*, or even Emma Woodhouse, she might find herself the prey of fortune hunters like Wickham or Willoughby, or the social-climbing Mr Elton. As women's property rights were increasingly eroded, a wealthy woman's fortune generally benefited her new husband and their future progeny. In the case of Emma, an heiress whose family estate adjoins that of another wealthy landowner, her eventual marriage to this neighbour satisfies the laws of accumulation as well as fulfilling the requirements of love, although it dashes the prospects of her husband's nephew.

Hypocrisy, as so often, being the fluid that fuels the social engine, the emphasis on property and income in marital arrangements was offensive to a Christian society, which prided itself on valuing morality and sentiment over the greed and acquisitiveness of the market place. The effect of this was to throw new emphasis on feeling in marriage, particularly where women were concerned. Whatever the realities of the situation, the public fantasy was that women married for love, a romantic dream that was encouraged by the fiction of the period. As the historian Ruth Perry explains:

> Fiction held out a promise that, in a world beset by greed, heroic fidelity to true love above all else was possible. For women, this message had a sexual dimension: to marry without love (or to love without marrying) were variations on the theme of prostitution. A woman could belong to only one man and so she had better choose well the first time. Everything else paled next to the importance of that choice, which was supposed to be made on the intangible ground of feeling rather than for any material advantage.[17]

In the light of such expectations, Elizabeth Bennet's repugnance in *Pride and Prejudice* at the marriage of her friend Charlotte Lucas to the obnoxious Mr Collins is all the more understandable. Even so, Jane Austen is too just and worldly wise to dodge the benefits to Charlotte of the arrangement: the acquisition of a home of her own, complete with garden and poultry and a full complement of furniture, household linen and china, and, perhaps most important of all, the opportunity to hold up her head in society as a married woman (even if her husband is a fool), the stigma and anxiety of spinsterhood gone for ever. As for passion, Charlotte clearly does her duty, since she becomes pregnant within a reasonable period of marriage, a promise of future happiness even if the begetting may have been a somewhat joyless affair.

The balance between love and money is the destiny Jane Austen's heroines are called on to affront, a negotiation admirably played out in *Pride and Prejudice*. Mrs Bennet's comic determination to marry off her five daughters masks her genuine anxiety about their future. Failing a male heir, the Longbourn estate is entailed outside the family, a modern arrangement criticised by Lady Catherine de Bourgh, the haughty representative of an aristocracy long accustomed to female heirs. In the event of her husband's death, Mrs Bennet and her girls will be thrown on the goodwill of Mr Bennet's successor, the unreliable churchman Mr Collins. Had Elizabeth been able to sink her scruples and marry this cousin, she would have been able to secure the family home for her mother and unmarried sisters. That she does not even consider this as an option is a sure indication that the reader is dealing with a romance, in which the heroine's compass is resolutely set towards true love. The financial difficulties of the female members of the family are compounded by Mr Bennet's lifelong failure to save any money from his income. Married to an extravagant wife, he has pride and independence enough to keep out of debt, but all that is available for the future maintenance of his family is the five thousand pounds settled on Mrs Bennet and her progeny when she married.

It is against this background of uncertainty that Elizabeth Bennet's refusal first of Mr Collins and then of the wealthy Mr Darcy, possessor of a superb house and extensive grounds in Derbyshire, and an income of ten thousand a year, has to be assessed. What drives this heroine, apparently, is a fastidiousness and emotional integrity that demand true love and mutual respect as the only acceptable bases for marriage. Like Fanny Price in *Mansfield Park*, who dares to refuse Mr Crawford despite the prospect he offers of financial security for herself and her siblings, Elizabeth stands by her own moral judgement. There is, moreover, the question of personal taste and Austen is quite clear about a woman's right to choose. In rejecting the arrogant Mr Darcy, Elizabeth might have echoed Fanny's indignant declaration of independence to Sir Thomas: 'Let him have all the perfections in the world, I think it ought not to be set down as certain, that a man must be acceptable to every woman he may happen to like himself.'[18] By upholding these values, Elizabeth is in tune with the moral *Zeitgeist* and, through a denouement that must have spoken to the secret dreams of penniless girls all over Europe, she is amply rewarded for her high standards. In Mr Darcy, she wins a husband with the intelligence to respond to her wit, the imagination to be captivated by her glowing eyes and vivid complexion, fresh from an energetic tramp across muddy fields to visit her sick sister, and a man generous enough to acknowledge his own arrogance and insensitivity. Gradually these complementary lovers come together, Elizabeth all fun and quickness and sparkle, Darcy reticent, upright and vulnerable to passion. When asked what first persuaded her to fall in love with Mr Darcy, Elizabeth jokes that it was seeing his splendid estates at Pemberley. Love *and* money: lucky Elizabeth, who manages to achieve both these desirable goals and, in doing so, sets a marker for aspiration for generations of needy heroines.

The debate about women, love and money is continued in *Sense and Sensibility*, where a mother and three sisters are again compelled by a father's thoughtlessness to face a future without income or property. The debate revolves wittily around popular ideals about falling in love, woman's constancy and the reliability of 'romantic' gestures. In balancing the impetuous sensibility of Marianne Dashwood, with her quivering response to music and poetry, and her love of solitary rambles through damp and picturesque landscapes, against the sense of Elinor, who silently and stoically suffers the misery of unfulfilled love, Austen homes in again on the question of appropriate female behaviour. How is Marianne's passion for the handsome Willoughby to be evaluated in the light of his subsequent treatment of her and pursuit of a wealthy bride? And what of woman's famous fidelity, given Marianne's eventual marriage and devotion to a second man? What is the reader to make of Willoughby as a suitable mate for Marianne? Like Frank Churchill in *Emma*, he is dependent on an older woman who controls his purse strings, but it is his own bad faith that alienates his mentor Mrs Smith, and causes the loss of Marianne. If women are expected to be constant in love, the message seems to be that they would be well advised to take care in whom they place their affections. The behaviour of sensible Elinor is similarly open to question, since she makes the mistake of falling for a man who is already secretly engaged. In her case fidelity is finally rewarded, although almost until the end of the novel her future remains in doubt. What is unquestionable is her loyalty and integrity. Quietly committed to Edward's well-being and reputation, she defends his behaviour, conceals her own pain and, with a sensibility as acute as any displayed by Marianne, does her best to secure him the living that will enable him to marry her rival. Their eventual union lacks the brio of Elizabeth's triumphant nuptials with Mr Darcy, but it satisfies the requirement that a young woman's virtue, loyalty and generosity should be rewarded by winning her heart's desire, even if this appears in the less than peerless guise of the unheroic Edward.

Jane Austen explored in her novels the possibilities of happiness and disappointment in love, balancing the needs of a woman's heart against the future requirements of her family coffers once she was a wife and mother to a brood of small children. Austen's ability to look at many sides of the marriage question is revealed in her letters to her niece Fanny Knight, written in November 1814 during the composition of *Emma*, a novel hugely concerned with the need for a woman to make the right choice in marriage. It is evident from the correspondence that Fanny had confessed her fluctuating feelings for a suitor whom she at first seemed to love, but for whom she lost enthusiasm as soon as she was sure she had secured his affection, a contrariness in human nature her tolerant aunt readily understands. 'What strange creatures we are!' she exclaims sympathetically. 'It seems as if your being secure of him (as you say yourself) had made you Indifferent . . . How shall we account for it?' Aunt Jane has no doubt where the problem lies: 'Your mistake has been one that thousands of women fall into. He was the *first* young Man who attached himself to you.' So much for popular cant about love at first sight, and the unchangeable affections of women. Even so, as she considers the character and virtues of Fanny's suitor, Austen cannot help feeling 'the sterling worth of such a young Man & the desirableness of your growing in love with him again'. Laughingly she advises her, 'I recommend this most thoroughly,' but continues more seriously, 'There *are* such beings in the World perhaps, one in a Thousand, as the Creature You & I should think perfection, where Grace & Spirit are united to Worth, where the Manners are equal to the Heart & Understanding, but such a person may not come in your way, or if he does, he may not be the eldest son of a Man of Fortune, the Brother of your particular friend, & belonging to your own County.'[19] Money, family connections and the advantages of locality are, Fanny's aunt suggests, significant factors in choosing a husband.

Writing a few days later in response to a further letter from her niece, Austen is now convinced of the inadvisability of Fanny's embarking on a long engagement with this young man, when her feelings are so 'very cool' and the chances of a speedy marriage so very slight. 'When I consider how few young Men you have yet seen much of—how capable you are . . . of being really in love—and how full of temptation the next 6 or 7 years of your Life will probably be,' she cannot recommend an engagement, she confesses with extraordinary candour and common sense. 'I should not be afraid of your *marrying* him,' she goes on, perhaps remembering her own Fanny Price in *Mansfield Park*, whom Austen predicted would undoubtedly have come to love Mr Crawford if the circumstances had been right. '[W]ith all his Worth, you would soon love him enough for the happiness of both; but I should dread the continuance of this sort of tacit engagement . . . Years may pass, before he is Independant.'[20]

In Mr Darcy, Jane Austen had begun to evolve the character of the man of worth, the 'Creature' she and Fanny 'should think perfection'. With Mr Knightley, fair, measured, generous and well-mannered, the clear-sighted mentor and critic of wilful Emma, she rounds the picture to fit more fully her own definition of the paragon best suited to win the heart of a clever, spirited woman. In *Persuasion*, the novel that was perhaps already in Austen's thoughts as she warned against the dangers of a long engagement, she added a dash of spice and obstinacy to the character of the freebooting Captain Wentworth, who returns from his adventures at sea with a pocket full of money, a desire to marry, and a resolute indifference to the woman he had once adored and who turned him down on the advice of a family friend. When Anne Elliot said goodbye with a heavy heart to Frederick Wentworth, it was not through any cooling of affection on her part, but precisely because Lady Russell had warned her, 'Years may pass, before he is Independant.'

All Jane Austen's heroines show pluck and resilience in handling the cards that fate has dealt them. Even Fanny Price, often dismissed as a tedious mouse and goody-goody, affronts her destiny with formidable courage. The re-imagining of Fanny as a roistering tomboy in Patricia Rozema's film treatment of the novel, while satisfying the contemporary fad for feisty women, does the original Fanny a grave disservice and misses the point of Austen's subtle study of this modest, shy, self-effacing girl. Considering her fear of attracting attention, her dependency on the goodwill of others and terror of giving offence, Fanny's bravery in standing up to her uncle and rejecting a man she neither loves nor can approve is staggering. It is driven by an impeccable moral judgement, whose source, given her parentage and upbringing, is mysterious, and which can only be attributed to something steely and true in her own nature. Fanny's protection of her integrity, her only defence against the corrupt values that increasingly undermine the security of her life at Mansfield Park, is matched by a similarly heroic act on the part of Anne Elliot in *Persuasion*. In refusing to agree to the uncertainty of a long engagement with Frederick Wentworth, a young naval captain without family or fortune, Anne had been guided by her mentor

Lady Russell's opinion that such a commitment was indiscreet and even improper. She had also been prompted by her own tender care for her lover, which urged that it was for his benefit that the relationship be given up, for the time being at least. Frederick Wentworth's refusal to see Anne's point of view meant that they had parted with anger and a sense of ill-usage on his side. For a girl of nineteen, deeply in love with a man in whom she found all the qualities of empathy, culture and taste that were lacking in her family, this was a heavy sacrifice, and one that Anne bitterly regretted as the years passed and Captain Wentworth rose irrepressibly up the ladder of social and financial success. Despite his rapid accession to a position where marriage would have been possible, Captain Wentworth had never renewed his suit and Anne was left to mourn his loss and the fading of her girlish bloom to a spinsterish nullity.[21]

Austen's clear-sighted view of the vulnerability of love and fidelity to circumstance is signposted very early in *Persuasion*, a novel whose central theme is constancy. The action begins seven years after Anne has parted from Wentworth, but in the intervening period very little has happened to wean Anne from the memory of her lover. Left alone to pine, without change of scene or occupation to distract her, she has been dependent on time alone to assuage her grief: '[N]o aid had been given in change of place . . . or in any novelty or enlargement of society.' As for finding a replacement for Captain Wentworth in the limited society of Kellynch, the Somerset village where her father, Sir Walter Elliot, presides over the family estates, 'No second attachment, the only thoroughly natural, happy, and sufficient cure, at her time of life' has been possible to a woman of Anne's fastidiousness and discrimination. With the memory of her loss ever present to her vivid and pensive imagination, how eloquently Anne could have spoken in support of taking a chance on 'early warm affection' and youthful energy and hope. 'She had been forced into prudence in her youth,' her creator comments, 'she learned romance as she grew older—the natural sequel of an unnatural beginning.' Thus simply does Jane Austen set down a sensible, sympathetic view of love: romance and optimism are natural in the young and to be encouraged. At the same time she pooh-poohs the idea of one love for a lifetime. Had Anne met a suitable replacement and fallen in love again, this would have been 'the only thoroughly natural, happy, and sufficient cure' for her early attachment to Frederick Wentworth. Since this doesn't happen, the isolation and tedium of her seven years' penance keeps Anne, like a maiden in a fairy tale, trapped in a past that Captain Wentworth's experience of bustle, activity and worldly success allows him successfully to bury.[22]

Again and again in Jane Austen's novels, women stagnate and suffer, trapped in lives whose central motif is immobility and power-lessness. Dependent daughters or sisters without means or occupa-tion, young women in love are forced to wait for men to make the advances. Jane Bennet cannot take the initiative to summon or visit her lover Mr Bingley when she is in London; she can only hope (fruitlessly) that his snobbish sisters will tell him that she is staying in the city. When Marianne Dashwood, in a similar situation, both writes to and publicly accosts Willoughby, she is humiliated and exposed to gossip and innuendo. Despite being an independent heiress, even Emma has to conform to the proprieties. When she discovers (in a night of pain and revelation that recalls Dorothea's physical writhing over Will Ladislaw in *Middlemarch*) that she is madly in love with Mr Knightley, modesty forbids her confessing her feelings and she steels herself to listen to his admission of love for another woman. Elinor Dashwood dons a mask of composure and indifference while the scandal of her lover Edward Ferrars's secret engagement unfolds around her. Fanny Price winces in secret, listening white-lipped to Edmund's anxieties about his attraction to Mary Crawford. Like all these muted heroines, pouring tea and engaging in social chit-chat while their hearts vibrate with passion and loss, Anne Elliot sits quietly in a drawing room, talking about fidelity to the genial Captain Harville, while her proud, tetchy, inconstant lover writes at a table only a few yards away.

In this crucial scene in *Persuasion* Captain Harville and Anne are discussing the fickleness of Harville's friend Captain Benwick. Apparently inconsolable after the death of his fiancée, Harville's sister, Benwick has fallen in love with Louisa Musgrove, a pretty, flirtatious girl whose vivacity has been quenched by a serious accident. (Louisa's sobering fall and subsequent marriage to the thoughtful Captain Benwick has interesting parallels with Marianne's near-fatal illness in *Sense and Sensibility* and its consequences.) Despite his friend's all too rapid change of heart, Harville insists that men have stronger feelings than women. While he cites the many instances in literature and history of woman's inconstancy, Anne speaks from her personal experience of woman's fate. 'We live at home, quiet, confined, and our feelings prey upon us,' she reminds him, while men are 'forced on exertion. You have always a profession, pursuits, business of some sort or other, to take you back into the world immediately[.]' As for books, Anne dismisses their testimony as one-sided: 'Men have had every advantage of us in telling their own story. Education has been theirs in so much higher a degree; the pen has been in their hands.' Harville urges the sorrow of the naval man, watching his wife and children sail back to shore in a dinghy at the start of a long sea voyage, and his excitement at the prospect of seeing them again on his safe return home. Here, the tender-hearted Anne can meet him completely. Men, she agrees, are capable of any good feeling 'so long as you have an object. I mean, while the woman you love lives, and lives for you.' Her voice faltering as she thinks of her own seven years' endurance, she says quietly, 'All the privilege I claim for my own sex (it is not a very enviable one, you need not covet it) is that of loving longest, when existence or when hope is gone.' It is a persuasive argument and inspires Captain Wentworth, listening at the desk nearby, to make a final bid at winning Anne.[23]

Like Jane Fairfax and Jane Bennet, like Catherine Morland and Elinor Dashwood, Anne Elliot is eventually united with the man she loves and wants to marry. In spite of adverse circumstances, true love does prevail and Cinderella does get to go to the ball. Elizabeth Bennet may suffer from vulgar relations and a lack of dowry, but she nets Mr Darcy, the biggest catch ever seen in the quiet neighbourhood of Longbourn. Fanny Price's mother married for love, but she chose unwisely, to 'disoblige her family' as society put it. Without energy or character to make the best of poverty, she ends up in squalor with a house full of children and a husband who retains little of his initial glamour. Her daughter also marries for love, but manages a match with a young man of family, property and intellect, even if he was temporarily bewitched by Mary Crawford. Anne Elliot, despite the disadvantages of fading looks and competition from younger, more confident women, recaptures the devotion of her handsome captain and embarks on the life of a sailor's wife, with all its uncertainties, novelty and rewards. These are fairy-tale endings, in which love and money, or at worst a decent competence, reward a heroine's virtue and tenacity or, in Elizabeth Bennet's case, her ability to learn from experience.

In none of these novels is there a hint of Mary Wollstonecraft's outspokenness about sex. Imlay's soft lips and warm cheek, the memory of passion that made Mary's skin glow, speak of sexual satisfactions that virginal girls were not expected to imagine and certainly not to anticipate before marriage. Ardour exists, however, in Austen's decorous novels, evident in Darcy's response to Elizabeth's bright eyes and Marianne's emotional abandonment to Willoughby. The new colour in Anne Elliot's complexion and her restoration to the bloom of nubile girlhood follow the rise of hope and of sexual energy. Courted by her eligible cousin, seen at advantage in Bath where her unshowy elegance finally attracts discriminating admirers, Anne exudes a desirability that mirrors her rising hopes of love's attainment. Where television and film productions of Austen's novels rely for sexual impact on throbbing bosoms and Mr Darcy in the seductive disarray of sodden shirt and damply clinging breeches, Austen evokes desire through the reader's empathy with her characters. No intelligent reader can be left in doubt as to the nature of Mr Bingley's response to Jane Bennet, or the honest farmer Robert Martin's attraction to Harriet Smith. Where women are concerned, her ability to set a scene and to delineate character (that famous deft, fine brush working on two inches' breadth of ivory) invite a participation so intense that the reader can feel on the pulse what is being represented on the page.[24] Austen's account of women's love describes an eroticism diffused through a wide range of feelings, involving shared tastes and sensibilities, and a mutual trust that invites the tenderest regard and secures intimacy. Elizabeth Bennet falls in love with Darcy because he is generous and reliable; Emma adores Mr Knightley because she has had years in which to test his character and find it faithful and true; Elinor loves Edward because she responds to the intelligent, steadfast man beneath his veneer of uncertainty. Yet none of these loves would be credible without passion, and that essential spark, acknowledged so sympathetically in Austen's letters to her niece, is what gives the adventures of her heroines their zest and perennial appeal.

A New Style of Heroine:
Jane Eyre and Lucy Snowe

No characters could be further from Austen's restrained heroines than Charlotte Brontë's Jane Eyre and Lucy Snowe, although money similarly plays a significant role in their struggles with love and fate. Indeed, Charlotte Brontë was immune to Austen's brilliance and charm. Writing to the critic G. H. Lewes, a great admirer of Austen's novels, Brontë deplored her predecessor's lack of *'poetry'* (her italics) and dismissed *Pride and Prejudice* as an 'accurate daguerreotyped portrait of a common-place face; a carefully-fenced, highly cultivated garden with neat borders and delicate flowers— but no glance of a bright vivid physiognomy—no open country— no fresh air—no blue hill—no bonny beck'. Puzzling over Lewes's admiration, she asked, 'Why do you like Jane Austen so very much? . . . I should hardly like to live with her ladies and gentlemen in their elegant but confined houses.'[25] Perhaps, like Maria Bertram in *Mansfield Park*, the conventional marriage plot left Brontë yearning to escape: to slip through the railing that fenced in the magnificent house and grounds, and plunge into the open landscape beyond.

Destined by financial necessity to work as a governess to the spoilt children of the wealthy, Brontë may instinctively have rebelled against sharing their confined lives. Born in 1816, and the eldest of four surviving children of Patrick Brontë, the perpetual curate at Haworth in Yorkshire, she was brought up in an atmosphere of frugality and endeavour. From her earliest childhood she read avidly and widely, taking in politics, poetry and novels in a household where children were encouraged to be attentive to national events. Sent to school with the Misses Wooler at Roe Head, her greed for knowledge and awareness that the time for formal education would be short-lived drove her to prodigies of effort. A school friend recalled Charlotte as always reading, peering short-sightedly at a book, her nose almost touching the page, even in the playground where her classmates played ball, bursting with energy after hours confined in the classroom. Yearning for culture, she 'picked up every scrap of information concerning painting, sculpture, poetry, music, etc., as if it were gold'.[26] Returning to Roe Head as a teacher, Charlotte raged against doltish girls too stupid or lazy to learn, and longed for private time and space to pursue her fantasy world, the saga of Angria, which she and her brother Branwell had been developing since childhood, and which Charlotte peopled with heroes and heroines shaped to her own idiosyncratic moulds. Like Edna St Vincent Millay, her youth wasting in drudgery, or Sybylla Melvyn, the stultified heroine of the Australian writer Miles Franklin's *My Brilliant Career*, who bewailed her teenage years consumed by the 'living death' of 'monotony, narrowness, and absolute uncongeniality', Charlotte Brontë rebelled against the frittering of youth, talent and ardour, and dreamt of being a writer or artist.[27] Desperate for recognition, she sent some poems to the Poet Laureate, Robert Southey, with a note confiding her ambitions. Months passed before the master's measured response. 'Literature cannot be the business of a woman's life,' was Southey's chilly advice. Marriage, babies, a woman's 'proper duties', should fill her time, and would dampen her enthusiasm for 'celebrity'.[28] Christina Rossetti's short story, 'Maude', records a young girl's anxiety and guilt about her poetic aspirations and desire to shine. Eventually she dies, a martyr to her inappropriate talent. Ambition in a woman was immodest and unseemly; no wonder that clever women from Florence Nightingale to Emily Dickinson found extreme methods of expressing their rage and resentment at the social straitjacket.[29]

Resolute in their determination to find an independent means of earning a living, the three Brontë sisters, Charlotte, Emily and Anne, resolved to set up a school together. In preparation, Charlotte and Emily went to Brussels, to polish up their foreign languages and acquire that veneer of 'superiority', which Charlotte felt was indispensable for success in an overcrowded market.[30] At the Pensionnat Heger she met the gifted teacher who was to become her mentor and the focus of her passionate need for many months to come. Unfortunately, Constantin Heger was already married to a watchful wife. An exacting teacher and critic, who was at first stimulated and excited by his brilliant pupils, Monsieur Heger withdrew from Charlotte's increasing demands on his attention and she eventually returned home, to wait like an Austen heroine for the letters that rarely came and finally stopped.

Although it is not known how often Monsieur Heger wrote to Charlotte, four of her own letters to 'Monsieur' survive, written in French, three of them in patched-together fragments. Their history is remarkable, testimony to Madame Heger's astuteness, or maybe her caution. On receiving Charlotte's letters, Monsieur Heger appears generally to have torn them into pieces and thrown them into the rubbish, whence they were retrieved by his wife, who carefully glued and stitched together the pieces, and kept them in her jewellery box. Years later, when both their parents were dead, two of the Hegers' children donated the rescued letters to the British Museum.[31] The story the letters tell is of memory and imagination feeding a growing desperation. As plans to start a school or fulfil her dreams of being a writer faded in the reality of Haworth Parsonage, Charlotte wrote nostalgically of life at the pensionnat and her longing to hear from her master. In January 1845, one year after she had left Belgium, her courage seemed finally to falter when friends returned from Brussels with no kindly note from Heger to warm her heart or stimulate her energies. Aware that she would be accused of hysteria and despondency, she begged for reassurance of his continued interest. 'If my master withdraws his friendship from me entirely I shall be absolutely without hope,' she declared, but it was better to know this for sure than to writhe in horrible uncertainty.[32] Her final surviving letter, written the following November, is even more bereft. Cut off from face-to-face contact with her teacher, Charlotte seems to have become obsessed with the idea of his importance to her. Attempts to control her thoughts prove unavailing. 'I have done everything, I have sought occupations, I have absolutely forbidden myself the pleasure of speaking about you,' she wails, but she cannot control her regrets or her impatience to hear from him. This is what humiliates her: 'not to know how to get the mastery over one's own thoughts, to be the slave of a regret, a memory, the slave of a dominant and fixed idea which has become a tyrant over one's mind.'[33] Is this love or fantasy, a rare friendship transformed by absence and silence into the dominant impulse of a woman's life? A writer to her fingertips, passionate to her heart's core, Charlotte could not help the image of Constantin Heger governing her imagination with recollections of precious comradeship and shared enthusiasms, of a stimulating relationship that recalls the working partnerships between Heloise and Abelard, Mary Wollstonecraft and William Godwin, and Miss Barrett talking poetry with Robert Browning. Unfortunately for Charlotte, as she knew only too well, her feelings for Monsieur Heger were not and indeed could not be reciprocated. The observant Madame Heger presided over her husband's activities, but her action in rescuing and repairing Charlotte's cast-aside letters may not simply have been motivated by jealousy, or a wish for ammunition should the situation get out of hand. If Madame Heger was the model for clever Madame Beck in Charlotte's *Villette*, a novel that draws richly on her experiences in Brussels, she would have had the intelligence and foresight to give an unusual pupil her due and to save her quirky, needy letters for whatever future use could be made of them.

It was not all solitude and longing. When Anne Brontë resigned her job as governess and returned home to Haworth, literary dreams flourished anew as three talented young women resumed their habits of talk, study and writing. Discovering a manuscript collection of Emily's poems, Charlotte found the energy to persuade her sisters to attempt joint publication of their work. *Poems* by Currer, Ellis and Acton Bell, the androgynous pseudonyms chosen by women anxious to mask their gender, was published in 1846, just after Charlotte's thirtieth birthday. *Jane Eyre* followed seventeen months later and was an instantaneous success for the mysterious 'Currer Bell'. In place of Constantin Heger, Charlotte had fed her imagination on more malleable heroes, Fairfax Rochester and the fascinating St John Rivers, and in Jane Eyre invented a heroine who became a model of what a woman without beauty, property or social position could achieve.

Given Charlotte's background, history and character, it is small wonder that her most famous heroine is a doughty seeker after independence, who struggles through want and hardship to claim a man capable of recognising her originality and spirit. Schooled to her own insignificance in the social pecking order and her lack of any compensatory beauty, Jane is indomitable in her sense of her own worth. Feeling herself to be soul sister to her employer, a wealthy man many years her senior, Jane dares to declare her love and assert its value. She is Rochester's equal in feeling and in her right to respect as one of God's creatures. 'I have as much soul as you,' she reminds him, '—and full as much heart!' Tossing aside the rules that govern sexual relations, she speaks to Rochester from a new dimension, a medium where custom, convention and even their physical bodies have been dissolved. '[I]t is my spirit that addresses your spirit,' she tells Rochester, 'just as if both had passed through the grave, and we stood at God's feet, equal,—as we are!'[34]

It is a revolutionary assertion of a woman's right to address her lover on equal terms. Disdainful of false modesty and feminine shrinking, Jane declares her feelings with honesty and passion. She is rewarded by an equally unequivocal response. Fairfax Rochester loves Jane for who she is, not for what she can bring him in terms of worldly goods, social status or even conventional feminine allure. Once he has found her, he is determined to have and to keep her, in defiance of public opinion and law. His passion recognises no checks or barriers. It is Jane, an impoverished chit of a girl without looks or connections, a lowly governess in Rochester's household at Thornfield, who places conditions on their alliance. When they are first betrothed, in the happy days before she knows the truth about her lover, she sets her conscience and integrity against the claims of desire, holding her besotted suitor at arm's length during their brief engagement. When Rochester is discovered to have a living wife, the raving Bertha, locked away in an upper storey of the house, Jane resolutely turns from temptation, running away in the night to an unknown future. It is a remarkable plot by a writer who, like her heroine, combined a lack of looks and position with defiance of her limitations, the strength and obstinacy to endure setbacks, and the bold imagination of genius.

Although Mrs Gaskell's daughter Marianne felt obliged to ask her mother's permission before reading such an immodest book, Charlotte's boldness won her many admirers.[35] In print if not in practice, her male readers at least were prepared to be fascinated by a daring woman. While some of Brontë's reviewers baulked at what they saw as the irreligiosity of *Jane Eyre*, many were in little doubt as to its heroine's appeal for her jaded employer. Rochester's 'curiosity is excited', commented the *Atlas* critic, 'his interest awakened; he is charmed—fascinated'. As for Jane's lack of looks, Currer Bell had 'too profound a knowledge of the sources of human passion' to make her 'a beauty of the first water'. It is precisely her originality that stimulates the world-weary Rochester 'into an intensity of love

and desire'.[36] Thackeray wept at some of the love passages, while
J. G. Lockhart, the biographer of Sir Walter Scott, called Jane a
'brazen Miss', who exemplified 'the duty of taking the initiative'.
She is 'a thin, little, unpretty slip of a governess', who falls in love
with a 'plain, stoutish Mr Burnand, aged twenty years above herself,
sits on his knee, lights his cigar for him, asks him flat one fine
evening' and, when his mad wife dies, 'at last fills that awful lady's
place'.[37] Lockhart's fun highlights Jane's attraction for many female
readers: her boldness in dealing with Rochester and the fact that
she gets away with it, qualities in a heroine that Georgette Heyer
was to exploit to stupendous success in *Frederica*, *Arabella* and *The
Grand Sophy* a century later. More soberly, G. H. Lewes, who
recommended the novels of Jane Austen to Charlotte, was in no
doubt of Jane's 'mortal excellencies'. 'We never lose sight of her
plainness,' he wrote in *Fraser's Magazine*, 'no extraordinary goodness
or cleverness appeals to your admiration; but you admire, you love
her,—love her for the strong will, honest mind, loving heart, and
peculiar but fascinating person.'[38]

Jane Eyre survives misfortune to win an inheritance of her own
and the joy of reunion with her beloved; Lucy Snowe in Brontë's
later novel *Villette* is not so fortunate. Like Jane she is forced to
earn her living, but no dark-browed Mr Rochester sweeps her off
her feet. Instead, she is gnawed by unfulfilled desire for handsome
Dr John, before embarking on an unpredictable, sour-sweet courtship with the prickly Paul Emanuel, a mentor-lover who recalls
Constantin Heger. Spiky and observant, Lucy is not an immediately
engaging heroine, but she diverts the reader by her plain speaking,
a blunt dryness that dissolves romance and its fictions in the acid of
reality. Her love affair, when it finally struggles into bud, is fraught
with difficulties and the lovers are all too quickly separated, perhaps
never to meet again. In the little house Monsieur Emanuel has
found and fitted out for her, Lucy runs her school, cultivates her
plants and builds a modest library against Paul's return from a

lengthy trip overseas. As autumn chills into winter, prosperous and confident in her love, she waits for him. A terrible storm devastates the Atlantic; ships falter, bodies strew the water. The conclusion to Lucy's long wait for happiness is left open to the reader's interpretation.

Jane Eyre and Lucy Snowe are workaday heroines with their way to make in the world. With her commitment to passion and authenticity, Jane recalls Mary Wollstonecraft's courage and originality. Lucy Snowe is a later, subtler study. Bruised by life and less open and optimistic than Jane, she has fewer resources to battle against loneliness and isolation. During a long autumn vacation at Madame Beck's school, left almost alone with a mentally disabled pupil, she is driven to the brink of madness by the lack of human warmth and conversation. Lucy's sufferings are not romantic, yet she feels with the same intensity as Jane Eyre. When, many months later, in anguish over the departure of Monsieur Emanuel for a prolonged and dangerous journey, and under the influence of a powerful drug, she rushes out late at night to the Grande Place in Villette, her need for a final word with her 'monsieur' has the same force as Jane's urge to communicate with Mr Rochester, or Charlotte's craving for a letter from Constantin Heger.

A longing for love drives Jane and Lucy, a capacity for passion that is balanced by their need to be independent, to fend for themselves by whatever means they can find. As was the case with their creator, talent, ambition and hard-won education are important resources for these portionless young women. Other heroines, less well equipped to withstand poverty, are forced to look to a prudent marriage, even if it means sacrificing love. As the century progressed, Jane Austen's optimistic romances gave place to harsher fantasies about the embattled heroine. Gwendolen Harleth in George Eliot's *Daniel Deronda* (1876) is that unfortunate creature, a young woman without resources whose best hope is to marry for money. This she succeeds in achieving, but at a terrible cost.

The Cost of Money: The Tragic Destinies of Gwendolen Harleth and Lily Bart

In developing the history of Isabel Archer, the heroine of *The Portrait of a Lady*, Henry James had in mind George Eliot's Gwendolen Harleth, the vulnerable girl whose struggle with destiny seems to matter so 'inordinately', as James described it. Beautiful and refined, and with a taste for pleasure and luxury, Gwendolen sustains a precarious position in English society as an attractive young woman who lacks personal fortune. Despite the advantages of making a good marriage, she prefers to be admired at a distance and to be free to follow her own tastes and amusements. In this she is very like Lily Bart in Edith Wharton's *The House of Mirth* (1905), a novel that exposes the claustrophobia, hypocrisy and cruelty of New York society at the turn of the century. Like Gwendolen, Lily is an exquisite young woman who wishes to enjoy the pleasures of money and leisure without securing her position by marrying. Lily is somewhat older than Gwendolen, living under the protection of her aunt, but with a circle of wealthy friends whose grand houses she visits, making herself useful so that she can linger at their expense without causing resentment. Gwendolen lives quietly in the country with her mother and sisters, dependent on her uncle's goodwill when the family is bankrupted by failed investments. Both women share a taste for gambling, a recklessness that leads indirectly to Lily's downfall, but which Gwendolen quickly abandons when a young man, Daniel Deronda, redeems the necklace she had sold to finance her gaming and returns it with an anonymous note. Deronda becomes a moral mentor to Gwendolen, just as Lawrence Selden in Wharton's novel influences Lily to struggle towards a higher standard of values than the corrupt socialites whose world she inhabits. Neither Selden nor Deronda is in a position to marry the woman he is so happy to advise, but they hover on the periphery, stepping in at crucial moments to prompt or console. Selden works as a lawyer and can afford bachelor rooms, a tasteful apartment where he receives letters from his mistress, one of Lily's married friends, and can indulge his enthusiasm for first editions. Deronda, who has similarly had the benefit of an excellent education, is also half-heartedly studying law and lives mainly with his guardian, a well-heeled member of the English aristocracy.

By contrast, neither Lily nor Gwendolen has adequate personal resources or any private space she can call her own. Social butterflies, they are always at the disposal of others and are ill equipped to earn a living. When she loses her place in society, Lily finds work as a milliner, but is swiftly sacked for incompetence. Threatened with the necessity of working as a governess, Gwendolen has fantasies of being an actress or a singer, but is advised by the uncompromising Herr Klesmer that she is totally unsuited to the life of an artist. In short, both she and Lily are educated solely to be charming, a function made explicit when each is invited to pose, exquisitely dressed and tellingly mute, in the tableaux vivants with which fashionable society liked to entertain itself. Marriage is the only respectable career open to either woman, but Lily seems almost wilfully to sabotage her opportunities. Adroit in the arts of pleasing, she brings her suitors to the brink of marriage, but then withdraws, apparently almost at a whim, although it rapidly dawns on the reader that Lily's behaviour is governed by a fastidiousness and self-respect at odds with her friends' social values. She abandons the shy millionaire Percy Gryce when he is on the verge of proposing for the charm of a quiet talk with Selden. She icily refuses Sim Rosedale, a wealthy arriviste in search of a well-connected wife, only to be rejected by him in turn when her social cachet collapses under an avalanche of gossip and innuendo. Naive about money, she accepts financial advice (and several cheques) from a friend's husband, who tries to call in the debt through sexual favours. Stubbornly loyal, she is made a scapegoat by a promiscuous friend anxious to save her marriage. At every step, Lily shows an almost culpable lack of self-protection, and her struggle to live up to Selden's ideal for her exposes her to scandal and poverty. Too honest to stoop to manipulation and blackmail, Lily is abandoned by her society friends without the skills to provide for herself. The love she might have shared with Selden, had either had the courage to make the commitment, comes to nothing. In the final scene, as he hovers over Lily's pale, still body, Selden acknowledges the purity and possibility of their love. It is all indescribably touching, but also quite fruitless. Lily is dead and whatever love she shared with Selden is no longer of any value to her, however much he may glorify its memory.

The House of Mirth is a brilliant analysis of the doomed career of a woman whose beauty is her major attribute. Wharton's nuanced study sympathetically explores Lily's nature and limited opportunities, while spelling out the hard economic truths of the marriage market. Gwendolen Harleth in Eliot's novel is similarly beautiful, vulnerable and lacking in worldly wisdom and, like Lily, she is both fastidious and virginal. Gwendolen's dislike of being touched is almost pathological and her decision to marry Grandcourt has nothing to do with passion. Aware that he already has a mistress and children with prior claims, Gwendolen at first rejects Grandcourt and only finally accepts him when she can no longer put off the bleak alternative. Even then, she drifts into agreement rather than making any firm decision, much as Lily Bart acts through inertia rather than reasoned choice. Gwendolen's moral qualms are suppressed as preparations for the marriage rush irresistibly forward and she hears Grandcourt's plans to care for her mother and sisters. She quells her physical repugnance by the consoling thought that it will be amusing to have a husband subject to her whims. Innocent and chaste, she has no concept of the sexual tastes of a man like Grandcourt. On her wedding night her husband's gift of the family diamonds arrives accompanied by her rival's curse. When he comes to take her in to dinner, Grandcourt finds her white and shrieking, the jewels scattered on the floor.

This horrifying scene suggests the pitch of excitement and denial that Gwendolen has reached in order to go through with the marriage. The scattered diamonds mark the end of her self-deception. The jewels had been given to Lydia Glasher, Grandcourt's mistress, and had for years been warmed by contact with Lydia's flesh, adorning her mature beauty in moments of intimacy and display. Now, in terrible retribution, their reassignment to Grandcourt's legal bride calls Gwendolen's bluff. She can no longer ignore her husband's history with Lydia, his moral commitment to his mistress and the long physical relationship that has resulted in their shared children. A Freudian interpretation might conclude that the jewel box represents Gwendolen's virginity, and the scattered jewels are the price she has to pay for accepting Grandcourt and ignoring Lydia's claims. The symbolic rupture of Gwendolen's hymen is accompanied by screaming and terror, hinting at the brutality with which Grandcourt takes possession of this shrinking girl. It is a matter of mental as much as physical control. Grandcourt's sadism and need to dominate are revealed to the reader early in the novel when he torments his water spaniel Fetch. His treatment of Lydia and the obliging Mr Lush follows the same pattern of humiliation and the callous exercise of power. Once she has become his wife, and his to command both in and out of the bedroom, Gwendolen can expect neither tenderness nor mercy.

Her distaste will only add piquancy to his epicene lovemaking, and she will wince again and again under her husband's languid command.

Dangerous Passions

Sexuality and its dangers provide a fascinating subtext in women's novels of the eighteenth and nineteenth centuries, a covert eroticism modern film-makers have been quick to exploit. Patricia Rozema's *Mansfield Park* (1999) is blatant in its sexual knowingness. Far from being modest and retiring as in Austen's novel, the heroine Fanny Price is dressed in vivid red, in a low-cut dress that barely conceals her swelling breasts. Travelling with her by coach from Portsmouth, her cousin Edmund falls asleep, his head nestling against Fanny's inviting flesh. Nubile and sprightly, Fanny is a magnet for other tastes at Mansfield Park. Harold Pinter's Sir Thomas glows with sexuality, a flushed and lustful figure almost barbarous in his frank appreciation of Fanny's complexion and womanly figure. Fanny's rival Mary Crawford also has her eye on this tasty feminine morsel, insisting that Fanny strip to her chemise after she has been drenched in a sudden shower. In one scene Fanny discovers sketches of the rape and sexual exploitation of black slaves on Sir Thomas's sugar plantations. In another she comes across Henry Crawford in bed with Maria Bertram, now Mrs Rushworth, all naked buttocks and thrashing limbs. These are not incidents conventionally associated with well-brought-up heroines. Rozema has produced a reversed image of the surface decorum of Austen's novel. Her steamy narrative, flowing as if from the pen of the scarlet Fanny, exposes an undercurrent of lust, violence and anarchy. The film reveals the heart of darkness that heroines must confront: the hidden desires of men, and women's secret yearnings, and the cruelty and viciousness that society smoothes over with a carapace of dances and poetry readings, and the insipid watercolours of vapid English virgins. 'Run mad, but do not faint,' Rozema's Fanny advises her sister Susan, words in the film appropriated along with Fanny's other scribblings from Austen's juvenile writings. The insane love affairs, escapades, seductions, elopements and foolish older women of the tyro novelist sound ridiculous and laughable, but they mirror the emotional tangles of the Crawfords and Bertrams and Rushworths, a bubbling cauldron of desire and rivalry, which the blindness and complaisance of Lady Bertram and Mrs Norris do little to cool down.

How far is Rozema's treatment anachronistic? What did the spinsterish Jane, that 'perpendicular, precise, taciturn piece of "single blessedness"' as Mary Russell Mitford described her, know of sex, lust and violence?[39] Recent critics have put forward cogent arguments for Austen's awareness of savage practices in her society, her knowledge through her brother of the navy's brutal disciplines, her almost certain familiarity with the cruelties of slavery and the arguments for abolition, of the indecencies of popular theatre and entertainment, as well as the sensationalist scenarios of the Gothic novel that she satirises so amusingly in *Northanger Abbey*. Even without these studies, and Fanny's breasts and Crawford's comely buttocks notwithstanding, a brief glance through the novel reveals that Jane Austen does not need this kind of help to convince the reader that she was cognisant of many aspects of the sexual lives of women that were not mentionable in respectable drawing rooms. The sexual desire, folly and disgrace of young women are everywhere in her novels, and her attitude is far from contemptuous. She reveals the agony that sexual misbehaviour can inflict, although it is the women who suffer most. The men get off almost scot-free. In Austen's version of *Mansfield Park* the history of Maria Bertram's passion for Henry Crawford is a quietly observed study of sexual temptation and jealousy. While Austen's heroines are prey to romantic love and its setbacks in more or less conventional ways, her sub-plots touch on the darker side of sexual passion. Bursting through the decorous storylines, like Bertha Rochester breaking out of her prison at Thornfield to harass Jane Eyre, are tales of girls who run away for love, are seduced and abandoned, and die in childbirth or abject poverty or of some horrible unidentified disease. Mr Darcy's sister in *Pride and Prejudice* almost elopes with the plausible Mr Wickham. Lydia Bennet does run away with him, exposing her family to scandal and embarrassment, although Lydia is as casual about her reputation as she is about paying her debts, or sponging off her sisters. Colonel Brandon in *Sense and Sensibility* confesses to Elinor the tragic story of the loss and ruin of the woman he adored, and her daughter's abandonment while pregnant by her seducer, the plausible and careless Willoughby. Even respectable Harriet Smith in *Emma* is a by-blow, giving imaginative Emma an excuse to invent distinguished parents for her protégée. Such stories remind us of the perils for women of following their desires, and highlight the good luck of Austen's Elizabeth and Anne and Emma, who manage to find marriage, money *and* true love.

George Eliot was writing half a century after Jane Austen, but social attitudes to women and the double standard in sexual behaviour had if anything become more entrenched under the repressive Victorian moral code. Like the novelist Mrs Gaskell, whose *Ruth* is a study of seduction and bastardy, Eliot was alert to the delights and dangers of sexuality, and not afraid to demonstrate its power. Eliot's real name was Mary Ann Evans but, like the Brontë sisters, she published under a male pseudonym in order to hide her gender and protect her privacy. As ardent as any of her heroines, and highly gifted and intellectual, Eliot achieved an independent life as editor, critic and translator, but her early experience of love was frequently unhappy. Naive and impetuous, she had a tendency to idolise the men with whom she fell in love. Her intensity and lack of coquetry, along with an unprepossessing appearance, alienated faint-hearted lovers. It was only when she met G. H. Lewes that she found a man prepared to appreciate and nurture her unusual gifts, although their relationship, a close working partnership as well as a love affair, came at great cost. Lewes was already married to an unfaithful wife, but by condoning Agnes's affair with her lover, the editor and writer Thornton Hunt, to the extent of caring for her children by Hunt, he sabotaged his chances of divorce and remarriage. Eliot bravely resolved to ignore the social consequences of her illicit relationship. When she and Lewes set up house together, she defiantly called herself 'Mrs Lewes' and spoke of her lover as her 'husband'. London society and Eliot's family were less emancipated. Her beloved brother Isaac refused to communicate with her and for many years Eliot was forced to lead the reclusive life of a woman outlawed on account of her dangerous passions. Lewes, of course, was permitted to socialise as usual. She used the long quiet hours to study and write, turning her early experience of life and love to good account in her stories of the struggles of men and women, caught in the toils of passion and ambition.

As Eliot was only too aware, women's desire can have terrible consequences. Hetty Sorrel in *Adam Bede* is a touching study of a romantic young girl's infatuation with a man from a different social class. Hetty's abandonment of her baby leads to her conviction for murder, although a last-minute pardon sentences her to deportation rather than the gallows. Eliot's sympathetic exploration of the experience and emotions of this naive girl challenges the period's clichés about the stupidity and depravity of rural workers, and particularly of women. Hetty's adoration of Arthur Donnithorne and his instinctive response to his charming admirer are ill advised, but neither deserves the retribution that follows their immature passion.

In *Daniel Deronda*, Lydia Glasher, a far more experienced and sophisticated woman than Hetty, leaves her husband for Grandcourt and suffers the misery of her lover's refusal to marry her or publicly acknowledge their children. Maggie in *The Mill on the Floss* is sexually enthralled by her cousin's fiancé, Stephen Guest, an erotic enchantment that holds him equally spellbound. Strolling together in the heated atmosphere of a conservatory, Stephen becomes mesmerised by the soft dimpled curve of Maggie's bare arm as she reaches for a rose and he impulsively seizes her wrist and showers her warm flesh with kisses. Straitjacketed by convention, Maggie responds with angry outrage. Soon afterwards she finds herself alone in a boat with Stephen, gliding rapidly along a river until, in a languor of feeling that leaves her indifferent to everything except the gentle motion of the boat and the rhythmic dip of Stephen's oars, they drift together far beyond the village that was their destination. Eliot's gentle description evokes the irresistible impulse towards sex of an impressionable, ardent young girl, although Stephen and Maggie barely touch. True to the spirit of the age, however, Maggie finds herself compromised because she has spent a night away from home unchaperoned and in the company of this attractive young man.

Dorothea Brooke in *Middlemarch* also falls in love with a handsome boy, the engaging Will Ladislaw, and is quite literally felled to the ground when she believes that Will is having an affair with pretty Rosamond, the wife of a local doctor. Alone at night in her room, racked by waves of grief and thwarted passion as she endures the blow to her secret hopes and to her belief in Will, Dorothea 'besought hardness and coldness and aching weariness to bring her relief from the mysterious incorporeal might of her anguish; she lay on the bare floor and let the night grow cold around her; while her grand woman's frame was shaken by sobs as if she had been a despairing child'.[40] Dorothea's passion for Will, so often derided by critics who feel that he has too slight a personality to win this exacting heroine, is carefully signalled throughout the novel, an assertion by George Eliot of the power and importance of sexual love in the relationship between men and women. Dorothea longed to commit herself to her first husband, the scholar Edward Casaubon, but, cautious and proud, he was unequal to her ardour, emotional or intellectual. With Will she chooses more wisely, recognising in his youth and sensitivity a man with whom she can develop the trust and intimacy her nature demands. Capable of powerful feeling, but also young and sexually responsive, Dorothea picks a man to whom she can truly cleave body and soul. She may, as George Eliot's closing obituary on her heroine declares, have 'lived faithfully a hidden life', an achievement not highly regarded according to the arduous standards of modern feminism, but, as Eliot points out, '[n]o life would have been possible to Dorothea which was not filled with emotion'. Dorothea and Will 'were bound to each other by a love stronger than any impulses which could have marred it'.[41] Sexual passion, as Eliot makes plain, was an irresistible component of their love.

Eliot's unconventional lifestyle and 'marriage' to G. H. Lewes gave her access to physical experience denied to Jane Austen and to Charlotte Brontë before her marriage. Not having actually experienced intercourse does not, of course, preclude erotic desire or imagining its fulfilment. Despite the polite convention that spinsters, and particularly young girls, were ignorant about sexual matters, many unmarried women writers during the Victorian period wrote powerfully about erotic love. Geraldine Jewsbury's *Zoe* was a *succès de scandale* when it was published in 1845, no doubt precisely because of the 'indecency' and 'want of reserve' of which it was accused. A fan of George Sand and her liberated lifestyle, Jewsbury never married although she had a number of love affairs. Mary E. Braddon made her name with the sensational *Lady Audley's Secret* (1862), which includes bigamy, attempted murder, arson and possibly madness, a potent cocktail for an unmarried woman writer. Braddon, avowedly a respectable spinster, was living at the time with her publisher, a married man with several children, and a wife in a lunatic asylum, and she bore him a son the same year as the publication of her best-seller.

Other spinster writers led more obviously celibate lives, whatever the speculation by biographers about their private romances. Both Emily Dickinson and Christina Rossetti wrote powerfully about erotic love, although in Dickinson's case no name has been indisputably attached to the mysterious correspondent whom she called 'Master' and who appears to have been the addressee of passionate poems. Although Christina Rossetti never married and may have had little personal experience of sex, in *Goblin Market*, she created one of the most extraordinary poems ever penned about the dangers of unbated desire.[42] Sometimes published as a children's poem because of its fairy-tale elements and sing-song metre, it was included by Rossetti as the title work in an adult collection, *Goblin Market and Other Poems* (1862), and its fanciful setting and storyline mask a fable about self-control and the advantages of sisterly love. While the good sister, Lizzie, refuses to try the goblins' forbidden fruits, Laura purchases their exotic offerings with a golden curl, cut from her maiden tresses. The outcome for Laura is deathly sickness, but she cannot resolve her craving by a second tasting. She has become blind and deaf to the goblin gang, and it is left to Lizzie to face the tempters on her sister's behalf. Enraged by her resistance to sampling their produce, the goblins smash the fruit against Lizzie's lips and body, and she runs home to Laura, begging her to suck and lick the dripping pulp and juice.

> 'Hug me, kiss me, suck my juices
> Squeezed from goblin fruits for you,
> Goblin pulp and goblin dew.
> Eat me, drink me, love me;
> Laura, make much of me:
> For your sake I have braved the glen
> And had to do with goblin merchant men.'

Laura is cured of her mania and restored to health and happiness, and both sisters live to enjoy the sweets of happy (and legitimate) wife- and motherhood.

Rossetti had little to say in explanation of her story of the two sisters and the deathly goblin fruit. Her brother William claimed that he 'more than once heard Christina say that she did not mean anything profound by this fairy tale—it is not a moral apologue', but modern critics have been delighted by its Freudian undertones.[43] The idea of a beautiful girl assailed by goblins has also appealed to illustrators, with Rackham's tastefully lubricious Lizzie, her skirts plucked by the tempters (1933), metamorphosing, according to the appetites and licence of the period, into Kinuko Craft's half-naked Lizzie for *Playboy* magazine (1973). Surrounded by fruits split like a vagina, or rounded and nippled like breasts, and attacked by monsters holding erect and spurting penises, Lizzie clings to the remnants of her white robe in a parody of Botticelli's Venus emerging from the waves. Craft's frank exposé of Rackham's pornographic subtext produces an obscene rendering of male lust, in which the girl seems a helpless and hapless participant, although there is a hint of queasy participation in Lizzie's averted face. George Gershinowitz's 1981 illustration of the line 'She kissed and kissed her with a hungry mouth' is, by contrast, an intimate evocation of female-to-female desire, in which Lizzie seems as spellbound by erotic trance as Laura, who is licking the crimson drops that fall from her sister's cheeks.[44] Do such interpretations represent Rossetti's intentions? Rossetti hints that the forbidden fruit does have a sexual meaning: the poem tells us that Jeanie, another girl who had eaten goblin fruit, fell sick and died 'for joys brides hope to have'. In 1859 Rossetti had become a volunteer at St Mary Magdalene Penitentiary in Highgate, working with young prostitutes, and *Goblin Market* may have been her imaginative response to the stories she had heard of the temptations and miseries of 'fallen' women.

Stories Fit for Girls

If the poem verges on the pornographic in its voluptuous evocation of the temptations and dangers of forbidden fruit, *Goblin Market* nevertheless concludes, like many conventional Victorian stories for girls, with happy wife- and motherhood, even if the sisters' husbands are somewhat left out of the picture. Two immensely popular writers for girls, Louisa May Alcott and Lucy Maud Montgomery, whose novels are still widely read today, typically uphold such family values while inventing heroines who are spirited, outspoken and brave as well as determinedly moral. Each writer communicates a distinctive emotional atmosphere, product of their separate times and differing backgrounds, which has nevertheless a similar effect of homely reassurance. Be true like Jo March, the author seems to be recommending, be generous like Anne Shirley, and the reader will find herself armed against fate's attacks and rewarded by life's sweets in the pleasing form of rosy-cheeked children, a devoted husband, enough of the world's wealth to get by and loving, loyal friends. In the case of Alcott's Jo March, fame will also come knocking at the door, even if the distinguished authoress has to shelter behind an apron and duster in order to avoid its grosser intrusions.

In *Little Women* (1868) the American writer Louisa May Alcott portrays the heroic struggle against poverty and self-centredness of the four March sisters and their beloved Marmee while Father is away fighting in the American Civil War. Taking *The Pilgrim's Progress* as their guide, the sisters treat life as a journey to be undertaken with courage, open-handedness and humour, and are appropriately rewarded as their story expands into several volumes. Gentle, domestic Meg marries devoted John Brooke; Amy finds art and romance in Europe; while tomboy Jo falls in love with an amiable middle-aged German professor, founds a school for boys and becomes an unexpected literary success. Only Beth, frail and timid, does not survive into adult life and love. Although her stories about the March girls offer a benign view of family relationships and marriage, Alcott's personal experience was rather grimmer. Like her most interesting heroines, she had to fend for herself in a world where money and beauty were a woman's most marketable assets.

Daughter of the Transcendentalist Amos Bronson Alcott, an educational reformer whose enthusiasms frequently took precedence over his obligations to wife and children, Alcott took early responsibility for helping her hard-working mother boost the family finances. Industrious and unpretentious, she found jobs as a teacher and seamstress, and even enrolled as an army nurse, a venture that permanently damaged her health when she was prescribed calomel (a substance containing mercury) for an attack of typhoid. Like Jo March, however, her metier was writing, and she tried her hand at many kinds of fiction including the popular 'sensation' stories, which get Jo into such hot water with her mentor Professor Bhaer. Alcott never married (although she may have been in love with the philosopher Henry David Thoreau, a close family friend), but just as the adventures of the March girls draw on her family experience, so Jo, her attractive, impulsive heroine hungry for life and recognition, reflects many aspects of her author's character and literary struggles. Indeed, however gripping the love affairs of her sisters may be, it is Jo's battle to be true to her nature and gifts that is the dominant theme in Alcott's March saga.

Tall, thin and plainly dressed, Jo scorns the womanly arts of pleasing whether in costume or manners. Her sole claim to beauty is her mane of thick chestnut hair, which she impulsively sells in order to finance Marmee's trip to Washington when Father falls dangerously ill. Despite her angularity, Jo's originality and energy attract the admiration and then the ardent love of her wealthy neighbour, the young and handsome Laurie, whose patient pursuit of reluctant Jo keeps readers on tenterhooks through many pages. Jo's refusal of Laurie (leaving the field open to her more polished sister Amy) is a terrible let-down, but Alcott's point, which she makes rather more melodramatically in her novel *Moods*, is that a woman who marries for friendship rather than passion is making a terrible mistake. Poor, lonely and deeply fond of 'the Laurence boy', Jo nevertheless finds the strength to refuse him, paving the way for her tender, droll, tentative courtship by the honest German professor. The scene when Friedrich finally proposes, with both partners up to their ankles in mud and drenched by rain, is a comic gem, which at the same time insists, with great sympathy and tenderness, on the transformative power of true love.

> Little they cared what anybody thought, for they were enjoying the happy hour that seldom comes but once in any life, the magical moment which bestows youth on the old, beauty on the plain, wealth on the poor, . . . the world had nothing more to offer him in the way of bliss; while Jo trudged beside him, feeling as if her place had always been there, and wondering how she ever could have chosen any other lot.[45]

Sentimental perhaps (and Alcott never hesitated to vibrate her readers' heartstrings), but Jo's embrace of her professor, watched by a flock of bedraggled sparrows, sets the seal on what will be a marriage of loving partners, whose unbewitching exteriors conceal honesty, integrity and passionate love.

The story of Jo and her sisters offers a gentle and inspirational model to penniless girls of how best a young woman may affront the challenges of a mercenary world. Alcott's thriller *Behind a Mask*, written under a pseudonym for a Washington weekly, *Flag of Our Union*, which specialised in sensationalist fiction, presents a very different view of what a girl has to do in order to survive. It is interesting to speculate how many of the girls who loved *Little Women* also took a peek at the more inflammatory pages of the *Flag*. I recall a running battle with my mother throughout my childhood over the suitability of certain magazine stories for a girl of my tender years. I read them anyway, under the bedclothes with a torch if all else failed, but parents and governesses cannot watch all the time, and no doubt inquisitive females of all ages pored over the spicy stories of 'A. M. Barnard' with as much guilty enthusiasm as I consumed the amorous adventures of the Julias, Roses and Patricias in *Woman's Journal*. *Behind a Mask* is a surprising and original version of the popular *Jane Eyre* theme of the governess who finds love and money. Behind the mask of its sensational plot, Alcott considers the limited power available to women in a society where men controlled wealth and its administration, where they took the lead in love, courtship and marriage, and where even a hint of sexual misbehaviour could ruin a woman's reputation for life. Faced with these social realities, the heroine draws on a considerable talent for play-acting and an even greater capacity for reading and manipulating human nature to make a bid for the security and respectability of a wealthy marriage. Jean Muir is a portrait in cynicism, a revelatory example of how a woman can beguile and deceive the gullible male.

Miss Muir's capacity to deceive at first hoodwinks the reader as well as the family who have employed her as governess. When she arrives at the great house, having walked from the station because no one took the trouble to provide a carriage, her manner and appearance are disarming. What the Coventry family and their cousin see is a 'pale-faced girl' in a 'plain black dress', with a simple silver cross about her neck. She is '[s]mall, thin, and colourless', and poverty has 'set its bond stamp upon her', although her face betrays strength and she has a remarkably compelling voice. She admits to being just nineteen years old. Despite her weariness, she charms them with a plaintive Scotch melody, then faints from lack of food. When the eldest son is sceptical, she challenges him with a glance and brief words that cause him to experience 'a new sensation, indefinable, yet strong'. For the first time in his life he is abashed. Miss Muir was clearly a novel phenomenon as far as her employers were concerned, but alone in her room this paragon took a bracing nip of 'some ardent cordial', then 'unbound and removed the long abundant braids from her head, wiped the pink from her face, took out several pearly teeth' and, removing her dress, 'appeared herself indeed, a haggard, worn, and moody woman of thirty at least'.[46] This battered wreck is only one of the many faces of the redoubtable Miss Muir, the tired woman who shelters behind her repertoire of masks. By the end of the novella she has caused mayhem in the family, setting the sons at odds, driving the cousin wild with jealousy and winning herself an elderly husband, Sir John Coventry, to whom she will make an admirable and devoted wife.

What gives Miss Muir her edge over the Coventry family is her intelligence and knowledge of the world. A rakish past as an actress might damage her prospects as bride or even as governess, but these were never promising anyway in the society to which she aspires to belong. As a woman on the make, her expertise in counterfeit and masquerade stands her in good stead, while her desperation – she really is at her last throw – drives her to a game of brinkmanship, which she plays with consummate skill. As a story fit for conformable American misses *Behind a Mask* was a non-starter, but its remarkable heroine is a superlative example of a woman who uses her brains to secure her future. As for love, Sir John may be elderly, but his loyalty and affection ensure his wife's safety and contentment, not a bad resolution to a rackety career.

In writing her 'sensation' stories, of which *Behind a Mask* is just one interesting example, Louisa May Alcott demonstrated a schizophrenia common among women writers. Respectable women were not supposed to know the risqué ways of the world, still less write about such matters, although the financial rewards for what we might today term 'pulp fiction' could be substantial. Alcott generally published such tales anonymously or under a pseudonym, happy to receive public recognition as the author of *Little Women* and its sequels, and to lay claim to her adult 'literary' novels *Moods* and *Work*.

L. M. Montgomery, the author of *Anne of Green Gables*, writing some decades later, was similarly adroit at negotiating a dual personality. Apparently at odds, her separate writing voices were, in fact, complementary. Her private journals allowed this compulsive writer to air the complaints and disappointments behind the respectable public façade she successfully maintained through most of her life. They also provided an apprenticeship in the polished narrative style that makes her writing such a pleasure to read. Despite her apparently conventional approach to courtship and marriage, in her novels and short stories she touched on many aspects of women's lives that were still considered unmentionable in polite society. She did this by the simple device of making gossip an integral component of her hugely popular stories, which were set mainly in small towns and villages in Prince Edward Island in Canada at the close of the nineteenth century. Comfortably jawing in kitchens and parlours, rambling along country lanes or picnicking in woods or on the seashore, her characters, mainly women, exchange news and information about the small communities among which they and their ancestors have lived for generations. Seductions, elopements and lovers' quarrels make up that 'slip-slop' of women's talk that Elizabeth Barrett so much enjoyed, and which enlivens the letters of writers from Jane Austen to Virginia Woolf. While the central plots of Montgomery's novels and short stories revolve around more or less decorous love affairs, there are casual references to infidelity and illegitimacy, and a wide range of other sexual misdemeanours, which Montgomery treats with humour and compassion.

Downtrodden Valancy in *The Blue Castle* shocks her family by leaving home to care for a dying girl, who has been shunned by the community because of her bastard child.[47] Initially Valancy's boldness and courage stem from the (mistaken) belief that she herself is about to die from a heart complaint, but her zest for life and willingness to laugh at convention eventually win her an adoring mate. *Anne's House of Dreams* is one of several novels continuing the saga of Anne Shirley, the orphan who transforms the lives of elderly siblings at Green Gables. Now happily married, Anne is dumbfounded when her neighbour, Leslie Moore, a woman tied to a hated husband, confesses that she has fallen in love with her summer lodger. Leslie finds the strength to reject temptation, and her integrity and good faith result in love and happiness. Anne herself has moments of anxiety when, after years of blissful marriage, she fears that Gilbert is hankering after a former girlfriend. As is the case with Valancy and Leslie and many other Montgomery heroines, Anne's doubts fade in the reassuring glow of steady, faithful love.

Hiding behind her fictitious characters, Montgomery is more outspoken about women's sexual lives than the decorous Louisa May Alcott of *Little Women* probably cared to be, although she is less obviously daring and original than the feminist Alcott of *Moods* and *Work*. Deeply romantic and essentially conservative about the possibilities open to women, however frank she may be about their most personal concerns, Montgomery's magic lies in her ability to capture personality, to pin down dialogue and to create a sense of environment with a dash of her pen. Plot and character interweave seamlessly with references to the woods and gardens and seashores of Prince Edward Island. Her attractive heroines, Valancy, the Story Girl, Mistress Pat and Kilmeny, and Anne Shirley herself, with her explosive temper and dangerous red hair, are imaginative and resourceful, fond of make-believe but equally fascinated by the lives of family and friends, and responsive to natural beauty.

Whatever the passions that may surge behind the pintucked 'waists' and neatly fitted jackets of these young women as they negotiate the treacherous stepping stones to true love, Montgomery is mistress of the happy ending, which frequently only comes about after years of separation or misunderstanding. Anne's 'will-they, won't-they' romance with her childhood rival keeps the reader guessing for several volumes until Gilbert's near-fatal attack of typhoid fever alerts Anne to her love for him. His proposal is couched in the homely terms that constitute high romance in Montgomery: 'I dream of a home with a hearth-fire in it, a cat and dog, the footsteps of friends—and *you!*'[48] How could Anne resist, even if her dreams of success as a writer are almost entirely swamped by her duties as a busy doctor's wife and mother of six children. The estranged parents in *Jane of Lantern Hill* are again brought together by illness, this time Jane's pneumonia after a mad dash through rain and mud to see her father, who she believes is about to marry another woman. Waking from fever, she hears Dad and Mother whispering on the stairs, '"Darling, I didn't mean a word ..." ... "My poor little love ...".'[49] Despite her auspicious name, Montgomery's alter ego, the writer Emily Starr, is perhaps the most star-crossed of her heroines. *Emily's Quest* is a catalogue of broken engagements, mismatched lovers and botched weddings, but when Emily finally hears Teddy Kent whistle from Lofty John's bush (locations are often named after people on the Island), she responds without hesitation, gliding into the night to meet the only man she has ever truly loved.

Nothing was wanting to bridge the years. There was no gulf. He put out his hands and drew her to him, with no conventional greeting. And spoke as if there were no years—no memories— between them.

'Don't tell me you can't love me—you can—you must—
why, Emily'—his eyes had met the moonlit brilliance of hers
for a moment—'you *do*.'[50]

Even 'baby' Rilla, Anne's youngest daughter, has a muted
romance, again conducted almost entirely in her own imagination,
since her lover is abroad fighting with the Canadian troops. *Rilla of
Ingleside* is a moving record of a remote community's experience of
the Great War, as the eligible men enlist in droves and sail off to
an unknown fate. A frivolous girl when the novel begins, prone
to childish lisping and indulged by all her family, Rilla is forced
into maturity when she adopts a war orphan, little Jims. As her
favourite brother Walter, a poet and dreamer, is killed in the fighting, and families all around her suffer loss and injury, she is sustained by a romantic dream: the fragile memory of a boy in a
lieutenant's uniform who snatched a kiss and a promise before he
marched briskly away. Four years later, when she has almost given
up hope, Kenneth returns to claim her.

'*Is* it Rilla-*my*-Rilla?' he asked, meaningly.
Emotion shook Rilla from head to foot. Joy—happiness—
sorrow—fear—every passion that had wrung her heart in those
four long years seemed to surge up in her soul . . . She tried to
speak; at first voice would not come. Then—
'Yeth,' said Rilla.[51]

Sympathetic, funny and romantic in her treatment of heroines
and their troubles, Montgomery was less generous with herself.
Perhaps because of the tension in her nature between the claims of
propriety and those of intense feeling, her personal history did not
follow a comfortable trajectory from love and courtship to years of
happy marriage. Aside from her fame as a writer, Montgomery's
adult life as wife of a Presbyterian minister and mother of two sons

seemed ordinary enough, until the recent publication of her journals revealed the suffering and self-suppression of this secretive woman. As a young woman she fell violently in love with a man whom she considered her intellectual inferior; many years later she made a 'suitable' marriage to a clergyman whose life and the lives of his family were made wretched by disabling depression. According to the codes of the day, both experiences had to be kept carefully hidden from public knowledge.

From an early age Montgomery had used her journal to exorcise painful or complex feelings. Her diaries for 1897 and 1898, when she was in her early twenties, record her unhappy engagement to Edwin Simpson, a conceited young man for whom she felt increasing repugnance, and her attraction to Herman Leard, the eldest son of the family with whom she boarded while teaching at a school in Lower Bedeque on the southern coast of Prince Edward Island. It was to some extent the old story of friendship versus love, which Alcott had explored in Jo March's relationships with Teddy Laurence and Professor Bhaer, and in Sylvia's dilemma over her rival suitors in *Moods*.

'Love is like the wild rose briar,' a plant whose blossoms fade in winter, warned Emily Brontë, and she recommended the perpetual green of the holly tree, her symbol for friendship. Most heroines, however, want passion as well as a reliable companion. *Moods* traces the misery for all concerned when a woman marries one man while desiring another, and in *Good Wives* Alcott rewarded Jo's honesty to Laurie by giving her a partner who was both companion and lover. Montgomery all too soon discovered that her intellectual rapport with Edwin was based on a faulty assessment of his character, but she was disconcerted to find her body a surer guide to her feelings. Increasingly she came to dread her fiancé's caresses, to turn a frigid cheek to his kiss and to suffer acute anxiety when expecting his letters during their long separations. Having consented impetuously to a secret engagement, she quickly acknowledged to herself that Edwin was a self-centred and obtuse young man, whom she found physically repellent. Terrified of his reaction if she withdrew from their agreement, she was even more horrified to find herself irresistibly attracted to the slight, dark Herman with his 'magnetic blue eyes'.[52]

Her account of their brief affair is taut with the tension of sexual yearning, which both partners knew, according to the social mores of the time, ought to be suppressed. As so often in these matters, the man made physical overtures, his touch a surer weapon than words to break down the woman's resistance. Again and again, Montgomery found herself seduced into giving more than she intended, although she baulked at crossing the final barrier. At first Herman seemed to her 'rather insignificant', then, quickly, 'wonderfully fascinating', even though she realised at once (and never reneged on this opinion) that he 'had no trace of intellect, culture, or education—no interest in anything beyond his farm and the circle of young people who composed the society he frequented. In plain, sober truth, he was only a very nice, attractive young animal! And yet!!!'[53] Her 'And yet' speaks volumes.

The first step on 'a pathway of passion and pain' came one moonlit night when, driving home from a Baptist Union meeting, 'with a subtly caressing movement' Herman drew her head down on his shoulder. She was about to draw away with some sharp comment, but 'there came over me like a *spell* the mysterious, irresistible *influence* which Herman Leard exercised over me from that date—an attraction I could neither escape nor overcome and against which all the resolution and will power in the world didn't weigh a feather's weight. It was indescribable and overwhelming.' She did not move and 'voiceless, motionless' they drove home.[54] The relationship progressed, through 'a kiss of fire and rapture' to her recognition that she loved Herman 'with a wild, passionate, unreasoning love' that in its intensity 'seemed little short of absolute madness'. Even so, she believed it would be the 'rankest folly to dream of marrying such a man'. She would be 'deliriously happy for a year or so—and wretched, discontented and unhappy' for the rest of her life.[55] Torn between the two sides of her family inheritance, her 'passionate Montgomery blood' and 'Puritan Macneill conscience', Montgomery was unable to break with her lover.[56] Matters reached a climax when they were alone one night, deeply embraced. She told him it was late, he must go. He stayed pressed close, his 'burning breath' on her face, his 'burning kisses' on her lips. His wish, 'veiled, half inaudible', was 'unmistakable'. 'The most horrible temptation swept over me ... to *yield*—to let him stay where he was—to be his body and soul if that one night at least!' What held her back was not morality, convention or even anxiety about pregnancy. It was the fear of her lover's contempt if she yielded. Almost swept away by 'instinctive passion', she clung to her need for Herman's respect.[57]

After this pivotal moment the lovers kept their distance and very soon Montgomery returned home. She finally managed to break with Edwin Simpson and struggled to put Herman out of her thoughts. Looking back on the experience a few months later, she reflected on it as a love that could never have reached fruition.

> And so it ends—yes, ends. For I will never go back to Bedeque and I expect and *hope* that I will never see Herman Leard again. I feel that no love can ever again be to me what mine for him was—that never again will I meet any man who will have the power to stir my heart and soul to their profoundest depths as did Herman Leard. And, all in all, I think it is best so for I believe that such love is hardly ever the forerunner of happiness—it is a 'challenge to fate' and she punishes it surely and severely. I have had my love dream and it is dead—or murdered—and I have buried it very deeply ...[58]

Months later came news that Herman was dead, from complications following influenza. Again alone at night, Montgomery 'unflinchingly' thought over every detail of her stay in Bedeque. No agony, she felt, not even grief at Herman's death, could equal the pain of their 'real parting', their last kiss before she left Bedeque, but then she bowed her head on the windowsill and 'wished that I were lying in Herman's arms, as cold in death as he, with all pain and loneliness lost forever in an unending, dreamless sleep, clasped to his heart in one last eternal embrace'.[59] It is a conclusion as moving as anything in her fiction. Montgomery's powers as a storyteller transform bitter experience, as she composes the history of her love affair into a gripping narrative of doomed love.

In her journal Montgomery's longing for Herman Leard provided the raw materials for narrative and reflection; there is often the sense of an audience even in this private writing, and shaping her experience into a 'story' helped her to assimilate emotions that might otherwise have been overpowering. Sitting down to record 'the stormy, passion-wrung life' of her stay in Bedeque, she commented, 'I have always found that the writing out of a pain makes it at least bearable.'[60]

Montgomery was correct in thinking that she would never love with such intensity again. What is fascinating, from the perspective of the permissive twenty-first century, is the depth of feeling these two young lovers managed to wring out of their experience of unconsummated desire. Was Montgomery right to deny her body's yearning? Should she have married Herman and seen whether sexual love could blossom into soul companionship? She was prepared to take the risk with Edwin that a vague intellectual compatibility would ripen into married love. In a society in which women were taught to fear and repress their sexual instincts, passion could seem both the most dangerous and the most desirable of responses, and the experience of sexual love could assume almost mythic significance. In Olive Schreiner's *The Story of an African Farm* (1883), about a young woman's rebellion against the restrictive Boer code for women, the heroine Lyndall attempts to analyse different kinds of love, and speaks of the love 'that blots out wisdom, that is sweet with the sweetness of life and bitter with the bitterness of death, lasting for an hour; but it is worth having lived a whole life for that hour'.[61] This seems to have been Montgomery's experience with Herman Leard and years later she was still looking back on its 'wild potent sweetness' as one of the supreme moments of her life.[62]

Love and Art:
The Dilemma of the Woman Artist

By the time she married the Reverend Ewan Macdonald at the comparatively late age of thirty-six, L. M. Montgomery had made her name with the publication of *Anne of Green Gables*. A committed writer, she was too professional to allow marriage or children to hamper her career and she continued to publish throughout her life. Louisa May Alcott never married and used her increasing popularity as a writer to fund her often needy family. When her writer-heroine Jo March marries, Professor Bhaer has long since made clear his disapproval of the colourful magazine fictions with which Jo had earned valuable funds. Like her creator, she eventually makes her name with domestic fiction, scribbling 'a little story' about the lives and adventures of herself and her sisters, which brings her unexpected 'gold and glory'.[63] While Jo carves out a reputation within a genre her husband can approve, Anne Shirley is content to subordinate her ambitions to the needs of Gilbert and the children, writing an occasional sketch for the local newspapers. For other women writers and artists in fiction, as in life, the choice between love and work was not so easily resolved, and it became a significant theme in women's writing. In Elizabeth Cambridge's low-key but beautifully balanced novel *Hostages to Fortune* (1933), the heroine Catherine thinks of the impulse to write as 'a caged beast that padded up and down and banged its head against the walls of its cage and fretted to be let out'.[64] The wife of a doctor in a busy rural practice, with small children and a limited budget, she has no time for serious writing. When the tattered manuscript of her novel is returned unwanted, she shuts it away in a drawer and gets on with the 'proper duties' that Southey had so blithely recommended to Charlotte Brontë.

An early exploration of the trials of the gifted woman burst on the reading public in the glorious form of Corinne, heroine of Madame de Staël's romantic novel *Corinne, or Italy*, first published in 1807. Half-English, half-Italian, Corinne is a woman of multiple talents as poet and painter, actress and musician, as dancer and a beautiful woman of culture and sensibility. She performs as an *improvisatrice*, a spontaneous composer of poetry, and is first seen in triumph at the Capitol in Rome where the senators gather to crown her with the myrtle and laurel wreath awarded to celebrated poets. It is her fate to fall in love with the conservative Oswald, an Englishman who is entranced by Corinne and captivated by the Italy she reveals to him in their tour through the country. Eventually, in one of those intricate plots involving the betrothals of the English aristocracy, which seemed so fascinating to the reading public in the early nineteenth century, Oswald learns that his father had intended him to marry Corinne's decorous and golden-haired half-sister, a more suitable wife for an English lord than a flamboyant raven-tressed genius. He returns home to follow the path of duty, but Corinne, having given her heart to Oswald, cannot survive without him. A fever consumes her energy and her beauty, she can no longer perform or even write; only God and the hope of immortality can sustain her, and she dies a broken woman. Her one revenge is an attempt to teach Oswald's little daughter the arts that her aunt must relinquish: she is to be a second Corinne.

De Staël's portrait of Corinne in glory impressed and influenced generations of women writers, who evidently thrilled to the allure of public display and universal acclaim (preferably when dressed in the flowing robes of a sibyl, with unbound hair and a captive audience). '[*Corinne*] is an immortal book,' rhapsodised Elizabeth Barrett, 'and deserves to be read ... once every year in the age of man.'[65] Madame de Staël herself was an impressive role model, a great talker and writer, and the adviser and confidante to powerful men in politics, literature and the arts. Her name, said George Eliot, 'rises first to the lips when we are asked to mention a woman of great intellectual power'.[66] Even so, her heroine sets an unfortunately low standard for talented women when faced with the conflict between art and love. Despite her great gifts, many friends and admirers and independent means, Corinne dies because her lover rejects her for another woman. In fiction as in life, the model of the truly independent woman had scarcely been invented, although throughout the century women writers made attempts to imagine what such a woman would be. Charlotte Brontë's Lucy Snowe is a sober exemplar; we can be sure that even if Monsieur Paul had perished at sea, Lucy would continue modestly running her school, tending her plants and improving her French. Jane Eyre is similarly resilient; will-power impels her flight from Thornfield and self-preservation keeps her lurking at the Rivers family's door until she is invited in. When it came to the woman writer and artist, the challenge was to invent a modus vivendi for such a woman that would allow her to practise her art while fulfilling the duties of courtship, matrimony and child-rearing. Mrs Gaskell balanced books and children, writing her first novel, *Mary Barton*, as a distraction from grief after the death of her baby son Willie from scarlet fever. Years later, giving advice to a young wife who wanted to write, she warned her not to neglect her family by becoming absorbed in fiction. Pursue 'an active & sympathetic life' was her advice; experience would give her books 'strength & vitality'.[67] George Sand wholeheartedly embraced the life of experience, juggling a successful writing career with children and a string of lovers, although she had first to cast off an uncongenial husband. Elizabeth

Barrett composed some of her most challenging poems as writer-wife of Robert Browning and doting mother of Pen.

In fiction, perhaps because the heroic model of Corinne was too tempting to ignore, the woman artist fails to find an equilibrium between love and her vocation. George Eliot's Princess Halm-Eberstein in *Daniel Deronda* is by any standards a formidable woman. The version of her life that she tells her son Daniel, when they meet at the Italia Hotel in Genoa, inspires awe rather than tenderness. Impressive in her black lace mantua and rich bracelets, when she kisses him, the son she has not seen since babyhood, 'it was something like a greeting between royalties'.[68] Almost her first words to her son are a declaration of her right to independence as an artist: 'I wanted to live out the life that was in me, and not to be hampered with other lives. . . . I was a great singer, and I acted as well as I sang. . . . I was living a myriad lives in one. I did not want a child.' Marriage was forced on her by her father, but it also offered some escape from bondage: 'I had a right to be free.' As for her child, 'I was glad to be freed from you.' Even as she states her position, defiant and uncompromising, her words and their expression are perfectly matched; she is a great actress acting out her own life drama.

Leonora had been born the daughter of a Jew, a strict adherent of the Law who required her to conform to the expected pattern for a Jewish woman. '[Y]ou can never imagine', she tells her son, 'what it is to have a man's force of genius in you, and yet to suffer the slavery of being a girl.' Once married and her father dead, she was able to have the career she wanted. Her husband devoted himself to her until his early death. Queenly in her stage persona as the renowned Alcharisi, she handed her two-year-old son to Sir Hugo Mallinger, one of her admirers, to educate as an English gentleman, an act of rebellion against her father who had yearned for a grandson to carry on his Jewish inheritance. Alcharisi continued the life of a great diva, but her career was cut short by what turned out to be a temporary faltering, a brief period when she sang out of tune and another woman challenged her ascendancy. Terrified of 'failure and decline', she left the stage, married a Russian nobleman and had many children. Her voice recovered, but she never returned to public performance. '[I]t was too late. I could not go back.'

Unlike Corinne, the Princess puts her career before any consideration of love, duty and family ties. 'I cannot make myself love the people I have never loved,' she tells Deronda in a moment of despair. She is referring to her Jewish inheritance, but her words encompass too the father and son whom she sacrificed to her vocation. What is pitiable is that the choices she had to make were so extreme. Rebellion and rejection were the weapons of this woman of genius, pride in her own talents and achievements, and the determination to play every role with consummate art, including that of wife and mother when all other paths seemed closed. The Princess is an astonishing creation, a tribute to female artistry, which acknowledges the appalling cost of genius in a woman and the energy required to follow a calling that demanded a casting off of the womanly virtues so valued by nineteenth-century European society. Glowing in the spotlight of fame and adulation, Alcharisi scorns conventions of female modesty and retirement; she rejects tenderness and self-sacrifice to husband and children. Eliot's portrait recalls that of the actress Vashti in *Villette*, an ambivalent homage to the real-life Rachel whom Charlotte Brontë had seen acting in London in a performance that had left her amazed and appalled.

Elizabeth Barrett Browning was also fascinated by the tension for the woman artist between love and talent. In her verse-novel *Aurora Leigh* (1857) she invented a heroine who looks back to de Staël's Corinne, a half-English, half-Italian poet with a strong sense of her own vocation. Aurora, however, is a feistier invention than Corinne, a woman prepared to fight for her right to equality and respect. The theme had occupied Barrett Browning for many years.

Very early in her correspondence with Robert Browning, in February 1845 just a few weeks after their first meeting, Elizabeth wrote to him about her plan to write a 'modern' poem, 'running into the midst of our conventions, & rushing into drawing-rooms & the like "where angels fear to tread";—& so, meeting face to face & without mask, the Humanity of the age, & speaking the truth as I conceive of it, out plainly'.[69] The result, over ten years later, was nine books of blank verse running to around 11,000 lines, in which Barrett Browning explored a lifetime's ideas about women's rights, the relationships between men and women, and the social function of poetry. She had told Browning that she wanted to be up to date, to drag poetry into contemporary drawing rooms. What is refreshing is precisely Aurora's modernity, shocking by nineteenth-century standards, in tune with more liberal times. Like any female artist worth her salt, she rejects her cousin's offer of a marriage in which she would relinquish poetry for good works and sets off to live alone in London, paying her bills by hack writing and burning the midnight oil while she wrestles with her Art.

The plot of *Aurora Leigh* is dense and sensational, travelling from Italy to England and back again, involving death, rape and illegitimacy, and lurid scenes of high and low life, all described with tremendous verve. The denouement is disappointing, since Aurora loses her single-mindedness and, when Romney is blinded in a fire (shades of Mr Rochester), consents to marry him in a high-minded rapprochement between poetry and social do-gooding. Despite Aurora's capitulation, there is no denying Barrett Browning's achievement in presenting a heroine who dares to stand up not just for her right to be a poet, but also to have her poetry duly valued and respected by the man who claims her as wife.

The battle for the woman artist was far from won. Humbled by experience, Romney was prepared to accede to Aurora's claims on behalf of poetry and to negotiate a more equitable partnership, but society as a whole remained unconvinced. Women continued to struggle against a prevailing mores that declared that woman's place was in the home and, even more damningly, that women were incapable of achievement in art. 'Women can't paint, can't write,' whispers the insidious voice of self-doubt in the artist Lily Briscoe's ear in Virginia Woolf's *To the Lighthouse*. Like the angel in the house whom Woolf had to murder before she could write with an unhampered pen, women had to conquer not simply the anxiety common to any act of creation, but more dauntingly the view that women were inferior creatures, whose work would only ever be second-rate. Often these negative voices came from lovers and husbands with a vested interest in seeing their partners fail. In *Aurora Leigh*, Romney is dismissive of Aurora's work and ambitions, anxious to annex her energies for his own pet projects. In L. M. Montgomery's *Emily's Quest*, Emily burns the only manuscript of her first novel because a jealous suitor, whose opinion she values, tells her that it is 'Pretty and flimsy and ephemeral as a rose-tinted cloud. Cobwebs—only cobwebs.'[70]

The American writer Constance Fenimore Woolson develops the theme of male discouragement in a short story, 'At the Château of Corinne', which describes the silencing of a woman poet by the man who professes to love her. John Ford's annihilation of Mrs Winthrop takes place at Coppet, the chateau where Madame de Staël held court on the shores of Lake Leman, and the differing fates of Corinne and her canny inventor act as a ghostly commentary on the unfolding action of the main plot. Ford's condemnation of Mrs Winthrop's work, like Dean Priest's dismissal of Emily Starr's novel, is presented as the honest opinion of a disinterested critic, who has the strongest regard for his victim's interests. His criticisms, however, reek of sexism, like Dean's dismissal of Emily's 'pretty cobwebs', and there is also the sour undertaste of begrudgingness at Mrs Winthrop's success, at her reputation and admiring public. Not only is she guilty of the subjectivity that limits all women's poems in Ford's opinion; he also accuses her, somewhat inconsistently, of brazenness and immodesty in daring to venture into 'the garish arena' where men contend.[71]

Faced with a woman's achievement, such critics cease to be lovers, friends, or even balanced judges. Competition is the keynote of their qualified praise, a wish to limit or even silence the woman who has dared to assert her individuality as poet, artist, or biographer. Commenting on his wife Lucy Madox Rossetti's biography of Mary Shelley, William Rossetti coldly conceded that it was 'a very readable book', but added that it was not the product of 'highly trained literary accomplishment'. Privately, as his diary reveals, he was piqued because Lucy had disagreed with him on some points of interpretation, a challenge to his own status as a Shelley scholar.[72] Woolson herself suffered the subtle disparagement of her friend Henry James's influential article 'Miss Woolson', which failed to mention her stories of artists, one of which, 'Miss Grief', would later give James the phrase the 'figure in the carpet', which he appropriated for one of his own tales.[73] In the case of John Ford in 'At the Château of Corinne', his 'love' for Mrs Winthrop requires her submission and withdrawal into womanly seclusion. Despite these humiliations, Mrs Winthrop eventually accepts her suitor and voluntarily relinquishes her muse. After their marriage the couple settle near New York, where their library displays a watercolour of the ageing chateau with the works of Madame de Staël ranged beneath in pride of place. No mention is made of the volumes of the former Mrs Katharine Winthrop.

Woolson's stories of women artists are nuanced attempts to chart the ebb and flow of power and feeling between men and women confronting a woman's attempt to enter the palace of art. Capitulation, compromise and loss are almost inevitably the woman's part in such negotiations. Edna Pontellier, the heroine of Kate Chopin's *The Awakening* (1899), goes one step further. Unable to find a solution to her search for selfhood and love, she swims out to sea, on and on towards the horizon, far beyond her strength to return.

Chopin's portrait of the wilful Mrs Pontellier was condemned on publication as a dangerous book, and its angry reception checked its author's willingness to write openly about the sexual lives and aspirations of women.[74] The story is exquisitely told, pursuing the transformation of an acquiescent wife and mother to a woman artist who dares to set up a separate home and studio, take a lover for the sake of experiencing sensation and confess to another man that she passionately desires him. Set in New Orleans and the fashionable resort of Grand Isle, off the coast of Louisiana, *The Awakening* evokes the lush but claustrophobic atmosphere in which Edna had been content to dream for so long. Her awakening to the possibilities for individuality and freedom coincides with learning to swim, a physical emancipation that is like a sudden sharpening of the senses after torpor. Indifferent to convention, she follows her impulse towards sensual experience and creativity, only to find that she is still clogged by society's expectations. Her decision to swim out to sea might seem like defeatism, but is described as an inevitable next step in her journey to free herself from all ties and commitments. It is, however, prefaced by the image of a bird with a broken wing, who flutters helplessly, 'circling disabled down, down to the water'.[75]

Edna's voyage into deeps from which she can never return is an extreme solution for the beleaguered woman artist. In *Night and Day*, the most conventional in form and romantic in theme of her novels, Virginia Woolf explored an alternative possibility, an enabling partnership between man and woman, which would allow for individual growth and development. It is a reworking of the relationship Heloise dreamt of sharing with Abelard, and which Mary Wollstonecraft lovingly developed with William Godwin. The novel begins with a snapshot of a dutiful daughter trapped in the Victorian model of femalehood. By day Katharine Hilbery assists her mother with her biography of Katharine's grandfather, a distin-guished poet. In the afternoon she doles out tea and conversation to the family, friends and assorted hangers-on who gather in her parents' drawing room. Late at night, in the privacy of her bedroom, she studies mathematics, revelling in a system that requires concentration and logic rather than the groping after elusive words and slippery emotions that makes up the tedium of her days. When she meets the young lawyer Ralph Denham, Katharine finds herself cudgelled by his demands on her interest and attention. After a brief, panicky engagement to another man, she agrees to marry Ralph and to live with him in a cottage in the country, where he will write books and she will ponder equations. The working out of this restful solution involves numerous false starts, quarrels and entanglements with other young people in their circle who are equally in search of a goal in life and a partner to share their aspirations.

Woolf's model for the ideal relationship in *Night and Day* mirrors the partnership she eventually set up with her husband Leonard Woolf, a mutually supportive environment in which both could fulfil their aspirations as writers, publishers and thinkers. It was a twosome that permitted close friendships and, in Virginia's case, another kind of enabling partnership, her affectionate relationships with women.[76] One of these, her romance with Vita Sackville-West, was particularly fruitful, spawning a novel that imaginatively extends the possibilities of the woman artist. Her fantasy of the handsome young aristocrat Orlando, who changes gender as the centuries progress, is an experiment in androgyny in which writing, love and sexual identity are seen as fluid components of a consciousness that is both clearly defined and as evanescent as leaves blown in the wind. While *Night and Day* proposes a serviceable solution to the tension between love and work, *Orlando* is an essay in escapism, a romp through the unfettered spaces of the imagination in which anything is possible.

Mr Knightley and Mr Rochester

At the close of Rozema's *Mansfield Park*, Fanny and Edmund are sitting by the pool in front of the house, whose grandeur is mirrored in the water at their feet. Later the viewer will see that this impressive façade conceals a house in ruins, with workmen repairing its shattered wings while the family camp out on the lawn, symbolic, perhaps, of the collapse of this once proud family into uncertainty and cautious recovery. There is nothing mournful about Fanny. Vivid in her low-cut russet dress, she is busy with her manuscript while Edmund muses at her side, the couple presenting a charming vignette of the writing woman with her supportive partner. This is the serene moment when Edmund finally makes his declaration. 'I love you, Fanny,' he tells her, 'as a man loves a woman; as a hero loves a heroine.' It is a pleasing finale, as two attractive young people find happiness together after the turmoil of Edmund's passion for Mary Crawford, his brother's illness and his sister's disgrace.

Edmund's words, while not actually scripted by Jane Austen, have the ring of a truth, universally acknowledged, about the proper feelings of a hero towards a heroine. Even so, given the misunderstandings between men and women, the mismatch in aspiration and expectation, his view of what is right and proper in the emotional line may be different from Fanny's. Just how does a hero love a heroine? To put the question another way, what kinds of heroes have women writers invented, and what is their relation to the young women with whom they fall in love and in some cases eventually marry? Jane Austen's novels are crammed with heroes, many of whom lose heroic status and are exposed as cads and bounders as the story proceeds. Take Willoughby, for example, in *Sense and Sensibility*. He is handsome, young, cultured and charming, yet he turns out to be reckless with money and a seducer of young girls. Wickham in *Pride and Prejudice* is fashioned along similar lines, and Mr Elliot who pursues Anne in *Persuasion* and Mr Crawford in *Mansfield Park* are also discovered to be unreliable. Among the genuine heroes, Mr Bingley lacks self-confidence and is easily persuaded, Mr Darcy is proud and shy, Edmund Bertram is hoodwinked by beauty and a witty tongue, and Elinor Dashwood's lover Edward Ferrars allows himself to be entangled by the wily Lucy Steele. Even sensible Henry Tilney in *Northanger Abbey* has his failings as a romantic hero. He falls in love with Catherine out of gratitude for her affection towards him, a circumstance Jane Austen admits is new in romance 'and dreadfully derogatory of an heroine's dignity'.[77]

To borrow Chaucer's graceful tribute, the one 'verray, parfit gentil knyght' in Jane Austen's novels is the aptly named Mr Knightley in *Emma*, a paragon whose common sense and plain speaking make him an uncomfortable companion at times, but whose honesty and generosity are reassuring. His claims to the status of romantic hero extend far beyond these homely virtues. Financially, he is a tremendous catch. He is a substantial property owner and farmer, with a large house, Donwell Abbey, and extensive estates. Of his appearance little is known except that he is tall and looks like a gentleman, while his abstemious habits and fondness for walking suggest an attractive athleticism. Although wary of social frivolity, he is able to acquit himself without shame on the dance floor and is an excellent host. He is attentive and respectful to old ladies, careful of his tenants' welfare and the kind of employer in whom younger men confide. He is fond of domesticity, preferring to stay at home with a newspaper to noisy evening parties, and he is deeply attached to his younger brother and his family. At thirty-eight, he is still an eligible bachelor, and the fact that he has not so far married suggests discrimination and self-sufficiency. He is indeed far from indifferent to women, alert to Jane Fairfax's claims to admiration and attention, kind to Harriet Smith when Mr Elton slights her, and a loyal friend and mentor to Emma. When he finally proposes to her, it is with a modesty and openness that are truly engaging. 'I have blamed you, and lectured you,' he acknowledges, 'God knows, I have been a very indifferent lover.' He manages, even so, to say enough about his feelings to satisfy Emma that to him she is the 'sweetest and best of all creatures, faultless in spite of all her faults'.[78] In his soberness and integrity Mr Knightley may not suit all tastes, but lucky the woman who can appreciate and win him. 'Imaginist' Emma, a woman whose lively fancy is irresistibly drawn to pairing off her friends, is in no doubt of her own good fortune.

Perhaps surprisingly, Mr Knightley has not become an obvious model for heroes in female fictions, although aspects of his character and relationship with Emma turn up in surprising places, not least in detective fiction and in the novels of Georgette Heyer, where his integrity and capacity for devotion become virtues in waiting. In *Emma* Mr Knightley is always himself, while the emphasis of the story is on Emma's matchmaking for others. In his later metamorphoses he becomes the plot: a cynic, rake or dilettante transformed by his passion for a worthy woman. Interestingly and quite unlike the prototype, this new breed of hero often appears in public masquerading as a fashion plate. Sir Percy Blakeney in Baroness Orczy's *The Scarlet Pimpernel* (1905) sets the trend for the foppish hero whose vapidity is a front for courage and trustworthiness. Young, tall, 'broad-shouldered and massively built', with 'deep-set blue eyes' and a 'strong, clearly cut mouth', his good looks are marred by laziness and a 'perpetual inane laugh'. He is also immensely rich and 'leader of all the fashions'. Under his perfectly fitting jackets, satin breeches and mask of languor and stupidity, however, Sir Percy conceals intelligence, probity and a concern for his fellow creatures that echo Mr Knightley's merits. His sensitivity is betrayed by his slender, feminine hands, and by the 'deep and hopeless passion' with which he secretly worships his beautiful, clever and estranged French wife. The 'inane' Sir Percy turns out to be the intrepid Scarlet Pimpernel, who dares to snatch members of the French aristocracy from the very steps of the guillotine and convey them safely to England.[79]

Sir Percy is Mr Knightley recast as a hero of the French Revolution and the misunderstood husband of Marguerite, whose perils allow him the pleasure of rescue, reconciliation and mastery. The type reappears in the less sensational form of Lord Peter Wimsey, Dorothy Sayers's canny detective, who similarly conceals strong passions and a formidable intellect under a dandified exterior. Here again, Lord Peter's powerful body is civilised by exquisite tailoring and his piercing gaze concealed behind an affected monocle. In his love and concern for Miss Harriet Vane, whom he rescues from a murder charge and pursues assiduously during the course of several cases in which she acts as junior sleuth, he recalls Mr Knightley's watchful care of Emma, although Lord Peter, unsure of his place in her affections, never dares to lecture Harriet.

Georgette Heyer, in her Regency novels, developed the foppish hero into an art form, retaining his links to the exemplary owner of Donwell Abbey in his social class and willingness to fall in love with a spirited woman. Hero after hero is presented in highly polished boots, immaculate neckcloth and a coat that appears to have been moulded to his (magnificent) form. Typically wealthy young bachelors, intelligent but bored, her leaders of fashion are cynical about the ploys of young girls and their mamas to entrap them into marriage. Like Jane Austen's Henry Crawford, they have too much time on their hands and too little to engage their interest; unlike Mr Knightley, the care of their farms and tenants is often rather low on their list of priorities. Faced with a sprightly heroine, a Frederica or Arabella, or the daring Mary Challoner in *Devil's*

Cub, such men are at first dismissive, then challenged and finally disarmed into passionate love. Married to clever women, they will lead productive and fulfilled lives. The plots of Heyer's novels may follow a familiar trajectory, but their working out is so elegant, romantic, ingenious and witty that the reader returns again and again, sure of happy hours of intrigue and suspense.

Heyer's heroes are the product of escapism, the wonderful realm of make-believe, which is one of the most powerful lures to reading and writing novels. P. D. James's detective hero Adam Dalgliesh belongs to a harsher, more unforgiving world, where jealousy, hatred, greed and revenge are played out in plots that rarely lead to a happy ending. Dalgliesh, with his alternative career as a poet, his taste for fine wine and good music, his tact and manners and moral probity, is a throwback to an earlier period, a gentleman in the old-fashioned sense of the word. His connections to Mr Knightley are subtly signposted in his courtship of his own Emma, a young woman academic whom he meets in the course of an investigation. There is not simply the coincidence (surely intentional) of Emma's name. There are other parallels, in Dalgliesh's reserved, upright character and his mode of courting Emma, which is reticent and attentive. Just as Mr Knightley suffered from jealousy of Frank Churchill, in *Death in Holy Orders* Dalgliesh frets about possible rivals, and accepts the risk of trouble and failure. His feeling for Emma is not, however, the result of 'friendship melting into love', a gradual fruition based on daily, familiar contact as was Mr Knightley's for Emma Woodhouse. A modern, deracinated hero, with a tragic past and an impressive internal barricade against too much feeling, he gropes his way into commitment, advancing with the caution of the chastened Mr Darcy, Captain Wentworth, or even Mr Knightley himself, fearful of rejection, yet determined to make a bid for happiness. In *The Murder Room*, like Frederick Wentworth in *Persuasion*, he writes a letter declaring his passion, but months later, in *The Lighthouse*, although the couple now seem united as lovers, his marriage to Emma is still undecided. It is her initiative that will finally set the date.

Mr Knightley is perhaps too perfect a specimen for cloning. Mr Rochester in *Jane Eyre* proved more susceptible to reinterpretation, a flawed 'Dark Hero' whose all too human grasp at happiness attracts fellow feeling along with condemnation. His anarchic passion for a plain, impoverished governess appeals to female romanticism, while his mad wife and the secret chamber where he keeps her tap into legends of Bluebeard and other demonic husbands, dark spirits whom the heroine has to tame or outwit if she is to survive. Although physically powerful (and hence menacing), his body shape is simian rather than Apollonian, 'of middle height, and considerable breadth of chest', as Jane swiftly observes when she first meets him, a stranger whose horse has slipped on a sheet of ice on a lonely road.[80] His customary expression is grim rather than genial; his head is massive and his features 'granite-hewn', although he has very fine eyes, 'great dark eyes' with an occasional glimmer in their depths that speaks of tenderness. The 'sable waves' of his hair conceal a forehead whose configuration suggests intellect, but lacks benevolence.[81] In short, Mr Rochester is not handsome, a deficiency with which Jane delights to tease him, although she secretly relishes his ruggedness. As to his character, in a letter to her publisher's reader, William Smith Williams, Charlotte Brontë wrote a revealing sketch of the man she had intended to portray:

> Mr. Rochester has a thoughtful nature and a very feeling heart; he is neither selfish nor self-indulgent; he is ill-educated, misguided, errs, when he does err, through rashness and inexperience: he lives for a time as too many other men live—but being radically better than most men he does not like that degraded life, and is never happy in it. He is taught the severe lessons of Experience and has sense to learn wisdom from them—years improve him—the effervescence of youth foamed away, what

is really good in him still remains—his nature is like wine of a good vintage, time cannot sour—but only mellows him.[82]

She goes on to compare him to another unconventional hero, the rebellious Heathcliff in her sister Emily's novel, *Wuthering Heights*.

> Heathcliffe [*sic*] . . . is quite another creation. He exemplifies the effects which a life of continued injustice and hard usage may produce on a naturally perverse, vindictive and inexorable disposition. Carefully trained and kindly treated, the black gipsey-cub might possibly have been reared into a human being, but tyranny and ignorance made of him a mere demon. The worst of it is, some of his spirit seems breathed through the whole narrative in which he figures: it haunts every moor and glen, and beckons in every fir-tree of the 'Heights.'[83]

Charlotte always had problems with Emily's novel, which she felt she had to defend against public accusations of grossness and unfemininity. Her assessment of Heathcliff is astute but unsympathetic, and her comparison of their respective heroes suggests the difference between the two sisters' views of life: Charlotte's essentially humanitarian, social vision and Emily's fearless embrace of the stark and elemental impulses in human nature. (It is illuminating to compare Charlotte's sympathetic description of her hero with the repressed and cruel Rochester of Jean Rhys's *Wide Sargasso Sea* (1966). Rhys's novel tells the 'back story' of the mad wife in the attic, the Creole heiress, Bertha Mason, and the young Englishman who became infatuated with her, and convicts Rochester of prejudice and hypocrisy.)

For years in her early writings, the Glass Town stories and the romance of Angria, Charlotte Brontë had been experimenting with the idea of the hero. Mr Rochester is the distillation of these early fictions, which were shaped and influenced by her copious reading.

Her quick imagination feasted on fairy tales and the *Arabian Nights'*
Entertainments, on Sir Walter Scott's dashing adventurers and
Byron's picturesque Don Juan. The newspapers and journals, which
were an essential component of Brontë family reading, contributed
real-life accounts of the quirks and personalities of politicians, statesmen and soldiers, and in particular of Charlotte's hero, the Duke
of Wellington. The Bible provided models of masculine power and
intransigence, of high aspiration and human failing, of the dreams
and visions of apocalyptic writers. All these sources came together
in Charlotte's vision of the mate fit for a heroine and in her bold
sketch of the man who might steal Jane away from Rochester, the
ascetic St John Rivers. Her portrait of St John is so vivid and detailed
that he almost persuades the reader by the steely glitter of his eye,
the energy of his obsession. He is too cold for Jane, too cold for any
woman, but Charlotte understood and dared to reproduce his
zealot's eloquence and the force of his terrible will. It is St John's
history that ends the novel, a farewell to the man whom Jane
compares to Greatheart in *The Pilgrim's Progress*, to Christ's apostle
shouldering the cross of self-denial, to the 'high masterspirit' who
aims to stand at last, his life's work complete, a spotless soul before
the throne of God.

Whatever St John Rivers's claims to respect, he did not, in Hollywood parlance, 'get the girl'. The honours went to flawed Mr
Rochester, a hero so potent where women were concerned that his
progeny entranced generations of novel readers and thrilled cinema
audiences in the twentieth century. Reviewing L. M. Alcott's novel
Moods in July 1865, just a few years after the publication of *Jane*
Eyre, Henry James satirised the type of the masterful lover without
attempting to analyse his appeal. Describing Alcott's Adam War-
wick, one of two rival suitors for the heroine Sylvia, James protested:

> He is the inevitable *cavaliere servente* of the precocious little girl;
> the laconical, satirical, dogmatical lover, of about thirty-five,

with the 'brown mane', the 'quiet smile', the 'masterful soul', and the 'commanding eye.' Do not all novel-readers remember a figure, a hundred figures, analogous to this? Can they not, one of his properties being given,—the 'quiet smile' for instance,—reconstruct the whole monstrous shape? When the 'quiet smile' is suggested, we know what is coming: we foresee the cynical bachelor or widower, the amateur of human nature, . . . who has travelled all over the world, lives on a mysterious patrimony, and spends his time in breaking the hearts and the wills of demure little school-girls, who answer him with 'Yes, sir', and 'No, sir.'[84]

James's acidity notwithstanding, the 'cynical bachelor or widower' has long been favoured by female novelists and their readers, and his capitulation to a young woman who is generally too spunky for the compliant 'Yes, sir/No, sir' that James so disdains drives the plot to its satisfactory conclusion. The genre was polished to perfection by Georgette Heyer and reworked with fascinating variation in inter-war novels from E. M. Hull's *The Sheik* (1919) to Margaret Mitchell's *Gone With the Wind* (1936) and Daphne du Maurier's *Rebecca* (1938). With their reticent but passionate heroes, it may be that such novels reflect the anxieties of women faced with damaged, taciturn men returned from the 1914–18 war. The intensity that lurks behind Maxim de Winter's sangfroid and Rhett Butler's insouciance is a reminder that men are capable of strong feeling, even if the plots in which these heroes play a leading role are hardly reassuring. For sheer nastiness *The Sheik*, written by the wife of a Derbyshire pig farmer while her husband was fighting in the First World War, is unrivalled, but the novel was an immediate success, combining a far-fetched plot in an exotic locality with erotic adventure of almost pornographic lubricity.

Rudolph Valentino's performance as Sheik Ahmed in Jesse L. Lasky's film version of *The Sheik*, directed by George Melford, confirmed the rising star's reputation for sexual menace and Oriental allure. Crowds thronged to the Rivoli and Rialto theatres in New York when the film opened in October 1921. Within a year of its release, the gross income at the box office exceeded a million dollars (the picture cost under 200,000 dollars to make). Encouraged by Melford to play up the melodramatic elements in the Sheik's character, Valentino seems at times like a caricature of an Eastern lover, his eyes widening with pseudo-passion, his burning gaze subverted by a beguiling air of mischief and camp flirtation as he ogles the hapless Lady Diana Mayo, the Englishwoman he kidnaps and carries off to his desert hideaway. Fear of the censors meant a softening of E. M. Hull's brutal plot, in which the Sheik masters Lady Diana by rape, breaking her will and bringing her eventually to a point of abject adoration. The film reverses the balance of power, with the Sheik capitulating to tenderness for his resistant captive, who is of course by now madly in love in return. The prevailing image, however, and one which the promoters relentlessly plugged is that of the magnificent Valentino storming Lady Diana's horse in the desert and bearing her away on his white Arabian steed with a laugh of triumph and the immortal words, 'Lie still, you little fool.'[85]

Although played by the rather droopy Agnes Ayres in the movie, Lady Diana in the novel is athletic and bold, a feminist who abhors marriage and is determined to flout the silly conventions that limit the behaviour of young unmarried women. An expert horsewoman and happy to tote a gun, she sets out to explore the desert accompanied only by native camel drivers and an Arab guide, to the horror of English matrons left behind to gossip in Biskra. The account of her rape in the novel is both titillating and horrific. If the Sheik had been physically repulsive, the scene would have been stripped of any glamour or eroticism. Even so, its unpleasantness is scarcely softened by Hull's insistence on the Sheik's good looks and ruthless desire. Unwrapped from the cloak that has blinded her during her abduction, Diana is confronted by a tall, broad-shouldered man, with 'the handsomest and the cruellest face that she had ever seen'. His gaze leaves her in no doubt of his intentions; his 'fierce burning eyes' seem to strip away her boyish riding clothes, 'leaving the beautiful white body bare under his passionate stare'.[86] His physical assault terrifies and hurts her; sickened by his ardent gaze, crushed by his clasping arms and scorched by his kiss, the first she has ever known from a man, she is robbed of all power to resist.

Hull is reported to have responded to criticisms of her 'caveman' depiction of Ahmed Ben Hassan by saying that she was 'old fashioned enough' to believe that 'a woman's best love is given to the man . . . she recognizes as her master'.[87] The appeal of her novel is not in any parley about the power relations between men and women, but in its insistence on masculine desire and the lure of female beauty. Not only does Ahmed have to have Diana, he goes on wanting (and having) her time and time again. Like Shakespeare's Antony with Cleopatra, he never seems to tire of her and pays her amorous attention which, however forceful, leaves her in no doubt of her own attractions. In the end the couple are mad for one another and Diana opts happily to live in the desert with her ravisher: 'I am not afraid of anything with your arms round me, my desert lover. Ahmed! Monseigneur!'[88]

At first glance Sheik Ahmed Ben Hassan seems to bear little relation to the owner of Thornfield who enjoys verbal sparring with Jane Eyre and can host a house party of the local aristocracy with style and brio, but there are fascinating parallels. The Sheik, it turns out, had an English father and was partly educated in Europe before assuming his adopted father's position as head of his tribe. Unlike Rochester, it was not marriage that tainted his optimistic youth, but the revelation that he was the son of an English viscount. His father had treated his mother abominably, and Ahmed was born in the desert and brought up by the previous Sheik Ahmed as his heir. The knowledge of his history devastates the young man. Rejecting his European heritage and the culture that went with it, he becomes 'cruel' and 'merciless'.[89] Like Rochester's love for Jane, Ahmed's relationship with Lady Diana penetrates his barrier of reserve and self-protection and, again like Rochester, when he finds the woman he wants, he adores her. In direct opposition to Charlotte Brontë's novel, however, *The Sheik* celebrates woman's physical attributes, not her wit and originality. It is Diana's beauty that captivates her abductor; her feminism is redundant, although her courage in taking on the life of a desert bride ensures the continuation of their love affair (and a lucrative sequel to their story). Extravagant and ridiculous, and steeped in quasi-racist mythology of the glamorous, dangerous East, *The Sheik* plays on the fantasy of woman's atavistic desire to be mastered by a powerful and erotic lover. The romantic pay-off is that her lover becomes besotted in return.

Edith Maude Hull created a lover whose character and history are risible; even Valentino could barely keep a straight face. Despite this, the story had tremendous appeal for women, evoking that need for reciprocal passion that clamours through women's words of love since Heloise begged Abelard to respond to her again with all his former ardour. Sheik Ahmed is a curious hybrid, a romantic hero (or villain) who belongs in the pages of fiction. Rhett Butler in Margaret Mitchell's *Gone With the Wind* provided frisson of a more reliable nature. Not only was he the kind of wealthy sophisticate who so irritated Henry James, he was also ardent, brave, handsome and kind. Just as he sweeps aside Scarlett's conservatism with his breezy honesty and frank appreciation of life's pleasures, so he beguiles the reader by his boldness and self-confidence.

Gone With the Wind tells the story of a conventional Southern belle's metamorphosis into a hard-nosed businesswoman, a canny negotiator impatient at the scruples of men and women enervated by centuries of good breeding. The Civil War liberates Scarlett O'Hara, releasing her talent for bargaining and management and, despite society's and her author's condemnation (Mitchell is unsparing in her criticisms of Scarlett's lapses from her Catholic mother's standards of young-ladyhood), revealing her courage, loyalty and aptitude for hard work. Faced with a baby to midwife, a crumbling estate to repair, fields to plough or a renegade soldier to slaughter, she never hesitates, however weary or repulsive the task. She is a true heroine, although it ruins her character. She is also a romantic, clinging to her dream of being loved by sensitive Ashley Wilkes long after she has married debonair, bootlegging Rhett. The saga of Rhett's patient courtship of Scarlett and her blindness to his devotion is only one theme in Mitchell's intricate jigsaw, a work of such popular appeal that it sold millions of copies all over the world, and is still in print seventy years on. Not only did people read and reread Mitchell's novel, they also wrote to her in their thousands, wanting to know more about characters whom they experienced as real people. Disturbed by the ending of the novel in which Rhett finally dismisses his wife with the chilling 'My dear, I don't give a damn', readers enquired anxiously whether they would ever be reunited. The estrangement between Rhett and Scarlett alerted husbands and wives to fracture lines in their own marriages, while men damaged by the Depression wrote of their sympathy for Ashley. Scarlett's efforts to support her many dependants won praise from readers who understood how far a woman would stoop to protect beloved family and friends.[90]

In her novel Mitchell traces the histories of two contrasting heroes, gentle dreamy Ashley, unable to adapt to the new, mercantile world of post-war Atlanta, and swashbuckling Rhett, a rebel who despises cant and the stuffy regulations of a society that buries its young widows in black crêpe and quells the energy and appetites of its young girls. Played by Clark Gable in David Selznick's film version, another smash hit at the box office, Rhett, like Rochester, is powerful rather than handsome, a man who clearly knows what a woman looks like 'without her shimmy', as Scarlett complains, pretending to be scandalised by Rhett's appraising gaze. Rejected by his family and polite society in Charleston for compromising a young girl,

Rhett makes his own way in the world, acquiring huge wealth by astute trading during the Civil War. His passion for Scarlett resembles that of Mr Rochester for Jane Eyre, an intelligent man's recognition of a twin soul, the woman who is his match. Unfortunately Scarlett, so astute in other matters, fails to understand Rhett or to interpret her own response to him. She is blind to his love and indifferent to his attentions in bed, and eventually refuses to sleep with him, fearing the inconvenience of another pregnancy. When he finally takes possession of her in a night of uninhibited passion, Scarlett is aroused and receptive, but it is all too late, and from here their relationship dwindles into misunderstanding and tragedy, and finally Rhett's exhausted departure in search of more civilised values, the old world he was once so eager to renounce.

Rhett's essential decency, his clear-sighted love for Scarlett, his kindness to her children by previous marriages and his suffering when their own daughter Bonnie dies, are unappreciated by his wife. Greedy and unimaginative, lacking subtlety and insensitive to the ideals that underlie the restrictive practices of genteel Southerners, Scarlett only loves Rhett when, like Ahmed Ben Hassan with Diana, he 'masters' her sexually in an orgy of rage and self-indulgence. Mitchell's message seems as blatant as Edith Hull's: woman's 'best love' is given to the man whom she recognises as boss. Vivien Leigh, the unknown actress who made her name through *Gone With the Wind*, plays Scarlett's waking up after Rhett's 'rape' as a recollection of physical bliss, but also as a moment of triumph. Alone in her huge bed, she stretches voluptuously, smiling with sexual satiety and the satisfaction of knowing her power over the husband who has dealt her such delight. In this, as so often, Scarlett misjudges her man; Rhett apologises for his conduct and decamps on a long journey, and the couple remain as estranged as ever.

Mitchell's sensitive portrayal of Rhett Butler recalls Charlotte Brontë's description of Mr Rochester, the man with 'a thoughtful nature and a very feeling heart', who has the sense to learn wisdom from experience. Daphne du Maurier's Maxim de Winter in *Rebecca* is a more sinister character, whose good-heartedness remains in question, especially when the reader has discovered his dark secret. Like Rochester, he has a skeleton in his closet, in his case a dead wife who mysteriously drowned at sea. The arrival of a young woman at a widower's house is an intriguing circumstance, offering opportunities for menace and humour, which women writers have exploited to great effect. Elizabeth von Arnim's *Vera* is a horrifying tale of wifely subjection. In *Palladian*, Elizabeth Taylor challenges romantic cliché with the adventures of a modern Jane Eyre. Miss Mole, in E. H. Young's novel of that name, is a middle-aged waif who sees through the pretensions of her employer, the pompous Reverend Corder, and finds a far more suitable and unexpected lover. These are all more or less sophisticated reworkings of the familiar scenario. Du Maurier's girl, however, the heroine who is never named in *Rebecca*, is a true ingénue, an orphan who artlessly falls in love with and marries a man whom she meets in Monte Carlo while working as a companion to a wealthy woman. The novel in which her story is told is neither pastiche nor satire; it is a thriller in which events are recorded from the perspective of the girl, whose innocence and integrity are never in question, although, like Jane Austen's Emma, she is an 'imaginist', endlessly fantasising alternative scenarios to improve on the life she lives with such gaucherie and self-doubt.

What kind of hero is Maxim de Winter? He has none of Mr Rochester's self-knowledge or fire; he lacks Rhett's warmth and understanding. He appears unaware and self-absorbed, falling in love with the girl because of her youth and naivety, but insensitive to her anxieties when expected to take over as chatelaine of Manderley, and self-condemned as the murderer of his first wife. Rebecca had goaded him throughout their farce of a marriage; her final taunt was intended to take him over the edge of control. Even so, like Bluebeard, he killed his wife and the girl will have to live with that knowledge as the couple eke out dreary days abroad after Manderley burns down, staying in dull hotels, reading outdated newspapers, making a treat of finding out the cricket score. Why does she fall in love with him? Their first days together are a record of the agony and ecstasy of first love, her fascination with his 'medieval' appearance, which already seems to her a little sinister, her awkwardness when she is invited to sit with him at lunch, or is driven out in his motor for trips around the coast. She longs to be thirty-six, in black satin and a string of pearls; he laughs at her fantasy and asks her to marry him as if they were chums, playmates, childish companions whose innocence can erase the memory of Rebecca's betrayal and falsehood. She longs to be grown up for him; he loves the funny little lost look on her face.

Maxim is not an ideal hero; he is secretive, dark, hidden and unknowable. Even when he has bared his heart to the girl, she is the one who is transformed, from girl bride to watchful wife, even mother in her solicitousness to spare him pain. At no stage does he seek her out in the way Rochester sought out Jane; he is patronising rather than inquisitive, perhaps not wanting to know further than he can imagine, frightened of revelations that may damage him as Rebecca destroyed his ideals and happiness so soon after their marriage. Companionable but not intimate, caring but hardly passionate, the couple seem by the end of the novel to have lapsed into a state of wariness in which he dares not look back, she cannot look forward. Where will the girl make her proper home with Maxim and what of the children she might have had, the friends her lonely, sociable nature requires? Maxim's personality dominates *Rebecca*, but as a hero his charms are limited. It is the girl who gives and he who takes; a reversal of their roles when he brought her back to Manderley, a wealthy man introducing a penniless girl to a life of luxury, ease and contentment.

How does a hero love a heroine? How does a woman artist

accommodate the tension between love and work? How does a young woman affront her destiny and tackle the challenge of wife- and motherhood? Explored repeatedly in women's fiction, these themes continue to be as unresolved as they had been for Heloise in twelfth-century France or Mary Wroth in Renaissance England. For a young woman growing up in America in the 1940s, the questions remained as pressing as ever. In her brief life the writer Sylvia Plath struggled to accommodate the demands of her physical nature, her great talent and the society in which she yearned to shine. Her story, too, had a 'Dark Hero', a brilliant man who, like Charlotte Brontë's Mr Rochester, might be described as possessing a thoughtful nature. But this was not fiction. It was real life, in the troubled climate of the mid-twentieth century, a period when women battled to realise their natures and desires within narrow definitions of female capacity and destiny.

PART 6

Sylvia Plath: Passion and Poetry

'I accept the idea of a creative marriage now as I never did before; I believe I could paint, write, and keep a home and husband too. Ambitious, wot?'[1]

A Woman's Proper Duties

When Charlotte Brontë was writing *Jane Eyre*, she had little idea of creating a love story that would influence generations of women readers and writers. Poor, plain and almost by definition socially invisible, a teenage governess dared to love a wealthy, talented, world-weary man, and in turn inspired a passion that challenged custom and breached the frontiers of the rational world. This was romance with a vengeance, but Brontë's book is also original, gripping and deeply persuasive. Many readings do not exhaust the novel's power to enchant and surprise, but it could so easily not have happened. 'Literature cannot be the business of a woman's life,' Robert Southey had warned Charlotte ten years previously, 'and it ought not to be.' A woman's 'proper duties', he advised, would make her 'less eager for celebrity'.

The tension for the woman writer between love, ambition and a woman's 'proper duties' has still not been resolved, despite the efforts of feminism and the lip-service paid to sexual equality. For Sylvia Plath, a gifted young woman growing up in the repressive atmosphere of conservative America, the struggle to express her nature as lover, writer, wife and mother was as challenging as Charlotte Brontë's battle against the forces of reactionary Victorianism. Like Mary Wollstonecraft, Elizabeth Barrett and Virginia Woolf, Plath was lucky enough to find a lover/husband with the imagination and energy to help her redefine a woman's 'proper duties' and fulfil her longing to be a writer. Her story ended, however, in tragedy: a suicide that came to be seen as the defining gesture of Plath's life, obliterating her aspirations and achievements. Just as Heloise is remembered for the unhappy outcome of her love affair with Abelard, so Plath is recalled as the woman who punished her faithless husband with poems as shimmering and corrosive as quicklime, and then gassed herself. This reading of Plath as both love's victim and its scourge does her (and her survivors) a great disservice, denies her virtuosity and accomplishment, and plays into still current myths of woman's weakness, hysteria and tendency towards self-destruction. Plath's story is remarkable not because of its sad conclusion, but for the energy, courage and determination with which she lived. It was a life in which love, writing and being female were essential elements, sometimes complementary, often reactive and at odds.

The Female Self

'[C]an the female self be expressed through plot or must it be conceived in resistance to plot? Must it lodge "between the acts"?'

Gillian Beer[2]

'O, only left to myself, what a poet I will flay myself into,' wrote Sylvia Plath in her journal, in a rare moment of exhilaration and confidence.[3] 'Flaying' is an apt image for Plath to use of her struggle with writing, suggesting the need for painful exposure in order to reach emotional truth, and also her relentless self-criticism. In choosing this word, she may have been thinking of the classical story of the satyr Marsyas, who challenged Apollo, god of music and poetry, to a musical competition. Marsyas, not surprisingly, lost the contest, and was suspended from a tree and skinned alive as punishment. It was a favourite theme of Renaissance artists, who interpreted it as an allegory of spiritual purification. Titian's *The Flaying of Marsyas* (1575–6) in the State Museum in Kromeriz, Czechoslovakia, depicts the satyr hanging from his ankles, helpless to resist his tormentors: a reminder of the fate of those who presume to challenge the gods. Plath's identification with the upstart flautist was probably intentional (she was fascinated by mythology) and is consonant with the legends that have evolved since her suicide in 1963. She too, it is claimed, was an overreacher, a clever American college girl who dared to marry the godlike Ted Hughes, and expressed her rage and grief at his desertion in poems so savage that she lost her sanity and died. This story and its many variants, which have cast Hughes and Plath alternately in the roles of demon and victim, have become as fascinating to the popular imagination as the story of Heloise and Abelard was to their contemporaries.

There is more, however, to Plath's apparently casual exclamation. In defining herself as Apollo as well as Marsyas, flayer as well as flayed, Plath penetrates the deeper meaning of this ancient contest. Inscribed on Apollo's temple at Delphi were the words 'Know thyself', which Socrates adopted as his credo. As the art critic Edgar Wind pointed out, an idea of catharsis is implicit in the myth: according to Plato, the 'terrestrial Marsyas' (the body) is tortured in order to crown the 'heavenly Apollo' who dwells within the soul. Dante, too, saw Marsyas's agony as an essential condition of achieving the poet's crown.[4] Just as the poetic intelligence represented by Apollo has to overcome the anarchic Dionysian forces embodied by Marsyas if culture and reason are to prevail, so Plath's determination to 'flay' herself into poetic excellence is dependent on discipline and self-understanding. As her journals reveal, the task at times seemed overwhelming. Dogged by self-doubt and a nagging perfectionism, the simple act of setting pen to paper or typing a few tentative words could plunge her into despair.

Who, she continually asks herself, is this 'self' she wishes to be 'left to', 'this particular individual which is spelled "I" and "You" and "Sylvia"', and how is she to cope with its vociferous demands for recognition?[5] 'I am' is the refrain that tolls her into madness as a twenty-year-old student and, as she recalls in her brief memoir 'Ocean 1212–W', it is a voice she first heard as a tiny child, when she learnt, to her resentment, that she had a baby brother. 'As from a star I saw, coldly and soberly, the *separateness* of everything. I felt the wall of my skin: I am I. That stone is a stone. My beautiful fusion with the things of this world was over.'[6] In her novel *The Bell Jar*, a fictionalised account of her breakdown and first suicide attempt, Plath described how the burden of 'I am' became relentless. Swimming out to sea in a fruitless attempt to drown herself, the heroine hears her heartbeat boom 'like a dull motor' in her ears: 'I am I am I am.'[7]

The nature and management of this 'I' is the quest of Plath's journals, an adventure in introspection whose rawness, honesty, desperation and wit catch the breath. In place of rumour and gossip, the reader finds the unmediated voice of a young woman wrestling with academic grades and the sexual double standard, greedy for success, love and experience, and the 'strong potential powerful mate who can counter my vibrant dynamic self'.[8] Written as a personal resource and not intended for publication, Plath's record of her youthful affairs, the hard graft to become a writer, and her eventual meeting and marriage with Ted Hughes is deeply moving. Compared to Abelard's polished *post facto* autobiography, this is life caught in the act of breathing, a privileged insight into a gifted young woman's dreams of love and artistic fulfilment.

'There is nothing between us': Aurelia Plath and Her Daughter[9]

'Read Freud's "Mourning and Melancholia" this morning ... An almost exact description of my feelings and reasons for suicide: a transferred murderous impulse from my mother onto myself: the "vampire" metaphor Freud uses, "draining the ego": that is exactly the feeling I have getting in the way of my writing: mother's clutch.'

Sylvia Plath, 27 December 1958[10]

In a BBC radio interview in 1961, Sylvia Plath explained that she turned to writing as a young girl because she was rather depressed and introverted.[11] By the time she was seventeen her journal records that writing and the search for a suitable mate had become the twin goals of her life. These aspirations and the dedication with which she pursued them were inevitably influenced by her family inheritance and upbringing. What is striking is the extent to which public opinion and deference to what others might say about her behaviour featured in Plath's plans, and were the subject of considerable private anxiety. The struggle between the need to conform and her rebellion against society's expectations of women, which Plath repeatedly recorded in her journals, contrasts with Heloise's unconventionality in her letters to Abelard. Nobody could call Heloise a 'liberated woman' in the modern sense, and her dream of a mutually supportive partnership derived from male classical models. But this twelfth-century bluestocking appears to have had a self-confidence in pursuing individuality that Sylvia Plath lacked. Plath's insecurity and hunger for acceptance may well have derived from her parents' history as first- and second-generation immigrants, and the premature death of her father Otto, which left her mother Aurelia responsible for two young children. Plath's family history and early years are movingly described by Aurelia in the introduction and commentary to *Letters Home*, the selection of Plath's letters that Aurelia published in 1975. Her memoir suggests the continuities between mother and daughter that nourished Plath, but were also a source of dread. Perhaps every daughter secretly fears that she may end up like her mother; in Plath's case her mother's influence was particularly difficult to resist because of the role played by Aurelia and her own mother, 'Grammy' Schober, in the upbringing of the Plath children.

Aurelia was born in 1906 to Austrian immigrants, and grew up in a predominantly Italian-Irish neighbourhood in Winthrop, Massachusetts during the First World War. Although her parents were ardent patriots and Republicans, Aurelia was bullied and ostracised as a child because of her German-sounding surname. An incident in Plath's poem 'The Disquieting Muses' illuminates the ways in which defining events in Aurelia's childhood impacted on her daughter's imagination. One stanza in the poem describes a troupe of schoolgirls, dancing on tiptoe, flashing lights like fireflies and chanting a glow-worm song. Despite her 'twinkle-dress', the writer cannot join in their revelry, but lurks 'heavy-footed' on the sidelines, in the shadow cast by three malevolent godmothers.[12] While her mother weeps, their umbra advances, until it obliterates the fairy lights. Writing about her daughter long after Plath's death, Aurelia baulked at what she described as 'the picture of an ambitious mother sending her protesting, awkward child to ballet school'. In fact, 'Sylvia never took ballet lessons'; Aurelia herself had been the firefly child, one of a chorus of thirty children, and she had told Plath that she felt 'exalted' by the performance. Her parents were sitting in the front row and 'I was for *them* the prima ballerina!'[13]

In objecting to this 'violation of actual circumstances', Aurelia, like many of Plath's critics, identified the persona of the poem with its author.[14] However, treating Plath's poems as straight autobiography obscures the subtlety of her imagination and its power to transform experience. In the context of a poem about maternal haunting, Plath's 'borrowing' of the firefly dance testifies to the shared memory bank between mother and daughter, and derives from a perception of her mother that reaches beyond the little girl deliriously pirouetting in front of her parents. What Plath seems to have intuited is the pain of a childhood blasted by a sense of difference. This subliminal narrative reflects another more distressing story Aurelia told about her early life. As the daughter of recent immigrants, she spoke German at home and later recalled her sense of isolation on her first day at school, standing by herself in a corner of the yard at recess, while her classmates shouted to one another in an unfamiliar language.[15] The shy girl, made outcast by her alien mother tongue, prefigures the ill-wished child in Plath's poem, whose clumsy feet disqualify her from the firefly dance. Plath collates two contrasting stories about her mother in a poem which, like many traditional fairy tales, reflects on a mother's inability or failure to shield her child from hardship.

There is a further element to Plath's 'recollection' of difference and threat in 'The Disquieting Muses', which relates to her own childhood experience, and again demonstrates the subconscious play of memory and feeling between mother and daughter. Two of Plath's short stories, 'The Shadow' and 'Superman and Paula Brown's New Snowsuit', are set in the early 1940s, at the time when America became actively involved in World War Two. In both, the heroine is accused of acts of aggression towards other children and is socially condemned. It is clear, however, that what is at stake is not neighbourhood gossip about childish pranks, but the Germanic origins of the heroine's family. As children mimic the Nazi goose-step and a horrific film about a Japanese prisoner of war camp plays at the local cinema as B-movie to *Snow White*, the taint of nationality hovers over the young girl like the malevolent shadow of the three bad fairies. In both stories it is a defining moment for the heroine when she realises that the forces of good represented by her favourite champions, Superman and the Shadow, have no status in the real world. Justice and truth do not necessarily prevail, and the parched men in iron cages, watching their Japanese guards gulp water at a fountain just beyond their reach, are a harsh reality of adult life.

The affection of her parents and her own success in the classroom helped Aurelia Schober through her childhood challenges, and she found refuge in what she calls 'sugar-coated fiction', the comforting saga of the March girls in Louisa May Alcott's *Little Women* in which 'the poor and the virtuous always ultimately triumphed', and the romantic historical novels she sought out in the public library.[16] Although Aurelia writes deprecatingly about popular fiction, it was a genre in which she and Sylvia shared a continuing interest. Sylvia constantly tried out story ideas and plots in an attempt to break into what she called the 'slicks', the women's magazine market in the States and Britain. In August 1960 she wrote to Aurelia to urge her, too, to try her hand at magazine stories: 'Get a plot, imagine it in several scenes, with a character changing through events and finding something out about life and resolving problems. I'll edit anything you do for what it's worth ... Get to it, mummy!'[17] As she grew up, Aurelia turned to the literary classics, to Dickens, Jane Austen, Hardy and Henry James, and the poems of Emily Dickinson, to feed her fascination with stories and poetry, an interest that flowed to and fro between generations of women in the Schober and Plath households. When Aurelia was at college her mother read her set texts, two educations for the price of one, a doubling-up of learning that was to be mirrored later by Aurelia and *her* daughter, as Aurelia caught up with modern literature and art through Sylvia's studies at Smith College.

There were other parallels between the experiences of Aurelia and Grammy Schober, and the Plaths. When Aurelia was in her early teens her father plunged the family into financial catastrophe as the result of unwise investment on the stock market. From that time Grammy managed the family affairs, so that Aurelia's younger siblings grew up in what amounted to a matriarchy. After the death of Otto Plath when Sylvia was eight, the Plaths and senior Schobers joined forces to save money. This meant that Sylvia too experienced a transition from a traditional male-dominated family to a household managed by strong, competent and assertive women. Later, when her marriage to Ted Hughes broke up, Plath's anger and distress were compounded by the thought that she had ended up like her mother, a single mother responsible for the welfare of two young children. Her horror at this idea suggests the burden she had carried as the daughter of a mother struggling to clothe, educate and feed her children, and to instil in them the cheerful endurance that Aurelia in turn had learnt from her hard-working, struggling, civic-minded mother.

Plath's legacy from her father was similarly complicated. Otto Plath was born in 1885 in Grabow, a country town in Polish Corridor territory. His grandparents had emigrated to the United States, and offered to educate the scholarly Otto at Northwestern College in Wisconsin as a preparation for the Lutheran ministry. When he arrived in New York at the age of sixteen, Otto stubbornly worked his way through the grades at a local school until he had mastered English, a process which, astonishingly, he completed in a year. He did well at college, majoring in classical languages, but was disillusioned by the hypocrisy and narrow-mindedness of the Lutheran seminary he attended to please his grandparents. His rejection of the ministry led to a severing of links with his sponsors – his name was struck from the family Bible – and Otto spent many years teaching German and studying for a doctorate in entomology, which he was awarded in 1928. When he met Aurelia the following year, Otto was lecturing in German and biology at Boston University where Aurelia was studying for an MA. Despite the difference in their ages, their shared enthusiasm for learning and hard work, as well, perhaps, as Aurelia's admiration for Otto's vivid blue eyes and fair, ruddy complexion, drew them together and they married in January 1932, after Otto had acquired a Reno divorce from a first wife discarded somewhere along the route of his climb to academic honours.

So much has been written about Otto Plath in his role as 'buried male muse & god-creator risen to be my mate in Ted', as Plath described him, that his imagined influence over his daughter and her poetic development tends to overshadow the reality of their relationship and its afterlife.[18] According to Aurelia's brief account in *Letters Home*, her marriage was dominated by Otto's work and interests. Always wholehearted in whatever she set out to achieve, Aurelia recalls that she was 'totally imbued with the desire to be a good wife and mother', an ambition she passed on to her daughter as woman's supreme goal in life.[19] Twenty-one years younger than her husband, she had not allowed for the problems Otto would have in adapting to domestic life after years of living in college dormitories or lodgings, and having only himself to think about. His attitude of 'rightful' dominance led to storms, particularly since Otto seemed never to have learnt the value of talking things through to resolve problems. The result was an act of conscious self-suppression on Aurelia's part: 'I would simply have to become more submissive, although it was not my nature to be so.'[20] Particularly important in their domestic life was what Aurelia calls THE BOOK, Otto's adaptation of his doctoral thesis into *Bumblebees and Their Ways*, published in 1934. This was followed by THE CHAPTER, a section on 'Insect Societies' for *A Handbook of Social Psychology*, in which Aurelia actively collaborated, reading and note-taking along lines directed by Otto, and writing the first draft. All this took place while Aurelia was pregnant with Sylvia and during her daughter's first year, with Grammy and Grampy living in and providing much-needed 'humor, love, and laughter' to soften the 'academic' atmosphere of the Plath menage.[21]

While Aurelia never openly criticises her husband, the stories she chooses to tell about him skilfully reveal his character, the flavour of their domestic arrangements and Otto's attitude to his children. Sylvia was born on 27 October 1932 and Warren on 27 April 1935, more or less exactly as prescribed by Otto, who had told his colleagues after Sylvia's birth that a son, two and a half years from that date, would fulfil his dearest hopes. As Aurelia noted, when news spread of Warren's punctual arrival, Otto was greeted as 'the man who gets what he wants when he wants it'.[22] Otto got what he wanted in other ways from his anxiously accommodating wife. The sociable Aurelia's dreams of entertaining students and friends were confounded when Otto decided that the dining room was the most suitable place for his work on 'Insect Societies'. The sideboard was stacked with reference works, the table neatly covered with books and papers, none of which was to be moved from its position. On evenings when Otto taught night school at Harvard, Aurelia would occasionally invite friends to dinner, first drawing a plan of the current arrangement of the table top, and meticulously returning each item to its correct place before Otto came home. His lifelong habit of thrift meant that Otto took charge of family expenditure, including the weekly purchase of fish, vegetables and meat. It seems that an experienced manly eye was required to identify the best food at the lowest prices. Whether he ever cooked this food (or indeed washed up afterwards) Aurelia does not reveal, although she says tellingly that his premarital enthusiasm for 'fifty-fifty' relationships did not survive their wedding vows.[23]

Otto's approach to bringing up his children was equally selective. He enjoyed discussing theories of child-rearing with Aurelia,

favouring a 'natural' approach, which Aurelia appears to have interpreted as demand feeding (unfashionable in the 1930s), cuddles
when they cried, and songs and poems to soothe and entertain.[24]
Years later Sylvia brought up her own baby daughter, Frieda, on a
similar diet of nursery rhymes and songs, many of which probably
derived from Aurelia.[25] But Otto's Darwinian delight in the tendency of baby Sylvia to use toes as well as fingers when invited to
cling to a rope did not spill over into active involvement in tending
or playing with his children. What pleased him was their attractiveness and progress in acquiring skills. As Otto began increasingly to
suffer from the mysterious debility that attacked him when Sylvia
was nearly four, Aurelia instituted an 'upstairs-downstairs' arrangement to ensure that the children's games and noise did not disturb
their father. The largest bedroom became a playroom where they
ate supper and listened to the next exciting instalment of a saga
invented by Aurelia, 'The Adventures of Mixie Blackshort', whose
nightly escapades ran for years. In the evening the two children
would be brought into the living room to perform for their father.
Sylvia would play the piano or dance, and she and Warren would
show Otto their drawings, or recite poems and rhymes. This ritual
of 'showing off' for Otto made a deep impression on his daughter.
In a long passage of self-analysis in her journal in June 1950, when
Plath was seventeen, she ponders the genetic influence of her 'dead
father', and recalls that 'you were his favourite when your [*sic*] were
little, and you used to make up dances to do for him as he lay on
the living room couch after supper'.[26]

  Aurelia's description of this scene, the mother hovering in attendance and the small girl prancing for her daddy, recalls her delight
in dancing for *her* parents in the firefly chorus. It has, however, a
darker resonance of anxiety and placation, which Plath herself seems
to intuit in her journal entry. The artist Paula Rego's treatment of
a similar theme illuminates the subtext of these performances. In
one of a series of lithographs illustrating scenes from Charlotte

Brontë's novel *Jane Eyre*, Rego depicts the half-French love child, Adèle, dancing for Mr Rochester in the drawing room at Thornfield after supper. Entitled 'Pleasing Mr Rochester', the lithograph shows the little girl displaying her legs for her guardian in a parody of an older woman's provocative gesture, while the dogs fawn and tumble at Rochester's feet and a maid, or maybe Jane herself, arranges a chair for the master to sit on.[27] Rochester stands upright, arms aggressively crossed, legs braced in polished riding boots and his head tilted back in an arrogant sneer. Nobody could suppose that Otto treated his family with similar lordliness, but Adèle's anxiety to please, the pressure on the child to perform for an adult male, and the psychological gulf between herself and her guardian reflect the situation of the Plath children in relation to a father determined to be what Aurelia described as *'der Herr des Hauses* (head of the house)'.[28]

There may have been another equally troubling aspect to Sylvia's attempt to charm her father. In a poem written some years after her death, Ted Hughes reflected on Plath's need as a young woman at Cambridge to win friends and admiration by 'performance' as a poet, an act of fruitless self-display (her poems were panned by the coterie of bombastic young male poets of which Hughes was himself an active member), which he connected to her dancing for Otto. Hughes saw Plath's dance for her father as an attempt to offer her abundant life as a prophylactic against the bitterness of her father's 'raging death'. It was an act of propitiation against chaos and death, which she was to repeat again and again, but in chauvinistic Cambridge 'Nobody wanted your dance, / Nobody wanted your strange glitter'.[29] Whatever the truth of Hughes's insight, and it is a persuasive reading of her almost psychotic need for approval, Sylvia's ploys to grab Otto's attention and praise might understandably have become frenetic when faced with a father withdrawing into fear, sickness and finally an unnecessary death.

Plath's fictionalised account of Otto's illness and death, 'Among the Bumblebees', written in the early 1950s, emphasises the child's trust in her father's godlike nature and invincibility. He is 'a giant of a man', who favours his daughter, named Alice in the story (Plath enjoyed the adventures of Lewis Carroll's Alice), over her younger brother, the sickly Warren, and lords it like a king over his intimidated students.[30] In the end he fails her, first by submitting to the 'plump silly doctor' with his silver needle, and then by withdrawing into the weakness and self-absorption of the dying.[31] 'Lost and betrayed' after he fails to respond to her appeal for notice, Alice never sees her father again.[32] Otto's death *was* in a sense a betrayal of his family. His illness turned out not to be cancer as he had feared, but a treatable form of diabetes. The disease was far advanced, however, by the time he agreed to see a doctor, and he died from an embolism after the amputation of a gangrened foot and leg. It was just after Sylvia's eighth birthday.

Looking back on her early love of the Atlantic in 'Ocean 1212-W', Plath recalls that her 'seaside childhood' in Winthrop, Massachusetts ended after her father's death when they moved inland to Wellesley. 'Whereon those nine first years of my life sealed themselves off like a ship in a bottle – beautiful, inaccessible, obsolete, a fine, white flying myth.'[33] This sense of childhood as a magical, lost, paradisiac past was an experience she shared with Ted Hughes. In their radio interview in 1961, *Two of a Kind*, Hughes talks about his own move away from the village of Mytholmroyd in the Yorkshire Pennines to a 'depressed' and 'dirty' place, the industrial town of Mexborough in south Yorkshire. As a result, his first seven years became 'sealed off' as a 'subsidiary brain' for him, a place of special reference. Like Plath, he coped with the change by plunging himself into writing, his childhood memories preserved as a reservoir of experience on which he was to draw for the rest of his life.

Plath's salvation by the pen from teenage blues and possibly more serious depression owed much to Aurelia's love of reading. Just as mastery of English had been her parents' gateway to academic success and social integration, Sylvia was encouraged from early childhood to engage with the world through her expert manipulation of language. The fact that this was often associated with good behaviour and parental approval was something Plath pondered in December 1958 during her therapy with Ruth Beuscher, when she was wrestling with the problem of writer's block and its sources in her relationship with her mother. 'Nothing I do,' she wails in her therapy notebook, '(marrying . . . writing: "here is a book for you, it is yours, like my toidy products and you can praise and love me now") can change her way of being with me which I experience as a total absence of love.'[34] Burdened by a demanding husband and a new baby, Aurelia used words to comfort and distract her bustling toddler. Sylvia discovered the alphabet from the capital letters on grocery packets in the pantry and was encouraged to 'read' a newspaper while Aurelia nursed Warren. In this way she learnt that being 'good with words' (in both senses of the phrase) was a way of winning her mother's approval, and praise became a substitute for play and cuddling. Later Aurelia encouraged the children to invent their own rhymes and limericks, copying what was read to them, an exercise in controlled self-expression, which came in handy for those evening 'performances' for Daddy. Her daughter's response to poetry was everything she could have wished. Hearing Matthew Arnold's 'The Forsaken Merman' for the first time, Sylvia recalled that '[a] spark flew off Arnold and shook me, like a chill. I wanted to cry; I felt very odd. I had fallen into a new way of being happy.'[35] Millay's 'Renascence' also seems to have gripped her imagination.[36] By the time she was at junior high school, she was keeping a diary, writing book reports and composing verses, accompanied by her own illustrations. She and Warren were also encouraged by Aurelia to express their opinions about books, music and paintings. As Aurelia explains, these family discussions were disciplined analyses rather than sloppy effusions (although her description of the process is interestingly convoluted): 'We were critical of our verbal and written expression, for we shared a love of words and considered them as a tool used to achieve precise expression, a necessity for accuracy in describing our emotions, as well as for mutual understanding.'[37] Aurelia's careful training in self-expression seems also to have been an education in censorship. Encouraged always to be bright and cheerful, to be frugal and hard-working, to cherish high ideals of public service and personal achievement, Plath was left with a residue of 'negative' feelings – jealousy, anger, hatred, fear – which she was unable to explore with her mother. There were some emotions Aurelia did not wish to hear about, however accurately they were described.

Aurelia's influence on her daughter cannot be overestimated. Throughout her life Plath wrote compulsively to her mother, sharing every triumph and woe. Their enthusiasm for words was the strongest bond between them, with letters winging their way back and forth even at the time when Plath was writing to her brother, after the breakdown of her marriage, to beg him to 'tactfully convey' to Aurelia 'that we should not meet for at least a year'.[38] It was often more comfortable for both of them to write rather than meet. 'Both Sylvia and I were more at ease in *writing* words of appreciation, admiration, and love than in expressing these emotions verbally,' Aurelia says in *Letters Home* and adds, 'thank goodness, write them to each other we did!'[39] Sylvia's analysis in her journal is more clear-sighted: 'One reason I could keep up such a satisfactory letter-relationship with [Mother] while in England was we could both verbalize our desired images of ourselves in relation to each other: interest and sincere love, and never feel the emotional currents at war with these verbally expressed feelings.' At the heart of Plath's disquiet is the fear that she will never meet her mother's exacting standards: 'I feel her disapproval. But I feel it countries away too.'[40] The 'Sivvy' of the letters to Aurelia is very different from the percipient, self-mocking 'I' of the journals. Tart, observant and ruthlessly self-analytical, Plath's journals are a study in soul making that invites the reader's pity, respect and admiration. The anxious, manipulative Sivvy of *Letters Home* derives from the complex inter-action between mother and daughter, which Aurelia described as 'a sort of psychic osmosis which, at times, was very wonderful and comforting; at other times an unwelcome invasion of privacy'.[41] Again, Sylvia's journal reflects more honestly the pain and muddle of the mother-daughter dyad: 'When she dies, what will I feel? I wish her death so I could be sure of what I am: so I could know that what feelings I have, even though some resemble hers, are really my own. Now I find it hard to distinguish between the semblance and the reality.'[42] Plath's dilemma is dramatised in 'Medusa', a poem that reflects savagely on the power of the umbilical bond and ends with the ambiguous declaration, 'There is nothing between us.'[43]

'A passionate, fragmentary girl'

> 'I want so obviously, so desperately to be loved, and
> to be capable of love ... I know pretty much what
> I like and dislike; but please, don't ask me who I
> am. "A passionate, fragmentary girl," maybe?'
>
> Sylvia Plath, 25 January 1953[44]

Sylvia Plath's college room-mate, Nancy Hunter (later Steiner),
recalled her eagerness to present herself as 'the typical American
girl, the product of a hundred years of middle-class propriety'.[45]
Plath's passionate need for social acceptance may be partly explained
by her family background, but she also grew up in a period of
repression for women. The psychologist Betty Friedan's *The Feminine Mystique* drew on the lives of young women who, like Plath,
were growing up, going to college and getting married in the 1950s.
Her book sets out their social expectations and in particular what
Friedan calls 'the problem with no name', the sense of emptiness
and lack of identity that overwhelmed vast numbers of American
women, who found themselves trapped at home with young children, a sinkful of dishes and a lifelong prospect of repetitive domestic chores. The cause of the problem, according to Friedan, was
the limited role allocated to women in the reactionary period after
the Second World War. Regardless of their talents, interests, or
education, women were expected to be perfect wives and mothers;
any other role was regarded as 'unfeminine':

> Over and over women heard in voices of tradition and of
> Freudian sophistication that they could desire no greater destiny
> than to glory in their own femininity. Experts told them how
> to catch a man and keep him, how to breastfeed children and
> handle their toilet training, how to cope with sibling rivalry and
> adolescent rebellion; how to buy a dishwasher, bake bread, cook
> gourmet snails, and build a swimming pool with their own
> hands; how to dress, look, and act more feminine and make
> marriage more exciting[.][46]

Women who aspired to be poets, physicists or political leaders
were derided as neurotic and unfeminine; the independence and
opportunities for which older feminists had struggled were cast
aside. As Friedan points out, by the end of the 1950s the average
age of marriage for women in America was twenty, while the
proportion of women attending college compared to men had fallen
from 47 per cent in 1920 to 35 per cent in 1958. Girls went to college
to get a husband rather than an education, and many dropped out
prematurely because they were afraid that men would fight shy of
marrying a 'brainy' woman.[47] Plath herself was to write acerbically
about the female dons who were her supervisors at Newnham
College as 'bluestocking grotesques, who know about life second-
hand'.[48] Her poem 'Two Sisters of Persephone', also written in
Cambridge in 1956, contrasts two women, one a golden child of
nature who weds the sun and gives birth to a king, the other a
lemon-sallow spinster, devoted to mathematics, who goes to her
grave 'Worm-husbanded, yet no woman'.[49] These polarities may
today seem rather quaint, but they reflect the very real anxieties of
scholarly girls in the Fifties. The writer A. S. Byatt, who was an
undergraduate at Cambridge during the time Plath was there as a
Fulbright scholar, later recalled the conflict between her dreams of
being 'normal', of having romantic love and marriage and children,
and her ambition for the kind of working life that men took for

granted. The attitude of the women dons only exacerbated the dilemma. Byatt went on to do postgraduate research at Oxford, but her tutor, the distinguished scholar Helen Gardner, insisted that 'a woman had to be dedicated like a nun, to achieve anything as a mind'. Byatt's grant was taken away when she married; men, as she pointed out, had *their* grants increased, to provide for their households.[50]

Plath, with her longing for academic *and* social acceptance, was particularly fraught at the idea of being identified as a bluestocking, an anxiety that dogged her high-school ventures into flirtation and dating. Aurelia Plath describes how she learnt to hide 'behind a facade of light-hearted wit' when meeting boys and relates a telling incident, reported to her by an exultant Sylvia:

'Rod asked me what grades I got. I said airily, "All A's, of course." "Yeah," he replied, grinning, as he led me out to the dance floor, "You *look* like a greasy grind!" Oh, Mummy, they didn't believe me; they didn't believe me!'[51]

The effects on women of the collective scramble into early marriage and childbearing were, as Friedan reports, devastating. The poet Anne Stevenson, Plath's authorised (and often unsympathetic) biographer, suffered as a young wife in England from 'the problem with no name' and was later to explore the anguish of women's unfulfilled lives in her verse-novel *Correspondences*, which looks at several generations of women in a Vermont family. The young wife, Kathy Chattle, struggling to conform to Fifties idealism of blissful wife- and motherhood, takes refuge in drink and, when she runs away from her screaming baby, is confined in a mental asylum. But she can see no way out of the impasse, as her desperate letter to her mother reveals:

Can't you get me out of here?

I'll try, I'll try, really,
I'll try again. The marriage.
The baby. The house. The whole damn bore!

Because for me, what the hell else is there?
Mother, what more? What more?[52]

In the mindless conformity of the 1950s it was as if a century of female protest had been wiped from memory. Even highly educated women succumbed to the rhetoric of compliant womanhood and blamed themselves for any deviation from 'normal' feelings. George Eliot's plea for female individuality in *Daniel Deronda* (1876) might never have been penned. In Eliot's critique of the limited roles allocated to women in Victorian society, the Princess Halm-Eberstein boldly justifies her willing sacrifice of her child for her vocation:

'Every woman is supposed to have the same set of motives, or else to be a monster. I am not a monster, but I have not felt exactly what other women feel – or say they feel, for fear of being thought unlike others.'[53]

The Princess is an artist – other women in Eliot are not allowed such latitude in their behaviour – but her words must have rung true for generations of women readers, trapped in the Christian dogma of submissive motherhood. Invoked for centuries, this mythology found new converts in the women of Plath's generation, with dire consequences for their mental health and well-being. As Friedan reports, the women she interviewed for her survey wept at the relief of confessing that they too did not feel exactly what the social legislators – whose mouthpiece was the popular press and, in particular, the influential women's magazines – said that women were 'supposed' to feel.[54] Like the Princess, Stevenson's Kathy is also an artist and survives to metamorphose into the self-sufficient writer Kay Boyd, just as Plath's real-life contemporary Anne Sexton, burrowing out from atrophy and despair, transformed herself from neurotic housewife into a feisty, outspoken, witchy poet, whose willingness to delve into taboo areas of female sexuality and consciousness made her an icon for Sixties feminism. But for Kathy/Kay and Anne Sexton, and thousands of women like them, the cost of daring to think beyond the acceptable norms of female behaviour was disapproval, mental illness and sometimes even death.[55]

This, then, was the social atmosphere in which Sylvia Plath grew up, but it was further complicated by her father's death and the necessity for Aurelia Plath to become the family breadwinner. The dominant role model in the Plath household was not a woman trapped at home, suffering from 'the problem with no name', but a mother who worked to keep her family. For Aurelia's children this meant domestic frugality, the need to win academic scholarships and awards, and also a burden of guilt at their mother's sacrifices on their behalf and her bouts of possibly stress-related ill health. There was, too, the consciousness of having been born somehow on the wrong side of town, of being less wealthy than many of the kids the Plaths met at high school and college, and the embarrassment of a mother who didn't conform to the American ideal of happy wifehood.[56] All these pressures are worked out in Plath's *Journals*, as she struggled to come to terms with the dichotomy between marriage and children and her glorious future as a writer. But there was yet another social pitfall she had to negotiate: the paradox that unmarried girls were required to be both sexually enticing and chillingly chaste.

The story of Plath's life is often told as if her meeting and marriage with Ted Hughes were the sole events, apart from her earlier breakdown, of any significance to her life, both as a woman and a writer. But Plath's journals reveal a very different emphasis, giving an account of her sexual relationships before she met Ted Hughes, the picaresque adventures of, to use her own words, 'the American virgin, dressed to seduce'.[57] What is striking is Plath's honesty in describing her sexuality and the dilemmas she faced in exploring her appetites in the moral climate of the early 1950s. The cultural ideal of 'the American virgin' chafed Plath as a young woman in search of physical satisfaction, and also constrained her choice of subject matter as an aspiring writer. It was an impasse that Virginia Woolf, one of Plath's revered foremothers, had defined for her generation and foreseen as a curb on female creativity for decades to come. It would be fifty years, Woolf had hypothesised in 1931, before men became 'so civilized' that they could hear a woman speak freely about her body without being shocked.[58] Both Sylvia Plath and Heloise wrote frankly about women's sexual and physical needs: Heloise in her passionate letters to Abelard and in her recommendations for adapting the Benedictine rule to suit female physiology, while Plath kept intimate journals. Both faced censorship or even downright denial when their private writings were published. Male critics insisted that Heloise's letters must have been written by Abelard because of their shameless sexuality. When Sylvia Plath's journals were first published in 1982, about the time that Woolf had fixed on for civilised freedom of expression for women, Plath's editor Frances McCullough noted in her foreword the cutting of 'intimacies', which had the effect (she clearly meant the intention) of diminishing Plath's 'eroticism' which was 'quite strong'.[59] These 'intimacies' were not available to a wide readership until Karen Kukil's edition of the unexpurgated journals appeared in 2000.

There is no evidence that Plath wrote her journals with publication in mind, although she recognised their value as a means of exploring ideas and techniques, and pinning down descriptions of people and events as they occurred. Consequently, she felt free to write whatever came into her head, about her body and its desires, as well as a wide range of other observations, during the fifteen years or so in which she kept a record. In spite of this, her private writings reflect the tension between truth and propriety so feelingly described by Virginia Woolf, a conflict that seems to have dominated Plath's relationships with men, and her ambition to be both a perfect wife and mother *and* a successful writer. 'Having it all', later to be a rallying call for feminists, was an ambition Plath explored again and again in her journals, during a period in which women had been pushed back more firmly than ever into the traditional roles of homemaker and helpmate. As Rosemary Dinnage points out in *Alone! Alone!*, her study of 'Outsider Women', the 'trouble with trying to . . . "have it all" is that it demands a firm sense of self'.[60] Plath's uncertain sense of self was the cause of painful psychic disorder, but also enriched her achievement as a writer. In dating and 'love' affairs, as for so many young women of her generation, it led to heartache and humiliation, as she struggled to squeeze her erotic impulses into the moral straitjacket that confined 'the American virgin' and secretly raged against the double standard that denied women's right to sexual desire.

An incident when Plath was working on a farm during the summer of 1950, when she was seventeen, brings into focus the young girl's conflict between public opinion and desire. A handsome Estonian refugee, Ilo, is working in the strawberry fields with her, and amuses Plath with his talk of Renaissance painters and Picasso, and his teasing about the 'sendimental Frank Sinatra'.[61] Ilo is himself something of an artist and one day he invites Plath to the barn where he is living for the summer to see one of his sketches. As they walk together through the farmyard the other kids roar and jeer, 'Oh, Sylvia.' In his bedroom studio Ilo kisses Plath, his 'tongue darting between [her] lips, his arms like iron'. She backs away, frightened and crying, but also 'flooded with longing, electric, shivering'.[62] Later she drives home with a group of boys from the farm, and is shamingly conscious of their teasing and curiosity, and her sense of public exposure. Shortly after this she records preparing for a date with a young man she calls Emile, dressing slowly, 'smoothing, perfuming, powdering', anticipating the evening ahead: 'This is I, I thought, the American virgin, dressed to seduce. I know I'm in for an evening of sexual pleasure. We go on dates, we play around, and if we're nice girls, we demure [*sic*] at a certain point.'[63] As they sit in a bar talking, she is aware of 'the strong smell of masculinity which creates the ideal medium for me to exist in'. But Sylvia guesses that Emile only wants her for sex and so, being a nice girl, she lets him go after a goodnight kiss. Alone in her room, she ponders their encounter: 'fifteen thousand years—of what? We're still nothing but animals.'[64] Babysitting a 'family of beautiful children', she is still brooding about Emile, imagining him watching baseball or television, sharing a dirty joke with the boys in a litter of beer cans and used ashtrays, while she dissolves in sexual longing and rages against the rules that constrain female behaviour: 'I can only lean enviously against the boundary and hate, hate, hate the boys who can dispel sexual hunger freely, without misgiving, and be whole, while I drag out from date to date in soggy desire, always unfulfilled.'[65] As for popular songs (Ilo's quip about Sinatra may have been in her mind), if 'they substituted the word "Lust" for "Love" . . . it would come nearer the truth'.[66] What is remarkable about these stories is Plath's ability to be both in and out of the experience, the young woman tingling with erotic excitement, and the writer observing and recording. Earlier, she had written about her wish to inhabit other people's lives and then be able to record her thoughts and emotions as that person, but 'I have to live my life, and it is the only one I'll ever have. And you cannot regard your own life with objective curiosity all the time . . .'[67] Maybe not, but Plath's skill in capturing the dramatic essence of her experiences and her willingness to investigate her own responses transform the raw materials of her life into compelling autobiography.

Plath entered Smith College in the autumn of 1950 as a scholarship student, funded by the romantic novelist Olive Higgins Prouty, but her years of academic supremacy and increasing success in placing her writing with reputable magazines and journals, a remarkable achievement for a high-school girl, seemed to count for nothing in the new environment, and she immediately plunged into loneliness and isolation. Throughout her life Plath was to be fazed by unfamiliar scenes. Despite her zest for experience, her stability depended on routine and public recognition of her talents. Threatened by the wealthy, self-confident girls who thronged the campus at Smith, she was unable to sustain herself by memories of past success and family affection. Fastidiously resistant to mingling with the crowd, she had a painful sense of herself as negligible, 'one more drop in the great sea of matter'.[68] Sitting in the library, faceless among a herd of avidly reading girls, she felt ungrounded in some essential, devastating way. Paradoxically, the problem of identity had never seemed so pressing. 'There is no living being on earth at this moment except myself,' she recorded sombrely, alone in her room, and more ominously, 'if you have no past or future . . . you may as well dispose of the empty shell of present and commit suicide.'[69] Somewhere, she knew, there was the possibility of 'joy, fulfillment and companionship', but 'the loneliness of the soul in it's [*sic*] appalling self-consciousness, is horrible and over-powering'.[70] This burden of the inescapable self returns again and again at moments of change or crisis in Plath's life, robbing her of sleep and the ability to work. And yet, even in her darkest moments, Plath's capacity for 'objective curiosity' allows her to reflect on her misery with characteristic humour and self-mockery. She ends one bout of wretched introspection with the bracing reminder that in three days' time she has her first mid-year exam, and ruefully hectors herself into self-discipline: 'you'd much rather read anything but what you have to, but you <u>do</u> have to, and you will, although you've already wasted two hours writing stream-of-consciousness stuff in here when your stream isn't even much to brag about, after all.'[71]

Part of Plath's difficulty was the pressure to be seen at weekends with a string of attractive men. Tall and slim, with light-brown hair worn in a long bob, her expression characteristically alert and attentive, she caught the eye by her vitality, the mobility of her flexible mouth and long, slim, gesturing fingers. Her charm, however, depended on a receptive audience and in her first months at Smith she struggled against being a social misfit. Unable at first to find suitable escorts, she was forced to fall back on blind dates arranged by other girls, or to stay at home studying, which earned her an unwelcome reputation as a swot. Always prone to paranoia, she was convinced that the girls in her residential hall gossiped maliciously behind her back and she winced at their barbed civilities. 'I never see you,' says one spitefully saccharine adversary. 'You're always <u>studying</u> in your <u>rooom</u>!'[72] Forced to take whatever man was on offer, Plath once again made good use of her experiences in her journal and her account of a date with the 'fatherly' war veteran Bill is a wryly comic exposé of the pitfalls of the mating game. Primed to make the most of an unpromising partner, Plath was at her most winsome and womanly, only to find her illusions of intimacy shattered when Bill crudely attempted to have sex with her. Frustrated by her resistance, he was grumpily prepared to settle for her masturbating him, which Plath also indignantly rejected. The experience shocked her, but she was able, too, to laugh at Bill and herself for the mismatch in their expectations.[73] Plath's sense of the ridiculousness of human behaviour, including her own, is a thread of humour and self-mockery that runs through her journals, and underlies the deadpan comedy of her novel *The Bell Jar*.

Even when more satisfactory partners came her way, Plath remained perplexed by the dating game, partly because of her own ambivalence about marriage. On the one hand she cynically observed that 'most American males worship woman as a sex machine . . . a painted doll who shouldn't have a thought in her pretty head other than cooking a steak dinner and comforting him in bed after a hard 9–5 day at a routine business job', but, as women have been for centuries, she was trained to see herself as a helper rather than the prime mover in marriage.[74] 'I must pour my energies through the direction and force of my mate,' she angrily reminded herself. 'My only free act is choosing or refusing that mate.'[75] At the same time she yearned to find her male counterpart, 'a strong potential powerful mate who can counter my vibrant dynamic self', and could not commit herself to a life of cooking scrambled eggs for some man, feeding his 'insatiable guts and begetting children', when what she really wanted was to write.[76] 'If I did not have this time to be myself, to write here, to be alone, I would somehow, inexplicably, lose a part of my integrity,' she confided to her journal, at the end of her first year at Smith.[77] Would marriage sap her creative energy, or would childbearing lead to a fuller expression in art?[78] When, in March 1951, she started seriously dating Dick Norton, a former high-school friend some years older than Plath, her journal recorded the escalating tension between Dick's conservative notions of the all-consuming demands of wife- and motherhood, and Plath's dream of the enabling relationship that would stimulate her productivity in writing and art.[79]

In her novel *The Bell Jar*, published in the United Kingdom just before her death, Plath penned a wickedly perceptive portrait of the stuffiness and hypocrisy of the Norton family. *The Bell Jar* is fiction rather than autobiography, a *Bildungsroman* in which Plath transformed the horrific experience of breakdown into a blackly comic account of a young girl's coming of age in Fifties America. However, in creating her naive and in some ways autistic heroine, Esther Greenwood, she drew on many of her own experiences and frustrations, and the line between fact and fiction is often very thinly drawn. In the book, Dick is re-created as the self-important Buddy Willard, whose genitals resemble turkey gizzards and whose opinions on the relative roles of the sexes in marriage come straight from his mother. 'What a man is is an arrow into the future and what a woman is is the place the arrow shoots off from,' he constantly reminds the heroine.[80] But Esther, like Plath, wants to be the arrow herself, and not just one arrow, but a whole clutch of brightly coloured missiles, a Fourth of July rocket shooting off in different directions. Like the real-life Dick, Buddy attempts to colonise Esther, on the one hand telling her that poetry is 'dust', on the other proudly showing her a toe-curlingly awful poem written by himself and published in a minor arts magazine.[81] The relationship reaches a crisis when Dick/Buddy confesses that he had slept with a waitress during the 1952 summer break. As Plath tells it in *The Bell Jar*, Esther's anger stems from Buddy's duplicity. Why, she rages, should there be one standard of purity for men and another for women? Why should Buddy be allowed to lead a double life while she, Esther, as his future wife, is expected to save herself for marriage? And what will this marriage offer her? A lifetime of being a doormat, like her own mother and Mrs Willard: 'when you were married and had children it was like being brainwashed, and afterwards you went about numb as a slave in some private, totalitarian state.'[82]

Plath was furious and humiliated when Dick confessed to his affair with the waitress. Her resentment at his self-indulgence may have been exacerbated by her own reluctant chastity during the same period. At home in August, recovering from a sinus infection, she dated a handsome Princeton boy, and her journal records her excitement during an evening together at the cinema and the romantic, tantalising drive home to her house. Plath's evocation of this meeting includes a virtuoso analysis of the role of the silver screen as the new religion of middle-class America, but she also conveys the delight of being young, beautiful and seductive. Plath's love of pretty clothes and dressing up is a persistent theme in her journal and on this occasion she relishes her own delightful appearance, 'fresh and apple-scented in the lovely shimmering tie-silk dress with the lavendar [sic] design'. Her escort is chivalrous and protective, helping her in and out of the car, 'and you think of Southern breeding'. After he has driven her home, he whispers loving words, his boyish cheek pressed against hers. 'She let him kiss her once, pulled reluctantly away, thinking: The power, the power of the life force. Exulting inwardly, she walked to the door with him. . . . In her, beating loudly, strongly, was the neutral fact: the potent sex drive.' For men, fulfilling this urge was the gateway to experience and adventure; but, as Plath melodramatically exclaims, her sexual instinct could be used for 'her triumph or her downfall'. The 'adorably opinionated' Princetonian has to be satisfied with that lingering kiss.[83]

Plath's attempted suicide in the summer of 1953 appears to have been the result of a slow accretion of pressures, which finally paralysed her hyperactive mind and plunged her into breakdown. There had been warning signs from the beginning of her third year at Smith. Looking through her journal and family letters for the period, there is a sense that she felt overwhelmed by the lack of unambiguous goals in her life. Every area of activity – her studies, her relationship with Dick Norton, her creative ambitions – seemed fraught with uncertainty and she was oppressed by the sheer weight of tasks that she expected herself to accomplish each day. Immobilised by depression, Esther Greenwood in *The Bell Jar* gives up washing her clothes and hair 'because it seemed so silly'. Why 'wash one day when I would only have to wash again the next', she wonders. Exhausted at the mere thought of pointless daily rituals, she 'wanted to do everything once and for all and be through with it'.[84] This sense of the burden of routine recurs in Plath's writings, compounded by the high level of achievement she set herself. Throughout her years at Smith she endeavoured to impress her initial sponsor Mrs Prouty, her family and the college staff with her image as a brilliant all-rounder, excelling equally in her class assignments, her commitment to College societies and journals, and the poems and stories she submitted for publication to a variety of magazines. In the autumn of 1952 she moved to Lawrence House, where she eked out the cost of board and lodging by waitressing in the dining room and similar chores. A required science course tested her patience and mental capacities to the hilt, and there were medieval literature and creative writing assignments as well as her work for the Smith College Press Board and the *Smith Review* to fulfil to her customary exacting standard.

On 3 November, groggy from lack of sleep, she enumerated the tasks awaiting her: 'The list mounted, obstacle after fiendish obstacle, they jarred, they leered, they fell apart in chaos[.]' Hollowed out by exhaustion, her mind felt numb and paralysed: 'I want to kill myself, to escape from responsibility . . . I do not know who I am, where I am going[.]'[85] Her only recourse was a pretence at coping: 'Masks are the order of the day – and the least I can do is cultivate the illusion that I am gay, serene, not hollow and afraid.'[86] At the same time Plath's support network had collapsed: her close friend Marcia Brown was living off-campus and was less available for comforting sessions of soul-searching and reassurance, and Dick Norton had contracted tuberculosis and been sent off to a sanatorium for a protracted recovery. Her postal confidant, Eddie Cohen, who for years acted as Plath's private counsellor, urged her to seek professional help for her panic and despair, but Plath soldiered on, although she did confess her suicidal urges to Aurelia. A visit to Dick over the Christmas holiday did nothing to improve Sylvia's foundering feelings for her potential future mate and she broke her leg in a skiing accident, which meant weeks of hobbling to classes across icy walkways with her leg in plaster. The crown of her academic year should have been the invitation to work in June 1953 as guest editor on one of New York's glossiest fashion magazines, but the experience at *Mademoiselle* seems to have stretched Plath's already fragile sense of identity to snapping point.

In fictionalising the story of her breakdown and recovery in *The Bell Jar*, Plath foregrounds the dilemma of the intelligent woman in post-war America. The heroine, Esther Greenwood, is one of twelve clever girls who have won the chance to edit one month's issue of a fashion magazine. Corralled together at night in a hotel ironically named the Amazon, the girls spend their days working on the magazine, going out to lunches, receptions and movies, and receiving showers of free gifts: clothes, make-up, ballet tickets and styling sessions at a famous hair salon. For most of the young women the emphasis is on frivolity and fun, but Esther is assigned to the formidable editor who runs the fiction pages of the magazine and she is expected to turn in quality copy. Some years after Plath, the writer Sandra M. Gilbert similarly worked at *Mademoiselle*, under the editor who was the model for Esther's 'Jay Cee'. It was a bewildering experience. The hard-working college girls were over-whelmed by the identity of 'Woman' projected by the magazine. The offices were 'pastel, intricately feminine, full of clicking spikey heels'. They were staffed by glitzy 'career gals', and there was a sense that the floors were swabbed down at midnight with Chanel No. 5. 'Jay Cee', however, was made in a sterner mould. A 'serious, unfashionable, professional woman', she seemed out of place in the stylish corridors of the magazine, 'like a warning of what might happen to you if you threw away the clothes and entered the nun-nery of art'.[87] The editor chivvied the girls with questions about their futures and, in *The Bell Jar*, she similarly demoralises Esther with her merciless probing, reducing her girlish achievements and ambitions to dust.

The impact of the New York experience on Plath was to exacer-bate her anxiety about her future. None of the available role models was appealing and she was as yet unable to formulate the kind of woman she wanted to be. Trapped by her need for conformity, her bright, adventurous spirit was powerless to challenge the models for female behaviour that confronted her at *Mademoiselle*. In *The Bell Jar*, Esther describes her impasse as starving to death in the fork of a fig tree, because she couldn't decide which of the figs to choose: 'One fig was a husband and a happy home and children, and another fig was a famous poet and another fig was a brilliant professor, and another fig was Ee Gee, the amazing editor[.]'[88] But the problem seems to have been not so much the difficulty of choice, as a sense of inertia and emptiness at the prospect of any of the roles on offer. Plath's final gesture, brilliantly described in *The Bell Jar*, was to cast her expensive new garments out of the window of her hotel, a symbolic shedding of the delusory sophistication of her month at *Mademoiselle*: 'Piece by piece, I fed my wardrobe to the night wind, and flutteringly, like a loved one's ashes, the grey scraps were ferried off, to settle here, there, exactly where I would never know, in the dark heart of New York.'[89]

When Plath returned home, she learnt that she had unexpectedly been turned down for a creative writing course at Harvard Summer School. This was a further blow to her ego and left her with a terrifyingly blank space before the autumn term began at Smith. Unscheduled time was always a problem for Plath. One of the hardest tasks she faced as a writer was how to be productive without the external pressures of timetables and deadlines, an experience she likened to lifting a sealed bell jar off a 'clockwork-like functioning community' and watching all the busy people float into the air, arms impotently flailing.[90] In an unsent letter to Eddie Cohen, written from McLean Hospital in December 1953, Plath described the state of mind that culminated in the serious and almost successful bid to kill herself in August 1953. Her confidence in her literary ability shattered, Plath felt 'sterile, empty, unlived, unwise, and UNREAD', and toppled into a cycle of sleepless nights and aimless days.[91] An attempt to drown herself was unsuccessful: the old, familiar 'I am I am I am' pounded in her ears, and her body stubbornly refused to yield to the waves.[92] Finally she climbed into a dark recess under the family home in Wellesley where she took quantities of sleeping pills. She was only discovered two days later, when Warren heard her moaning after she had vomited up some of the pills and smashed her face against the low roof of her hiding place.

Plath's breakdown freed her temporarily from family and college pressures, and in hospital she met a young psychiatrist, Dr Ruth Beuscher, who was to play an important role in her attempts to understand her inner conflicts. But the trauma of mental collapse, her initial terrifying experience of ECT treatment and the lack of understanding typically awarded to mental patients, which the novelists Antonia White, Janet Frame and Jennifer Dawson similarly record in their accounts of female breakdown, marked Plath for the rest of her life.[93] In particular, the terror of not being able to think clearly or to read haunted her, and may have returned during the period of depression prior to her successful suicide nearly ten years later. It was a fear of her brain spinning out of control that she shared with Virginia Woolf, who committed suicide when, after a sustained period of strain, she dreaded the onset of disabling madness. Perhaps most tellingly, Plath writes in her letter to Cohen of her need to have someone to love her, 'to be with me at night when I wake up in shuddering horror and fear'.[94] In her memoir of Plath's last days, her friend Jillian Becker recalls Plath weeping in the night and needing Jillian to sit with her and reassure her. The writer Sarah Kane, who for many years was prone to depression and finally committed suicide, dramatised in her play *4.48 Psychosis* the mental confusion of the depressive: 'my mind is the subject of these bewildered fragments'.[95] Kane pinpointed 4.48 a.m., the time when she habitually found herself lying wide awake in bed, as paradoxically a moment of lucid clarity. For someone of Plath's sensitivity to feelings of isolation and unfriendedness, the dark hour just before dawn, with its freight of bitter insight, must have seemed to stretch into eternity.

Plath survived her breakdown and returned to Smith to take up her studies with renewed zest and dedication. Nancy Hunter Steiner describes Plath at this time as beautiful, with her impressive, almost statuesque height, her shoulder-length blonded hair, and her dark, deeply set eyes under heavy lids. The two girls roomed together in the summer and Steiner records Plath's almost manic determination to savour life to the full. Having disentangled herself from Dick, she embarked on a fresh round of sexual experiments with men willing to take on the vivacious, brilliant young woman. This was the time of her grotesque relationship with the 'strange, morose, determined' Irwin, a professor of biology at an Eastern college.[96] Their encounter was both comic and traumatic: Irwin seems to have been a determined seducer, the type to notch his conquests into the bedpost, but with Plath he almost met his nemesis. It is unclear quite what happened between them, assault or consensual sex, but it led to a vaginal tear, which haemorrhaged for hours. Sylvia was hysterical with fear by the time Nancy got her to the emergency room at hospital. Whether Irwin was responsible for Plath losing her virginity is not certain, but she seems to have taken the decision during this summer to enjoy her sexuality to the full.

Despite Plath's attempts to forge an identity for herself as a modern, independent woman, little had changed in the social environment. She collected a fistful of awards and prizes during the course of her final year for her poems and articles, won the Alpha Phi Kappa Psi award at Smith College and graduated in June 1955 with a two-year Fulbright Scholarship to study English at Cambridge University in England. The departing students were cheered on their way by a speech from Adlai Stevenson in which, as Steiner reports, he spoke in dauntingly conventional terms about the future of Smith girls as 'thoughtful, discriminating wives and mothers who would use what we had learned . . . to influence our husbands and children in the direction of rationality'.[97] Woman's role was defined as homemaker and helpmate. Writing in her journal in January 1953, Plath had attempted once again to wrestle with the problem of 'I am' and had perceptively defined herself as a 'passionate, fragmentary girl', an identity still in the making.[98] Her struggle to balance the conflicting demands of her ardent, ambitious nature had led to breakdown and an attempt to silence her relentless self-scrutiny by suicide. Eighteen months after her return to a busy, active life as writer, student and lover of men, Plath still hadn't resolved the questions that had troubled her most deeply during the *Mademoiselle* summer. What kind of woman was she meant to be? What would she make of her talents and experiences, and how would she balance her dreams of love and marriage with her determination to succeed as a writer? And, perhaps most important, where would she find the male counterpart of herself, the superman who would fulfil her vision of a creative partnership, spawning books and babies with a zest to equal her own?

'Singer, story-teller, lion ... a vagabond who will never stop': Ted Hughes

> '[I]n the last two months I have fallen terribly in love, which can only lead to great hurt. I met the strongest man in the world, ex-Cambridge, brilliant poet ... a large, hulking, healthy Adam ... with a voice like the thunder of God – a singer, story-teller, lion and world-wanderer, a vagabond who will never stop'
>
> Sylvia Plath, 17 April 1956[99]

By the beginning of October 1955, Plath was settling in at Whitstead, a residential home for foreigners in the grounds of Newnham College in Cambridge. Her letters home tell a reassuring story of bright, positive 'Sivvy' plunging herself into the attractions of student life. She joined the prestigious Amateur Dramatic Club, went punting and took tea with a string of charming young men (there was a ratio of ten men to every female student, as she gleefully told Aurelia), and seemed to be coping with the rigorous reading programme required for her English studies. At the same time she was pursuing her customary campaign of sending out poems and articles to literary magazines.

Despite her carefully upbeat letters, there are hints that all was not well. She had opted for practical criticism for one of her courses, but found herself outclassed by fellow students when it came to

dating prose and poetry from the sixteenth, seventeenth and eighteenth centuries, periods in which Plath's reading had been negligible. At first glance she dismissed the female dons as 'grotesques'
(although she was later to discover in Dorothea Krook a most
sympathetic tutor), and she found her own eager, inquisitive
approach to literature as a background and stimulus to her writing
was at odds with 'the grubbing detail' of the Ph.D. that was the
logical next step in her career.[100] Used to American standards of
comfort and healthy eating, she was appalled by the stodgy, unappe-
tising food at Whitstead and devastated by the spartan approach to
heating. 'Our rooms are cool enough to keep butter and milk in,'
she tells Aurelia with jovial dismay. When she goes to the bathroom
to wash, 'my breath hangs white in the air in frosty clouds!'[101] As
Christmas approached, she felt increasingly lonely and homesick,
and fell ill with a sinus infection, often a physical symptom of
acute mental anxiety in Plath. And much as she enjoyed the genial,
attentive boys who thronged the streets and bars at Cambridge,
none of them fed her longing for a soulmate.

Part of the problem was Plath's characteristic insecurity when
faced with a new situation, a replay of that first difficult term at
Smith, when she hid in her room from the hostile whispers of the
girls in her rooming house. Her journal reveals a similar build-up
of paranoia in Cambridge. When small boys bombard her with
snowballs, she feels that they have sensed the fear and condemnation
that lurk behind her smiling mask. Soon she suspects that the girls
in Whitstead are shunning her and gossiping behind her back, and
the awesome list of tasks to be completed paralyses her into familiar
inertia. She yearns for an older, wiser confidant, a father- or mother-
confessor, and sensibly arranges to see the college psychiatrist, just
'to know he's there'.[102] In the meantime the scar on her cheek from
her suicide bid seems to grow more prominent and she broods
obsessively on her Lazarus-like resurrection from the grave.[103]

There was another reason for Plath's discontent during her early months at Cambridge. Since the spring of her senior year at Smith, she had been involved in a volatile relationship with a fascinating and elusive lover. Younger than Plath, Richard Sassoon had been brought up in Europe and appeared tantalisingly sophisticated and self-assured. When they met, he was studying history and philosophy at Yale, and delighted Plath with his radical ideas, facility in French, and cosmopolitan taste for fine wines and gourmet meals. Brooding and dark-eyed, Sassoon embodied the mystery, melancholia and sardonic brilliance of the Byronic hero.[104] Slender and barely taller than the physically robust Plath, he failed to match her ideal of manhood, which conformed to the Hollywood stereotype of a man capable literally of sweeping her off her feet. After her skiing accident an earlier lover had delighted her by lifting her, plaster cast and all, into his arms to move her from place to place. 'I feel so feminine and light ... the carrying is a symbol of his virility,' confided Plath approvingly to her journal.[105] By contrast, Sassoon was 'thin, nervous, little, moody, sickly'. Unlike many of the young American males whom Plath dated, he had no enthusiasm for athletic self-display through swimming, sailing and prowess on the ski slopes; his power rested in his 'strong soul'.[106] Nevertheless, he represented the complex intellectual and emotional partnership that Plath craved, and she relished their exchange of extravagant, sometimes drunken letters, in which both partners could pour out an uncensored stream of poetic ideas and images to a responsive correspondent.

During her first Christmas in Cambridge she travelled to Paris to visit Sassoon, who was studying at the Sorbonne, and kept a diary of their journey south together to Nice and the Côte d'Azur, where she was ravished by her first glimpse of 'the red sun rising like the eye of God out of a screaming blue sea', an image that she was to resurrect later to great effect in her poem 'Ariel'.[107] This visit seems, however, to have initiated a withdrawal on Richard's part, which Plath explored in anguished entries in her journal. Although she had vacillated over her commitment to the relationship, when Sassoon appeared finally to have distanced himself, her response was to mourn his loss and to long for someone 'to blast over Richard; . . . some sort of blazing love that I can live with'.[108] She did not have long to wait. On the day that she wrote those words, 25 February 1956, Plath finally met the man who could provide the dynamic partnership that she craved, 'a large, hulking, healthy Adam . . . with a voice like the thunder of God', the poet Ted Hughes.[109]

It is perhaps ironic that while Plath was agonising over what her housemates might be thinking about her, she had made an impact on a group of male Cambridge poets, one of whom, Daniel Huws, had written a corrosive attack on two poems, 'Epitaph in Three Parts' and the cumbrously named 'Three Caryatids Without a Portico by Hugh Robus: A Study in Sculptural Dimensions', which Plath had published in *Chequer*, a Cambridge student magazine. Recalling the circumstances in his own poem, 'Caryatids (2)' in *Birthday Letters*, Ted Hughes evokes the circle of confident, still childish young men, who laughingly concocted a 'dismemberment' of the flamboyant American pretender.[110] At the time Plath was experimenting with a highly worked, rather precious style and, as Hughes's close friend Lucas Myers put it, the coterie objected to Plath's poems precisely because they were too 'well made' and, in their view, reeked of ambition. Poetry 'should come down on the poet from somewhere', not be written 'out of sheer will'.[111] But the young men were also suspicious of Plath's exuberance and gush, the public persona that Hughes astutely described as her 'misfit self-display', in reality a mask to conceal anxiety and fear.[112] To the critical eyes of her fellow students, with their British traditions of reticence and ironic self-effacement, Plath's ostentatiously casual clothes, her neat sweaters and skirts and loafers, combined with her 'flaring gestures', her 'dance of . . . blond veils' and 'Veronica Lake bang', seemed exotic and even crude.[113] Even Plath's fellow Americans backed away from her fervour. Jane Baltzell, also a postgraduate student living at Whitstead, wrote coldly of Plath's embarrassing showiness, as she pedalled into town on her bicycle, demanding directions from a Cambridge policeman to 'somewhere really picturesque and collegiate' where she might eat.[114] She noticed Plath's physical restlessness, her foot swinging as she sat, legs aristocratically crossed, her long fingers locking and unlocking in her lap.

It is easy to see, with hindsight, why Hughes's friends should have been so hostile to Plath. From recollections of their time at Cambridge, a picture emerges of male camaraderie and bonding, a resistance to the 'establishment' that chimes intriguingly with Sassoon's bravado iconoclasm, and a boyish (and possibly ineffectual) strategy towards women of 'seduce' and 'subjugate', which Hughes himself seems to have instigated. (A fellow student, Michael Boddy, recalled that Hughes's advice was gradually to assert dominance, 'until, I suppose, the woman was cooking a five-course meal, feeding the goldfish, walking the dog, and doing the laundry without argument'.)[115] Any woman who seriously challenged their masculine stronghold was likely to meet a forest of spears. Hughes himself was not so aggressively defended. A character still in the making, he was romantically open to the charm and possibilities of Plath's New World allure. Although he had graduated the previous year, Hughes was still hovering on the peripheries of student life, while he tried to decide his future. He was older than many of the group, already twenty-one when he went up to Pembroke College to read English in October 1951. A grammar-school boy, with an extensive knowledge of the natural world developed during his childhood in the Yorkshire Pennines, Hughes coped with Cambridge snobbery and pretension by developing his own idiosyncratic lifestyle, roasting meat on the fire in his room, playing Beethoven very loudly on his gramophone and pursuing his fascination with astrology, the Ouija board and the occult.

Dedicated to writing, he found the English syllabus, with its emphasis on critical assessment, creatively stultifying and, in his third year, he transferred to reading Archaeology and Anthropology. The stimulus for this change was a strange dream, which Hughes refers to in his poem 'The Thought-Fox' and later described in a short article. After several days' toiling to write a critical essay, Hughes dreamt that a wolf-size fox appeared in his room, walking on its hind legs, its body charred and bleeding as if it had just stepped out of a furnace, its eyes 'dazzled with the intensity of the pain'. Approaching Hughes where he sat at his desk, it laid its human hand palm down on the unwritten page. 'Stop this – you are destroying us,' it instructed Hughes. Deeply superstitious, Hughes read the bloody handprint, the lines as clear as a palmist's sample, as an image of the damage he was doing to his nature by pursuing a constricting discipline.[116] In contrast to Plath, he seems to have known instinctively how to listen and respond to his deepest needs, and had the courage to follow his own path. What he lacked was the focus and practical ambition that Plath had applied to her writing since she started sending out poems and stories for publication as a schoolgirl.

After he went down from Cambridge, Hughes took odd jobs as a security guard and gardener, washed dishes in the cafeteria of a zoo and read novels for J. Arthur Rank, so that he could concentrate his energies on writing poetry.[117] Physically imposing (Hughes was over six foot tall and large-boned), he wore smelly old corduroys and was indifferent to the creature comforts that Plath saw as essential to civilised living. But their differences would help to cement the bond between them. Of his meeting with Plath, Hughes was to say quite simply, 'the solar system married us'.[118] Whatever influences were at work that evening, it seems undeniable that two highly gifted, unusual people recognised one another and formed an intuitive connection that was dramatically to affect their lives. Both were, in a sense, lost souls looking for direction, although each pursued his or her quest with characteristic difference, Plath busily seeking the perfect mate, while the laid-back Hughes relied on his 'blind-man's-buff / Internal torch of search'.[119] Their immediate response seems to have been a powerful sexual attraction. As far as Plath was concerned, Ted's intelligence, charisma and striking physique suggested that here, finally, might be the man large enough to take her on.

They met at a party, held in the Women's Union at Falcon's Yard, to celebrate the launch of a new literary magazine, the *St Botolph's Review*. Hughes arrived with his current girlfriend, a student named Shirley, who shared a supervision with Plath and inflamed Hughes's imagination by venomous descriptions of her rival. Plath turned up with a Canadian boyfriend, already euphoric on the Whiskey Macs she had been gulping to stave off a cold and perhaps to give herself courage for the ordeal ahead. In the account she wrote the next day, adrenalin still flaring, she described the 'Bohemian' gathering, the 'boys in turtle-neck sweaters and girls being blue-eye-lidded or elegant in black'.[120] Plath herself was strikingly turned out, with red shoes, a thickly lipsticked mouth and a scarlet bandeau to hold back her shoulder-length hair. There was a jazz band composed of Hughes's cronies, 'the syncopated strut of a piano upstairs', and a steady flow of alcohol to fuel the excitement.[121]

Eager to impress the *St Botolph's* poets, Plath had memorised Hughes's and Myers's contributions, and now started to dance with Myers, reciting one of his poems as they writhed disharmoniously to the end of the number. Seconds later she was face to face with Ted Hughes, 'that big, dark, hunky boy, the only one there huge enough for me', and they retreated into a neighbouring room, where they sloshed down brandy and yelled together 'as if in a high wind' about poetry, and Daniel Huws's malevolent critique of Sylvia, and Ted's ten-pound-a-week job.[122] It ended, inevitably, in a kiss, Hughes ripping off her headband and silver earrings as keepsakes, and Plath biting him deeply on the cheek. She had wanted to make her mark and she did it quite literally. Hughes was to bear the 'swelling ring-moat of tooth-marks' on his cheek for days to come and felt that Plath's gesture symbolically branded him for life.[123]

Plath's next-day account of their meeting evokes a clash of Titans on some mountain peak or skeletal building exposed to the elements, the huge man with his poems 'strong and blasting like a high wind in steel girders', and the woman screaming to give herself 'crashing, fighting' to the one man 'who could blast Richard'.[124] It is an extraordinary piece of writing, apparently spontaneous and full of energy, but also stylish, crafty, artily self-conscious. Just before the party Plath had been reflecting on the 'dialogue between my Writing and my Life', and the 'slithering shifting of responsibility' from one to the other. If life got out of hand, she gave it order by writing about it, while she justified her writing on the grounds that it would give her 'life' through publication and prestige.[125] Now, she dealt with the excitement and emotion of meeting Hughes by describing it in dramatic, even sensationalist, terms. 'Such violence, and I can see how women lie down for artists,' she exults.[126] She was later to rework her diary description into a story, 'Stone Boy with Dolphin', which recreates the events of the evening through the eyes of Dody Ventura, a heroine who, like Esther Greenwood, shares many of Plath's thoughts and experiences, but through whom Plath objectifies and distances life's messiness into the 'order, form, beauty' of writing.[127] But at the same time, sitting in her room the next day, 'demure and tired in brown', she felt 'slightly sick at heart'. The downside to her euphoria was a familiar dread of public humiliation, of being seen as 'the world's whore' and the fear that Hughes would not seek her out again.[128] For his part, he was bewitched by her vivacity and elegance, her 'long, perfect, American legs', her expressive face and 'balletic' fingers, her dark eyes like 'a crush of diamonds', a 'crush of tears'.[129]

Plath channelled her sexual excitement into a remarkable poem, 'Pursuit', inspired by a quotation from Racine: *'Dans le fond des forêts votre image me suit.*' She had been reading Racine's *Phèdre*, a tragedy about a queen's forbidden lust for her stepson, and her imagination was gripped by the fierce shame and pride that inhibit Phèdre from confessing her love. In the poem Plath inverts her own sexual yearning into a dramatic fantasy of the chase: a panther sleekly hunting down its human prey through a menacing forest. The fleeing woman both fears and desires her 'black marauder', whose radiance ravishes her even as she escapes into a tower, fruit-lessly bolting the doors against her pursuer as she mounts the stairs.[130] Plath told Aurelia that the poem was partly influenced by Blake's poem 'The Tiger', and was 'a symbol of the terrible beauty of death, and the paradox that the more intensely one lives, the more one burns and consumes oneself'. Racine's idea of 'passion as destiny' was also in her thoughts.[131] But Plath's sensual evocation of the pursuit, with its heat and danger and panting desire, also cap-tures a longing to be forced and taken, like the rapturous rape by the sun that she had imagined as a young girl, pressed against burning rocks beside the glittering ocean.[132] It is an erotic dream that has its roots in ancient myth and fairy tale, and finds its happiest culmination in the story of Beauty and the Beast, where terror ends in tenderness, and the reciprocity of a tried and tested love. Angela Carter found the theme of woman and beast fascinating, returning to the story again and again to explore its possibilities. Her short story 'The Tiger's Bride', one of the subtlest and most touching of these versions, recognises the beast's magnificence and sexual power, but also the humility and self-restraint that make fearless love poss-ible.[133] In Plath's darker version of the fable the panther's desire is all-consuming and only 'total sacrifice' will glut his need. She dedi-cated the poem to Ted Hughes, but it could equally represent her frustrated passion for Richard Sassoon.

In the light of all that subsequently happened between them, Plath's meeting with Hughes seems momentous. At the time, how-ever, the little she knew about him increased her uncertainty that they would meet again. He had 'obligations' (to his girlfriend Shirley and maybe a stream of other women for all she knew – 'the biggest seducer in Cambridge' was a male friend's assessment of Hughes), he was living in London and was involved in Cambridge with a group who had shown hostility to Plath.[134] She was in any case still committed to Sassoon, to whom she continued to draft agonised letters in her journal, and was at the same time actively looking for a suitable mate among other possible contenders. Her journal and letters to Aurelia during the next four months, until her sudden marriage to Hughes on Bloomsday, 16 June 1956, are a kaleidoscope of Plath's hopes and fears, as the relationship with Hughes gradually assumed dominance over other possibilities.

Sassoon's continued withdrawal – in March he wrote to insist on a clean break – crystallised her wavering feelings into a torrent of love and longing, mixed with chagrin at the thought of how long it would take to find another, equally vibrant love. What she wants, she wails in a long, passionate, heartfelt letter, is the right man to share her life. 'I am inclined to babies and bed and brilliant friends and a magnificent stimulating home where geniuses drink gin in the kitchen after a delectable dinner and read their own novels . . . and discuss scientific mysticism (which, by the way, is intriguing . . .),' she adds, irresistibly inquisitive even when in despair.[135] But Sassoon remained elusive. When Plath travelled to Paris at the end of March, hoping to confront him with arguments why their affair should continue, she found that he was away for several weeks and had left no forwarding address. Worse, Plath found her letters unopened at his lodgings, 'lying there blue and unread'. '[N]ever before had a man gone off to leave me to cry after,' she wrote bitterly in her journal.[136]

She managed nevertheless to have a productive time in Paris, reading and sketching, making friends with Giovanni, an Italian journalist, and teaming up with the 'fearfully bright and game and witty' Tony, 'the kind of English chap who would be all daisy-fresh at eight in the morning and leap over tennisnets in immaculate white shorts his blond hair shining in the early sun saying "Tennis anyone" in a fearfully Oxford accent'.[137] Although she finds him boring (and an easy butt for her sarcasm), they end up in bed together, mellowed by a bottle of iced white wine, but Tony changes his mind about sex, and Plath forgivingly attributes his reticence to class-consciousness and goes with him to the cinema to see Grace Kelly in Hitchcock's *To Catch a Thief*. All the time her mind is revolving the problem of men and her future. 'Is it some dread lack which makes my alternatives so deadly?' she asks herself on her last day in Paris, weighing up the options. 'Some feeble dependence on men which makes me throw myself on their protection and care and tenderness?'[138] She is planning to travel to Munich the next day with safe, reliable Gordon Lameyer, a former boyfriend from her Smith days, and yet her spirit rebels against accepting 'the boring daily bread' that such men represent. Precious time seems to be slipping through her fingers: 'it is my life which is passing, my life which is smutched and battered and running, each heartbeat; each clocktick being a fatal subtraction from the total number I was allowed in the beginning[.]'[139]

Plath's search for the 'strong potential powerful mate who can counter my vibrant dynamic self' was almost at an end.[140] Despite her fear that Ted would not follow up their meeting at the *St Botolph's* party, he had come to Whitstead with Lucas Myers some days later to throw stones at Plath's window. Unfortunately, they chose the wrong window and Plath was, in any case, out drinking with a friend, but Hughes's approach threw her into a tumult of longing. 'Oh, he is here; my black marauder; oh hungry hungry. I am so hungry for a big smashing creative burgeoning burdened love,' she wrote in her journal when she heard the news of his escapade.[141] Later, dressed in 'violent, fierce colors', she waited in her room for the panther's step on the stair, only to be frustrated when Myers and Hughes arrived in the early hours once again to throw mud in error at a fellow student's window.[142] Charitably, the girl got up and tried to waken Plath, but she slept through the rumpus. She finally saw Ted in London, at his lodgings in Rugby Street in Bloomsbury, on the night before she travelled to Paris. Plath's brief comment in her journal mentions a 'sleepless holocaust night', which left her with a bruised face and 'raw and wounded' neck.[143] Adrift in Paris, she continued to feel that Hughes was unknown territory. 'One night is not enough,' she told herself, but she sent him a postcard of Rousseau's *Snakecharmer*, and when she flew back from Rome, after a fractious week travelling with Lameyer, she 'renounced Gordon, Sassoon – my old life – & took up Ted'.[144]

Hughes recalled his first night with Plath in a poem, '18 Rugby Street', written perhaps many years after her death and included in the *Birthday Letters* collection. It begins on a note of foreboding, as the decrepit Victorian house is imagined as a stage set for the tragic fates that will, over the years, befall its female lodgers. Hughes dates their meeting as 13 April, the anniversary of Plath's father's birthday and the day when she actually returned from her holiday, perhaps simply a misremembering on his part, a collation of the two nights together that bracketed her travels, or a deliberate ploy to link his fate to Otto's, a device he uses repeatedly in the *Birthday Letters* poems. This time he is the one waiting for the step on the stairs and he hears Plath babbling breathlessly as she climbs towards him, before she emerges like a 'great bird', ruffling her plumage in a flare of cobalt-blue electricity. Now at last he can look at her, can take in her 'elvish' brown eyes and 'aboriginal' lips, and the broad 'Apache' nose that 'made every camera your enemy'. Most of all, it is the mobility of her face that he registers, a surface as changeable and responsive as the sea. Later she smuggles him into her hotel and they make love: 'So this is America, I marvelled. / Beautiful, beautiful America!'[145]

Once Plath had met up again with Hughes, events moved with

remarkable speed, although she continued to feel anxious that it
was only a temporary passion on his part. Hughes had been planning
to emigrate to Australia, where his beloved older brother Gerald
was already living, and the fear of loss haunts Plath's writing at this
period. In a letter to Aurelia on 17 April she announces that she
has fallen in love with a 'singer, story-teller, lion and world-
wanderer', but predicts it 'can only lead to great hurt'.[146] On 18 April
there is an angry entry in her journal, apparently addressed to
Sassoon, in which she says 'something very terrifying' has happened
as a result of his desertion, and now she is living 'in a kind of
present hell'.[147] She confided to Warren, 'I am . . . in love with the
only man in the world who is my match and whom I shall no doubt
never see after this summer as he is going to Australia.'[148] She was
overwhelmed by the delight of finding a man whom she could meet
on equal terms. 'For the first time in my life I can use *all* my
knowing and laughing and force and writing to the hilt,' she exulted
to Aurelia.[149] In a radio interview some years later, Hughes laughingly described how he blew his savings on his three-month courtship of Plath, an investment in the future that acknowledged the
impact of their meeting.[150] For her it was a period of blossoming
after the long, wretched, lonely winter: 'my resurrection came about
with that green and incredible Cambridge spring[.]'[151]

   After Sylvia's return to Whitstead she and Ted became close
companions, taking long walks in the fens and talking about poetry.
They read each other's work, shared criticism and ideas, and poured
out new poems. It was a remarkable beginning to their long working
relationship. 'Daily I am full of poems; my joy whirls in tongues
of words,' crowed Sylvia, dashing in to write to her mother after
time out with Ted, exploring the habits of coots and cows and
whatever other animal life they encountered in their rambles.[152]
Hughes saw quite simply that 'she was a genius of some kind. Quite
suddenly we were completely committed to each other and to each
other's writing . . . I see now that when we met, my writing, like

hers, left its old path and started to circle and search. To me, of course, she was not only herself: she was America and American literature in person.'[153] Jane Baltzell, observing their comings and goings from the house at Whitstead, described Ted's calming effect on the volatile Sylvia: 'Before, she had been gushing and a little silly, restless, self-divided, always striving in several directions to "achieve" . . . but at a stroke she became private, serious, and seemingly centered.'[154]

Almost immediately, Plath took charge of Hughes's literary career, typing up poems and sending them to literary magazines, and managing to get two published in an American journal. Her knowledge of the American literary world was to be invaluable in getting Hughes's work known and published in the USA, and her approach to writing as a commodity to be ruthlessly marketed propelled him willy-nilly into the life of a professional writer. Her friend Jillian Becker kept Plath's neat handwritten list of periodicals that published poetry and remembers her advice that a 'serious writer' should take care to submit work 'correctly typed, with double spacing, on clean paper'.[155] It was Plath's initiative that secured the publication of Hughes's first book of poems, *The Hawk in the Rain*, which won a poetry competition sponsored by Harper Brothers Publishers in New York, a prestigious beginning that opened many doors. Although Hughes's fellow poet Lucas Myers personally benefited from Plath's practical approach (she sent out a bunch of his poems and offered to type up a long prose piece for him), he viewed her with suspicion, shrewdly identifying her difference from Hughes in their attitudes to poetry: 'Sylvia was determined that it should be read. Ted was determined that it should exist.'[156] Watching the relationship move irresistibly towards marriage, Myers feared that Sylvia would pull Hughes into the 'struggle for income, shoes, tableware, functioning appliances, perhaps into the American English Literature Establishment . . . or else that he would make a stand against all this and the marriage would explode.'[157]

Like so many published commentators on the Plath–Hughes relationship, Myers was writing with the benefit of hindsight, but there is no doubt that Plath had been programmed throughout her formative years towards the idea of marriage, children and a home, a public display of successful womanhood which she continued to see through the conventional eyes of the Wellesley community among whom she had grown up. While her letters celebrated Ted's refreshing Bohemianism, the old black sweater and 'corduroy jacket with pockets full of poems, fresh trout and horoscopes', her lover's delightful disregard for his appearance was the subject of increasingly anxious messages to Aurelia, who was planning a visit to England that June.[158] 'He may shock you at first,' warned Plath, 'unless you imagine a big, unruly Huckleberry Finn. He hasn't even a suit of clothes . . . .'[159] When Warren visited, he was to be roped into the task of civilising Ted, helping Sylvia 'very subtly' to wean him 'into shopping for clothes for himself and giving him "man information" about America'.[160] The extent of Plath's concern with public opinion can be judged from her 'most cherished dream' of presenting Ted to all her friends and neighbours at a huge barbecue the following summer.[161] Recognising that Hughes's 'rugged self' was rather different from the clean-cut aspirational American boys whom she had been dating at Smith, she wistfully begged Aurelia, 'If only you [and Warren] will just take him for what he is . . . without wealth or a slick 10-year guarantee for a secure job, of a house and car[.]'[162]

Ted's indifference to conventional patterns of getting and spending continued to be a source of tension throughout his relationship with Plath. 'What is so terrible about earning a regular wage?' she exclaimed mutinously during a particularly freewheeling period in Boston.[163] Being socially invisible can, of course, be very useful to the aspiring writer. The reclusive Emily Dickinson wrote wittily about its advantages:

I'm Nobody! Who are you?
Are you – Nobody – Too?
Then there's a pair of us?
Don't tell! they'd advertise – you know![164]

Whereas Hughes wasn't bothered about being a Nobody, happy to
lead a hobo existence while he learnt his craft as a poet, Plath's
training in the necessity of keeping up appearances and her craving
for recognition as a writer made her the driving force in homemaking and earning money to fund her aspirations. Her need for security
and the tangible proofs of success may well have put a strain on the
relationship, pushing both partners too quickly into responsibilities
that could have waited. They were young, in love, creative writers
committed to their calling. Even so, the dreams of travelling light,
living in Spain or Italy, observing and recording, which she and
Hughes shared in that first golden spring, fed perhaps by their
enthusiasm for D. H. Lawrence and his peripatetic existence, were
laid aside while Plath spent a year teaching at Smith College, and
were further postponed when she became pregnant with their first
child, named Frieda after Otto Plath's sister, but also in homage to
Lawrence's wife. Although Hughes for several years fell in with
Plath's determined life plan, the infatuation with another woman
that broke up his marriage may have been due partly to a wish to
free himself from family ties. In one of the many memoirs written
by friends and critics after Plath's death, Jillian Becker recalls Ted
'complaining' at the grim meal that followed Plath's funeral, 'She
made me professional.' Becker dismisses this as 'fiddle-faddle', an
example of English respect for amateurism fastidiously at odds
with materialistic America. In her view Ted relished his status and
developing reputation as a poet, and simply disliked being *seen* as
commercially minded, but she suggests that Hughes might also have
been referring to the duties required by marriage and fatherhood.[165]

So why, then, did Hughes succumb to Plath's pressure to marry?

The answer lies perhaps in his personality, a willingness to 'wait and see' how circumstances would unfold that was an essential part of his receptivity as an artist. In several of the poems in *Birthday Letters*, referring to the two years he and Plath spent in America, Hughes writes about 'sleepwalking' his way into disaster, a reading of events closely tied to the fatalistic interpretation of his marriage that he developed in these poems.[166] Whatever the truth of Hughes's *post facto* theories about his wife (and 'truth' is a notoriously slippery concept when dealing with memory and emotion), it is clear that Plath's need for order and control was very different from Hughes's more instinctual, relaxed approach. In these early days in Cambridge Plath's enthusiasm quickly pushed their love affair towards what she regarded as its only logical conclusion. For her, marrying Ted was the culmination of years of dreaming and hard effort. Once she felt sure of his acquiescence, she simply took over and organised their lives to fit her fantasy. Hughes's attitude was more pragmatic. His account of how they decided to marry is an example of their contrasting styles: 'She wanted to teach, I wanted to go off round the world. I didn't even ask her to marry me. She suggested it as a good idea and I said OK, why not?'[167] Whatever his later reservations about Plath's energetic steering of his career, Ted acknowledged their meeting was providential. If he had gone to Australia, he wrote to Aurelia Plath in the 1970s, he 'might have been lost altogether'.[168]

Aurelia arrived at Southampton on 13 June 1956 after the long sea voyage across the Atlantic and to her astonishment found herself, the sole representative of family and friends, attending Sylvia's and Ted's wedding three days later. Anxious to pin down this marvellous man, her 'male counterpart' as she described him to Warren, but terrified that she would lose her Fulbright scholarship if she married, Plath had pledged Hughes to secrecy.[169] Her worries turned out to be unfounded. When she later 'confessed' her clandestine marriage to her tutor, there was no question of losing her award and she was readily given permission to move out of Whitstead to live with Ted.[170] Her fears were not illusory. Hughes's biographer, Elaine Feinstein, herself a student at Newnham in the Fifties, recalls that, whatever the regulations actually stipulated, Newnham women 'certainly *believed* they risked a serious penalty if they chose to get married'. It was a marker of those benighted times for intellectual women that several sought illegal abortions believing that matrimony was not an option if they wanted to continue their studies.[171]

Hughes's poem 'A Pink Wool Knitted Dress' evokes the magical, dreamlike quality of the wedding ceremony and Plath's brimming delight. Dressed in his scruffy 'uniform' of thrice-dyed black corduroy jacket and an RAF tie from his National Service days, Hughes felt like the swineherd in the fairy tale, stealing the 'pedigree' Plath from her carefully guarded future.[172] Aurelia, gallant as ever, rose to the occasion, providing Plath with the 'lovely pink knitted suit dress' she wore as her bridal gown, and doing her best to stand in for all the non-invited guests.[173] The sexton acted as best man, temporarily abandoning the busload of children he was escorting to the zoo. As for Sylvia, she wept for joy, predicting the golden future poised to shower down upon them, her eyes sparkling with tears and happiness like 'great cut jewels'.[174]

In a loving memoir, a remarkable tribute to her pupil, Dorothea Krook, the dedicated young woman who supervised Plath's English Moralists paper at Cambridge, recalled her happiness after her marriage. 'What would happen', Krook wondered, obscurely troubled by such radiance, 'if something should ever *go wrong* with this marriage of true minds? Nothing of course would, nothing *could*, go wrong,' she reassured herself. 'Yet if, inconceivably, it should, she would suffer terribly; I held my breath to think how she would suffer.'[175]

The Afterlife of the Beloved:
Ted Hughes and Sylvia Plath

'[T]he *single* poetic theme of Life and Death . . . the
question of what survives of the beloved'

Welsh poet Alun Lewis, quoted in Robert Graves,
The White Goddess[176]

The marriage lasted six years before Hughes and Plath separated
in October 1962. It was an astonishingly busy time for both partners.
After Plath had finished her degree at Newnham in 1957 they
travelled to America, where she taught literature at her Alma Mater,
Smith College, and Ted worked briefly at the University of Massachusetts. Both then decided to take the gamble of living on their
earnings as freelance writers and moved to Boston in autumn 1958.
Always anxious without formal work schedules, Plath took a clerical
job in a hospital and attended Robert Lowell's poetry class, where
she met the poet Anne Sexton. After a period of travelling and a
visit to the artists' community at Yaddo in Saratoga Springs, she
and Hughes returned to England late in 1959 and rented a flat near
Primrose Hill in north London. Their daughter Frieda was born
the following April. On 31 August 1961 they were on the move
again, to Court Green, a substantial family house in North Tawton
in Devon. Their second child, Nicholas, was born in January 1962.
Later that spring, a weekend visit from Assia and David Wevill,

the couple who had rented their London flat, sparked a powerful attraction between Ted and Assia. By the autumn he had moved out of Court Green and Plath was talking about divorce. She committed suicide on 11 February 1963.

These are the bare bones of what was both a marriage and a creative partnership. During this time Hughes's reputation was established. His prizewinning poetry collection, *The Hawk in the Rain*, was published by Harper Brothers in 1957 and went on to gain a Somerset Maugham award. *Lupercal*, published in March 1960, won the Hawthornden Prize. At the same time, once he was back in London, Hughes developed a productive connection with the BBC, writing scripts for radio plays and giving readings of his own and other writers' work. Plath's career moved more slowly. It took time to wean herself away from her ambition to teach and she suffered months of agonising block when she committed herself to full-time writing. Homemaking and babies ate into her time. Her first poetry collection, *The Colossus*, was published in England in October 1960 and in a slightly different version in the USA in May 1962. Her novel, *The Bell Jar*, appeared under the pseudonym Victoria Lucas just a few weeks before she died. Both were modestly reviewed: her serious acclaim as a writer depended on the *Ariel* poems, published posthumously.[177] It was more than a decade after the publication of *Ariel* that selections from Plath's short stories and other prose pieces, and her edited journals and letters to her family, finally appeared in print. Their importance in evaluating Plath's achievement as a writer has still to be fully recognised.

Throughout this period Hughes and Plath shared a dialogue about their writing, which was conducted on a number of levels. There was, most importantly, the day-to-day discussion about reading and writing, and what each partner was attempting. Both were totally committed to poetry, but their approaches to the task of writing were very different. Hughes's more laid-back, intuitive attitude helped to free Plath from the iron grip of obligation and ambition. Desperate to write, she found herself sitting day after day in front of a blank page, paralysed by the self-imposed requirement to produce brilliant, fresh, innovative work. When Plath's 'Panic Bird' stultified her imagination, Hughes suggested writing exercises to free her mind, an external discipline to satisfy the Cerberus who guarded the gates of her creativity.[178] Writing 'to order' released her from the anxiety of composition, while hypnosis and play with tarot cards and a Ouija board uncovered the secret processes of the subconscious. Plath's and Hughes's mutual openness about their work extended to the communal use of writing paper. They frequently sketched out new work on the unused side of discarded drafts of each other's writing, a subterranean conversation that sometimes had intriguing effects. A typed page of what seems to be Sylvia's projected Cambridge novel, in which 'Sheila' receives a letter from 'Sassoon' and describes the view from her bedroom window at college, was later reused by Ted for a handwritten draft of his short story 'Harvesting'.[179]

Their working partnership benefited both poets. Plath turned Hughes into a professional money-making writer. She effectively acted as his literary agent, typing up work to be submitted for publication, rattling on her typewriter at a rate of eighty words a minute, and methodically sending out poems and manuscripts to magazines, journals and publishers. Her commitment to poetry and to Hughes extended far beyond this practical assistance, which she would in any case have regarded as part of her function as an enabling mate. Jillian Becker, in her memoir of Plath, makes the point that 'Sylvia was an intellectual', something that is often forgotten in discussions that focus on her emotional lability.[180] Plath's trained intelligence made her a stimulating partner; she was, in addition, supremely well equipped to talk to Hughes as an equal about poetry. She provided him, too, with a subtler resource, which he described in a BBC radio interview, *Two of a Kind*, transmitted in January 1961. Asked about the wellsprings of his inspiration,

Hughes mentioned the telepathic union he enjoyed with Plath. Drawing on what he called their 'single shared mind', he had access to her experience as well as his own, and could use it in new ways in his writing. Plath's response to the same question was more down to earth. Sidestepping any airy-fairy discussion about spiritual rapport, she said simply that Ted had a practical influence on her choice of subject matter. His interest in animals, for example, had made her think back to her childhood and to her father's fascination with bees. Interestingly, given subsequent speculation about her relationship with Otto, she didn't dwell on her father, moving smoothly on to talk about painting and sculpture, and the importance of visual influences on her work.

Listening in a soundproofed booth at the British Library to the recording of this long-past discussion is a moving experience. The poets' voices are rich and warm and tantalisingly present, Plath's beautifully modulated and self-possessed, as she talks about her public persona as housewife and mother, and the positive influence of Frieda on their lives and work. Far from finding herself 'swallowed up in motherhood', Plath relishes her baby daughter: '[S]he's fitted in beautifully and is amazingly little trouble ... she doesn't yell and cry and she plays by herself and is very amusing, and I think both of us have written a good many poems to her[.]' Plath sounds calm and competent and in control, while Ted is more hesitant and reflective, at his most communicative when he can talk about what interests him: the functioning of the creative process. His friend Lucas Myers has suggested that writing poetry and nurturing his receptivity were inextricable in Ted. 'Poetry was the expression and the inner life was the substance. He attended to and developed his inner life more consistently than anyone I have encountered apart from advanced Buddhist practitioners.'[181]

Ted returned to the subject of his partnership with Plath many years later. In an interview with the journalist Eilat Negev, first published just after Hughes's death, he emphasised how much he and Sylvia worked as a team. They were young and ambitious; they pushed each other to achieve. Hughes made sure that Plath had time each morning to write; later in the day he worked while she cared for the children. He saw their shared commitment to writing as an advantage. Being the sole writer in the family can lead to jealousy and opposition. '[W]hen there are two of you,' Hughes explained, 'the atmosphere is supportive. It's easier to concentrate on what you are doing, because both of you do the same thing. It's like singing together in the dark.'[182] This is a curious analogy for Hughes to make, implying that the effort 'to woo the muse', as he earlier describes the creative process, is essentially an act of faith, a groping in fog. But the image also hints at the continued professional relationship after Plath's death, when Hughes gradually made her work available through a steady drip-feed of publications, a process that involved his reading, assessing and in some cases editing the manuscripts she had left, including her journals. It also invokes his private conversation with his wife, the attempt to understand why their promising love affair ended with her suicide in a London flat during one of the coldest English winters on record.

One of Hughes's ways of finding a thread through the darkness following Plath's death was to explore their relationship in a series of poems, which were finally published in 1998, some months before his death, as *Birthday Letters*. Several of the poems are a tribute to Plath's vivacity and brilliance, and Hughes's passion for his wife. They also place Plath in a carefully constructed narrative, in which her death is seen as a consequence of her early experiences, and quite specifically the loss of her father Otto Plath. Hughes had always been interested in the operations of the subconscious mind, and had encouraged Plath to make use of astrology, tarot cards and the cryptic utterances of the Ouija board to get in touch with her imagination and the hidden forces that drove her destiny. According to his account, Otto Plath played a significant role in these negotiations with unseen forces:

I n this anonymous late 15th-century panel painting, *The Love Charm*, a beautiful naked girl casts a spell on a captive heart, while a young man spies on her through the open door. The flowers, fire, fluffy dog and perching parakeet all play a part in love's witchery.

In these paired portraits of the Brownings, Robert glows with health and intellectual curiosity, while Elizabeth, despite the masses of dark hair that girlishly frame her face, seems more reserved, her firmly modelled lips suggesting suffering and self-restraint.

Edna St Vincent Millay having fun with Eugen Boissevain (*standing*) and her close friend Arthur Ficke, and recovering from a serious operation soon after her wedding in the summer of 1923.

This sumptuous portrait shows Madame de Staël posing as her heroine Corinne, the poet, lyrist and *improvisatrice* who captivated audiences across Europe.

George Sand's fondness for cross-dressing exposed her to public mockery, as in this cartoon by Alade Joseph Lorentz, but as an unknown writer it freed her to wander the streets of Paris without check or comment.

Mrs Dashwood and her three daughters, heroines in the making, from Ang Lee's film of *Sense and Sensibility*.

Jane Austen's niece, Fanny, to whom she wrote about love and marriage, painted by Cassandra Austen (*top left*).

Charlotte Brontë's 'Woman in leopard fur', who may represent her heroine Caroline Vernon (*top right*).

The first portrait of L. M. Montgomery's popular heroine, Anne of Green Gables, 1908 (*right*).

'White and golden Lizzie stood': Arthur Rackham's disturbing 1933 illustration to Christina Rossetti's *Goblin Market*.

Rudolph Valentino abducts
Agnes Eyres in the 1921
film of *The Sheik*.

Richard E. Grant as
Sir Percy Blakeney in one
of several screen versions
of *The Scarlet Pimpernel*.

Judy Davis as Sybylla Melvyn in the 1979
film version of *My Brilliant Career*.

Vita Sackville-West in June 1916.

Laurence Olivier and Joan Fontaine
in Hitchcock's *Rebecca*.

Clark Gable and Vivien Leigh
in the 1939 film version of
Gone With the Wind.

Sylvia Plath with Joan Cantor in
Cape Cod, 1952.

Sylvia Plath interviewing Elizabeth
Bowen for *Mademoiselle* in 1953.

'Pleasing Mr Rochester': Paula Rego's lithograph for her *Jane Eyre* series.

Sylvia Plath and Ted Hughes in Yorkshire soon after their marriage, 1956.

Sylvia Plath with Frieda in 1962.

She would describe her suicide attempt [in 1953] as a bid to get back to her father, and one can imagine that in her case this was a routine reconstruction from a psychoanalytical point of view. But she made much of it, and it played an increasingly dominant role in her recovery ... Some of the implications might be divined from her occasional dealings with the Ouija board, during the late fifties. Her father's name was Otto, and 'spirits' would regularly arrive with instructions for her from one Prince Otto, who was said to be a great power in the underworld. When she pressed for a more personal communication, she would be told that Prince Otto could not speak to her directly, because he was under orders from the Colossus. And when she pressed for an audience with the Colossus, they would say he was inaccessible.

Hughes believed that Plath's effort 'to come to terms with the meaning this Colossus held for her, in her poetry, became more and more central as the years passed'.[183] In pondering the enigma of Plath's life and death, he interpreted the events of their brief marriage as stages in an inevitable progress towards its abrupt end. Seen from this perspective, Hughes was little more than fate's patsy, 'sleepwalking' his way into a destiny he could have done little to avert. This is, however, an oversimplification of what is happening in *Birthday Letters*. Written possibly over many years, the poems reflect the dilemma of those who survive the suicide of a partner or close family member: the replaying of past events to see what might have been done to avert the tragedy, the painful 'what ifs' with which the shared life is interrogated. Too late for remedy, the survivor must still obsessively ask, 'How did it all happen? What might I have done?' These two strands, destiny and the possibility of deflecting it into new paths, twist in and out of the poems, a conflict that is resolved only by the irrefutable fact of Plath's death.

The triangular relationship between Plath, Otto and Hughes,

which is explored to such dramatic effect in *Birthday Letters*, can be read as a response to Plath's own identification of Hughes with her father. In a journal entry during the second year of their marriage she refers to Otto as 'the buried male muse & god-creator risen to be my mate in Ted', an image that is associated with 'the sea-father neptune'.[184] This benign vision darkens in the poem 'Daddy', where the speaker (who is not, of course, necessarily Plath) creates her dead father's double, a 'man in black with a Meinkampf look', to whom she says, 'I do, I do'.[185] In a series of disquieting snapshots Hughes draws on these hints to build up a picture of Plath as haunted by her father, and himself as both victim and unwitting instrument of Otto's determination to reclaim his daughter. In 'The Shot' Plath becomes a high-velocity bullet that plunges straight through Hughes to find its resting place in the heart of her father-god. In 'Trophies' Hughes sees himself as the real target of the panther, Otto in feline guise, from Plath's poem 'Pursuit'. In 'Black Coat' he recalls walking along the North Shore, during their stay in America. For him it is a moment of peaceful introspection, an attempt to rediscover his identity after a stressful period of exile and adjustment. In Hughes's re-creation of this incident Plath is watching him. As she observes her husband from a distance, her dead father crawls out of the ocean behind him and, in her mind's eye, Ted and Otto fuse into one. There are other disturbing portents. When Plath has her portrait painted, the artist includes a hunched, gloating figure, who suddenly appears, lurking behind her shoulder.[186] In Devon, the haunting reaches crisis point, when Sylvia smashes an heirloom table top, furious with Ted for arriving late for babysitting. 'Pour all that fury into your poems,' is his response, but unwittingly he has offered her the thread that will lead through the labyrinth to the 'horned, bellowing / Grave of your risen father – / And your own corpse in it'.[187] When Ted starts to suffer strange poundings of the heart, he feels that an 'alien joker' is sharing his skin, planning to evict him from his own life.[188]

Could he have stopped Plath's 'perfect' trajectory towards Daddy, the 'god with the smoking gun'?[189] In 'The Shot' he laments that the 'right witchdoctor' might have caught her in flight; in 'Fishing Bridge' they seem on the very brink of happiness, but somehow they turn away from its bright promise, sleepwalking their way into the deadly labyrinth.[190] Childbirth invites her into the 'sorority' of flowers and insects, and in 'Flounders', again they are offered a vision of the simple life, in tune with nature, that might have kept them together.[191] But poetry draws them on to their fate. 'Shall we be famous?' Hughes asks the Ouija board one evening and is stunned by Plath's bursting into tears, as if she had heard a whisper from the future:

> 'Fame will come. Fame especially for you.
> Fame cannot be avoided. And when it comes
> You will have paid for it with your happiness,
> Your husband and your life.'[192]

Birthday Letters is a literary account of a marriage, and Hughes's careful structuring of Plath's life and death begs the question of how far it reflects the reality, for example, of Plath's relationship with her dead father. Is 'Daddy' to be read as a statement by Plath of vicious feelings about Otto and her husband, or is it to be seen, as one critic has suggested, as a poem that asks disturbing questions about power relations, and in particular their operation during the Holocaust?[193] In his doom-laden reading of their marriage, how far does Hughes project his own fascination with the occult on to events that might bear a rather different interpretation? What was the effect of his own inner life during this period (he admits to a range of powerful emotions, including the fear of death from heart failure) on his perception of events? The poetry and radio plays he was writing during the early Sixties testify to Hughes's dark and power-ful imagination. *The Wound*, first broadcast in 1962, was inspired by his reading of the *Bardo Thodol, The Tibetan Book of the Dead*. Symbolising the journey through death into the underworld and then rebirth, it describes a violent and bloody encounter between soldiers and a group of maenad women in a castle in the woods. How far did Hughes's concern with such themes affect his responses to his private life? Plath's journals from their return to England in late 1959 until her death are not available (Hughes wrote that he destroyed the final journal and another somehow disappeared).[194] If the journals that do survive are read in parallel with Hughes's account in *Birthday Letters*, a rather different picture emerges of Plath's thoughts and preoccupations. What, then, would she have made of *Birthday Letters* and, indeed, of Hughes's earlier claim that her poems similarly followed a definable pattern, 'chapters in a mythology where the plot, seen as a whole and in retrospect, is strong and clear'?[195]

What seems to have been at stake for Hughes was the question of his own responsibility, and the need to come to terms with the past and his grief over what had happened. He was not alone in his attempt to do this through poetry. He was working in a long tradition of male poets who celebrated dead women in remarkable verse collections. In *La Vita Nuova*, Dante used the death of Beatrice, a married woman whom he had venerated from a distance, as inspiration for the development of his craft as a poet, and the book was intended as a handbook for fellow poets, a model of the interaction between theory and practice. Here, the element of guilt is almost entirely absent: the dead woman can be dreamt about and mourned in much the same way as the troubadours fantasised about the women they 'loved'. From the woman's point of view it is imaginary emotion, celebrating a cipher who has no true subjectivity. Her feelings, even her corporeality in any real sense, are not so much denied as simply never considered.

Thomas Hardy similarly turned to poetry to deal with his conflicted feelings over the sudden death of his wife Emma. Like

Hughes, Hardy had the uncomfortable experience after his wife died of reading her diaries, which were increasingly unflattering about her husband's behaviour and literary achievements. He and Emma had long been estranged, although they continued to live together, and his unkindness and indifference had aroused her considerable resentment. The effect on Hardy of her death was not, as in Hughes's case, to go back over their life together, seeking explanations to justify the outcome. Instead he returned to the early days of their marriage, 'when each was much to the other ... intensely much'.[196] Soon after she died, he travelled to St Juliot in Cornwall, the scene of their meeting forty-three years previously. This period of remembering his first passion for Emma flowered into a series of haunting poems, recalling the fearless young woman, who used to wait on the edge of town for him in her 'air-blue gown'.[197] The poems celebrate an intensity of emotion that is lost for ever and are steeped in nostalgia, but at the same time, by the act of writing, Hardy is able to relive his feelings as vividly as when they were first experienced.

In 'At Castle Boterel' he remembers climbing a hill with Emma:

> was there ever
> A time of such quality, since or before,
> In that hill's story?

The primeval rocks that border the road have witnessed many scenes now long gone:

> But what they record in colour and cast
> Is – that we two passed.

Now, after revisiting the hill as an old man, he looks back and sees a phantom figure on the slope:

I look and see it there, shrinking, shrinking,
   I look back at it amid the rain
For the very last time; for my sand is sinking,
   And I shall traverse old love's domain
      Never again.[198]

Hardy's need to communicate the uniqueness of the experience, and his feeling of loss, as a lover and an old man himself approaching death (he was in fact to live for another fifteen years), speak to the heart. As with Hughes, there is no doubting the sincerity of his love, or his regret. Would these poems have compensated Emma for years of neglect? An impossible question: they only exist because she died. Florence Dugdale, the young woman whom Hardy had been clandestinely courting for several years, wrote rather tartly of his expedition to Cornwall: 'He says that he is going down for the sake of the girl he married, & who died more than twenty years ago. His family say *that* girl never existed, but she did exist to him, no doubt.'[199] It is an irony of poor Florence's often disappointing life that no sooner had her rival died than Hardy transferred the interest and attention he had been devoting to his *bonne amie* to his dead wife. For Hardy, the pull of early feeling and the need to communicate it while it was still fresh and pure overcame all other considerations. The poet came first, before the human reality of domestic arrangements and the jealousy, disappointment and distress of the woman he was soon to marry.

As in Hardy's memorial to Emma, Hughes's poetic imagination and his need to impose order and meaning on Plath's unexpected death, are important elements in the story he tells in *Birthday Letters*, as is the fantasy of the woman revivified by the poet's voice. What is equally apparent is that Plath retained a claim on Hughes's life, which could only be appeased by trying to make sense of their relationship through writing. Hughes confronted the theme of the dead wife's hold over the living husband in his version of Euripides' play *Alcestis*. As Euripides tells the story, Admetos, the King of Thessaly, is doomed to die prematurely unless one of his family agrees to take his place. His wife Alcestis offers to stand in for her husband, but after her death she is unexpectedly rescued from the underworld and returned to Admetos by the god Heracles. It is an ending, as in *The Winter's Tale*, in which a husband learns a lesson from his wife's selflessness and dignity. With its story of a wife who willingly accepts death in order to save her husband, it had resonance for Hughes and also for Robert Browning, who similarly reworked the play some years after the death of Elizabeth Barrett Browning.

In Hughes's version of the play the Chorus speak prophetically of what Alcestis's death will mean to Admetos:

> He does not know what loss is.
> Nothing has ever hurt him.
> But when she has gone he will know it.
> When everything is too late
> Then he will know it.
> When he has to live in what has happened.[200]

Their forebodings prove correct. Admetos *does* suffer cruelly, although Hughes follows Euripides in not flinching from the self-pity that undermines Admetos's tragic stature. Does he deserve Alcestis's loyalty? The question remains in doubt in both Euripides' and Hughes's versions. When Browning tackled the story, with the image of his poet wife in mind, he radically changed its moral emphasis by giving an alternative ending in which Admetos is genuinely deserving of Alcestis's love.[201]

The play offered Hughes and Browning an opportunity to write about what in life could never happen: the return of a beloved wife from the dead. In *Balaustion's Adventure*, Browning reinforces this theme by creating a vivid memorial to his wife in the frame story. Balaustion is a young woman refugee from war, whose ship seeks shelter in the harbour at Syracuse. Caught between the threat of pirates on the high seas and the hostility of the Syracusans, the resourceful girl offers to tell the story of Alcestis in return for the life of her comrades. A gifted raconteur, she wins their freedom by her account of Euripides' play, adding an alternative ending that stresses the death-defying love of husband and wife. As was the case with Hughes and Plath, the core of Browning's relationship with Elizabeth Barrett was their shared commitment to poetry, their close engagement with one another's work and the intellectual partnership that enriched their years together. In *Balaustion's Adventure* Browning found a way to continue that dialogue with his wife through the heroine's passionate engagement with poetry and politics.

The story of Alcestis may have been in Heloise's mind when she assured Abelard that she would have had no hesitation in going ahead of him, at his bidding, into the flames of hell.[202] If he had required it, she would have been happy to take on the wife's sacrificial role. In the event, Heloise's 'death' in the convent worked in a similar fashion: her acquiescence in Abelard's demands enabled him to look forward with confidence to his forgiveness and salvation in Christ. Abelard was another husband who attempted to come to terms with the past by writing about painful events. His carefully constructed memoir of Heloise in the *Historia calamitatum* has parallels with Hughes's summing up of his courtship and marriage to Plath in *Birthday Letters*. In both cases the authors reinvent the past as a story in which events are directed by some external force beyond human control. Abelard saw his affair with Heloise and his castration as acts of God. Through God's grace the lovers were shown the error of their ways and brought to redemption. In *Birthday Letters* it was fate that took control: Hughes's marriage was doomed from the start by Plath's allegiance to her dead father. Assia Wevill seems similarly to have been wished on him. In 'Dreamers' he says that he and Sylvia didn't find Assia; she tracked them down, to fulfil her own predetermined narrative. Luckily for posterity, Heloise survived and was able to contest Abelard's neat packaging of their turbulent relationship. In Hughes's case neither woman survived to disagree with his version of events (Assia gassed herself and her little daughter some years after Sylvia's death), but both would almost certainly have objected to the way in which the 'facts' of their lives were appropriated and cast into the public arena.

'Warm, eager, living life'

A few days before her death from tuberculosis in October 1922 Katherine Mansfield wrote in her diary of her longing to be well. In attempting to define what health meant for her, she set down a blueprint for living that recalls the excitement and aspirations of Sylvia Plath's early journal entries:

> By health I mean the power to live a full, adult, living, breathing life in close contact with what I love—the earth and the wonders thereof—the sea—the sun. All that we mean when we speak of the external world. I want to enter into it, to be part of it, to live in it, to learn from it, to lose all that is superficial and acquired in me and to become a conscious, direct human being. I want, by understanding myself, to understand others. I want to be all that I am capable of becoming so that I may be . . . *a child of the sun.* . . .
>
> Then I want to *work*. At what? I want so to live that I work with my hands and my feeling and my brain. I want a garden, a small house, grass, animals, books, pictures, music. And out of this, the expression of this, I want to be writing. (Though I may write about cabmen. That's no matter.)
>
> But warm, eager, living life—to be rooted in life—to learn, to desire to know, to feel, to think, to act. That is what I want. And nothing less.[203]

Mansfield died at the age of thirty-five, her greed for life undiminished by sickness, the world's indifference, and her husband's failure to comfort and support her through her final illness. She died desperately wanting to live. Sylvia Plath, sharing almost identical hopes and dreams, killed herself at the point where she was finally writing with fluency and confidence. 'I am a genius of a writer; I have it in me,' she wrote to Aurelia in October 1962, soon after Hughes had left Court Green.[204] Plath's death, like that of Katherine Mansfield, was a terrible loss to art, and to the 'warm, eager, living life' both women might have enjoyed. They died so young, at the beginning of their achievement and Plath left two tiny children whose futures she would never share. Mansfield's life was very different from Plath's. She was experimental, less conventional in her love affairs, seeming to see life as a series of improvisations through which she felt her way, always observant, alert to nuance and subtle shifts of feeling. What her blueprint lacks is the eagerness for public recognition that was so important in Plath's life plan, which she wrote about so jubilantly to her mother. What she also omits are the other great desires of Plath's life: marriage to the 'strong potential powerful mate who can counter my vibrant dynamic self', and the children who would complement that partnership of creative Titans.[205]

By early 1962 Plath had achieved almost all her ambitions and during the course of that year she was to write many of the poems that would, as she had anticipated, eventually establish her reputation. So where did it all go wrong? Why did she die and how now is she to be remembered? Did she, as Fay Weldon claims with deceptive simplicity, die 'for love'?[206] It is impossible for anyone to know exactly what was in Plath's mind when she made the final preparations that were to end her life: sealing up doors so that the gas would not seep through to the children sleeping upstairs; placing some bread and milk by their bedside, presumably so Frieda, then almost three, could feed herself and look after baby Nicholas; then kneeling in front of the gas oven, her head on a folded cloth, and turning the taps full on. By now, Plath was living with the children in a flat near Primrose Hill in north London, in a house where Yeats had once lived, an omen that had filled her with jubilation when she moved in.

It was bitterly cold, the coldest winter in London for many years, and Plath and the children had been ill with colds and influenza. Always eager to put experience to good use, she wrote an amusing sketch, 'Snow Blitz', about the horrors of dirty snow, frozen pipes and a roof that leaked water into the tub in her newly painted bathroom. There was a three-month waiting list for a home telephone, so Plath had to run out to a kiosk to call the plumber, and 'Snow Blitz' ends with a power cut. A neighbour lends her a hot-water bottle for Frieda and she dresses Nicholas in a snowsuit while they wait for the electricity to be restored. Plath hated the grey, dank English winters; most of all, a child of the sun like Katherine Mansfield, she loathed the cold, but 'Snow Blitz' is an entertaining piece, which ends on a note that is both upbeat and, in the light of Plath's death, curiously ironic:

And what if there *is* another snow blitz?
And another?
My children will grow up resolute, independent and tough, fighting through queues for candles for me in my aguey old age. While I brew waterless tea – *that* at least the future should bring – on a gas ring in the corner. If the gas, too, is not kaput.[207]

Her death is, of course, the problem. It makes everything that happened before seem highly charged and suspect. Rather than part of the steady stream of a life suddenly cut off in mid flow, events are seen as prophetic, doom-laden, the end anticipated and read back into Plath's life and work. By the beginning of 1963, in fact,

Plath's life had taken a more promising turn. In turmoil and unable to sleep after Hughes had left Court Green, she had risen in the blue dawn day after day to write, and now had a folderful of poems lying on her desk: 'the best poems of my life; they will make my name'.[208] Although she and Hughes were still estranged, she had been seeing him and apparently even talking to him about her work. Hughes later wrote that after a brief respite following the period of intense creativity in October and November, 'on 28 January she began to write again. She considered these poems a fresh start. She liked the different, cooler inspiration (as she described it) and the denser pattern, of the first of these, as they took shape.'[209] Hughes's account of Plath's calm, measured assessment of her work suggests confidence and tranquillity, and the continuation of a professional dialogue with her husband, which infidelity, jealousy and domestic separation had not apparently entirely disrupted. On 23 January she had published her novel *The Bell Jar* under a pseudonym and was due to meet her editor at Heinemann for lunch on the day she died. After months of turbulence and intense distress, Plath's life seemed poised to enter a more positive phase. So why, *then*, did she commit suicide?

Hughes writes of a 'perverse number . . . of varied crises', but does not elaborate on what these were.[210] In *Birthday Letters* he hints at upsetting tittle-tattle by false friends. Lucas Myers reports that Ted believed that he and Sylvia were on the brink of reconciliation.[211] Whatever the truth of her situation with Hughes, there were many reasons why Plath might feel disturbed. New circumstances always threw her and, even more than during her first term at Smith and the months of adjustment at Cambridge, Plath had faced what she experienced as catastrophic change during the previous year. Her dream of love had crumbled, and with it her fantasy of herself as the perfect wife and mother, making an impeccable home for her husband and children. This ambition was so deeply ingrained in Plath, so important to her self-esteem and her need to please and impress her mother, that its failure struck at the roots of her identity. Pride carried her through the difficult first months, and the poems she carved out in the early hours of the day replenished her sense of herself, but Plath's craving for affirmation and reassurance was beyond what friends and family could offer. In the end she was thrown back on the relentless 'I am I am I am' that had tortured her as a young woman, watching the sun blaze down on Egg Rock.

In her memoir *Giving Up* Jillian Becker, who with her husband Gerry offered Plath and the children generous support, records Plath's feelings of isolation and distress during her final weekend. She had been staying with the Beckers, but insisted on returning with the children to her own flat on the Sunday evening. On the brink of a serious depression, she had been prescribed drugs that required time to take effect, and Jillian recalls her wakefulness at night over the weekend, the stream of thoughts about Ted and Assia, and about Ted's enthusiasm for their 'ideal life' at Court Green. Just before three, for Plath, was the 'worst time', when the pills seemed to lose their effect and the dawn seemed very far off.[212] Back home and alone in the early hours of the Monday morning she took her life. The pain of depression can be intense, like a physical wound in the heart or breast; the sense of loneliness and despair can seem irremediable. In Plath's case the burden of consciousness, which she described so acutely in *The Bell Jar*, may simply have been too much to bear.

In her first novel, *The Shadow of the Sun*, finished when she was a 'very desperate faculty wife in Durham', a housebound mother cut off from the intellectual life she craved, A. S. Byatt wrote about 'the female belief in, or illusion of, the need to be "in love" which was the danger which most threatened the autonomy' of her heroine, Anna.[213] 'All those desiderata of the feminine mystique, the lover, the house, the nursery, the kitchen' were, in the words of the poem by Sir Walter Ralegh that Byatt used as the epigraph to her book, a 'goal of grief for which the wisest run'.[214] Claire Tomalin, writing about the difficulty Plath would have had adjusting 'from competitive and high-achieving girl to subjugated wife and mother', recalls her own life after graduating from Cambridge:

> one of my most vivid memories of the mid 1950s is of crying into a washbasin full of soapy grey baby clothes – there were no washing machines – while my handsome and adored husband was off playing football in the park on Sunday morning with all the delightful young men who had been friends to both of us at Cambridge three years earlier.[215]

Tomalin and her generation of Leavis-educated young marrieds were imbued with the Lawrentian idea of sex within marriage as 'passionate, serious and sacramental'. In Plath's case she hypothesises that the 'breaking of the sacramental marriage bond between her and her husband just as she was so vulnerable with the two small children was crucial'.[216]

The poet Ruth Fainlight, in an article about her friendships with Plath and with the writer Jane Bowles, observed that all three of them, in their 'obsessive domesticity', were the product of ideas about femininity current in the USA in the first half of the twentieth century. Plath 'tormented herself with impossible goals of domestic achievement' and all three women struggled with 'the dichotomy of being writers' wives as well as writers'.[217] Fainlight and Plath met in 1961, at the presentation of the Hawthornden award by Ruth's husband, Alan Sillitoe, the current holder, to Hughes as the new recipient. Ruth's first impression of Sylvia was almost comic: 'a burningly ambitious and intelligent young woman trying to look like a conventional, devoted wife but not quite succeeding'. There was 'something almost excessive' about Plath's 'disguise', suggests the canny Ruth: the 'small hat pressed onto elaborately dressed hair, and a tight-bodiced, full-skirted dark green shiny dress, the sort of costume one of my New York aunts might have worn for a cocktail party'.[218]

Plath was born too soon to benefit from the changes in women's lives brought about by the Women's Movement. Although one might argue that now women are busier than ever, juggling jobs and careers as well as husbands, homes and children, at least the women of today in Europe and the United States are not committed to the 'obsessive domesticity' that tortured Fainlight and her fellow women writers. The revolution in women's studies, with the publication of forgotten work by women writers and the re-evaluation of their achievement and contribution, might also have heartened Plath, who placed herself firmly in the tradition of women poets: 'Well, in history – Sappho, Elizabeth Barrett Browning, Christina Rossetti, Amy Lowell, Emily Dickinson, Edna St Vincent Millay', and among the living, 'Edith Sitwell & Marianne Moore, the ageing giantesses & poetic godmothers', and her nearest rival, Adrienne Cecile Rich.[219]

Marriage and motherhood did, however, bring Plath that 'warm, eager, living life' which Katherine Mansfield wrote about so yearningly. Nobody reading the account in her journals of her marriage to Ted Hughes, particularly the nine months at Smith and then living in Boston, can fail to understand the dynamics of their relationship, or to pity Plath for the psychological conflicts she endured and strove against with such persistence and courage. Nobody could doubt, either, how much she loved Ted, revelled in him physically, depended on him, and struggled against that dependency. Again and again, she records her resolutions to stand alone, not to confide too much, to work at her problems on her own. Their close working relationship survived quarrels about domestic chores (Plath's refusal to sew on buttons), atrophy and writer's block, and the claustrophobia of two writers living and working in a cramped apartment. Motherhood brought joy and fulfilment, and new subjects for her poems: 'Morning Song' with its vivid first line,

'Love set you going like a fat gold watch', and Plath's radio play *Three Women*, a sensitive exploration of women in a maternity ward.[220] Country living at Court Green similarly opened new vistas. Plath threw herself into the challenge of harvesting banks of daffodils, cultivating vegetables and the rituals of beekeeping.

The publication of the *Ariel* poems in 1965, combined with Plath's suicide, fixed her reputation as the author of 'personal, confessional, felt' poems, so probing that they were 'playing Russian roulette with six cartridges in the cylinder' (Robert Lowell's Foreword to the first edition). Al Alvarez described the *Ariel* poems as 'murderous art'; George Steiner saw them as 'taking tremendous risks . . . She could not return from them.'[221] But the body of work that Plath left belies these grim assessments of her writing and approach. Heloise's account of her love affair with Abelard is confined to a handful of letters; in Plath's case there is a treasure trove of material, covering every aspect of her life, in the form of journals, letters, poems, short stories and articles. There are also numerous sketches, paintings, scrapbooks and other artefacts, including the hundred and eighteen paper dolls in the Lilly Library, with their wardrobe of Hollywood-style gowns, designed and beautifully handmade by Plath.[222] These materials are accessible to the specialist researcher in university archives, an edition of her collected poems is available and her prose writings have been selectively published for the general public. Reading the journals in parallel with her poems, letters, short stories and articles gives the lie to the idea of Plath as an agonised 'confessional' poet, whose poems took her over the edge of sanity and of life itself. Such an approach offers, instead, a perspective on Plath's work that suggests her complexity and originality, the humour and irony that enrich her social commentary, her mocking feminism, and the richness and strangeness of her surreal imagination. The breadth and variety of her output indicate that she could have developed in a number of directions. If Virginia Woolf had died at the age of thirty, we would have had only her reviews to fall back on, along with the early notebooks and her letters. *The Voyage Out*, Woolf's first novel, wasn't published until she was thirty-two and her major writing followed: a great flood of novels, articles, reviews, the non-fiction feminist books, the letters and journals. Who knows what Plath might have produced, had she lived longer, grown older and wiser, had time to see her children develop and the opportunity to find new loves, new friendships?

Looking back to what was perhaps one of the happiest times of Plath's life, her brief courtship by Ted Hughes at Cambridge and their first year of marriage when she was finishing her degree, her image seems to shimmer in an aura of energy and enthusiasm. Jane Baltzell, her fellow resident at Whitstead, recalled Plath's vitality and the mobility of expression that attracted Hughes: 'Her face was invariably lit by interest in or attention to something or someone.' Her complexion seemed to give off 'a kind of sheen, even a radiance'.[223] Her élan was reflected in her clothes and domestic decor. In her journal she describes herself wearing bright, sexy clothes – dramatic red and black – while she waits for Ted's step on the stairs, and her attic room at Cambridge reflected her style, taste and individuality. Baltzell recalled its 'almost professional sense of interior design' and 'daring use of color'. Costly art books were cleverly stacked and propped open; a black pottery tea set suggested 'taste and luxury'; her studio couch, which doubled as a bed, was drawn up close to the gas fire and piled with bright cushions.[224] Wendy Campbell, who sat in on Sylvia's supervisions with Dorothea Krook at Cambridge, memorably described Plath's compelling physical presence. Her 'quality, her personal style of being, her vitality' were 'summed up' in the floodlit image of the Winged Victory in the Louvre: 'She strides, her robes fly out, beautiful and huge.'[225] Campbell's striking tribute embodies the contradictions that continue to intrigue and bewilder commentators on Plath's life and achievement. For all her illusion of life and movement, the Winged Victory is carved in marble, frozen for eternity like Keats's exquisite figures on the Grecian vase, and chillingly divorced from the vibrant experience that Sylvia Plath so eagerly embraced. In this sense the statue aptly embodies both the finality of Plath's sudden death and her subsequent literary immortality. Yet Campbell clearly intended to create an image of the living Sylvia as a massive presence, vigorous, formidable and bathed in light. Her description is a magnificent memorial, a testimony to Plath's charisma and achievement, and a lament for the 'warm, eager, living life' that was so prematurely cut short.

Select Bibliography and Notes

A list of references and further reading is given for each section, followed by notes that refer to authors/titles listed.

PART 1 'Farewell, my only love': The Passion of Heloise

Bibliography

Brooke, Christopher N. L., *The Medieval Idea of Marriage*, Oxford: Oxford University Press, 1989

Brundage, James A., *Law, Sex, and Christian Society in Medieval Europe*, Chicago and London: University of Chicago Press, 1987, paperback edition, 1990

Burgess, Glyn S. and Keith Busby (trans. and intro.), *The Lais of Marie de France*, Harmondsworth: Penguin Books, 1986

Cartlidge, Neil, *Medieval Marriage: Literary Approaches, 1100–1300*, Cambridge: D. S. Brewer, 1997

Charrier, Charlotte, *Héloïse dans l'histoire et dans la légende*, Paris: Librairie Ancienne Honoré Champion, 1933

Chaucer, Geoffrey (F. N. Robinson, ed.), *The Works of Geoffrey Chaucer*, Boston: Houghton Mifflin Company, Riverside Press, Cambridge, second edition, 1961

Cicero, 'Laelius: On Friendship', in Michael Grant (trans. and intro.), *On the Good Life*, Harmondsworth: Penguin Books, 1971

Clanchy, M. T., *Abelard: A Medieval Life*, Oxford UK and Cambridge USA: Blackwell, 1997, paperback edition, 1999

Davies, Hilary, *In a Valley of This Restless Mind*, London: Enitharmon Press, 1997

De Beauvoir, Simone (H. M. Parshley, trans. and ed.), *The Second Sex*, London: Jonathan Cape, 1953; Harmondsworth: Penguin, 1972

De Lorris, Guillaume and Jean de Meun (Frances Horgan, trans., intro. and notes), *The Romance of the Rose*, Oxford and New York: Oxford University Press, 1994

De Troyes, Chrétien (William W. Kibler, trans., intro. and notes), (*Erec and Enide*, trans. Carleton W. Carroll), *Arthurian Romances*, Harmondsworth: Penguin Books, 1991

Dronke, Peter, 'Abelard and Heloise in Medieval Testimonies', in *Intellectuals and Poets in Medieval Europe*, Roma: Edizioni di Storia e Letteratura, 1992

——, 'Francesca and Heloise', in *The Medieval Poet and His World*, Roma: Edizioni di Storia e Letteratura, 1984

——, 'Heloise's *Problemata* and *Letters*: Some Questions of Form and Content', in *Intellectuals and Poets in Medieval Europe*, Roma: Edizioni di Storia e Letteratura, 1992

——, *Medieval Latin and the Rise of European Love-Lyric*, Vols I and II, Oxford: Oxford at the Clarendon Press, second edition, 1968; 1999 reprint

——, *Women Writers of the Middle Ages*, Cambridge: Cambridge University Press, 1984

Duby, Georges (Jean Birrell, trans.), *Women of the Twelfth Century*, Vol. 1, Cambridge: Polity Press, 1997

Duggan, Joseph J., *The Romances of Chrétien de Troyes*, New Haven and London: Yale University Press, 2001

Eliot, George (Barbara Hardy, ed. and intro.), *Daniel Deronda*, Harmondsworth: Penguin Books, 1967; Penguin Classics edition, 1986

Gilson, Étienne (L. K. Shook, trans.), *Heloise and Abelard*, London: Hollis & Carter, 1953

Godwin, William, *Memoirs of The Author of 'The Rights of Woman'*, in Mary Wollstonecraft and William Godwin (Richard Holmes, intro. and notes), *A Short Residence in Sweden* . . . and *Memoirs of The Author of 'The Rights of Woman'*, Harmondsworth: Penguin Books, 1987

Gotfredsen, Lise (Anne Born, trans.), *The Unicorn*, London: Harvill Press, 1999

Jaeger, C. Stephen, *Ennobling Love: In Search of a Lost Sensibility*, Philadelphia: University of Pennsylvania Press, 1999

Jager, Eric, *The Book of the Heart*, Chicago and London: University of Chicago Press, 2000

Kauffman, Linda S., *Discourses of Desire: Gender, Genre, and Epistolary Fictions*, Ithaca and London: Cornell University Press, 1986

Laven, Mary, *Virgins of Venice: Enclosed Lives and Broken Vows in the Renaissance Convent*, London: Viking, Penguin Books, 2002

Leclerq, Jean, *Monks and Love in Twelfth-Century France: psycho-historical essays*, Oxford: Clarendon Press, 1979

Marenbon, John, *The Philosophy of Peter Abelard*, Cambridge: Cambridge University Press, 1997, paperback edition, 1999

McLeod, Enid, *Héloïse: A Biography*, London: Chatto & Windus, second edition, 1971

McNamer, Elizabeth Mary, *The Education of Heloise: Methods, Content, and Purpose of Learning in the Twelfth-Century* [sic], Medieval Studies 8, Lewiston, New York: Edwin Mellen Press, 1991

Menon, Patricia, *Austen, Eliot, Charlotte Brontë and the Mentor-Lover*, Basingstoke and New York, Palgrave Macmillan, 2003

Mews, Constant J. (Neville Chiavaroli and Constant J. Mews, trans.), *The Lost Love Letters of Heloise and Abelard: Perceptions of Dialogue in Twelfth-Century France*, Basingstoke: Macmillan, 1999, Palgrave paperback edition, 2001

Minnis, Alastair, *Magister amoris: The* Roman de la Rose *and Vernacular Hermeneutics*, Oxford and New York: Oxford University Press, 2001

Muckle, J. T., C. S. B., 'Abelard's Letter of Consolation to a Friend' (*Historia Calamitatum*), in *Mediaeval Studies*, Vol. XII, Toronto, Canada: Pontifical Institute of Medieval Studies, 1950

——, 'The Letter of Heloise on Religious Life and Abelard's First Reply', in *Mediaeval Studies*, Vol. XVII, Toronto, Canada: Pontifical Institute of Medieval Studies, 1955

——, 'The Personal Letters Between Abelard and Heloise: Introduction, Authenticity and Text', in *Mediaeval Studies*, Vol. XV, Toronto, Canada: Pontifical Institute of Medieval Studies, 1953

Newman, Barbara, 'Authority, Authenticity, and the Repression of Heloise', in *From Virile Woman to WomanChrist* [sic]: *Studies in Medieval Religion and Literature*, Philadelphia: University of Pennsylvania Press, 1995

Nichols, Stephen G., 'An Intellectual Anthropology of Marriage in the Middle Ages', in Marina S. Brownlee, Kevin Brownlee and Stephen G. Nichols (eds), *The New Medievalism*, Baltimore and London: Johns Hopkins University Press, 1991

Norris, Pamela, *The Story of Eve*, London and Basingstoke: Picador, 1998, published in USA as *Eve: A Biography*, New York: New York University Press, 1999

Olson, Linda and Kathryn Kerby-Fulton (eds), *Voices in Dialogue: Reading Women in the Middle Ages*, Notre Dame, Indiana: University of Notre Dame Press, 2005

Ovid (Harold Isbell, trans., intro. and notes), *Heroides*, Harmondsworth: Penguin Books, 1990

Purcell, Sally (Peter Jay, ed., Marina Warner, preface), *Collected Poems*, London: Anvil Press Poetry, 2002

Radice, Betty (trans. and intro.), *The Letters of Abelard and Heloise*, Harmondsworth: Penguin Books, 1974

Robertson, D. W., Jr., *Abelard and Heloise*, New York: Dial Press, 1972

Sinclair, John D. (trans. and comment), *The Divine Comedy of Dante Alighieri: Inferno*, New York: Oxford University Press, 1939, paperback edition, 1961

Southern, R. W., 'The Letters of Abelard and Heloise', in *Medieval Humanism and Other Studies*, Oxford: Basil Blackwell, 1970

Stevenson, Jane, *Women Latin Poets: Language, Gender, & Authority, from Antiquity to the Eighteenth Century*, Oxford and New York: Oxford University Press, 2005

Thiébaux, Marcelle, *Dhuoda, Handbook for Her Warrior Son: Liber Manualis*, Cambridge: Cambridge University Press, 1998

Unterkircher, F. (intro. and commentaries), *King René's Book of Love (Le Cueur d'Amours Espris)*, New York: George Braziller, 1980

Wardle, Ralph M. (ed.), *Collected Letters of Mary Wollstonecraft*, Ithaca and London: Cornell University Press, 1979

Wheeler, Bonnie (ed.), *Listening to Heloise: The Voice of a Twelfth-Century Woman*, Basingstoke: Macmillan, 2000

White, Antonia, *Frost in May*, London: Desmond Harmsworth, 1933

Woolf, Virginia (Morag Shiach, ed., intro. and notes), *A Room of One's Own*, in *A Room of One's Own* and *Three Guineas*, Oxford and New York: Oxford University Press, 1998

Notes

1 Radice, p. 114. Summaries and translations of the letters are based on this edition unless otherwise indicated.
2 For a translation of *Historia calamitatum* see Radice, pp. 57–106. Quotations and summaries of the text are from this edition.
3 *Hist. cal.*, Radice, p. 65.
4 Ibid., p. 66.
5 Clanchy, pp. 173–4, 340.
6 Dronke points out the maliciousness of Fulco's letter ('Abelard and Heloise in Medieval Testimonies', pp. 272–4).
7 *Hist. cal.*, Radice, pp. 65, 66.
8 Godwin, p. 258.
9 Ibid.

10 *Hist. cal.*, Radice, p. 67.

11 Ibid.

12 See Dante, *Inferno*, Canto v, ll.73–142; Francesca da Polenta of Ravenna and her lover Paolo were incited to commit adultery by reading the story of Lancelot's passion for King Arthur's wife, Guinevere. Alone together with this dangerous book, they were tempted to gaze deep into one another's eyes, and then to kiss. They were discovered and murdered by her husband and, according to Dante, confined to the second circle of hell, a vast space inhabited by fierce winds, where they were blown hither and thither for all eternity, the punishment for those 'carnal sinners who subject reason to desire'. Dante's point is that sexual desire is as powerful, random and destructive as the wind, a belief that reflects Christian teaching on its dangers and illuminates Abelard's later repudiation of his passion for Heloise. Dronke, 'Francesca and Heloise', discusses parallels between Dante's treatment of Francesca and Jean de Meun's portrayal of Heloise in the *Roman de la Rose*.

13 *Hist. cal.*, Radice, p. 67.

14 Ibid., p. 68.

15 Radice, p. 149.

16 *Hist. cal.*, Radice, p. 74.

17 Ibid., p. 75. Clanchy, p. 199, points out that the men who castrated Abelard were likely to have been professionals rather than thugs: Fulbert would not have wanted to lay himself open to a charge of murder.

18 For a summary of the authenticity debate see John Marenbon, 'Authenticity Revisited', in Wheeler, pp. 19–33. See, too, Mews, pp. 47–53.

19 Dronke suggests that Abelard may have arranged for her to see it (*Women Writers*, pp. 112–13).

20 Southern, p. 96.

21 Radice, p. 113.

22 Quoted by Abelard in *Hist. cal.*, Radice, p. 71.

23 Radice, p. 113.

24 Ibid., p. 114.

25 Ibid.

26 Ibid., p. 115.

27 Ibid., pp. 115–16.

28 Ibid., p. 116.

29 Ibid., p. 117.

30 Ibid.

31 Muckle, 'The Personal Letters', p. 73.

32 Radice, p. 118; Clanchy, p. 335; Dronke, *Women Writers*, p. 121.

33 Radice, p. 133.

34 Ibid., p. 137. Abelard's reference suggests that he has heard this complaint from her on many previous occasions, implying that they may have met and talked privately, or

previously exchanged letters. It also mirrors Heloise's words in her second letter.

35 Ibid., p. 146.

36 Ibid., pp. 146–7.

37 Ibid., p. 147.

38 Ibid., p. 149.

39 Ibid.

40 Ibid., p. 150.

41 Ibid., p. 153.

42 Ibid., p. 154.

43 Ibid.

44 Ibid., p. 156.

45 For Heloise's achievement at the Paraclete, see Mary Martin McLaughlin, 'Heloise the Abbess: The Expansion of the Paraclete', in Wheeler, pp. 1–17.

46 Dronke, 'Abelard and Heloise in Medieval Testimonies', p. 276.

47 Mews, p. 41.

48 Dronke, 'Abelard and Heloise in Medieval Testimonies', p. 290.

49 Menon, pp. 12–13.

50 De Beauvoir, p. 653.

51 Mews, p. 85.

52 *Hist. cal.*, Radice, p. 58.

53 Clanchy, pp. 131–4.

54 *Hist. cal.*, Radice, p. 65.

55 For Heloise's family background and placement at Argenteuil as a young girl see John O. Ward and Neville Chiavaroli, 'The Young Heloise and Latin Rhetoric: Some Preliminary Comments on the "Lost" Love Letters and Their Significance', in Wheeler, pp. 60–2.

56 See Laven.

57 Mews, p. 64.

58 Radice, p. 160.

59 Woolf, pp. 101–2.

60 A rare and moving example of the effect on a mother of early separation from her children is the manual of conduct written in the ninth century by a Carolingian noblewoman, Dhuoda, for her teenage son. The boy had been committed to the court of Charles the Bald as a hostage for his father's good behaviour. Dhuoda's love and concern for William encouraged her to write her guide, a handbook to survival, which she hoped would provide a physical, emotional and moral bridge between herself and her absent child. See Thiébaux.

61 Dronke, *Medieval Latin*, p. 222, although he queries the Regensburg setting.

62 Introduction, Radice, p. 32.

63 Poem VI, in the sequence 'In a Valley of This Restless Mind', Davies, p. 53.

64 Muckle, 'The Letter of Heloise', p. 241; Dronke, 'Abelard and Heloise in Medieval Testimonies', p. 251.

65 Dronke, *Women Writers*, pp. 126–7.

66 Ecclesiastes VII:26; Radice, pp. 130–1.

67 Cicero, p. 227.
68 Ambrose, *De Officiis*, III:22, quoted in Dronke, *Medieval Latin*, p. 195.
69 Brooke, p. 105.
70 Heloise's yearning for some personal word from Abelard resonates with Charlotte's letters to her teacher Constantin Heger after her return to Haworth. 'If my master withdraws his friendship from me entirely I shall be absolutely without hope – if he gives me a little friendship – a very little – I shall be content – happy, I would have a motive for living – for working,' she wrote in desperation on 8 January 1845, twelve months after she had left Brussels. Heloise wrote to Abelard in Latin, the formal language of communication and scholarship in medieval Europe; Charlotte wrote to Monsieur Heger in French, the language she had been studying under her mentor. See Margaret Smith (ed.), *The Letters of Charlotte Brontë, Vol. 1: 1829–1847*, Oxford: Clarendon Press, 1995, p. 379.
71 Eliot, p. 280.
72 For letters and poems exchanged between men and women in the medieval period see Mews, Ch. 4, 'Traditions of Dialogue'; Dronke, *Women Writers*, Ch. 4, 'Personal Poetry by Women: the Eleventh and Twelfth Centuries'.
73 Dronke, *Women Writers*, p. 86.
74 Ibid., p. 88.
75 Ibid., p. 89. In his commentary on this exchange, Dronke hints at Constance's possible discomfort with this jesting wordplay, pp. 90–1.
76 For discussion of the Regensburg texts, see Dronke, *Medieval Latin*, pp. 221–9; for texts and translation, pp. 422–47.
77 For texts and translation see ibid., pp. 472–82.
78 Ibid., p. 475.
79 For a summary of the letters see Mews, pp. 15–25; for text and translation, ibid., pp. 190–289.
80 Edward Könsgen first made the suggestion in his edition of the letters (Leiden: E. J. Brill, 1974). For support of the attribution, see Mews's detailed analysis (which contains useful background material); Jaeger, pp. 157–73. Dronke (among others) disagrees: see 'Abelard and Heloise in Medieval Testimonies', pp. 270–2; *Women Writers*, pp. 93–7; see, too, opposing views from C. Stephen Jaeger and Giles Constable in Olson and Kerby-Fulton.
81 Wardle, letter 213, 1 July 1796, p. 331. Interestingly, this letter is written in the context of

sending Godwin the last
volume of Rousseau's novel
Julie; ou, La Nouvelle Héloïse.

82 Clanchy, p. 199 and see note 17
above.

83 Ibid., p. 224.

84 Burgess and Busby, p. 108.

85 Clanchy, pp. 147–8.

86 Ibid., p. 223.

87 Dronke, 'Abelard and Heloise
in Medieval Testimonies',
p. 257.

88 See note 60 above.

89 Radice, p. 284.

90 Ibid., pp. 135–6.

PART 2 Shimmerings of a Summer Sky: The Transient
Loves of the Japanese Court

Bibliography

Arntzen, Sonja (trans., with intro. and notes), *The Kagerō Diary: A
Woman's Autobiographical Text from Tenth-Century Japan*, Ann Arbor:
Center for Japanese Studies, University of Michigan, 1997

Austen, Jane (R. W. Chapman, ed.), *Minor Works*, Vol. VI of *The Works of
Jane Austen*, London, New York and Toronto: Oxford University Press,
revised edition, 1963

Bowring, Richard (trans. and intro.), *The Diary of Lady Murasaki*, London:
Penguin Books, 1996

Brookner, Anita, *A Start in Life*, London: Jonathan Cape, 1981; London:
Triad Granada paperback edition, 1982

Carter, Angela, 'Murasaki Shikibu: *The Tale of Genji*', in *Expletives
Deleted: Selected Writings*, London: Chatto & Windus, 1992

Cranston, E. (trans. and intro.), *The Izumi Shikibu Diary: A Romance of the
Heian Court*, Cambridge, Massachusetts: Harvard University Press,
1969

Du Cane, Ella (illus.) and Florence du Cane, *The Flowers and Gardens of
Japan*, London: Adam & Charles Black, 1908

Eliot, George (Barbara Hardy, ed. and intro.), *Daniel Deronda*,
Harmondsworth: Penguin Books, 1967; Penguin Classics edition, 1986

Field, Norma, *The Splendor of Longing in the Tale of Genji*, Princeton and
Guildford: Princeton University Press, 1987

Hirshfield, Jane (trans.), with Mariko Aratani, *The Ink Dark Moon: Love
Poems by Ono No Komachi and Izumi Shikibu: Women of the Ancient
Court of Japan*, New York: Vintage Books, Random House, 1990

Keene, Donald, *Seeds in the Heart: Japanese Literature from Earliest Times*

to the Late Sixteenth Century, *A History of Japanese Literature*, Vol. 1,
New York: Henry Holt, 1995 paperback edition

Lessing, Doris, 'He', in *To Room Nineteen*, London: HarperCollins, 2002

McCullough, Helen Craig (study and trans.), *Ōkagami: The Great Mirror: Fujiwara Michinaga (966–1027) and His Times*, New Jersey: Princeton University Press; Tokyo: University of Tokyo Press, 1980

McCullough, William H. and Helen Craig McCullough (trans., with intro. and notes), *A Tale of Flowering Fortunes: Annals of Japanese Aristocratic Life in the Heian Period*, Vols 1 and 2, Stanford, California: Stanford University Press, 1980

Morris, Ivan (trans. and intro.), *As I Crossed a Bridge of Dreams: Recollections of a Woman in Eleventh-Century Japan*, Harmondsworth: Penguin Books, 1975

—— (trans. and ed.), *The Pillow Book of Sei Shōnagon*, London: Oxford University Press, 1967

——, *The Pillow Book of Sei Shōnagon: A Companion Volume*, London: Oxford University Press, 1967

——, *The World of the Shining Prince: Court Life in Ancient Japan*, London: Oxford University Press, 1964

Murase, Miyeko (intro.), *The Tale of Genji: Legends and Paintings*, London: British Museum Press, 2001

Omori, Annie Shepley and Kochi Doi (trans.), *Diaries of Court Ladies of Old Japan*, London: Constable, n.d.

Sarra, Edith, *Fictions of Femininity: Literary Inventions of Gender in Japanese Court Women's Memoirs*, Stanford, California: Stanford University Press, 1999

Seidensticker, Edward (trans.), *The Gossamer Years (Kagerō Nikki): The Diary of a Noblewoman of Heian Japan*, Tokyo, Japan and Rutland, Vermont: Charles E. Tuttle, 1981

Shikibu, Murasaki (Edward G. Seidensticker, trans. and intro.), *The Tale of Genji*, London: Martin Secker & Warburg, 1976; Harmondsworth: Penguin Books, 1981

Stevenson, Barbara and Cynthia Ho, *Crossing the Bridge: Comparative Essays on Medieval European and Heian Japanese Women Writers*, New York and Basingstoke: Palgrave, 2000

Waley, Arthur, 'The Chinese Cinderella Story', *Folk-Lore*, Vol. LVIII, March 1947, pp. 226–38

—— (trans.), *The Lady who Loved Insects*, London: Blackamore Press, 1929

—— (intro. and trans.), *The Sacred Tree: Being the Second Part of 'The Tale of Genji'*, London: George Allen & Unwin, 1926

Whitehouse, Wilfrid and Eizo Yanagisawa (trans.), *Ochikubo Monogatari: The Tale of the Lady Ochikubo: A Tenth Century Japanese Novel*, London: Peter Owen, 1970

Notes

1 Bowring, p. 59.
2 I refer to the fictitious heroine as Lady Murasaki, to distinguish her from her creator, Murasaki Shikibu.
3 Shikibu, p. 699.
4 She says that her manuscript copy of the *Tale* has been taken from her room (without permission) to give to someone's daughter to read (Bowring, p. 33).
5 Morris, *World*, p. 252, note 2.
6 Bowring, p. 58.
7 Shikibu, p. 36.
8 Austen, p. 253.
9 Bowring, p. xxxv.
10 Morris, *Pillow Book*, pp. 124–5; *Pillow Book Companion*, p. 101, note 554.
11 She mentions a collection of Chinese books whose owner is now dead (Bowring, p. 55).
12 Ibid., p. 57.
13 Ibid., p. 56.
14 The commonly used name in English, *The Pillow Book*, comes from the Japanese title, which literally translated means 'notes of the pillow'. This was probably used to describe an informal notebook in which men and women jotted down thoughts and impressions, and which may have been kept in the drawers of the wooden pillows on which they slept (Morris, *Pillow Book*, p. xi). See, too, pp. 89–90 of this book.
15 Morris, *World*, p. 255.
16 Ibid., pp. 262–3.
17 Translation by Morris, ibid., p. 262; for an alternative version see Bowring, p. 61.
18 Morris, *World*, p. 200.
19 See, for example, the story of Lady Akashi, a young woman from a seaside village in the provinces. She is elegant, talented and extremely sensitive, but can only be a minor wife to Genji. Her father's ambition throws them together and a child is born. When she comes to the capital to live near Genji, she is persuaded to hand over her daughter to Lady Murasaki to bring up. The child will have a better future if she is sponsored by the more important consort.
20 Morris, *World*, p. 60.
21 McCullough, *Tale*, Vol. 1, pp. 43–7, for attribution to Akazome Emon and a brief biography of the poet.
22 Morris, *World*, p. 48.

23 For Ichijō's history see Morris, *World*, pp. 44–5.

24 Ibid., p. 256.

25 She was an aunt of the author of *The Sarashina Diary*, a sister was married to a great-uncle of Murasaki Shikibu and a brother was married to a sister of Sei Shōnagon (Seidensticker, p. 9).

26 It is difficult to be absolutely precise about the meaning of a Heian text. This is Morris's translation (*World*, pp. 309–10). Interested readers may like to compare it with Seidensticker's version (Shikibu, p. 437).

27 Ibid., p. 438.

28 Ibid., pp. 438–9.

29 Ibid., p. 83. Morris (*World*, p. 310, note 1) discusses Genji's attempt to relate the good and evil in fiction to Buddhist teaching, which embraces every aspect of human life. Everything has its purposes. Murasaki, similarly, makes a case for seeing her hero 'in the round'.

30 Shikibu, p. 699.

31 Carter, p. 197. There were earlier romantic heroes: Gilgamesh in the Babylonian epic written thousands of years before *The Tale of Genji* can perhaps lay claim to this title, although his romantic passion was reserved for the young man, Enkidu, whose death inspired Gilgamesh's search for the plant of immortality. Paris in the *Iliad* might also be seen as the prototypical romantic lover, even though the goddess Aphrodite was responsible for igniting the passion that launched a thousand ships. Genji is a more rounded character than either of these mythical heroes. His creator leavened the Heian ideal of manhood with a substantial pinch of all too human sentimentality, self-indulgence and sometimes wilful blindness to others' pain.

32 Du Cane, p. 151.

33 Shikibu, pp. 352–3.

34 Eliot, p. 171.

35 Robert H. Brower and Earl Miner, *Japanese Court Poetry*, Stanford: Stanford University Press, 1961, p. 431, quoted in Morris, *World*, p. 243.

36 The taboo on jealousy persisted long after Heian culture had been superseded. As Ivan Morris relates, in the seventeenth century upper-class women evolved the *Rinki Kō* (Jealousy Meeting), in which wives met privately to complain about their unfaithful husbands and their mistresses. The novelist Ihara Saikaku describes such a meeting in *The Life of an Amorous Woman* (1686). Each woman relates her grievances, then vents her anger on a beautiful doll, but

the doll suddenly comes to life, terrifying the ladies. See Morris, *World*, p. 243, note 3, and Ihara Saikaku, Ivan Morris (ed. and trans.), *The Life of an Amorous Woman and Other Writings*, London: Chapman and Hall, 1963, pp. 164–72.

Increasingly, the taboo was associated with proper female submissiveness. The eighteenth-century *Greater Learning for Women* (*Onna Daigaku*) warned Japanese wives: 'Let her never even dream of jealousy. If her husband be dissolute, she must expostulate with him, but never either nurse or vent her anger. If her jealousy be extreme, it will render her countenance frightful and her accents repulsive, and can only result in completely alienating her husband from her, and making her intolerable in his eyes.' See Rebecca L. Copeland, *The Sound of the Wind: The Life and Works of Uno Chiyo*, London: Peter Owen, 1992, p. 71.

Fear of the evil effects of female jealousy persisted into the twentieth century, with the wearing of a *tsunokakushi* (horn-hider) during the wedding ceremony. The *tsunokakushi* is a white triangular band worn by women 'to conceal their "horn of jealousy" and to immunize their husband against the effects of this morbid emotion. Although male jealousy was fully recognized in Japan ... it was never believed to have the same sinister implications as the female variety' (Morris, *World*, p. 250, note 3).

37 Murasaki Shikibu's diary includes a classic example of the use of exorcists in her description of the birth of the Empress's son (Bowring, pp. 8–13). Sei Shōnagon describes a medium brought in to relieve a seriously ill patient (Morris, *Pillow Book*, pp. 264–5).

38 Shikibu, p. 609.

39 The personal names of women were not generally recorded in genealogical records of the period, unless they were the consorts, mothers or grandmothers of emperors. Personal names were in any case rarely used in daily life. A person was generally referred to by his or her title or role. See Arntzen, pp. 25–6.

40 Seidensticker, pp. 39, 170, note 23. I have generally quoted from Seidensticker's translation, unless otherwise noted. Arntzen's robust, accessible translation is also well worth reading.

41 Arntzen, p. 29.

42 Seidensticker, p. 71.

43 Ibid., p. 9.

44 Ibid., pp. 15, 73.
45 See Bowring, pp. xxiv–viii and Morris, *World*, pp. 28–35 for Heian domestic architecture.
46 Morris, *World*, p. 205.
47 Ibid., p. 119.
48 Seidensticker, p. 8.
49 Ibid., p. 33.
50 See Keene, pp. 433–76, for a summary of the *monogatari* tradition.
51 See Whitehouse and Yanagisawa for an English translation.
52 See Waley, 'The Chinese Cinderella Story'.
53 Seidensticker, p. 33.
54 Ibid.
55 This pounding breaks off the diary, as the messenger from Porlock put an end to Coleridge's dream about Kubla Khan. Lady Gossamer is so skilled and subtle a narrator that it is possible to imagine that the pounding is Kaneie himself, come to pay her a New Year's visit, thus beginning the cycle of waiting and hoping all over again.
56 Seidensticker, p. 41.
57 Ibid., p. 44.
58 Ibid.
59 Ibid., p. 45.
60 Ibid., pp. 46–7.
61 Ibid., p. 197, note 108.
62 Ibid., p. 151.
63 Ibid., p. 166 and see note 55 above for the abrupt ending of the diary.
64 Arntzen, pp. 6–7.
65 McCullough, *Ōkagami*, p. 166; Arntzen, pp. 33–4. Arntzen, pp. 383ff, includes a short collection of poetry appended to extant manuscripts of *The Gossamer Diary*. These include courtship poems apparently written for her son and poems written for competitions.
66 Seidensticker, p. 69.
67 Morris, *World*, p. 311; Arntzen, pp. 5–8.
68 Seidensticker, p. 8; Arntzen, pp. x, 162.
69 Lessing, p. 90.
70 Seidensticker, p. 33.
71 Morris, *Pillow Book*, pp. 63–4.
72 Ibid., pp. 267–8.
73 Morris, *Pillow Book Companion*, pp. 194–5, note 1156; Keene, pp. 415–16.
74 Morris, *Pillow Book Companion*, p. 195, note 1156; Keene, pp. 1, 412.
75 Morris, *Pillow Book*, p. 20.
76 Ibid., pp. 65–6.
77 Ibid., p. 30.
78 Ibid., pp. 261–2, 40–2, for these two incidents.
79 McCullough, *Ōkagami*, p. 166.
80 Bowring, p. 53.
81 Morris, *Pillow Book Companion*, p. 53, note 260; Morris, *World*, pp. 201–5, for Heian standards of female beauty.
82 Bowring, pp. 47, 48, 49.
83 Morris, *Pillow Book*, p. 31.
84 Ibid., p. 76. She was about thirty at the time, getting on

but not yet 'past it' by Heian standards. Thirty-seven was the seriously dangerous age for women, when sudden death or illness might strike.

85 Morris, *World*, pp. 203–4; Morris, *Pillow Book Companion*, p. 34, note 149.

86 Morris, *Pillow Book*, p. 32.

87 See Waley, *Lady*, for translation.

88 Morris, *World*, p. 202, notes Heian indifference to the aesthetic qualities of the naked body.

89 See Bowring, pp. xxviii–xxx, for his description and illustration of formal court dress for the Heian lady-in-waiting. See, too, Morris, *World*, pp. 204–5; Seidensticker, p. 22, who sums up the appearance of the typical Heian lady as 'a shapeless and almost inert bundle of clothes surmounted by a spectral white face and masses of streaming black hair'.

90 Bowring, pp. 24–5.

91 Morris, *Pillow Book*, pp. 18–19.

92 Hirshfield, p. xiii.

93 See Cranston, pp. 3–30, for details of Izumi Shikibu's biography, on which I have drawn for this summary.

94 McCullough, *Ōkagami*, pp. 165–6, for the three princes; McCullough, *Tale*, p. 139, for Kaneie's relationship with his grandsons.

95 Ibid., pp. 163–4.

96 Ibid., p. 164.

97 If a wife disliked her marriage or her role as 'second wife', she could end the relationship through divorce or by moving to a new location (Hirshfield, p. xv).

98 McCullough, *Tale*, p. 166.

99 McCullough, *Ōkagami*, p. 170.

100 McCullough, *Tale*, p. 197; McCullough, *Ōkagami*, p. 170.

101 McCullough, *Tale*, p. 305.

102 See Cranston for English translation.

103 Hirshfield, p. 69, for translation; pp. xix, 191, note to p. 70, for commentary. A poet in her own right, Jane Hirshfield, working with Mariko Aratani, has made English translations of a selection of Izumi Shikibu's poems. I have drawn on these for my references to the poems.

104 Hirshfield, pp. 165, 168, 169. For a useful summary of the tradition see 'On Japanese Poetry and the Process of Translation', Hirshfield, pp. 161–73.

105 Ibid., p. 51.

106 Ibid., p. 50.

107 Ibid., p. 49.

108 Ibid., p. 187, note to p. 49.

109 Ibid., p. 133.

110 Ibid., p. 205, note to p. 144.

111 Ibid., p. 147.

112 Ibid., p. 157. Cranston, p. 6, says that she was 'probably a very young woman' at the time of the poem's composition; Hirshfield, p. 208, discusses the poem as a possible deathbed work.

113 Hirshfield, p. 208.

114 Ibid., pp. 89, 139.

115 Brookner, p. 7.

116 Scholars gave the book this title for purposes of identification, although Sarashina, a mountainous district in central Japan, is not directly mentioned (Morris, *Bridge of Dreams*, p. 13).

117 Although now regarded as one of the treasures of Heian literature, the book was earlier dismissed by scholars, because the ancient holograph manuscript by Fujiwara no Teika had been rebound in the early seventeenth century with several sections in the wrong order. The mistake was discovered in 1924 by Professor Tamai, an expert on Heian literature. His description of examining the manuscript might have charmed Lady Sarashina, with her love of the romantic, the curious, and the thrilling:

It was 1 August, a day I shall never forget. Early in the morning I was taken to the Ministry of the Imperial Household by Dr [Sasaki] and followed him into ... Hōmei Hall ... where a number of treasures had been laid on a table. From among them the assistant in charge took out a box containing the manuscript of *Sarashina Nikki* in the hand of Lord Teika. The outer box, the silk wrapper, the middle box, and the book pouch were removed one by one until finally I saw the precious little [inner] box decorated with a pattern of blue waves and with a moon embossed in lacquer. This too was opened and there lay the book, its cover still dyed in the ancient colours that had lasted for seven hundred years. Just then a faint breeze blew through the window and the splendid fragrance of the old paper was wafted towards me.

Dr [Sasaki] and I started to examine the book ... and presently in the seam of the binding I detected the first of the clues that I had expected to find ... Ah, so the origin of all the confusion really lay in this manuscript! I felt my heart pounding. For some time I had been wondering whether the disorder of the sections was not the result of some carelessness at the time when the manuscript was being re-bound. Now I had the proof before my eyes ...

(Quoted in Morris, *Bridge of Dreams*, pp. 24–5).
118 Morris, *Pillow Book*, p. 174.
119 Morris, *Bridge of Dreams*, p. 31.
120 Ibid., p. 44.
121 Ibid., p. 46.
122 Ibid., p. 47.
123 Ibid., p. 64.
124 Ibid., p. 135, note 142.
125 Ibid., p. 88.
126 Ibid., pp. 79–80.
127 Ibid., p. 107.
128 Shikibu, p. 1069.

PART 3   The Heart's Desire: Medieval Women Write About Love

Bibliography

Akehurst, F. R. P. and Judith M. Davis (eds), *A Handbook of the Troubadours*, Berkeley, Los Angeles and London: University of California Press, 1995

Baruch, Elaine Hoffman, *Women, Love & Power: Literary and Psychoanalytic Perspectives*, New York and London: New York University Press, 1991

Beer, Frances, *Women and Mystical Experience in the Middle Ages*, Woodbridge: The Boydell Press, 1992

Benton, John, 'Clio and Venus: a Historical View of Medieval Love', in John F. Benton (Thomas N. Bisson, ed.), *Culture, Power and Personality in Medieval France*, London and Rio Grande: Hambledon Press, 1991

Boase, Roger, *The Origin and Meaning of Courtly Love: A critical study of European scholarship*, Manchester: Manchester University Press; New Jersey: Rowman and Littlefield, 1977

Bogin, Meg, *The Women Troubadours*, New York and London: Paddington Press, 1976

Bond, Gerald A. (ed. and trans.), *The Poetry of William VII, Count of Poitiers, IX Duke of Aquitaine*, New York and London: Garland, 1982

Bonner, Anthony (ed. and trans.), *Songs of the Troubadours*, London: George Allen & Unwin, 1973

Brooke, Christopher, *The Medieval Idea of Marriage*, Oxford: Oxford University Press, 1989

Bruckner, Matilda Tomaryn, Laurie Shepard, Sarah White (eds and trans.), *Songs of the Women Troubadours*, New York and London: Garland, 1995

Burgess, Glyn S. and Keith Busby, *The Lais of Marie de France*, Harmondsworth: Penguin Books, 1986

Byatt, A. S., *Possession: A Romance*, London: Chatto & Windus, 1990

Camille, Michael, *The Medieval Art of Love: Objects and Subjects of Desire*, London: Laurence King, 1998

Chaucer, Geoffrey (David Wright, trans.), *The Canterbury Tales*, Oxford and New York: Oxford University Press, 1986

Coldwell, Maria V., 'Jougleresses and Trobairitz: Secular Musicians in Medieval France', in Jane Bowers and Judith Tick, *Women Making Music: The Western Art Tradition, 1150–1950*, Basingstoke and London: Macmillan Press, 1986

Cooper, Helen, *The English Romance in Time: Transforming motifs from Geoffrey of Monmouth to the death of Shakespeare*, Oxford: Oxford University Press, 2004

De Lafayette, Madame (Terence Cave, trans.), *The Princesse de Clèves*, Oxford: Oxford University Press, 1992

De Lorris, Guillaume and Jean de Meun (Frances Horgan, trans. and ed.), *The Romance of the Rose*, Oxford and New York: Oxford University Press, 1994

De Pizan, Christine (Rosalind Brown-Grant, trans. and intro.), *The Book of the City of Ladies*, Harmondsworth: Penguin Books, 1999

—— (Thelma S. Fenster, trans., with lyric poetry Nadia Margolis, trans.), *The Book of the Duke of True Lovers*, New York: Persea Books, 1991

De Rougemont, Denis (Montgomery Belgion, trans.), *Passion and Society*, revised and augmented edition, London: Faber & Faber, 1956

De Silva-Vigier, Anil (trans. and annot.), *Christine de Pisan: Autobiography Of A Medieval Woman (1363–1430)*, Montreux, London and Washington: Minerva Press, 1996

De Troyes, Chrétien (Dorothy Gilbert, trans.), *Erec and Enide*, Berkeley, Los Angeles and Oxford: University of California Press, 1992

—— (William W. Kibler, trans.), *Arthurian Romances*, Harmondsworth: Penguin Books, 1991

Dimmick, Jeremy, 'Ovid in the Middle Ages: authority and poetry', in Philip Hardie (ed.), *The Cambridge Companion to Ovid*, Cambridge: Cambridge University Press, 2002

Dronke, Peter, *Medieval Latin and the Rise of European Love-Lyric*, Vols I and II, Oxford: Oxford at the Clarendon Press, second edition, 1968; one-volume edition, 1999

——, 'The Provençal Trobairitz Castelloza', in *Intellectuals and Poets in Medieval Europe*, Roma: Edizioni di Storia e Letteratura, 1992

——, *Women Writers of the Middle Ages*, Cambridge: Cambridge University Press, 1984

Ewert, Alfred (ed.), Glyn S. Burgess (intro. and bibliog.), *Marie de France Lais*, London: Bristol Classical Press, 1995

Fowles, John, *The Ebony Tower*, London: Vintage, 1996

Gaunt, Simon and Sarah Kay (eds), *The Troubadours: An Introduction*, Cambridge: Cambridge University Press, 1999

Hanning, Robert and Joan Ferrante (trans.), *The Lais of Marie de France*, Durham, North Carolina: Labyrinth Press, 1978

Hubert, Merton Jerome (trans.), Marion E. Porter (revised Provençal text), *The Romance of Flamenca: A Provençal Poem of the Thirteenth Century*, New Jersey: Princeton University Press, 1962

Ibn Hazm (A. J. Arberry, trans.), *The Ring of the Dove: A Treatise on the Art and Practice of Arab Love*, London: Luzac, 1953

Jaeger, C. Stephen, *Ennobling Love: In Search of a Lost Sensibility*, Philadelphia: University of Pennsylvania Press, 1999

Jankowiak, William (ed.), *Romantic Passion: A Universal Experience?*, New York: Columbia University Press, 1995

King, Margaret L., *Women of the Renaissance*, Chicago and London: University of Chicago Press, 1991

Krueger, Roberta L. (ed.), *The Cambridge Companion to Medieval Romance*, Cambridge: Cambridge University Press, 2000

Larrington, Carolyne, *Women and Writing in Medieval Europe: A sourcebook*, London and New York: Routledge, 1995

Leclerq, Jean, *Monks and Love in Twelfth-Century France: psycho-historical essays*, Oxford: Clarendon Press, 1979

Lewis, C. S., *The Allegory of Love: A Study in Medieval Tradition*, Oxford: Oxford University Press, 1936

Mechthild of Magdeburg (Frank Tobin, trans. and intro.), *The Flowing Light of the Godhead*, New York: Paulist Press, c.1998

Merwin, W. S., *The Mays of Ventadorn*, Washington DC: National Geographic, 2002

Mitchell, Juliet, 'Romantic Love', in *Women: the Longest Revolution: Essays on Feminism, Literature and Psychoanalysis*, London: Virago, 1984

Owen, D. D. R., *Eleanor of Aquitaine: Queen and Legend*, Oxford: Blackwell, 1996

Paden, William (ed.), *The Voice of the Trobairitz: Perspectives on the Women Troubadours*, Philadelphia: University of Pennsylvania Press, 1989

Paterson, Linda M., *The World of the Troubadours: Medieval Occitan society, c. 1100–c. 1300*, Cambridge: Cambridge University Press, 1995

Porter, Andrew, 'Attuned to the Lady of Tripoli', *The Times Literary Supplement*, 29 November 2002, p. 20

Pound, Ezra, *The Cantos of Ezra Pound*, London: Faber & Faber, 1975

Press, Alan R. (ed. and trans.), *Anthology of Troubadour Lyric Poetry*, Edinburgh: Edinburgh University Press, 1971

Runciman, Steven, *A History of the Crusades*, Vol. II, *The Kingdom of Jerusalem and the Frankish East, 1100–1187*, Harmondsworth: Penguin Books, 1990

Smith, Lesley and Jane H. M. Taylor (eds), *Women and the Book: Assessing the Visual Evidence*, London and Toronto: British Library and University of Toronto Press, 1997

Spiegel, Harriet (ed. and trans.), *Marie de France: Fables*, Toronto and Buffalo and London: University of Toronto Press, 1987

Stevens, John, *Medieval Romance: Themes and Approaches*, London: Hutchinson University Library, 1973

Thiébaux, Marcelle (trans. and intros), *The Writings of Medieval Women: An Anthology*, second edition, New York and London: Garland, 1994

Topsfield, L. T., *Troubadours and Love*, Cambridge: Cambridge University Press, 1975

Wack, Mary Frances, *Lovesickness in the Middle Ages: The* Viaticum *and Its Commentaries*, Philadelphia: University of Pennsylvania Press, 1990

Walsh, P. G. (ed. and trans.), *Andreas Capellanus On Love*, London: Duckworth, 1982

Wardle, Ralph M. (ed.), *Collected Letters of Mary Wollstonecraft*, Ithaca and London: Cornell University Press, 1979

Wavell, A. P., Field Marshal Earl Wavell, *Other Men's Flowers*, Harmondsworth: Penguin Books, 1960

Weir, Alison, *Eleanor of Aquitaine: By the Wrath of God, Queen of England*, London: Jonathan Cape, 1999

Willard, Charity Cannon, *Christine de Pizan: Her Life and Works*, New York: Persea Books, 1984

Wilson, Katharina M., *Medieval Women Writers*, Manchester: Manchester University Press, 1984

Wolf, George and Roy Rosenstein (eds and trans.), *The Poetry of Cercamon and Jaufre Rudel*, New York and London: Garland, 1983

Woolf, Virginia (Morag Shiach, ed., intro. and notes), *A Room of One's Own*, in *A Room of One's Own* and *Three Guineas*, Oxford and New York: Oxford University Press, 1998

Notes

1 De Pizan, *Duke*, p. 116.
2 Bonner, p. 88, lines 53–4. From 'Tant ai mo cor ple de joya' ('My heart is so full of joy'), Bonner, pp. 87–9. Bonner's selection and English translation of troubadour poems is informative and accessible; Press's anthology usefully offers parallel texts in Occitan and a literal prose translation in English.
3 Dante was probably the first person to refer to the language of Occitan as *lingua d'oco*, the language which used *oco* for 'yes' as opposed to French *oïl* and Italian *si* (Paterson, p. 3).
4 Lewis, Chapter 1, argues his 'theory of adultery'. Denis de Rougemont similarly believed that passion and marriage were incompatible. His reading of the literature of love and in particular the story of Tristram and Yseult proposed that love and death were the two great affinities. More recent scholars have questioned both perspectives. For a broad-ranging survey of theories on 'courtly love' see Boase.
5 Bonner, p. 31.
6 My translation. For the poem see Bonner, pp. 33–4; Press, pp. 12–13.
7 Bonner, p. 36.
8 Ibid., p. 31.

9 Ibid., pp. 38–9.
10 Ibid., p. 39.
11 Ibid., p. 61.
12 Runciman, pp. 332–3.
13 'Qan lo rius de la fontana' ('When the fountain's flow'), Wolf and Rosenstein, pp. 138, 139, line 8.
14 Ibid., pp. 138–41; Bonner, pp. 64–5; Press, pp. 30–31.
15 'Lanqan li jorn son lonc en mai' ('When the days are long in May'), Wolf and Rosenstein, pp. 146–9; Bonner, pp. 63–4; Press, pp. 32–5.
16 Wolf and Rosenstein, pp. 146, 147, line 22.
17 'No sap chantar qui so non di' ('He cannot sing who makes no tune'), Wolf and Rosenstein, pp. 134–7, line 11; Press, pp. 34–7.
18 Wavell, p. 110. According to Porter, the critic Edmund Gosse suggested that Rudel was really a religious poet, writing in metaphorical terms about his adoration of the Church of Christ. This is not an entirely fanciful notion, given the enthusiasm with which Bernard of Clairvaux, almost a contemporary of Rudel's, appropriated the languorous phrases of the Song of Songs as an expression of Christ's love for his spouse, the Church. As Porter mentions, the spiritual undertones of Rudel's quest were not lost on

Kaija Saariaho, who concluded her opera, *L'Amour de loin*, on a note of exaltation, as the heroine Clémence, the Countess of Tripoli, renounces the world for God: '*Seigneur, c'est toi l'amour, c'est toi l'amour de loin.*'

19 For poem and commentary see Wavell, pp. 109–10.

20 For *vida* see Bonner, pp. 82–3.

21 Bonner, p. 257; Pound, Canto vi, lines 41–7.

22 'Can l'erba fresch'e.lh folha par' ('When the fresh grass and the leaf appears'), Press, pp. 78–81, lines 5–6. I have slightly amended Press's translation and inserted line breaks.

23 Bonner, pp. 91–3; Press, pp. 76–9. There are a number of modern recordings of this beautiful song and of other troubadour compositions.

24 Bonner, p. 91, line 16.

25 Ibid., p. 93, lines 59–60.

26 Woolf, pp. 56–7.

27 Letter to Godwin, 1 July 1796, Wardle, p. 331; Samuel Butler, *Hudibras*, Part ii, Canto i, lines 591–2.

28 For Occitan women's political and economic power see Paterson, pp. 221–8.

29 For the carefully orchestrated adulation of Elizabeth i see Roy Strong, *The Cult of Elizabeth: Elizabethan Portraiture and Pageantry*, London: Thames & Hudson, 1987. Strong refers to this poem, p. 48.

30 On kissing as a courteous greeting among the nobility see Benton, pp. 112–13. His essay is a corrective to anachronistic and romanticised readings of so-called 'courtly love'.

31 S. Gaunt, cited in Paterson, p. 236.

32 My translation. For the song see Bruckner, pp. 6–9. For Occitan texts and translations of thirty-six trobairitz songs, see Bruckner et al.'s edition. Meg Bogin's pioneer study of the trobairitz includes texts and translations, and offers an excellent introduction for the general reader.

33 Maria de Ventadorn and Gui d'Ussel, Domna H. and Rofin, Domna and Raimbaut d'Aurenga (Bruckner, pp. 38–41, 78–83, 88–91).

34 Ibid., pp. 138–9.

35 Ibid., pp. 30–1.

36 Ibid., pp. 18–21; see, too, Dronke, 'The Provençal *Trobairitz* Castelloza', for discussion and translation of her songs, pp. 407–29.

37 Almuc de Castelnou and Iseut de Capion (Bruckner, pp. 48–9).

38 Ibid., pp. 32–3.

39 Bruckner reads this as a poem between two women, pp. 96–7, but see Bogin, pp. 144–5, and Dronke, *Women Writers*, pp. 101–3, who both read it as

a conversation between three women.

40 Bruckner, pp. 6–9, for poem. My translation.

41 Bruckner, p. 7, lines 19–20.

42 Bogin, pp. 163–4.

43 Bruckner, pp. 10–11, for poem. My translation.

44 Lines 17–18. My translation.

45 Byatt, p. 122.

46 Woolf, pp. 88–90.

47 Bruckner, pp. 12–13, for poem. My translation.

48 Bruckner, pp. 2–5, for poem. My translation.

49 Dante, *Purgatorio*, xxvi, line 117.

50 Bonner, pp. 159–61; Press, pp. 176–9.

51 The romance of *Floire et Blancheflor*, which appeared in various versions from the mid twelfth century (Hubert, p. 253, line 4479).

52 Ibid., p. 247, line 4370.

53 For the visual imagery and symbolism of love see Camille. For a discussion of gifts and their significance see Camille, 'Love's Gifts', pp. 51–72.

54 Ibid., p. 51.

55 Ibid., pp. 57, 55–6, 61, 88–9.

56 Jankowiak, p. 3.

57 The original Belle Dame appeared in Alain Chartier's *Belle Dame sans mercy* (1424). Influenced by Christine de Pizan's *The Book of the Duke of True Lovers* (see later in this section), Chartier's Belle Dame refuses her exemplary lover on the grounds of self-protection: he may be like the false lovers who abandon women and then boast about their conquests. See de Pizan, *Duke*, pp. 27–8.

58 Wack, p. 149.

59 Ibid., p. 151.

60 Dronke, 'The Provençal *Trobairitz* Castelloza', pp. 425–6.

61 Spiegel, pp. 256, 257 for text and English translation.

62 Ibid., p. 4. I have slightly amended her translation.

63 Burgess and Busby, p. 43.

64 Paris, BN, MS Arsenal 3142; see Susan L. Ward, 'Fables for the Court: Illustrations of Marie de France's *Fables* in Paris', in Smith and Taylor, pp. 190–203.

65 The trials of Katharine Hilbery in Virginia Woolf's *Night and Day* recall those of the Stephen sisters, the future Vanessa Bell and Virginia Woolf, ambitious girls yearning to be working at easel or desk. Her days are taken up with meaningless social duties and helping her mother to write the biography of Katharine's grandfather, a famous poet. At night, she sits up late to work at mathematics.

66 Quoted in Burgess and Busby, p. 11.

67 Fowles, p. 120.

68 Stevens also makes this connection (pp. 114–15).

69 Fowles, p. 120.

70 London, British Library,
Harley MS 4431.

71 Woolf, p. 92, compares
Tolstoy's youthful experience of
love, travel and adventure with

the secluded life of George
Eliot, ostracised from society
because of her relationship with
a married man.

72 Beer, p. 95.

PART 4 The Heat and Violence of the Poet's Heart:
Women and the Love Sonnet

Bibliography

Beilin, Elaine V., *Redeeming Eve: Women Writers of the English Renaissance*,
Princeton and Oxford: Princeton University Press, 1987, paperback
edition, 1990

Bogan, Louise: *Selected Criticism*, New York: Noonday Press, 1955

Boyd, Nancy (Edna St Vincent Millay), *Distressing Dialogues*, New York
and London: Harper & Brothers, 1924

Browning, Elizabeth Barrett, *The Poetical Works of Elizabeth Barrett
Browning*, London: Henry Frowde, 1910

—— (Karen Hill, intro.), *The Works of Elizabeth Barrett Browning*, Ware:
Wordsworth Poetry Library, 1994

Browning, Robert and Elizabeth Barrett Browning (Philip Kelley and
Ronald Hudson, eds), *The Brownings' Correspondence*, Winfield, Kansas:
Wedgestone Press, Vol. 10, c. 1992

Camille, Michael, *The Medieval Art of Love: Objects and Subjects of Desire*,
London: Laurence King, 1998

Croft, P. J. (ed.), *The Poems of Robert Sidney: Edited from the Poet's
Autograph Notebook with Introduction and Commentary*, Oxford:
Clarendon Press, 1984

Crump, R. W. (ed.), *The Complete Poems of Christina Rossetti: A Variorum
Edition*, Vol. II, Baton Rouge and London: Louisiana State University
Press, 1986

Duncan-Jones, Katherine, *Sir Philip Sidney: Courtier Poet*, London:
Hamish Hamilton, 1991

——, *Sir Philip Sidney: Selected Poems*, Oxford: Clarendon Press, 1973

Durling, Robert M. (ed. and trans.), *Petrarch's Lyric Poems: The* Rime
sparse *and Other Lyrics*, Cambridge, Massachusetts and London:
Harvard University Press, 1976

Elizabeth 1, Leah S. Marcus, Janel Mueller and Mary Beth Rose (eds),

Collected Works, Chicago and London: University of Chicago Press, 2000

Epstein, Daniel Mark, *What Lips My Lips Have Kissed: The Loves and Love Poems of Edna St Vincent Millay*, New York: Henry Holt, 2002

Forster, Margaret, *Elizabeth Barrett Browning: A Biography*, London: Chatto & Windus, 1988

Fraser, Antonia, *Mary Queen of Scots*, London: Weidenfeld & Nicolson, 1969

——, *The Six Wives of Henry VIII*, London: Weidenfeld & Nicolson, 1992

Freedman, Diane P. (ed.), *Millay at 100: A Critical Reappraisal*, Carbondale and Edwardsville: Southern Illinois University Press, 1995

Gibson, Jonathan, 'Cherchez la femme: Mary Wroth and Shakespeare's Sonnets', in *The Times Literary Supplement*, 13 August 2004, pp. 12–13

Gilbert, Sandra M. and Susan Gubar, *No Man's Land: The Place of the Woman Writer in the Twentieth Century*, Vol. 3, *Letters from the Front*, New Haven and London: Yale University Press, 1994

Graves, Robert, *The White Goddess: A historical grammar of poetic myth*, amended and enlarged edition, London: Faber & Faber, 1961

Greer, Germaine, *Slip-Shod Sibyls: Recognition, Rejection and the Woman Poet*, Harmondsworth: Viking, 1995

Hackett, Helen, *Women and Romance Fiction in the English Renaissance*, Cambridge: Cambridge University Press, 2000

Hannay, Margaret Patterson, 'Mary Sidney: Lady Wroth', in Katharina M. Wilson (ed.), *Women Writers of the Renaissance and Reformation*, Athens and London: University of Georgia Press, 1987

——, *Philip's Phoenix: Mary Sidney, Countess of Pembroke*, New York and Oxford: Oxford University Press, 1990

Hay, Millicent V., *The Life of Robert Sidney: Earl of Leicester (1563–1626)*, Washington: Folger Shakespeare Library; London and Toronto: Associated University Presses, 1984

Hearn, Karen (ed.), *Dynasties: Painting in Tudor and Jacobean England 1530–1630*, London: Tate Publishing, 1995

Ives, Eric, *The Life and Death of Anne Boleyn: 'The Most Happy'*, Oxford: Blackwell, 2004

Johnston, George Burke (ed.), *Poems of Ben Jonson*, London: Routledge & Kegan Paul, 1954

Karlin, Daniel (ed.), *Robert Browning and Elizabeth Barrett: The Courtship Correspondence 1845–1846, A Selection*, Oxford: Clarendon Press, 1989

Kelley, Philip and Ronald Hudson (eds), *Diary by E. B. B.: The*

Unpublished Diary of Elizabeth Barrett Barrett, 1831–1832, Athens, Ohio: Ohio University Press, 1969

Kukil, Karen V. (ed.), *The Journals of Sylvia Plath 1950–1962*, London: Faber & Faber, 2000

Lessing, Doris, *Love, Again*, London: Flamingo, HarperCollins, 1996

Lewis, Scott (ed.), *The Letters of Elizabeth Barrett Browning to Her Sister Arabella*, Vols 1 and 2, Texas: Wedgestone Press, 2002

Macdougall, Allan Ross (ed.), *Letters of Edna St Vincent Millay*, New York: Harper & Brothers, 1952

Milford, Nancy, *Savage Beauty: The Life of Edna St Vincent Millay*, New York: Random House, 2001

Millay, Edna St Vincent (Norma Millay, ed.), *Collected Poems*, Cutchogue, New York: Buccaneer Books, n.d.

Miller, Betty (ed.), *Elizabeth Barrett to Miss Mitford: The Unpublished Letters of Elizabeth Barrett Barrett to Mary Russell Mitford*, London: John Murray, 1954

Muir, Kenneth (ed.), *Collected Poems of Sir Thomas Wyatt*, London: Routledge & Kegan Paul, 1949, paperback edition, 1963

Pollock, Mary Sanders, *Elizabeth Barrett and Robert Browning: A Creative Partnership*, Aldershot: Ashgate, 2003

Reynolds, Margaret (ed.), *The Sappho Companion*, London: Chatto & Windus, 2000

Roberts, Josephine A. (ed.), *The First Part of The Countess of Montgomery's Urania* by *Lady Mary Wroth*, Binghampton, New York: Medieval & Renaissance Texts & Studies, 1995

—— (ed.), *The Poems of Lady Mary Wroth*, Baton Rouge: Louisiana State University Press, 1983, paperback edition, 1992

Ryals, Clyde de L., *The Life of Robert Browning: A Critical Biography*, Oxford UK and Cambridge USA: Blackwell, 1993

Shakespeare, William (John Kerrigan, ed.), *The Sonnets and A Lover's Complaint*, Harmondsworth: Penguin Books, 1986

Stanbrough, Jane, 'Edna St Vincent Millay and the Language of Vulnerability', in Sandra M. Gilbert and Susan Gubar (eds), *Shakespeare's Sisters: Feminist Essays on Women Poets*, Bloomington: Indiana University Press, 1979

Stephenson, Glennis, *Elizabeth Barrett Browning and the Poetry of Love*, Ann Arbor and London: UMI Research Press, 1989

Teague, Frances, 'Elizabeth 1: Queen of England', in Katharina M. Wilson (ed.), *Women Writers of the Renaissance and Reformation*, Athens and London: University of Georgia Press, 1987

Waller, Gary, *The Sidney Family Romance: Mary Wroth, William Herbert and the Early Modern Construction of Gender*, Detroit: Wayne State University Press, 1993

Warnicke, Retha M., *The Rise and Fall of Anne Boleyn: Family politics at the court of Henry VIII*, Cambridge, New York and Melbourne: Cambridge University Press, 1989

Wilson, Edmund, *The Shores of Light: A Literary Chronicle of the Twenties and Thirties*, London: W. H. Allen, 1952

—— (Leon Edel, ed. and intro.), *The Twenties: From Notebooks and Diaries of the Period*, London and Basingstoke: Macmillan, 1975

Woolf, Virginia (Morag Shiach, ed., intro. and notes), *A Room of One's Own*, in *A Room of One's Own* and *Three Guineas*, Oxford and New York: Oxford University Press, 1998

Notes

1 Woolf, p. 62.

2 Ibid., p. 62.

3 Louise Labé (1522?–1566), French poet, published twenty-four sonnets along with elegies and a prose dialogue in 1555; Gaspara Stampa (1524?–1554) lived mainly in Venice as a *cortigiana onesta* (honest courtesan). She was one of the great Italian sonneteers in the Petrarchan tradition, which, like Lady Mary Wroth, she modified to suit a woman's voice. See Frank J. Warnke, *Three Women Poets*, London and Toronto: Associated University Presses, 1987, for commentary and translations of Labé, Stampa and the Mexican poet Sor Juana Inés de la Cruz.

4 Roberts, *Urania*, I. iii, p. 390.

5 Rosalind Smith, in *Sonnets and the English Woman Writer, 1560–1621: The Politics of Absence*, Basingstoke: Palgrave Macmillan, 2005, argues that English women poets were put off by the ill fame attached to a sonnet sequence attributed to Mary Queen of Scots. Written in French, the sonnets reveal the rape and adultery of the female speaker. They were among incriminating papers allegedly found in a silver casket and used as evidence that Mary had been complicit in the murder of her second husband Lord Darnley. There has been much debate about the authenticity of the sonnets and other 'casket' papers. See, for example, Peter Davidson, 'The Casket Sonnets: New Evidence Concerning Mary Queen of Scots', in which he concludes on the basis of

recently identified documents that the sonnets were forgeries, part of a dossier put together to prove Mary guilty of murder (*History Scotland Magazine*, Vol. 1, No. 1, Winter 2001).

6 Love letter from Henry VIII to Anne Boleyn (Ives, p. 85).

7 Ibid., pp. 70–1.

8 Ibid., p. 21.

9 Retha M. Warnicke suggests that the child Anne miscarried shortly before her arrest was deformed. This would have laid her open to suspicion of illicit sexual acts and even witchcraft, factors in Henry's sudden repudiation of his wife and in the charges laid against her and her alleged 'lovers'. See Warnicke, pp. 191–233.

10 Fraser, *Wives*, p. 136, hypothesises that Anne permitted some form of *coitus interruptus*, to keep the King interested while guarding against an untimely pregnancy.

11 Camille, p. 88.

12 Ives, pp. 37–8.

13 Ibid., pp. 6–7.

14 Ibid., p. 67.

15 Shakespeare, Sonnet 130, p. 141.

16 The Petrarchan sonnet consisted of fourteen lines each of eleven syllables, and followed a rhyme scheme of abbaabba, with two or three different rhymes in the final six lines. There was generally a break in thought between the first eight lines, the octet, and the final sestet. The English sonnet generally had a ten-syllable line, and a rhyme scheme of ababcdcdefefgg, although there were many variants on this basic pattern.

17 Durling, pp. 336, 337, for sonnet and English translation.

18 See Graves.

19 Muir, p. 7.

20 Elizabeth 1, p. 46.

21 Wyatt borrows the phrase from Petrarch ('*Nessun mi tocchi*'), but repositions it within the poem and gives the taboo a very different emphasis.

22 Fraser, *Wives*, pp. 253–4.

23 For sonnets attributed to Mary Queen of Scots see note 5 above.

24 In a letter to the critic Henry Fothergill Chorley, *Correspondence*, Vol. 10: 14.

25 Kukil, *Journals*, p. 360.

26 'Apology for the Countess of Pembroke', p. 51, in *The Use of Poetry and the Use of Criticism: Studies in the Relation of Criticism to Poetry in England*, London: Faber & Faber, 1964 edition.

27 Roberts, *Poems*, p. 6.

28 This point is made by Margaret P. Hannay in her biography of Mary Sidney. When the Countess's husband died and the estates passed to her son, she lost her flatterers (*Philip's Phoenix*, pp. 106–7).

29 Croft, pp. 74, 77–8. He also mentions a tutor's rudeness to her, again perhaps connected with her comparative ill education.

30 Beilin, p. 209.

31 Roberts, *Poems*, p. 8.

32 Croft argues for an earlier meeting and a love match, pp. 72–3.

33 Hannay, 'Mary Sidney: Lady Wroth', p. 548.

34 Roberts, *Poems*, pp. 11–12.

35 Roberts comments on Lady Mary's interest in hunting and in women's participation in the sport (*Urania*, pp. lxiii–lxv).

36 Roberts, *Poems*, p. 11.

37 Beilin, p. 325, note 4.

38 Hearn, pp. 135, 164.

39 Roberts, *Poems*, p. 13.

40 Ibid., p. 16.

41 By the nineteenth-century critic, Frederick Fleay. See ibid.

42 Ibid., p. 17.

43 Percy A. Scholes, John Owen Ward (eds), *The Oxford Companion to Music*, Oxford and New York: Oxford University Press, tenth edition, 1970, p. 584.

44 Muir, p. 49.

45 Ibid., p. 50.

46 Beilin, p. 209.

47 Roberts, *Poems*, p. 23.

48 Portrait currently in the Powis Collection, Powis Castle (Hearn, pp. 204–6).

49 Ibid., p. 205.

50 Hannay, *Philip's Phoenix*, p. 169.

51 Ibid., pp. 169–71, for Pembroke and Fitton; Roberts, *Urania*, pp. lxxxi–lxxxiv, for Mary Fitton.

52 Roberts, *Poems*, p. 24.

53 For Lady Mary's illegitimate children see ibid., p. 25.

54 Ibid., p. 35, and see Appendix, p. 236, for her letter to Buckingham.

55 Roberts, *Urania*, p. xvii.

56 Ibid., p. cxxi.

57 Ibid., p. xxxix.

58 Ibid., p. 317.

59 Ibid., p. 440.

60 See Beilin, pp. 226–9, for parallels between Pamphilia's queenship and that of Elizabeth 1.

61 See Gibson.

62 See note 3 above.

63 Roberts, *Urania*, p. xxvii.

64 Ibid., p. 371.

65 Roberts, *Poems*, pp. 33, 34.

66 There are variations between the order of poems in the manuscript copy in Wroth's hand (now in the Folger Shakespeare Library in Washington) and the printed text of 1621. See Gibson and cf Roberts, *Poems*, pp. 62–5, 73–5. For this discussion I have followed the order in Roberts, *Poems*, which accords with the 1621 arrangement.

67 P1, Roberts, *Poems*, p. 85.

68 P78, ibid., p. 128.

69 Ibid.

70 P79, ibid., p. 129.

71 P90, ibid., p. 134.

72 Ibid.
73 See note 66 above.
74 P103, Roberts, *Poems*, p. 142.
75 Karlin, p. 1. In quotations from EBB, the two-dot ellipses are hers. Both she and Robert Browning often used a two-dot ellipsis to suggest a brief pause. My omissions are marked by a three-dot ellipsis within square brackets.
76 From Kelley and Hudson, quoted in Forster, p. 60.
77 See, for example, Stephenson, pp. 44–5, for critical reception of 'Bertha in the Lane'.
78 Karlin, p. 2.
79 Ibid., p. 19.
80 Ibid., p. 34.
81 Ryals, p. 82.
82 Karlin, pp. 216–8, for Elizabeth's candid account of women's idealism about love and her responses to Browning.
83 Ibid., pp. 55–6.
84 See ibid., pp. 56–7, and p. 149, where Browning writes that he burnt the letter.
85 Ibid., p. 57.
86 Pollock, p. 86.
87 Ibid., pp. 62–3.
88 Karlin, p. 97.
89 Lewis, Vol. 1, pp. 368–9.
90 Ibid., p. 371, note 14. For Elizabeth's sketch of the courtyard and mimosa tree see ibid., Letter 42, p. 263.
91 Karlin, p. 78.
92 Sonnets III, IV, VII and VI.
93 Sonnets VIII, X and XI.
94 Sonnet XXV.
95 Sonnet XXXIX.
96 An echo of Prospero's 'our little life / Is rounded with a sleep', Shakespeare, *The Tempest*, Act IV, scene 1.
97 Sonnet XLII.
98 Sonnets XV, XVI and XLIII.
99 Sonnet XXVIII.
100 Sonnets XXXI, XXIX, XXXIII.
101 Sonnet XXXVIII.
102 Sonnet XXXV.
103 Sonnet XLII.
104 Crump, p. 86.
105 The poet Sara Teasdale, in notes for an uncompleted biography of Rossetti, opposed the (still prevalent) view of critics and biographers that Rossetti's life was unhappy: 'She need not be pitied because of what is called her limited experience and because she chose to remain unmarried. She was an impassioned woman, but not a passionate one. Neither of the two men who wanted her in marriage would have made her happy; and with Dorothea in *Middlemarch*, she "liked giving up".'
  Teasdale makes the further point that Rossetti idolised her brother Dante Gabriel 'though she was well aware of his faults'. Her two suitors (James Collinson and Charles Cayley) were 'pale beside his flame', and marriage would have

separated her from her family, her poetry and 'her jealous God'. Quoted in Margaret Haley Carpenter, *Sara Teasdale: A Biography*, New York City: Schulte Publishing Company, 1960, p. 312.

Elizabeth Barrett had the advantage over Rossetti of being pursued by a lover who was determined to marry her, but her attachment to her family and her reclusive life as a writer were similar to Rossetti's. As *Sonnets from the Portuguese* testify, her notion of God did not involve the renunciation and self-denial which Rossetti used to such great effect in life and art.

106 For commentary on this intriguing painting, see Camille, pp. 117–19.

107 Tertullian, *On Female Dress*, I:1.

108 Edna St Vincent Millay, notebook, n.d., quoted in Milford, pp. 37–8. My omissions in quotations from Edna St Vincent Millay are marked by a three-dot ellipsis in square brackets. Millay's diaries and notebooks have not yet been published. Quotations from Milford and Epstein are credited accordingly.

109 Quoted in Milford, p. 7.

110 Divorce was granted in January 1904 on the grounds of 'cruel and abusive treatment', which Henry Millay did not contest. His brother Bert testified on Cora's behalf. Cora was awarded custody of the three children (Milford, p. 33).

111 Epstein, p. 33. The Millay girls' domestic creativity recalls Sylvia Plath's talent for art and design.

112 Milford, p. 52.

113 Epstein, p. 3.

114 Ibid., p. 4.

115 Milford, p. 52.

116 Ibid., pp. 54, 55.

117 Ibid., p. 57.

118 Ibid.

119 Ibid.

120 Ibid., p. 81; Epstein, p. 67.

121 Letter from O'Keeffe to Millay (Milford, p. 341).

122 Elizabeth Atkins, *Edna St Vincent Millay and Her Times*, New York: Russell & Russell, 1964, p. 70. Millay, p. 127.

123 Ibid., p. 129.

124 Wilson, *Shores*, p. 751.

125 Ibid., p. 754.

126 Wilson, *Twenties*, p. 72.

127 Ibid.

128 Wilson, *Shores*, p. 753.

129 Millay, p. 46.

130 Macdougall, pp. 99–100, note 23.

131 Boyd, pp. 111, 120–1.

132 Ibid., p. 174.

133 Ibid., pp. 41, 46, 41, 42.

134 Millay, p. 141.

135 'Edna St Vincent Millay Reads Her Poems at Literary Institute', *Christian Science Monitor*, n.p., 6 May 1925, quoted in Milford, pp. 271–2.

136 Used by the poet Louise Bogan to describe Millay; see Bogan, p. 154.

137 Epstein, p. 236.

138 Women writers have often been criticised for being too domestic, accessible, intimate and just downright 'female' in their subject matter and approach. Popularity with the reading public can also be a cause for opprobrium and trivialisation. Millay's reputation for sex would not have helped her with the 'serious' male critic. See John Crowe Ransom, 'The Poet as Woman', for a contemporary (male) assessment of Millay's work in which he criticises her for 'lack of intellectual interest' and 'deficiency in masculinity' (p. 98) (John Crowe Ransom, *The World's Body*, New York & London: Charles Scribner's Sons, 1938, pp. 76–110).

139 Millay was aware of some, at least, of her predecessors in the female 'tradition' of love writing: she knew the sonnets of Louise Labé and Elizabeth Barrett. She was also familiar with Marie de France, appearing as Marie at a pageant at Vassar where she recited Marie's lay, *Chaitivel*.

140 Millay, p. 568.

141 Ibid., p. 571.

142 Ibid., p. 601.

143 Jane Stanbrough writes interestingly about Millay's anxiety and vulnerability. See Stanbrough.

144 Millay, p. 631. All quotations from *Fatal Interview* are from Millay, pp. 630–81.

145 Millay, p. 671. Her ellipsis.

146 Millay, pp. 606–22.

147 Ibid., p. 160.

148 From 'Thoughts of any Poet at a Family Reunion', quoted in Milford, p. 10.

149 Millay, p. 34.

150 Milford, pp. 120–1.

151 Millay, p. 77.

PART 5   Dreams and Reality: Fictions of Love

Bibliography

Novels and short stories with dates of first publication (the majority are still in print, available in a variety of editions):

Alcott, Louisa May, *Behind a Mask* (1866, under the pseudonym A. M. Barnard)

——, *Good Wives* (1869, originally published as the second part of *Little Women*)

——, *Jo's Boys* (1886)

——, *Little Men* (1871)

——, *Little Women* (1868)

——, *Moods* (1864)

——, *Work* (1873)

Austen, Jane, *Emma* (1815)

——, 'Lady Susan' (1871)

——, *Mansfield Park* (1814)

——, *Northanger Abbey* (1817, dated 1818)

——, *Persuasion* (1817, dated 1818)

——, *Pride and Prejudice* (1813)

——, *Sense and Sensibility* (1811)

Brontë, Charlotte, *Jane Eyre* (1847)

——, *Villette* (1853)

Brontë, Emily, *Wuthering Heights* (1847)

Browning, Elizabeth Barrett, *Aurora Leigh* (1857)

Bunyan, John, *The Pilgrim's Progress* (1678)

Byatt, A. S., *Possession: A Romance* (1990)

Cambridge, Elizabeth, *Hostages to Fortune* (1933)

Chopin, Kate, *The Awakening* (1899)

De Staël, Madame, *Corinne, or Italy* (1807)

Du Maurier, Daphne, *Rebecca* (1938)

Eliot, George, *Adam Bede* (1859)

——, *Daniel Deronda* (1876)

——, *Middlemarch* (1871)

——, *The Mill on the Floss* (1860)

Franklin, Miles, *My Brilliant Career* (1901)

Gaskell, Mrs, *Mary Barton* (1848)

——, *Ruth* (1853)

Glaspell, Susan, *Brook Evans* (1928)
——, *Fidelity* (1915)
Heyer, Georgette, *Arabella* (1949)
——, *Devil's Cub* (1932)
——, *Frederica* (1965)
——, *The Grand Sophy* (1950)
Hull, E. M., *The Sheik* (1919)
James, Henry, *The Portrait of a Lady* (1881)
James, P. D., *Death in Holy Orders* (2001)
——, *The Lighthouse* (2005)
——, *The Murder Room* (2003)
Lessing, Doris, *Martha Quest* (1952) (the first of 5 volumes in the *Children of Violence* sequence)
Mitchell, Margaret, *Gone With the Wind* (1936)
Montgomery, L. M., *Anne of Green Gables* (1908)
——, *Anne of Ingleside* (1939)
——, *Anne's House of Dreams* (1917)
——, *The Blue Castle* (1926)
——, *Emily's Quest* (1925)
——, *Rilla of Ingleside* (1920)
Orczy, Baroness, *The Scarlet Pimpernel* (1905)
Paretsky, Sara, *Indemnity Only* (1982) (first of the V. I. Warshawski novels)
Rhys, Jean, *Wide Sargasso Sea* (1966)
Richardson, Samuel, *Clarissa* (1748)
Sayers, Dorothy L., *Busman's Honeymoon* (1937)
——, *Gaudy Night* (1935)
——, *Have His Carcase* (1932)
——, *Strong Poison* (1930)
Schreiner, Olive, *The Story of an African Farm* (1883)
Smith, Dodie, *I Capture the Castle* (1949)
Taylor, Elizabeth, *Palladian* (1946)
Von Arnim, Elizabeth, *Vera* (1921)
Wharton, Edith, *The House of Mirth* (1905)
Woolf, Virginia, *Night and Day* (1919)
——, *Orlando* (1928)
——, *To the Lighthouse* (1927)
Young, E. H., *Miss Mole* (1930)

Other references and useful publications:

Alcott, Louisa May (Doris Lessing, foreword), *Behind a Mask or A Woman's Power*, London: Hesperus Classics, 2004

——— (Madeleine Stern, ed. and intro.), *Louisa May Alcott Unmasked: Collected Thrillers*, Boston: Northeastern University Press, 1995

——— (Sarah Elbert, ed. and intro.), *Moods*, New Brunswick, New Jersey and London: Rutgers University Press, 1991

Alexander, Christine, *The Early Writings of Charlotte Brontë*, Oxford: Basil Blackwell, 1983

Alexander, Christine and Jane Sellars, *The art of the Brontës*, Cambridge: Cambridge University Press, 1995

Allott, Miriam (ed.), *The Brontës: The Critical Heritage*, London and Boston: Routledge & Kegan Paul, 1974

Austen, Jane (R. W. Chapman, ed.), *Minor Works*, Vol. VI of *The Works of Jane Austen*, London, New York and Toronto: Oxford University Press, revised edition, 1963

Barker, Juliet, *The Brontës*, London: Weidenfeld & Nicolson, 1994

Battiscombe, Georgina, *Christina Rossetti: A Divided Life*, London: Constable, 1981

Beauman, Nicola, *A Very Great Profession: The Woman's Novel 1914–39*, London: Virago, 1983

Berry, Paul and Mark Bostridge, *Vera Brittain: A Life*, London: Chatto & Windus, 1995

Cambridge, Elizabeth, *Hostages to Fortune*, London: Jonathan Cape, 1933, reprinted London: Persephone Books, 2003

Eliot, George (Barbara Hardy, ed. and intro.), *Daniel Deronda*, Harmondsworth: Penguin Books, 1986

Fairweather, Maria, *Madame de Staël*, London: Constable, 2005

Franklin, Miles (Carmen Callil, new intro.), *My Brilliant Career*, London: Virago, 1980

Gordon, Lyndall, *A Private Life of Henry James: Two Women and His Art*, London: Chatto & Windus, 1998

———, *Charlotte Brontë: A Passionate Life*, London: Chatto & Windus, 1994

———, *Mary Wollstonecraft: A New Genus*, London: Little, Brown, 2005

Hackett, Helen, *Women and Romance Fiction in the English Renaissance*, Cambridge: Cambridge University Press, 2000

Honan, Park, *Jane Austen: Her Life*, London: Weidenfeld & Nicolson, 1988

Jack, Belinda, *George Sand: A Woman's Life Writ Large*, London: Chatto & Windus, 1999

James, Henry, *The Portrait of a Lady*, Harmondsworth: Penguin Books, 1966

Karlin, Daniel (ed.), *Robert Browning and Elizabeth Barrett: The Courtship Correspondence 1845–1846*, Oxford: Clarendon Press, 1989

Kooistra, Lorraine Janzen, *Christina Rossetti and Illustration: A Publishing History*, Athens: Ohio University Press, 2002

Le Faye, Deidre (collected and ed.), *Jane Austen's Letters*, Oxford and New York: Oxford University Press, new edition 1996

Leider, Emily W., *Dark Lover: The Life and Death of Rudolph Valentino*, London: Faber & Faber, 2003

Marsh, Jan, *Christina Rossetti: A Literary Biography*, London: Jonathan Cape, 1994

Menon, Patricia, *Austen, Eliot, Charlotte Brontë and the Mentor-Lover*, Hampshire and New York: Palgrave Macmillan, 2003

Miller, Lucasta, *The Brontë Myth*, London: Jonathan Cape, 2001

Moers, Ellen, *Literary Women*, London: Women's Press, 1978

Nightingale, Florence, 'Cassandra', Appendix I of Ray Strachey, *'The Cause': A Short History of the Women's Movement in Great Britain*, London: G. Bell, 1928

Perry, Ruth, *Novel Relations: The Transformation of Kinship in English Literature and Culture, 1748–1818*, Cambridge: Cambridge University Press, 2004

Pyron, Darden Asbury, *Southern Daughter: The life of Margaret Mitchell and the making of Gone With the Wind*, Athens, Georgia: Hill Street Press, 2004

Rossetti, Christina, 'Goblin Market' in R. W. Crump (ed.), *The Complete Poems of Christina Rossetti*, Vol. 1, Baton Rouge and London: Louisiana State University Press, 1979

—— (Jan Marsh, ed.), *Poems and Prose*, London: J. M. Dent; Vermont: Charles E. Tuttle, Everyman edition, 1994

Rubio, Mary and Elizabeth Waterston (eds), *The Selected Journals of L. M. Montgomery, Vol. 1: 1889–1910*, Toronto: Oxford University Press, 1985

Rubio, Mary and Elizabeth Waterston, *Writing a Life: L. M. Montgomery*, Ontario: ECW Press, 1995

Satrapi, Marjane, *Embroideries*, London: Jonathan Cape, 2005

Showalter, Elaine, *A Literature of Their Own: British Women Novelists from Brontë to Lessing*, London: Virago Press, 1982 revised edition

Smith, Margaret (ed.), *The Letters of Charlotte Brontë*, Vol. 1, 1829–1847, Oxford: Clarendon Press, 1995

——, *The Letters of Charlotte Brontë*, Vol. 2, 1848–1851, Oxford: Clarendon Press, 2000

Stern, Madeleine B., *Louisa May Alcott: A Biography*, Boston: Northeastern University Press, 1999 (originally published in 1950)

Stevens, Joan (ed.), *Mary Taylor: Friend of Charlotte Brontë: Letters from New Zealand and Elsewhere*, Dunedin: Auckland University Press/ Oxford University Press, 1972

Stoneman, Patsy, *Brontë Transformations*: *The Cultural Dissemination of* Jane Eyre *and* Wuthering Heights, Hemel Hempstead: Prentice Hall/ Harvester Wheatsheaf, 1996

Strachey, Ray, *'The Cause': A Short History of the Women's Movement in Great Britain*, London: G. Bell, 1928

Tatar, Maria (ed. and intro.), *The Annotated Classic Fairy Tales*, New York and London: W. W. Norton, 2002

Tatar, Maria, *Secrets beyond the Door: The Story of Bluebeard and His Wives*, Princeton and Oxford: Princeton University Press, 2004

Thirlwell, Angela, *William and Lucy: The Other Rossettis*, New Haven and London: Yale University Press, 2003

Todd, Janet (ed.), *The Collected Letters of Mary Wollstonecraft*, London: Allen Lane, 2003

Tomalin, Claire, *Jane Austen: A Life*, London: Viking, 1997

Uglow, Jenny, *Elizabeth Gaskell: A Habit of Stories*, London and Boston: Faber & Faber, 1993

Wardle, Ralph M. (ed.), *Collected Letters of Mary Wollstonecraft*, Ithaca and London: Cornell University Press, 1979

——, *Godwin & Mary: Letters of William Godwin and Mary Wollstonecraft*, Lawrence, Kansas: University of Kansas Press, 1966; London: Constable, 1967

Wollstonecraft, Mary and William Godwin (Richard Holmes, intro. and notes), *A Short Residence in Sweden, Norway and Denmark* and *Memoirs of the Author of 'The Rights of Woman'*, Harmondsworth: Penguin Books, 1987

Woolf, Virginia (Michèle Barrett, intro.), *Women & Writing*, London: Women's Press, 1979

Woolson, Constance Fenimore (Joan Myers Weimer, ed. and intro.), *Women Artists, Women Exiles: 'Miss Grief' and Other Stories*, New Brunswick and London: Rutgers University Press, 1988

Wyndham, Francis and Diana Melly (eds), *Jean Rhys Letters, 1931–1966*, London: André Deutsch, 1984

Notes

1 James, Preface, pp. x–xi.

2 Eliot, p. 160. In his Preface, p. xi, James misquotes Eliot (an instance when he was less than precise about the use of someone else's language), writing, 'In these frail vessels is borne onward through the ages the treasure of human affection.'

3 Woolf, 'Professions for Women', p. 61.

4 This early novel was reworked and published as *Sense and Sensibility*.

5 Gordon, *Mary Wollstonecraft*, offers a considered and perceptive analysis of Mary Wollstonecraft's relationships with men.

6 Letter 124, *c.* December 1793, Wardle, *Collected Letters*, pp. 238–9.

7 Letter 122, *c.* September 1793, ibid., p. 236.

8 Godwin, *Memoirs*, in Wollstonecraft and Godwin, p. 258; Letter 251, 4 October 1796, Wardle, *Collected Letters*, p. 356.

9 Letter 243, 15 September 1796, ibid., p. 351.

10 Letter 250, 30 September 1796, ibid., pp. 355–6.

11 Letter 13, 17 August 1796, Wardle, *Godwin & Mary*, p. 17.

12 Letter 17, 19 August 1796, ibid., pp. 20–1.

13 Letter 18, 19 August 1796, ibid., p. 22.

14 Letter 258, 10 November 1796, Wardle, *Collected Letters*, p. 360.

15 Letter 251, 4 October 1796, ibid., p. 357; letter 259, 13 November 1796, ibid., p. 360.

16 Mary Russell Mitford, letter to Sir William Elford, December 1814, Tomalin, p. 312, note 13.

17 Perry, pp. 286–7.

18 *Mansfield Park*, Vol. 3, Ch. 4.

19 Letter 109, Le Faye, pp. 279–80, for these quotations.

20 Letter 114, ibid., p. 286.

21 For the implications of the word 'bloom' applied to a young woman in English fiction, see Amy M. King, *Bloom: The Botanical Vernacular in the English Novel*, Oxford: Oxford University Press, 2003.

22 *Persuasion*, Vol. 1, Ch. 4.

23 Ibid., Vol. 11, Ch. 11.

24 To James Edward Austen, December 1816, Letter 146, Le Faye, p. 323.

25 18 January 1848, 12 January 1848, Smith, Vol. 2, pp. 14, 10.

26 Mary Taylor, letters to Mrs Gaskell, Stevens, Appendix B, pp. 158, 163.

27 Franklin, (Author's) Introduction.

28 Robert Southey to Charlotte

Brontë, 12 March 1837, Smith, Vol. 1, pp. 166–7.

29 In her autobiographical fragment 'Cassandra' (1852), Nightingale expressed her frustration at the limitations on women: 'Passion, intellect, moral activity—these three have never been satisfied in a woman' (Strachey, Appendix I, p. 398). After her return from the Crimea, she took to her bed for long periods, apparently suffering from ill health, a form of passive resistance common among Victorian women. Emily Dickinson dressed in the white garments of a virgin or novice and led an increasingly reclusive life, which allowed her to write literally hundreds of poems, many of which were not published in her lifetime.

30 Charlotte's letter to Aunt Branwell, 29 September 1841, Smith, Vol. 1, p. 268.

31 Miller, p. 114.

32 Letter to Constantin Heger, 8 January 1845, Smith, Vol. 1, p. 379.

33 Ibid., 18 November 1845, ibid., p. 436.

34 *Jane Eyre*, Ch. 23.

35 Writing to Marianne in May–June 1854, Mrs Gaskell mentioned, 'I am afraid I never told you that I did not mind your reading Jane Eyre' (J. A. V. Chapple and Arthur Pollard (eds), *The Letters of Mrs Gaskell*, Manchester: Manchester University Press, 1966; Mandolin paperback edition, n.d., Letter 198a, p. 860.

36 Allott, pp. 68–9.

37 Ibid., pp. 70, 82.

38 Ibid., p. 85.

39 Letter to Sir William Elford, December 1814, Tomalin, p. 312, note 13.

40 *Middlemarch*, Book 8, Ch. 80.

41 Ibid., Finale.

42 Jan Marsh hypothesises that Christina may have been sexually abused by her father (Marsh, pp. 258–64), but this can only be speculation until real evidence emerges. As Marsh acknowledges, there may have been other reasons for Rossetti's teenage break-down. Elizabeth Barrett suffered from a mysterious and debilitating illness when in her teens. Perhaps both young women felt overwhelmed by the conflict between their gifts as writers and the docile lives imposed on girls from puberty. Christina's High Anglican leanings would also have taken their toll. As her semi-autobiographical story 'Maude' indicates, the longing to excel could traumatise a girl brought up on religious ideals of female self-suppression and obedience. Sexuality, with its implications

of loss of control and forbidden feelings, would have been similarly fraught.

43 W. M. Rossetti (ed.), *The Poetical Works of Christina Georgina Rossetti with Memoir and Notes*, London: Macmillan, 1904, p. 459.

44 See Kooistra for history of illustrations of Rossetti's poetry, prose and works for children.

45 *Good Wives*, Ch. 23.

46 All quotations from *Behind a Mask*, Ch. 1.

47 Maria Tatar reads *The Blue Castle* as a variant on the Bluebeard story: see Tatar, *Secrets*, pp. 164–7.

48 *Anne of the Island*, Ch. XLI.

49 *Jane of Lantern Hill*, Ch. XLII.

50 *Emily's Quest*, Ch. XXVII.

51 *Rilla of Ingleside*, Ch. XXXV.

52 Rubio and Waterston, *Journals*, p. 203.

53 Ibid., pp. 208–9.

54 Ibid., p. 209.

55 Ibid., pp. 209–10.

56 Ibid., p. 213.

57 Ibid., p. 217.

58 Ibid., p. 227.

59 Ibid., p. 241.

60 Ibid., p. 204.

61 *The Story of an African Farm*, Part 2, Ch. 21.

62 Rubio and Waterston, *Journals*, p. 392.

63 *Jo's Boys*, Ch. 3.

64 *Hostages to Fortune*, Ch. 2.

65 Moers, p. 173.

66 Ibid., pp. 173–4.

67 Uglow, p. 127.

68 See *Daniel Deronda*, Book 7, Ch. 51, for this meeting.

69 Karlin, p. 28.

70 *Emily's Quest*, Ch. VI.

71 Woolson, p. 233.

72 Thirlwell, pp. 265–6.

73 For 'Miss Woolson' see Woolson, pp. 270–9; 'figure in the carpet', Gordon, *A Private Life of Henry James*, p. 216; for James's denigration of Woolson in his article see ibid., pp. 213–16.

74 Edna's indifference to conventional moral values was both innovative and shocking. The writer Susan Glaspell's novels *Fidelity* (1915) and *Brook Evans* (1928) similarly dealt with a woman's attempt to be true to her feelings, but were better received, partly because of changes in social mores, but also, probably, because of Glaspell's attempt to grapple with concepts of honesty and integrity in love. These two novels have been republished by Persephone Books, London: *Fidelity* in 1999, *Brook Evans* in 2001.

75 *The Awakening*, Ch. XXXIX.

76 There have been many loving, creative partnerships between women. Lillian Faderman's *Surpassing the Love of Men: Romantic Friendship and Love between Women from the Renaissance to the Present*, New

York: William Morrow, 1981, remains a classic introduction to the history of women loving women.

Like Woolf, Vera Brittain attempted to establish a working partnership with her husband, George Catlin, a 'semi-detached' marriage in which both partners had freedom to pursue their careers. This was not always a happy arrangement, and it is interesting that Brittain's greatest success at maintaining an enabling partnership was with her friend, the writer Winifred Holtby. See Berry and Bostridge.

77 *Northanger Abbey*, Vol. 2, Ch. 15.
78 *Emma*, Vol. 3, Ch. 13.
79 Quotations from *The Scarlet Pimpernel*, Ch. vi.
80 *Jane Eyre*, Ch. 12.
81 Ibid., Ch. 14.
82 14 August 1848, Smith, Vol. 2, p. 99.
83 Ibid.
84 Republished in Alcott, *Moods*, p. 220.
85 See Leider, pp. 152–72, for Valentino's role in *The Sheik*.
86 *The Sheik*, Ch. 2.
87 Leider, pp. 165–6.
88 *The Sheik*, Ch. 10.
89 Ibid., Ch. 9.
90 For Mitchell's postbag, see Pyron, pp. 338–40.

PART 6   Sylvia Plath: Passion and Poetry

Bibliography

Alexander, Paul, *Ariel Ascending: Writings about Sylvia Plath*, New York: Harper & Row, 1985
——, *Rough Magic: A Biography of Sylvia Plath*, New York: Da Capo Press, 1999
Alvarez, Al, *The Savage God: A Study of Suicide*, London: Weidenfeld & Nicolson, 1971; London: Bloomsbury, paperback edition, 2002
——, *Where Did It All Go Right?*, London: Richard Cohen Books, 1999
Bayley, John, *Iris: A Memoir of Iris Murdoch*, London: Duckworth, 1998
Becker, Jillian, *Giving Up: The Last Days of Sylvia Plath*, London: Ferrington, 2002
Beer, Gillian, 'Beyond determinism: George Eliot and Virginia Woolf', in Mary Jacobus (ed.), *Women Writing and Writing about Women*, London and Sydney: Croom Helm; New Jersey: Barnes & Noble, 1979, 1984 reprint
Brain, Tracy, *The Other Sylvia Plath*, Harlow: Longman, 2001

Browning, Robert, *Balaustion's Adventure*, London: Smith, Elder, second edition, 1872

Butscher, Edward (ed.), *Sylvia Plath: The Woman and the Work*, New York: Dodd, Mead, 1977; London: Peter Owen, 1979

Byatt, A. S., Introduction to *The Shadow of the Sun: A Novel*, London: Vintage, 1991

Campbell, Wendy: 'Remembering Sylvia', in Newman, 1970

Carter, Angela, *Burning Your Boats: Collected Short Stories*, London: Vintage, 1996

Cleverdon, Douglas, 'On *Three Women*', in Newman, 1970

Dante Alighieri (Barbara Reynolds, trans.), *La Vita Nuova*, Harmondsworth: Penguin, 1969

Dawson, Jennifer, *The Ha-Ha*, London: Anthony Blond, 1961

Dinnage, Rosemary, *Alone! Alone! Lives of Some Outsider Women*, New York: New York Review of Books, 2004

Eliot, George (Barbara Hardy, ed. and intro.), *Daniel Deronda*, Harmondsworth: Penguin Books, 1986

Fainlight, Ruth, 'Sylvia and Jane: Women on the verge of fame and family', in *The Times Literary Supplement*, 12 December 2003

Feinstein, Elaine, *Ted Hughes: The Life of a Poet*, London: Weidenfeld & Nicolson, 2001

Fenton, James, 'Lady Lazarus', in *New York Review of Books*, 29 May 1997

Friedan, Betty, *The Feminine Mystique*, Harmondsworth: Penguin, 1965

Gibson, James (ed.), *The Complete Poems of Thomas Hardy*, London and Basingstoke: Macmillan, 1976; Papermac edition, 1981

Gilbert, Sandra M., 'A Fine, White Flying Myth: The Life/Work of Sylvia Plath', in Sandra M. Gilbert and Susan Gubar (eds), *Shakespeare's Sisters: Feminist Essays on Women Poets*, Bloomington: Indiana University Press, 1979

Graves, Robert, *The White Goddess: A historical grammar of poetic myth*, amended and enlarged edition, London: Faber & Faber, 1961

Hughes, Ted, Euripides, *Alcestis*, in a new version by Ted Hughes, London: Faber & Faber, 1999

——, *Birthday Letters*, London: Faber & Faber, 1998

——, 'The chronological order of Sylvia Plath's poems', in Newman, 1970

—— (Paul Keegan, ed.), *Collected Poems*, London: Faber & Faber, 2003

——, *The Coming of the Kings and Other Plays*, London: Faber & Faber, 1970

—— (William Scammell, ed.), *Winter Pollen: Occasional Prose*, London: Faber & Faber, 1994; paperback edition, 1995

——, 'The Wound', in *Difficulties of a Bridegroom: Collected Short Stories*, London: Faber & Faber, 1995

Johnson, Thomas H. (ed.), *The Complete Poems of Emily Dickinson*, London: Faber & Faber, 1970; paperback edition, 1975

Kane, Sarah, *Complete Plays*, London: Methuen, 2001

Kopp, Jane Baltzell, '"Gone, Very Gone Youth": Sylvia Plath at Cambridge', in Butscher, 1979

Kroll, Judith, *Chapters in a Mythology: The Poetry of Sylvia Plath*, New York: Harper & Row, 1976

Krook, Dorothea, 'Recollections of Sylvia Plath', in Butscher, 1977

Kukil, Karen V. (ed.), *The Journals of Sylvia Plath 1950–1962*, London: Faber & Faber, 2000

Malcolm, Janet, *The Silent Woman: Sylvia Plath and Ted Hughes*, London: Picador, 1994

McCullough, Frances (ed., Ted Hughes, consulting ed. and foreword), *The Journals of Sylvia Plath*, New York: Ballantine Books, 1983

Middlebrook, Diane Wood, *Anne Sexton: A Biography*, London: Virago Press, 1991

——, *Her Husband: Hughes and Plath – A Marriage*, New York: Viking Penguin, 2003

Millgate, Michael, *Thomas Hardy: A Biography*, Oxford: Clarendon Press, 1992

Murry, J. Middleton, *Journal of Katherine Mansfield*, definitive edition, London: Constable, 1954

Myers, Lucas, 'Ah, Youth . . . Ted Hughes and Sylvia Plath at Cambridge and After', Appendix 1, in Stevenson, 1989

——, *Crow Steered Bergs Appeared: A Memoir of Ted Hughes and Sylvia Plath*, Sewanee, Tennessee: Proctor's Hall Press, 2001

Negev, Eilat, 'My life with Sylvia Plath, by Ted Hughes', *Daily Telegraph*, 31 October 1998

Neville-Sington, Pamela, *Robert Browning: A Life After Death*, London: Weidenfeld & Nicolson, 2004

Newman, Charles (ed.), *The art of Sylvia Plath: A Symposium*, London: Faber & Faber, 1970

Orr, Peter, 'Sylvia Plath', in Peter Orr (ed.), *The Poet Speaks: Interviews with Contemporary Poets*, London: Routledge & Kegan Paul, 1966

Plath, Aurelia S., 'Letter Written in the Actuality of Spring', in Alexander, 1985

Plath, Sylvia, *Ariel*, London: Faber & Faber, 1965

—— (Frieda Hughes, foreword), *Ariel: The Restored Edition*, London: Faber & Faber, 2004

——, *The Bell Jar*, London: William Heinemann, 1963; London: Faber & Faber, paperback edition, 1966

—— (Ted Hughes, ed.), *Collected Poems*, London: Faber & Faber, 1981

——, *Johnny Panic and the Bible of Dreams and other prose writings*, London: Faber & Faber, 1977; paperback edition, 1979

—— (Aurelia Schober Plath, ed. with commentary), *Letters Home: Correspondence 1950–1963*, London: Faber & Faber, 1976; paperback edition, 1978

Pollock, Mary Sanders, *Elizabeth Barrett and Robert Browning: A Creative Partnership*, Hampshire: Ashgate, 2003

Radice, Betty (trans. and intro.), *The Letters of Abelard and Heloise*, Harmondsworth: Penguin Books, 1974

Radin, Grace, *Virginia Woolf's* The Years: *The Evolution of a Novel*, Knoxville: University of Tennessee Press, 1981

Rego, Paula, *Jane Eyre: A suite of 25 lithographs*, Marlborough Graphics Catalogue No. 581, London: Marlborough Graphics, n.d.

Rigney, Barbara Hill, *Madness and Sexual Politics in the Feminist Novel*, London and Wisconsin: University of Wisconsin Press, 1978

Roche, Clarissa, 'Sylvia Plath: Vignettes from England', in Butscher, 1977

Rose, Jacqueline, *The Haunting of Sylvia Plath*, London: Virago Press, 1991

——, 'Sylvia Plath – Again', in *On Not Being Able to Sleep: Psychoanalysis and the Modern World*, London: Chatto & Windus, 2003

Sagar, Keith (ed.), *The Achievement of Ted Hughes*, Manchester: Manchester University Press, 1983

Sexton, Anne, 'The Barfly Ought to Sing', in Alexander, 1985

Showalter, Elaine, *The Female Malady: Women, Madness and English Culture, 1830–1980*, London: Virago Press, 1987

Sigmund, Elizabeth, 'Sylvia in Devon: 1962', in Butscher, 1977

Steiner, Nancy Hunter, *A Closer Look at Ariel: a memory of Sylvia Plath*, London: Faber & Faber, 1974

Stevenson, Anne, *Bitter Fame: A Life of Sylvia Plath*, London: Viking, 1989

——, *Poems 1955–2005*, Northumberland: Bloodaxe Books, 2004

——, 'Sylvia Plath's Word Games', in *Poetry Review*, Vol. 86, No. 4, Winter 1996–7, pp. 28–34

——, 'Writing as a Woman', in Mary Jacobus (ed.), *Women Writing and Writing about Women*, London and Sydney: Croom Helm; New Jersey: Barnes & Noble, 1979, 1984 reprint

Tennant, Emma, *Burnt Diaries*, Edinburgh: Canongate Books, 1999

Tomalin, Claire, *Several Strangers: Writing from Three Decades*, Harmondsworth: Viking Penguin, 1999

Wagner, Erica, *Ariel's Gift: A Commentary on* Birthday Letters *by Ted Hughes*, London: Faber & Faber, 2000

Wagner-Martin, Linda, *Sylvia Plath: A Biography*, London: Chatto & Windus, 1988

Warner, Marina, *Signs & Wonders: Essays on Literature and Culture*, London: Chatto & Windus, 2003

Weldon, Fay, *Auto da Fay*, London: Flamingo, 2002

Wind, Edgar, *Pagan Mysteries in the Renaissance*, Oxford: Oxford University Press paperback edition, 1980

BBC Radio

Two of a Kind: Poets in Partnership, Ted Hughes and Sylvia Plath, interview with Owen Leeming, recorded 18 January 1961

Notes

1   22 January 1953, Kukil, p. 164.
2   Beer, p. 80.
3   11 May 1958, Kukil, p. 381.
4   Wind, pp. 173–4.; Dante, *Paradiso*, I, 19–21.
5   Kukil, p. 63.
6   Broadcast by the BBC in 1962. See Plath, *Johnny Panic*, p. 120.
7   Plath, *The Bell Jar*, p. 167. See, too, 'Suicide off Egg Rock', 1959, in Plath, *Collected Poems*, p. 115: 'his blood beating the old tattoo / I am, I am, I am.'
8   Kukil, p. 173.
9   'Medusa', Plath, *Collected Poems*, p. 226.
10   Kukil, p. 447.
11   *Two of a Kind.*
12   'The Disquieting Muses', Plath, *Collected Poems*, p. 75.
13   Aurelia Plath, 'Letter Written in the Actuality of Spring', p. 215.
14   A phrase Aurelia borrows from Richard Wilbur, ibid., pp. 214–15.
15   Plath, *Letters Home*, p. 4. Aurelia recalls that the first English words she learnt (through hearing them so often at school) were 'Shut up!'. Greeting her father proudly and uncomprehendingly with this phrase, she received her first and only spanking.
16   Ibid., p. 5.
17   Ibid., p. 393.
18   Kukil, p. 381.
19   Plath, *Letters Home*, p. 10.
20   Ibid., p. 13.
21   Ibid.
22   Ibid., p. 12.
23   Ibid., p. 13.
24   The struggle over how and when a baby should be fed

is fictionalised in Mary McCarthy's *The Group* (1963), about the lives and loves of a group of Vassar graduates in the 1930s.

25 *Two of a Kind*.
26 Kukil, p. 64.
27 Rego, lithograph 7.
28 Plath, *Letters Home*, p. 13.
29 'God Help the Wolf after Whom the Dogs Do Not Bark', Hughes, *Birthday Letters*, pp. 26–7.
30 Plath, *Johnny Panic*, p. 259.
31 Ibid., p. 265.
32 Ibid., p. 266.
33 Ibid., p. 124.
34 Kukil, p. 446.
35 'Ocean 1212-W', Plath, *Johnny Panic*, p. 118.
36 Plath, *Letters Home*, p. 32.
37 Ibid., p. 31.
38 Letter to Warren and Maggie Plath, ibid., p. 468.
39 Ibid., p. 32.
40 Kukil, p. 449.
41 Plath, *Letters Home*, p. 32.
42 Kukil, p. 449.
43 'Medusa', Plath, *Collected Poems*, p. 226.
44 Kukil, p. 165.
45 Steiner, pp. 18–19.
46 Friedan, p. 13.
47 Ibid., p. 14.
48 Letter to Aurelia Plath, Plath, *Letters Home*, p. 219.
49 Plath, *Collected Poems*, pp. 31–2.
50 Byatt, p. ix.
51 Plath, *Letters Home*, p. 38.

52 Stevenson, *Correspondences*, in *Poems*, p. 243.
53 Eliot, p. 691.
54 See, for example, Friedan, p. 17.
55 The prevalence of the Virgin Mary, well into the twentieth century, as a subconscious role model for even non-Catholic women is striking. What finally tips Kathy Chattle into madness is seeing a 'worm-eaten' statue of the Virgin Mary, with a headless baby Jesus, as Kathy wanders around New York, savouring her temporary escape from husband and child. The Madonna's gaze of 'perpetual suffering' pierces her 'like a blade', and she wakes from a blackout to find herself in a mental ward, deprived of her wedding ring. Stevenson's symbolism of the headless child and the appropriated ring confirm the hopelessness of Kathy's position. A child without a head cannot cry (therefore this Madonna can afford to be compliant). A 'mad' woman has no status: even her wedding ring, her entrée into society, is removed (Stevenson, *Correspondences*, in *Poems*, pp. 242–3).
56 'your side of town', Kukil, p. 36: the careless comment from the boy who drives Plath on a date in his father's 'latest chromium-plated convertible'.

57 Ibid., p. 13.
58 Typescript of Woolf's speech, 'Professions for Women', delivered to the London and National Society for Women's Service, 21 January 1931, see Radin, p. 7.
59 McCullough, p. xii.
60 Dinnage, p. 267.
61 Kukil, p. 8.
62 Ibid., pp. 10–11.
63 Ibid., p. 13. Plath's choice of the pseudonym Emile was based on Otto's second name (Plath, *Letters Home*, pp. 58–9). Discussing the sexual mores of American teenagers, Anne Stevenson commented, 'Middle-class teenage Americans in the 1950s subscribed to an amazing code of sexual frustration. Everything was permissible to girls in the way of intimacy except the one thing such intimacies were intended to bring about' (*Bitter Fame*, p. 19).
64 Kukil, pp. 14–15. Plath was quoting what her confidant Eddie Cohen had said in one of his letters.
65 Ibid., p. 20.
66 Ibid., p. 21.
67 Ibid., p. 9.
68 Ibid., pp. 30–1.
69 Ibid., pp. 31, 30.
70 Ibid., p. 31.
71 Ibid., p. 37.
72 Ibid.
73 Ibid., pp. 40–3.
74 Ibid., p. 36.
75 Ibid., p. 54.
76 Ibid., pp. 173, 88, 93.
77 Ibid., p. 83.
78 Ibid., pp. 55–6.
79 See, for example, ibid., p. 107, where Plath quotes Norton's anxiety that wife- and motherhood would prevent her painting and writing as much as she would like.
80 Plath, *The Bell Jar*, p. 74.
81 Ibid., pp. 58, 96.
82 Ibid., p. 89.
83 Kukil, pp. 109–11.
84 Plath, *The Bell Jar*, p. 135.
85 Kukil, p. 149.
86 Ibid., p. 151.
87 Gilbert, pp. 246–7.
88 Plath, *The Bell Jar*, p. 80.
89 Ibid., p. 117.
90 Kukil, p. 118.
91 Plath, *Letters Home*, p. 130.
92 Plath, *The Bell Jar*, p. 167; Plath, *Letters Home*, pp. 130–1.
93 See Janet Frame, *Faces in the Water* (1961), Antonia White, *Beyond the Glass* (1954). Plath was reading Jennifer Dawson's novel about mental breakdown, *The Ha-Ha* (1961), just before she died.
94 Plath, *Letters Home*, pp. 131–2.
95 Kane, p. 210.
96 Steiner, p. 33.
97 Ibid., p. 57.
98 Kukil, p. 165.
99 Letter to Aurelia Plath, Plath, *Letters Home*, p. 233.

100 Ibid., pp. 198, 195.
101 Ibid., p. 187.
102 Kukil, p. 199.
103 Ibid. In her poem 'Lady Lazarus' Plath makes a specific connection between her wincing sense of exposure to an unsympathetic crowd and her recall to life, describing the 'peanut-crunching crowd' who gape at the woman's body as it is unwrapped from the grave clothes (Plath, *Collected Poems*, p. 245). I am grateful to Lyndall Gordon for pointing out this connection.
104 Steiner, p. 32.
105 Kukil, p. 171; and see, too, her reservations about Dick Norton, ibid., p. 155, where she equates fragility (being able to be 'masterfully' lifted up) with femininity, and says that 'wearing flat heels always, feeling physically [Dick's] equal in size' disturbed her.
106 Ibid., pp. 198, 200.
107 Ibid., p. 549.
108 Ibid., p. 209.
109 Sylvia to Aurelia Plath, *Letters Home*, p. 233.
110 Hughes, *Birthday Letters*, p. 6.
111 Myers, 'Ah, Youth', p. 312.
112 'Caryatids (2)', *Birthday Letters*, p. 5.
113 'Caryatids (2)', 'Fulbright Scholars', ibid., pp. 5, 3.
114 Kopp, p. 62.
115 Feinstein, p. 37.
116 'The Burnt Fox', in Hughes, *Winter Pollen*, p. 9.
117 Plath's black, sexy, acidic poem 'Zoo Keeper's Wife' (1961) may have been stimulated by Hughes's work experience, as well as Sylvia's and Ted's proximity to Regent's Park Zoo when living in Chalcot Square in north London.
118 'St Botolph's', Hughes, *Birthday Letters*, p. 14.
119 'Visit', ibid., p. 7.
120 Kukil, p. 210.
121 Ibid.
122 Ibid., pp. 211–12.
123 'St Botolph's', Hughes, *Birthday Letters*, p. 15.
124 Kukil, p. 212.
125 Ibid., pp. 208–9.
126 Ibid., p. 212.
127 Ibid., pp. 208–9. Throughout the winter Plath had been visiting a statue in the gardens of Newnham, a bronze boy with a dolphin, which she identified with Sassoon. In the story Dody tells Leonard, a fictionalised version of Hughes, that she has a stone statue to break. When he rises to the challenge and kisses her, the stone boy in the garden cracks into a million splinters and Dody stands, victorious, 'on a dimpled stone arm' ('Stone Boy with Dolphin', Plath, *Johnny Panic*, p. 309).

128 Kukil, p. 212.
129 'St Botolph's', Hughes, *Birthday Letters*, p. 15.
130 'Pursuit', Plath, *Collected Poems*, pp. 22–3.
131 Plath, *Letters Home*, p. 222.
132 Kukil, p. 74.
133 'The Tiger's Bride', Carter, pp. 154–69. Ted Hughes gave his own version of Beauty and the Beast in a play for children, which emphasises the power of tenderness and love. A young girl's 'ailment' is cured by a bear who metamorphoses into a handsome young man ('Beauty and the Beast', Hughes, *The Coming of the Kings*, pp. 61–77).
134 Kukil, pp. 212, 213.
135 Ibid., p. 221.
136 Ibid., p. 553.
137 Ibid., pp. 556–7.
138 Ibid., p. 565.
139 Ibid., p. 564.
140 Ibid., p. 173.
141 Ibid., p. 233.
142 Ibid., pp. 233, 235.
143 Ibid., p. 552.
144 Ibid., pp. 565, 366.
145 '18 Rugby Street', Hughes, *Birthday Letters*, pp. 22–4.
146 Plath, *Letters Home*, p. 233.
147 Kukil, p. 236.
148 Plath, *Letters Home*, p. 240.
149 Ibid., p. 234.
150 *Two of a Kind*.
151 Kukil, p. 366. Plath had recently been reading D. H. Lawrence's short story 'The Man Who Died', with which she closely identified. In a letter to Aurelia she again compared herself to Lazarus (Plath, *Letters Home*, p. 243). The idea of resurrection was very much in her mind that spring.
152 Plath, *Letters Home*, p. 234.
153 Quoted in Feinstein, p. 59.
154 Kopp, p. 75.
155 Becker, p. 27.
156 Myers, 'Ah, Youth', p. 315.
157 Ibid.
158 Plath, *Letters Home*, pp. 243–4.
159 Ibid., p. 250.
160 Ibid., p. 257.
161 Ibid., p. 251.
162 Ibid.
163 Kukil, p. 451.
164 Poem 288, Johnson, p. 133.
165 Becker, pp. 26–7.
166 See, for example, the final lines of '9 Willow Street', Hughes, *Birthday Letters*, p. 74.
167 Letter to Aurelia Plath, Feinstein, p. 60.
168 Ibid., p. 45.
169 Plath, *Letters Home*, p. 264.
170 Krook, p. 55.
171 Feinstein, p. 61.
172 'A Pink Wool Knitted Dress', Hughes, *Birthday Letters*, p. 34.
173 Plath, *Letters Home*, p. 258.
174 'A Pink Wool Knitted Dress', Hughes, *Birthday Letters*, p. 35.
175 Krook, pp. 55–6. Krook's

memoir is worth reading for its alternative portrait of Plath: not as agonised and obsessional, but as a thinker, whose supervisor delighted in their exchange of ideas.

176 Graves, p. 21.

177 For publication of the *Ariel* poems see Frieda Hughes's Foreword to Plath, *Ariel: The Restored Edition*, pp. ix–xvii.

178 Plath writes about the 'Panic Bird' in her journal, see, for example, Kukil, p. 486: 'I feel that this month I have conquered my Panic Bird' (31 May 1959).

179 Manuscript in British Library: Add. 53784, f. 49r and f. 49v.

180 Becker, p. 16.

181 Myers, *Crow Steered*, p. 2.

182 See Negev article. Ted's phrase resonates oddly with Iris Murdoch's description of the effect of Alzheimer's disease on her writing: she said she felt that she was 'sailing into the darkness' (Bayley, p. 179). Her husband John Bayley recorded her words in a memoir, which operated rather like Hughes's *Birthday Letters*: a male writer's version of his wife's life, which she was unable to challenge. Murdoch's darkness was the fog of a disintegrating mind; Hughes's darkness is more suggestive of the primordial void,

tohu-wa-bohu, and the hush of suspense at the beginning of Creation before God said, 'Let there be light.' The idea of singing together in the darkness also recalls Odysseus and his companions singing through a storm at sea to keep up their spirits, or miners stranded in a tunnel under the ground, images that reflect the danger and challenge of exploration and digging deep.

183 Hughes, 'Sylvia Plath and Her Journals', in *Winter Pollen*, p. 180.

184 Kukil, p. 381.

185 'Daddy', Plath, *Collected Poems*, p. 224.

186 'Portraits', Hughes, *Birthday Letters*, p. 104.

187 'The Minotaur', ibid., p. 120.

188 'The Lodger', ibid., p. 126.

189 'The Shot', ibid., p. 17.

190 'The Shot', ibid., p. 17; 'Fishing Bridge', ibid. pp. 87–8.

191 'Remission', ibid., p. 109; 'Flounders', ibid., pp. 65–6.

192 'Ouija', ibid., pp. 55, 56.

193 See Jacqueline Rose, 'Daddy', in *The Haunting of Sylvia Plath*, pp. 205–38.

194 'Sylvia Plath and Her Journals', Hughes, *Winter Pollen*, p. 177.

195 'She faced a task in herself, and her poetry is the record of her progress in the task. The poems are chapters in a

mythology where the plot, seen as a whole and in retrospect, is strong and clear . . .' (Ted Hughes, 'Notes on the Chronological Order of Sylvia Plath's Poems', Newman, p. 187). For a mythological reading of Plath's work see Judith Kroll. In *The Haunting of Sylvia Plath* Jacqueline Rose questions Hughes's editing and interpretation of Plath's work.

196 Millgate, p. 487.
197 'The Voice', Gibson, p. 346.
198 'At Castle Boterel', ibid., p. 352.
199 Millgate, p. 488.
200 Hughes, *Alcestis*, pp. 10–11.
201 See Pollock, pp. 207–16 for *Balaustion's Adventure* and its relation to Browning's poetic dialogue with his wife.
202 Radice, p. 117.
203 Murry, pp. 333–4.
204 Plath, *Letters Home*, p. 468.
205 Kukil, p. 173.
206 Writing about what she calls the 'Ted-Sylvia-Assia saga', Weldon comments that it was 'one of those seminal events which brought forth the fruits of Seventies feminism. That such talented women should die for what – for love? Because that's what they died of, not depression, let alone "born to suicide" as is so often said of Sylvia' (Weldon, pp. 351–2).
207 'Snow Blitz', Plath, *Johnny Panic*, p. 133.
208 Plath, *Letters Home*, p. 468.
209 'Sylvia Plath and Her Journals', Hughes, *Winter Pollen*, p. 189.
210 Ibid., p. 189.
211 Myers, 'Ah, Youth', p. 320.
212 Becker, p. 7.
213 Byatt, pp. xiii, xii.
214 Ibid., pp. xii–xiii.
215 Tomalin, p. 204.
216 Ibid., pp. 204, 205.
217 Fainlight, p. 13.
218 Ibid., p. 14.
219 Kukil, p. 360.
220 Plath, *Collected Poems*, pp. 156–7, 176–87.
221 Quoted in Brain, pp. 6, 5.
222 Ibid., pp. 32–3.
223 Kopp, p. 65.
224 Ibid., p. 63.
225 Campbell, p. 186.

Illustration Acknowledgements

Part title illustrations

1. The dangers of reading romance
   Study for *Paolo and Francesca* by Dante Gabriel Rossetti
   The Trustees of The British Museum, London (ref: PD 1981–11-7–17)
2. Lady Sarashina absorbed in romantic tales
   Illustration to *The Sarashina Diary*, 1704 ed.
3. A young man presents his sweetheart with a comb
   The Walters Art Museum, Baltimore
4. The poet Edna St Vincent Millay
   *Library of Congress, Prints and Photographs Division (ref: LC-G432–
   755-A), Washington D.C. / The Edna St Vincent Millay Society*
5. Gillian Anderson as the elegant Lily Bart
   The Kobal Collection, London (ref: HOU158AH)
6. Sylvia Plath with a typewriter
   *Estate of Sylvia Plath / Mortimer Rare Book Room, Smith College,
   Massachusetts (ref: MRBR SP-39)*

First plate section

Abelard and Heloise in earnest debate
   *Le Roman de la Rose MS 482/665, f. 60v. Musée Condé, Chantilly,
   France / The Bridgeman Art Library, London (ref: CND 69217)*
The separation of Abelard and Heloise
   *The State Hermitage Museum, St Petersburg / AKG Images, London (ref:
   1FK-625-E1)*
The lovers Tristram and Yseult
   The Trustees of The British Museum, London (ref: M&ME 1856, 6–23, 166)
La Vue (Sight) from *The Lady and the Unicorn* tapestries, c. 1484
   *Musée National du Moyen Age, Cluny, Paris / Agence Photographique de la
   Réunion des Musées Nationaux (ref: 05–516340 NU)*

Jupiter castrating Saturn
   Le Roman de la Rose *MS Douce 195, f. 76v. Bodleian Library, University of Oxford, England*
Hope comes to the rescue of the knight Cueur
   Cod. 2597, f. 21v. Austrian National Library, Vienna (ref: E 20704-CD)
Oenone writing to faithless Paris
   MS Fr. 873, f. 27v. Bibliothèque Nationale, Paris
Amalthea, a female scribe
   MS Fr. 12420, f. 36r. Bibliothèque Nationale, Paris
The bustling convent parlour at San Lorenzo, by Petrus van der Aa, from J. G. Graevius, *Thesaurus antiquitatum et historiarum Italiae* (Leiden, 1722), vol. 5, part 2, following page 69
   Biblioteca Nazionale Marciana, Venezia, Italy
Genji talks to Lady Murasaki
   Chester Beatty Library, Dublin / The Bridgeman Art Library, London (ref: CBL 16289)
Genji spies on Utsusemi, from the studio of Tawaraya Sotatsu
   The Rockefeller Plaza, New York / Christie's Images, London (ref: lot no. 97 / sale no. 1353)
A maid brushes a court lady's long black hair
   Tokugawa Art Museum, Nagoya / The Art Archive, London (ref: AA405731)
Michinaga inspects the boats (illustration, c. 1230)
   Fujita Museum of Art, Osaka
Living for a time in a mountain village
   Illustration to *The Sarashina Diary*, 1704 ed.
On a snowy night, Prince Niou carries Ukifune off to the Islet of Oranges
   The Rockefeller Plaza, New York / Christie's Images, London (ref: lot no. 70 / sale no. 1210)

Second plate section

An imaginary 'portrait' of the trobairitz Castelloza
   MS Fr. 12473, f. 110v. Bibliothèque Nationale, Paris
A similar manuscript portrayal of the Countess of Dia
   MS Fr. 854, f. 141r. Bibliothèque Nationale, Paris
Jaufre Rudel expiring in the arms of the Countess of Tripoli
   Chansonier MS Fr. 854, f. 121v. Bibliothèque Nationale, Paris
A *joglaresa*
   St Martin's Codex. MS LAT, 1118, f. 114r. Bibliothèque Nationale, Paris

Marie de France portrayed at work on her *Fables*
   MS Arsenal 3142, f. 256r. Bibliothèque Nationale, Paris
A medieval guide to healthy living (illustration, c. 1285)
   MS Sloane 2435, f. 9v. The British Library, London
The adulterous Lancelot and Guinevere in bed together (illustration,
   c. 1320)
   Add. MS 10293, f. 312v. The British Library, London
Lovers in a garden
   The Victoria & Albert Museum, London (ref: CT39806)
The Duke courts the lady (illustration, c. 1410)
   MS Harley 4431, f. 145. The British Library, London
Christine de Pizan presents a beautifully bound copy of her work
   *MS Harley 4431, f. 3. The British Library, London / The Bridgeman Art
   Library, London (ref: BL 53284)*
A portrait of Anne Boleyn
   Hever Castle, Kent, England
Henry VIII's love note to Anne Boleyn
   King's MS 9, f. 66v. The British Library, London
Anne Boleyn's love note to Henry VIII
   King's MS 9, f. 231v. The British Library, London
Lady Mary Wroth elaborately gowned and holding her archlute (artist
   unknown)
   *By kind permission of Viscount De L'Isle from his private collection at
   Penshurst Place, England*
Her lover, William Herbert, 3rd Earl of Pembroke (after Daniel Mytens)
   The National Portrait Gallery, London (ref: NPG 5560)

Third plate section

The Love Charm
   *Museum der Bildenden Kunste, Germany / The Bridgeman Art Library,
   London (ref: BAL 7946)*
Robert Browning (Michele Gordigiani, 1858)
   The National Portrait Gallery, London (ref: NPG 1898)
Elizabeth Barrett Browning (Michele Gordigiani, 1858)
   The National Portrait Gallery, London (ref: NPG 1899)
Edna St Vincent Millay with Eugen Boissevain and Arthur Ficke
   *Library of Congress, Prints and Photographs Division, Washington D.C. /
   The Edna St Vincent Millay Society*
Edna St Vincent Millay recovering from a serious operation

*Library of Congress, Prints and Photographs Division, Washington D.C. /
The Edna St Vincent Millay Society*

Madame de Staël posing as her heroine Corinne (Firmin Massot, after
Elisabeth Vigée-Le Brun, 1808)

*Château de Coppet, Paris / The Bridgeman Art Library, London (ref: XIR
175927)*

Caricature of George Sand (c.1848)

*Musée de la Ville de Paris, Musée Carnavalet, Paris / The Bridgeman Art
Library (ref: CHT 187791)*

Mrs Dashwood (Gemma Jones) and her three daughters, Elinor (Emma
Thompson), Marianne (Kate Winslet) and Margaret (Emilie François)
(1995)

The Kobal Collection, London (ref: SEN023BV)

Jane Austen's niece, Fanny

The Bridgeman Art Library (ref: XZL 150402)

Charlotte Brontë's 'Woman in leopard fur' (1839)

*The Brontë Society, The Brontë Parsonage Museum, England (ref: BPM
Bonnell 24)*

The first portrait of L. M. Montgomery's popular heroine Anne of Green
Gables

*By kind permission from The L. M. Montgomery Archival and Special
Collections, University of Guelph Library, Canada. 'Anne of Green Gables'
and other indicia of Anne are trademarks of the Anne of Green Gables
Licensing Authority Inc. 'L. M. Montgomery' is a trademark of Heirs of
L. M. Montgomery Inc.*

'White and golden Lizzie stood'

*The Osborne Collection of Early Children's Books / Toronto Public Library,
Canada*

Rudolph Valentino abducts Agnes Eyres

The Kobal Collection, London (ref: SHE016CA)

Richard E. Grant as Sir Percy Blakeney (1999)

BBC, London

Judy Davis as Sybylla Melvyn

The Kobal Collection, London (ref: MYB006AL)

Vita Sackville-West (photo by Hoppé)

Corbis (ref: CA001505)

Clark Gable and Vivien Leigh

The Kobal Collection, London (ref: GON004PG)

Laurence Olivier and Joan Fontaine (1940)

The Kobal Collection, London (ref: REB003AE)

Sylvia Plath with Joan Cantor (photo by Mrs Cantor)
  Mortimer Rare Book Room, Smith College, Massachusetts (ref: MRBR SP-7)
Sylvia Plath interviewing Elizabeth Bowen (photo by James F. Coyne)
  James F. Coyne / Black Star / Mortimer Rare Book Room, Smith College, Massachusetts (ref: MRBR SP-11–5)
'Pleasing Mr Rochester' (2002)
  Reproduced with kind permission from Paula Rego. Photo courtesy Marlborough Fine Art Ltd, London
Sylvia Plath and Ted Hughes (photo by Walter Farrar)
  Estate of Ted Hughes / Mortimer Rare Book Room, Smith College, Massachusetts (ref: MRBR SP-17)
Sylvia Plath with Frieda (photo by Susan O'Neill-Roe)
  Susan O'Neill-Roe / The Lilly Library, Indiana University, Bloomington, Indiana

Author Acknowledgements

In researching this book, I benefited greatly from the book and manuscript resources of the British Library. The London Library was invaluable for the breadth of its collection and its generous lending policy. I also made good use of the medieval and American literature collections at the University of London Library in Senate House. Many thanks to the staff at all these institutions for their expertise and advice. I am grateful to Elizabeth Crawford for her skill in obtaining second-hand and out-of-print books for my personal library. Two exemplary local bookshops, Dulwich Books and Village Books, Dulwich, supplied many wants. My thanks to both. I am indebted to friends willing to report on work in progress. Hilary Laurie cast an acute editorial eye over drafts of parts 2 and 3. The biographer Lyndall Gordon read the final section with close attention, providing commentary and encouragement at a crucial stage. To both these expert readers, many thanks. My agent Derek Johns at A. P. Watt read the manuscript in several phases, responding with understanding and enthusiasm. I am deeply grateful for his continued interest and support. Thanks, too, to Anjali Pratap, also at A. P. Watt, who commented on early drafts as well as providing administrative services, and to Juliet Pickering. I have been particularly fortunate in my team at HarperCollins. My editor Arabella Pike remained calm and positive as a three-year schedule stretched to twice that length. Kate Hyde was a most congenial reader and guided me through the various stages of proofs, ably assisted by Annabel Wright. Caroline Noonan is a pearl among picture researchers, imaginative, resourceful and efficient. I am grateful to all for their kindness, patience and willingness to meet my requirements. I was also fortunate in having Helen Ellis to handle my publicity. Other people made important contributions. Ilsa Yardley copy-edited the manuscript. Douglas Matthews expertly compiled the index. Nicola Beauman at Persephone Books kindly allowed me to try out ideas on her readers, notably at the Virginia Woolf weekend at Newnham College. The photographer Mari Mahr generously agreed to take my author pictures. Fellow-writer Elizabeth Buchan cheered me with bracing phone calls.

Christine Casley died some months before completion of the work, but her wisdom and gaiety continue to sustain me. Heartfelt thanks to all. I am grateful to the many friends and family members, too numerous to list, who put up with my seclusion for what must have seemed a very long haul. Particular thanks are due to my husband, John Senter, for his steadfastness and humour, and his welcome talents as musician, cook, gardener and keeper of bees. His honey sweetened many a hardworking hour.

Grateful acknowledgement for permission to quote is made to the following:

Quotations from Richard Bowring (trans.), *The Diary of Lady Murasaki*, Penguin Books, London, 1996, translation copyright © Richard Bowring, 1996. All rights reserved. (For details of page references, see footnotes.) Reproduced by kind permission of Penguin Books Ltd.

Quotation from Hilary Davies, *In a Valley of This Restless Mind*, Enitharmon Press, 1997. By kind permission of Enitharmon Press.

Quotation from Emily Dickinson, Thomas H. Johnson (ed.), *The Complete Poems of Emily Dickinson*, Faber & Faber, 1975 edition. Held in copyright. Permission applied for.

Quotations from Peter Dronke's translation of letters of Baudri of Bourgueil and Constance, from Peter Dronke, *Women Writers of the Middle Ages*, Cambridge University Press, 1984. Copyright © Cambridge University Press, 1984. Reproduced by kind permission of Dr Peter Dronke and Cambridge University Press.

Quotation from T. S. Eliot, *The Use of Poetry and the Use of Criticism*, Faber & Faber, 1964. By kind permission of Faber & Faber, Ltd.

Quotations from *The Ink Dark Moon* by Jane Hirshfield and Mariko Aratani. Copyright © 1990 by Jane Hirshfield and Mariko Aratani. Used by kind permission of Vintage Books, a division of Random House, Inc.

Quotations from the writings of Ted Hughes: Euripides' *Alcestis*, in a new version, Faber & Faber, 1999; *Birthday Letters*, Faber & Faber, 1998; *The Coming of the Kings and Other Plays*, Faber & Faber, 1970; William Scammell (ed.), *Winter Pollen: Occasional Prose*, Faber & Faber, 1994. Held in copyright by The Estate of Ted Hughes. By kind permission of Faber & Faber, Ltd.

Quotation from Emily W. Leider, *Dark Lover: The Life and Death of Rudolph Valentino*, Faber & Faber, 2003. By kind permission of Faber & Faber, Ltd.

Quotations from the writings of Edna St Vincent Millay. Held in copyright by the Edna St Vincent Millay Society. All rights reserved. Used by kind permission of Elizabeth Barnett, Literary Executor.

Quotations from *The Selected Journals of L. M. Montgomery, Volume 1*, edited by Mary Rubio and Elizabeth Waterston. Copyright © 1985 University of Guelph. Copyright (introduction and notes) © 1985 Mary Rubio and Elizabeth Waterston. Reprinted by kind permission of Oxford University Press.

Quotations from Ivan Morris, *The World of the Shining Prince: Court Life in Ancient Japan*, Oxford University Press, 1964; Ivan Morris (trans. and ed.), *The Pillow Book of Sei Shōnagon*, Oxford University Press, 1967. By kind permission of Oxford University Press.

Quotations from the writings of Sylvia Plath: *The Bell Jar*, Faber & Faber, 1966; Ted Hughes (ed.), *Collected Poems*, Faber & Faber, 1981; *Johnny Panic and the Bible of Dreams and other prose writings,* Faber & Faber, 1977; Karin V. Kukil (ed.), *The Journals of Sylvia Plath 1950–1962*, Faber & Faber, 2000; Aurelia Schober Plath (ed.), *Letters Home: Correspondence 1950–1963*, Faber & Faber, 1976. Held in copyright by The Estate of Sylvia Plath. By kind permission of Faber & Faber, Ltd.

Quotation from 'Abelard Solus' from Sally Purcell, *Collected Poems*, edited by Peter Jay, Anvil Press Poetry, 2002. By kind permission of Anvil Press.

Quotations from Betty Radice (trans. and intro.), *The Letters of Abelard and Heloise*, Penguin Books, Harmondsworth, 1974, copyright © Betty Radice, 1974. All rights reserved. (For details of page references, see footnotes.) Reproduced by kind permission of Penguin Books Ltd.

Quotations from Edward Seidensticker (trans.), *The Gossamer Years: The Diary of a Noblewoman of Heian Japan*, Charles E. Tuttle Company, Inc., 1964; Tut Book edition, 1973. Reproduced by kind permission of Charles E. Tuttle Company, Inc.

Quotations from Nancy Hunter Steiner, *A Closer Look at Ariel: a memory of Sylvia Plath*, Faber & Faber, 1974. By kind permission of Faber & Faber, Ltd.

Quotation from Ezra Pound, *The Cantos of Ezra Pound*, Faber & Faber, 1975. By kind permission of Faber & Faber, Ltd.

Quotation from *Correspondences: A Family History in Letters* from Anne Stevenson, *Poems 1955–2005*, Bloodaxe Books, 2004. By kind permission of Bloodaxe Books.

Index

378; and Sylvia's 'Pursuit', 392; and
Sylvia's falling for Hughes, 396,
398; visits England, 398, 400; and
Sylvia's ambition, 420
Plath, Otto (Sylvia's father): effect of
death on Sylvia, 19, 352, 356, 361,
369, 405–9; background and
family life, 356–60
Plath, Sylvia: suicide, 2, 347–8, 403,
406–7, 417–20; depressions, 3, 409;
life and career, 7, 347, 349; effect
of father's death on, 19, 352, 356,
361, 369, 405–9; relations with Ted
Hughes, 19, 42, 88, 344, 348–51,
361, 369, 384, 387, 389–98; and
conflict between poetry and
woman's role, 22, 352–3, 369, 375,
379–80, 383, 398; and passion, 29;
as poet, 191, 255, 349, 422–3;
admires Edna St Vincent Millay,
254–5; introspection, 349–51, 352;
family background and
upbringing, 353–8, 360–3, 369;
marriage breakdown, 356, 363;
undergoes therapy, 362, 381;
longing for social acceptance, 365,
374, 398–9; at Cambridge
University, 366, 382, 384–8, 424; at
college in USA, 367, 372–5, 377–8,
380, 382; early sexual and romantic
experiences, 370–2, 374, 382, 386,
394; uncertain sense of self, 371,
373, 382–3, 419–20; appearance,
374, 381; breakdown and
attempted suicide (1953), 377–8,
380–1, 407; relations with Richard
Sassoon, 386–8, 392–3; dress style
and display, 387–8, 390, 421–2,
424; marriage to Hughes, 393,
400–1; helps Hughes with writing
and publication, 397, 404–6;

children, 399, 402, 405, 422;
separation from Hughes, 401, 419;
married life, 402–4, 409, 421–2,
424; teaches at Smith College, 402;
writer's block, 403–4; posthumous
effect on Hughes, 411–13;
eagerness for life, 416–17; paper
dolls, 423; charisma and
achievements, 424–5; 'Ariel'
(poem), 386; *Ariel* (collection), 403,
423; *The Bell Jar*, 350, 374–80, 403,
419–20; *The Colossus*, 403; 'The
Disquieting Muses', 354; 'Epitaph
in Three Parts', 387; *Journals*,
369–71, 375, 377, 386, 393, 410,
416; *Letters Home*, 353, 357, 363–4;
'Medusa', 564; 'Morning Song',
422; 'Ocean 1212-W', 350, 361;
'Pursuit', 391–2, 408; 'The
Shadow', 354; 'Snow Blitz', 418;
'Stone Boy with Dolphin', 391;
'Superman and Paula Brown's
New Snowsuit', 354; 'Three
Caryatids Without a Portico by
Hugh Robus', 387; *Three Women*
(radio play), 423; 'Two Sisters of
Persephone', 366
Plath, Warren (Sylvia's brother), 358,
361–2, 380, 398, 400
Plato, 350
plays (drama): women writers, 177
poetry: women writers, 177–8, 190–1
Polwhele, William, 203
Pope, Alexander: 'Eloisa to Abelard',
11, 30
Pound, Ezra, 131
Pre-Raphaelites, 1–2
Prouty, Olive Higgins, 372, 377

Racine, Jean, 391–2
Rackham, Arthur, 303